"Pete Williams takes you behind the curtain of the NFL draft with rare depth and perspective, documenting the months leading up to it through the eyes of team, player, school, and agent. The scouting report: A big but nimble book that accelerates well and hits the hole hard. Worthy of a first-round pick."

—Bill King, *Street & Smith's SportsBusiness Journal*

"The most comprehensive look at the draft ever."

—Dan Pompei, *The Sporting News*

"A must for your own draft room."   —SportsIllustrated.com

"Quite an insight into the thinking of NFL personnel executives."

—Jose Miguel Romero, *The Seattle Times*

"This behind-the-scenes look at the scouting and agent recruiting process makes for a fascinating read."

—Tony Grossi, *The Plain Dealer* (Cleveland)

THE
DRAFT

• A Year Inside the NFL's Search for Talent •

PETE WILLIAMS

 St. Martin's Griffin ⚏ New York

For Lance

www.stmartins.com

Book design by Michael Collica

LIBRARY OF CONGRESS CATALOGING-IN-PUBLICATION DATA

Williams, Pete, 1969–
    The draft : a year inside the NFL's search for talent / Pete Williams.
      p. cm.
    ISBN-13: 978-0-312-35439-8
    ISBN-10: 0-312-35439-8
    1. Football draft—United States. 2. Football players—United States—Recruiting. 3. National Football League. I. Title.

GV954.32.W55 2006
796.332'64—dc22

                                    2005057440

First St. Martin's Griffin Edition: March 2007

10 9 8 7 6 5 4 3 2 1

CONTENTS

THE
DRAFT

PROLOGUE

THE 2005 NFL DRAFT
Saturday, April 23, 2005

The citizens of Waycross, Georgia turned out in force to watch the 2005 NFL Draft. More than three hundred gathered at the city's new community center to honor Fred Gibson, who had gone from Waycross to stardom at the University of Georgia and now was looking at a big payday in the NFL.

Banners were posted, along with blown-up images from Gibson's Bulldogs career. There were wide-screen televisions tuned to ESPN, a giant, bouncy house set up for the kids, and an impressive spread of ribs, barbecue, chicken, potato salad, baked beans, and cake.

Gibson, a skinny six-four wide receiver, arrived at the community center an hour into the first round and couldn't believe the turnout. His immediate family was there, along with uncles, aunts, cousins, former coaches, and seemingly everyone he had known since early childhood.

NFL teams selected three wide receivers among the first picks—Braylon Edwards of Michigan, South Carolina's Troy Williamson, and Mike Williams of Southern Cal—but Gibson was not concerned. He didn't expect to get picked that early.

His agents Doug Hendrickson and Demetro Stephens of Octagon were not on hand but offered encouragement over the phone. They believed Gibson could go as early as the end of the first round, certainly no later than the third.

It was a festive atmosphere at the Waycross community center. The guest of honor played the role of gracious host, all the while keeping an eye on ESPN. The draft proceeded slowly during the first round, with selections trickling out every fifteen minutes.

Gibson grew a little anxious at the end of the round when the Baltimore Ravens chose Oklahoma's Mark Clayton at number twenty-two and the hometown Atlanta Falcons opted for Roddy White of Alabama-Birmingham at number twenty-seven. Gibson had worked out alongside Clayton and White at the Senior Bowl, the late-January all-star game in Mobile, Alabama. He couldn't begrudge the teams for drafting such talented receivers.

The party grew silent early in the second round when the Philadelphia Eagles selected Reggie Brown, who also was a wide receiver out of the University of Georgia. The two Bulldogs were linked together, though for much of their careers Gibson was viewed as the better pro prospect.

Gibson pumped his fist and smiled. "Good for Reggie," he said.

The draft moved more quickly now, just ten minutes per pick starting with the second round, and Gibson paid closer attention. "Just sit tight," Hendrickson told him over the phone.

More receivers came off the board. The Chicago Bears selected Oklahoma's Mark Bradley. Roscoe Parrish, a speedy five-ten receiver from Miami, went to the Buffalo Bills. The Green Bay Packers picked up Terrence Murphy from Texas A&M and the San Diego Chargers grabbed Northern Colorado's Vincent Jackson.

Gibson stood in disbelief as the second round ended. He checked his cell phone to make sure he hadn't missed anything. Friends did their best to distract him. Surely he would go soon.

The third round got underway shortly after 9:00 P.M. The Tennessee Titans, with the fourth pick in the round, chose Indiana's Courtney Roby. Teams were drafting quickly now, but it seemed nobody wanted a wide receiver. Fourteen selections passed. Much of the Waycross crowd dispersed, but Gibson remained. Surely the call would come soon.

The Cincinnati Bengals were on the clock now, having already selected two of Gibson's Georgia teammates: defensive end David Pollack in the first and linebacker Odell Thurman in the second. The Bengals chose a wide receiver in the third round, but it was Chris Henry of West Virginia.

Two picks later, the Seattle Seahawks selected Georgia quarterback David Greene. Gibson was happy for "Greeney." Like the rest of his

Bulldogs teammates, Greene was picked at or before where most of the endless mock drafts projected him in the weeks leading up to the draft.

The next ten selections yielded no receivers. It was approaching 11:00 P.M. when Tennessee drafted Brandon Jones. Gibson couldn't believe it. Did the entire NFL really consider *three* wide receivers from Oklahoma better than him?

The crowd had all but departed by the time the Denver Broncos ended the first day of the draft by selecting Maurice Clarett, a controversial figure for his failed attempt to challenge the NFL's draft-eligibility rules and for accusing Ohio State, his former school, of all manner of wrongdoing.

There would be four more rounds tomorrow. Gibson put on a brave face and accepted encouragement from the stragglers. As he drove his white GMC Yukon back to his grandmother's house, he pondered how much money he had lost in the last twelve hours.

A year earlier, the last pick in the second round—defensive end Marquis Hill of Louisiana State University—received a signing bonus of $1.15 million from the New England Patriots. The final draftee in the third round—Purdue linebacker Landon Johnson, taken by the Cincinnati Bengals—received a signing bonus of $441,000. Gibson didn't even want to think about first-round cash.

But it wasn't just the money. Gibson knew that where a player was drafted influenced the direction of his career. Sure, plenty of low draft picks went on to stardom; New England Patriots quarterback Tom Brady, a sixth-round pick, was the NFL's most visible example. Still, the higher a player was drafted, the more slack teams would give him to learn complex schemes and make an impact. Teams found it easier to cut ties with players in which they had invested little.

How, Gibson wondered, did teams forget about him? Had he not done everything he could have since his college career ended on New Year's Day, when Georgia defeated Wisconsin in the Outback Bowl in Tampa?

Gibson excelled at the Senior Bowl and performed decently at the NFL scouting combine in February. Admittedly, his time in the forty-yard dash (4.55 seconds) was nothing to brag about, but he had run faster for scouts during the University of Georgia's "pro day" in March. Over the last four months, he had undergone dozens of interviews with NFL teams and always came across as gregarious, confident yet humble. Everyone loved "Freddy G."

At least that's how it seemed to Gibson. Surely, NFL teams did not view *thirteen* wide receivers in a better light. Did they?

Back home, Gibson broke down in front of his grandmother, Delores Bethea, who had raised him after her daughter, Brenda, gave birth to him at age thirteen. It was the first time he had cried in front of Bethea in years.

"They're telling me I can't play football," he sobbed. "Am I not good enough to play?"

Bethea comforted her grandson. Tomorrow would be another day.

In Charlotte, Chris Canty tried not to watch the draft. It was like passing an automobile accident; he knew it was ugly but had to know what was happening. Unlike Fred Gibson, he kept the day a low-key affair. He wisely did not invite friends over, preferring to watch with family. As the day wore on, his parents, both brothers, and assorted uncles and aunts tried to turn the topic of conversation elsewhere.

The last eight months had been a roller coaster for Canty, a six-seven defensive end who had played at the University of Virginia. Before the 2004 season, many scouts viewed Canty as a potential first-round pick. A month into the year, he shredded three of the four ligaments in his left knee during a game against Syracuse. He underwent grueling rehabilitation to restore the knee and by late January was feeling close to 100 percent.

That's when he walked into a nightclub in Scottsdale and ended up in a scuffle. Words were exchanged. In the darkness, someone smashed a bottle in Canty's face. He suffered a detached left retina. Even now, three months later, there still were bruises.

Some teams worried about the eye. Others had concerns about the knee. Some wondered about both. Still, Canty believed he could go as high as the second round, at least that's what he said agent Ethan Lock had led him to think.

Canty had spent the last month trying to eliminate the concern teams had about his knee and eye. It didn't help that he did not work out at the University of Virginia's pro day in Charlottesville on March 23, taking a few extra weeks to prepare for a private workout at his former high school in Charlotte. Since he missed the first day of the NFL combine, where players are physically examined, tested, and interviewed before all thirty-two teams in Indianapolis, he had to travel back to Indianapolis in early April for a physical. The knee checked out fine, but the eye doctor expressed concern about the retina. Those reservations became part of the official league file.

A dozen teams sent representatives to Canty's workout on April 14. The Baltimore Ravens and Dallas Cowboys also flew him in for interviews. Canty performed all of the familiar combine drills, but concerns lingered.

"There's not much market for a one-legged, one-eyed defensive end," one general manager said before the draft.

So Canty watched as teams selected five defensive ends in the first round. He couldn't argue with the picks, though it still hurt to see guys he once was rated alongside go high. At Virginia, Canty had played a key role in head coach Al Groh's 3-4 defense, an increasingly popular scheme in the NFL that featured three down lineman and four linebackers.

Groh had spent much of his coaching career as an NFL assistant under Bill Parcells, who was remodeling his Dallas Cowboys defense into the 3-4. Parcells wielded two picks in the first round and chose a pair of defensive ends with no major physical ailments, Troy State's Demarcus Ware and Marcus Spears of LSU.

The second round featured just two defensive ends. The Miami Dolphins grabbed Iowa's Matt Roth with the fourteenth pick. Canty figured his best hope was the Ravens, and they did select an end with the twenty-first pick, but it was Oklahoma's Dan Cody.

By the third round, Canty began thinking the wait could go into Sunday. Only two teams took ends. Those players, Notre Dame's Justin Tuck (New York Giants) and Vincent Burns of Kentucky (Indianapolis Colts), were rated below Canty, at least before the eye injury.

Few players had fallen as far as Canty, who sighed as the Broncos picked the ultimate damaged goods, former Ohio State running back Maurice Clarett, to close ESPN's first day of draft coverage.

Shirley Canty tried to console her son. A tall, striking woman, she served as pastor of the Calvary United Methodist Church in Charlotte. "You have to trust God's plan for your life," she said.

Chris nodded. Tomorrow was Sunday, the second day of the NFL Draft. They would pray about it in the morning. Perhaps later that day God's plan would materialize.

For now, Chris stared at the wide-screen television in the corner of the living room. Throughout the room were framed news clippings from his career at the University of Virginia, along with a handsome display of his oversized diploma, and a photo taken from the center of the school's historic grounds, an area designed by school founder Thomas Jefferson

ESPN analysts were recapping the day's events. Canty watched the names scroll along the bottom. There were former University of Virginia teammates, along with opposing players he had outplayed. There were guys he had trained with in Arizona before the NFL scouting combine, and a few names that didn't ring a bell.

All told, one hundred and one players heard from NFL teams on the first day of the NFL Draft. Sixteen months earlier, after Canty's junior season, there were agents and draft experts projecting him as a second-round pick for the 2004 draft if he left school early. Even an NFL advisory committee rated him a potential first-day selection.

Instead, Canty bypassed the draft, hung around to earn the diploma, enrolled in graduate school, and now was staring blankly at Chris Berman, wondering how so much could change so quickly.

Chapter One:

FIRST CONTACTS

E d Hawthorne and Ed Walsh looked at the young football agent sitting across the table from them and chuckled. Jack Scharf seemed right out of central casting. With a lantern jaw, bleached-white teeth, and jelled dark hair, he looked like a taller Tom Cruise. The forty-five-hundred-dollar, custom-tailored Armani suit, cuff links and white monogrammed shirt he wore covered a lean physique, shaved to accentuate the muscles. Scharf's rented Jaguar XJ8 sat outside Walsh's law office in New Haven, Connecticut.

"Say it, Jack," Hawthorne said.

Scharf shook his head. "C'mon guys."

Hawthorne raised an eyebrow. "Jack?"

"All right," Scharf said, taking a deep breath. "Show me the money."

Walsh and Hawthorne laughed. "Not bad," Hawthorne said. "Louder."

"Show Me the Money!" Scharf yelled, channeling Cruise. *"Show . . . Me . . . the . . . Mon-ey!"*

The Eds cackled. It was early September 2004, and Scharf was among the first agents to make a presentation in the hopes of representing Hawthorne's nephew, Anttaj, a 312-pound defensive tackle at the University of Wisconsin, for the 2005 NFL Draft.

There was little resemblance between Ed and Anttaj. Walsh, the family attorney, liked to greet agents in a conference room first and then introduce Ed Hawthorne to gauge the response. Most agents showed little reaction, though the recruiting process did have its amusing moments.

Whenever agents reached Anttaj on his cell phone in Wisconsin, he directed them to Uncle Ed. One agent called Uncle Ed and immediately dealt the race card.

"You know, Ed," the agent said. "All of our brothers are coming out of the NFL today and they're broke. Why? Because of the white agents, that's why; and I'm here to make sure that doesn't happen to 'Taj."

Hawthorne paused. "Do you realize I'm white?"

Ed's sister, Eileen, had raised her biracial son alone.

"Well, you know," the agent said after an awkward pause, "I've got white family, too."

That agent never got a meeting with the Eds, who vetted potential representatives for Anttaj, allowing him to spend his senior season focused on football and not on who might guide him through the NFL Draft in April.

The Eds liked what they saw of Jack Scharf, who beneath the slick, Jerry Maguire veneer had, at thirty-five, established himself as a legitimate player in the brutal world of football agents. He had flown from his office in San Antonio to New Haven armed with binders full of spreadsheets and contract information, showing how his company— Momentum Sports—had skillfully landed contracts for its clients at better than the market rate.

Scharf's presentation included testimonials from clients such as Nick Barnett, a linebacker drafted in the first round out of Oregon State by the Green Bay Packers in 2003. There were DVDs outlining the marketing efforts Momentum would undertake on behalf of Anttaj, and the trainers the company would employ to get Anttaj ready for the February NFL scouting combine in Indianapolis, where draft hopefuls are tested physically and psychologically by NFL teams.

The Eds flipped through Scharf's literature. His clients from the previous year were a mix of third- and fourth-round selections, though the Denver Broncos selected Tatum Bell, a running back from Oklahoma State, in the second round.

"You do all of this for a third-round pick?" Hawthorne asked. Anttaj Hawthorne was considered, at this early stage, a likely first-round choice.

"Absolutely," Scharf said.

The meeting, which had begun late in the afternoon, continued for three hours. At this early juncture, the Eds had met with only a few agents and were still in the information-gathering stage, learning how contracts were negotiated and what the process leading up to the NFL Draft entailed.

In the coming weeks, the Eds would investigate Scharf and the rest of the agents they interviewed. They would start on the Internet, searching through Google, and follow up with calls to the NFL Players Association to determine if any agents had been disciplined or engaged in unethical activity.

For now, they liked what they saw of Jack Scharf—or "Show Me," as they would call him throughout Walsh's firm. The ladies in the office would become fond of Show Me, though the older ones tended to prefer Tom Condon, the former Kansas City Chiefs lineman-turned-lawyer and agent, who, at fifty-two, looked like an older version of Jack Scharf.

NFL playing experience was the least of the advantages Condon held over Scharf, a graduate of UCLA and the Southwestern University School of Law in Los Angeles, who had been a licensed NFL agent for less than three years. As head of the football division for the International Management Group (IMG), the world's largest sports agency, Condon was the most powerful agent in football, with a lengthy list of clients that included Indianapolis Colts quarterback Peyton Manning and his brother Eli, who had been the top pick in the 2004 draft.

Condon also was a New Haven native whose high school, Notre Dame of West Haven, was a rival of Anttaj's Hamden High. Condon had scored a July meeting with the Eds that included Anttaj, who had not yet returned to Wisconsin.

For now, Condon was the leader in the race to secure Anttaj, though the Eds had other agents to interview. There would be more to learn about contracts, marketing, and the NFL draft process.

But as they said good-bye to Jack Scharf, sending him on his way in the Jaguar XJ8, they concluded that "Show Me" definitely was in the running.

On a late afternoon in mid-September, Pat Dye Jr. looked out the window of his sixteenth-floor office overlooking Lenox Square in Atlanta's upscale Buckhead district. Already the city's notorious traffic was beginning to thicken on the surrounding arteries.

Though it was just a week after Labor Day, the recruiting season for the 2005 NFL Draft was well underway, and already Dye knew his Pro-

Files Sports Management firm was in a dogfight for talent in its own backyard.

The son of the former longtime Auburn football coach, Pat Dye Jr. had over the previous seventeen years parlayed a childhood spent around college football and his dad's vast network of connections into a lucrative agent practice.

Now Dye Jr. and his business partner, Bill Johnson, represented forty NFL players, nearly all of which attended college in the southeast. Almost half of their clients had played at Auburn or the University of Georgia, located an hour away in Athens.

Atlanta had become a popular base of operations for sports agents. The NFL Players Association counted forty-seven registered agents from greater Atlanta. Most of the schools in the football-rich Southeastern Conference were within a four-hour drive, along with much of the Atlantic Coast Conference. Three prominent precombine training centers are based in Atlanta, along with the NFL's Falcons, who train out of palatial digs in the northeastern suburb of Flowery Branch.

Auburn and Georgia figured to be the nation's most fertile agent-recruiting grounds for the 2005 NFL Draft. Auburn had three players projected as likely first-rounders—running backs Ronnie Brown and Carnell "Cadillac" Williams, along with defensive back Carlos Rogers. Quarterback Jason Campbell's stock also was rising.

At Georgia, fiery defensive end David Pollack had surprised many people by not turning pro after his junior season. Dye, like other agents, had conceded Pollack to IMG and Tom Condon, who made inroads with the player as a junior. Pollack, under NCAA rules, could not commit to an agent, even orally, but the rest of the field knew better than to waste their time.

Dye was in the hunt for Pollack's roommate, quarterback David Greene, along with Georgia's two wide receivers, Reggie Brown and Fred Gibson. But the player Dye and his competitors lusted after was Thomas Davis, a 220-pound safety who NFL scouts projected as a future All-Pro linebacker in the mold of Ray Lewis, the Baltimore Ravens star. Davis and linebacker Odell Thurman were juniors, but, like Pollack a year earlier, they faced the tantalizing prospect of turning pro early.

Dye organized his recruiting by starting with a list of thirty to forty prospects in May. Some, such as Greene, Brown, Rogers, and Williams, he had recruited for more than two years. From there, he contacted twenty players via phone or mail, figuring he would have a serious shot with a dozen and sign five or six.

At forty-two, Dye came across as younger, with a thick mane of light brown hair, a slight Southern drawl, and a perpetual smile. "If agent recruiting was a beauty contest," said agent Ken Harris, a friendly rival based in Tampa, "Pat Dye would win every time."

Dye didn't fit the profile of a football agent, at least not in the Jerry Maguire or Jack Scharf sense, but his route was not an unfamiliar one. After graduating from Auburn in 1984 and Samford University's law school in 1987, he went to work at the Birmingham firm of Burr and Forman, serving as an attorney while building a football representation business on the side.

Two months after receiving his agent certification by the NFL Players Association, Dye traveled to Mobile, Alabama, for the Senior Bowl, the annual postseason meat market of draft-eligible talent. He arrived at the hotel lobby conservatively dressed in a pinstripe suit and wingtips, and encountered every sleazy stereotype he'd feared. There were agents dressed like pimps, openly paying players. There were agent "runners" promising women and even drugs to potential clients. It was everything Pat Dye Sr. had warned him about and more.

"There's nothing a college football coach hates more than dealing with agents," Dye Jr. says. "They distract the player, potentially jeopardize eligibility. And, I told my father, for those reasons I wanted to go into it. The industry needed more honest, reputable people, and I know that sounds self-righteous. He warned me. 'If you did it the right way, and I know you will, it's going to be a long uphill battle getting players, because I know the kind of things that go on in this business.' And he was right."

Dye almost got back in the car and returned to Birmingham. Instead, he stayed, vowing to build his business aboveboard. His name helped, along with his father's network of contacts. Within eighteen months, Dye Jr. had built a practice of about a dozen clients. Recognizing that the process of recruiting NFL clients was akin to solicitation in the law field, Dye took his clients to Atlanta and the sports entertainment division of Robinson-Humphrey, a major financial services firm.

There Dye worked under Richard Howell, who represented just one NFL player, former Georgia Tech linebacker Pat Swilling of the New Orleans Saints. Howell was better known for his NBA clients, and over the next four years Dye helped Howell land Tech point guard Kenny Anderson, Clemson center Elden Campbell, and Tom Gugliotta, a forward from North Carolina State.

The football practice also thrived. Dye and Howell signed running backs Emmitt Smith and Garrison Hearst, defensive end Tony Bennett, and defensive tackle Kelvin Pritchett. Soon the entrepreneurial bug bit Dye, and in January of 1994 he and an assistant left Howell, setting up shop on Dye's dining room table before dividing his basement into two offices.

Dye signed everything away to get a bank line of credit. Within two months he had negotiated nearly $20 million in new contracts, including a $12 million deal for Bennett with the Colts that included a $3 million signing bonus. That enabled Dye to lease office space in Buckhead.

It was an amicable departure; Dye had, after all, brought a football business to Robinson-Humphrey. Swilling stayed with Howell. So did Smith, who was in the midst of a long-term deal with Dallas. Hearst joined Dye two years later after his contract expired.

Now, nearly a decade later, Dye's client list included few superstars, but plenty of solid veterans such as Atlanta Falcons linebacker Keith Brooking and defensive tackle Rod Coleman, Minnesota Vikings running back Michael Bennett, and Dexter Coakley, the Dallas Cowboys linebacker. Dye represented Jon and Matt Stinchcomb, offensive tackles out of the University of Georgia who, during the 2004 season, played for the New Orleans Saints and Tampa Bay Buccaneers respectively.

Dye loved his work, though it was a brutal business, especially for a father of two children under the age of four. Many of his competitors were single or had a staff of young agents to handle the bulk of the recruiting. Dye still was struggling with the transition to fatherhood while working in a business where clients demand round-the-clock attention.

"I had my first meeting with a recruit and his family this past weekend," Dye said. "I can always be called slow out of the gate. May and June are the only months to catch your breath. I have two young kids, and obviously we're here for existing clients, but I try not to beat the bushes in those months. Then July comes and we have rookie negotiations. In August, you're just monitoring players and hoping they make their teams. Yeah, you're assessing your recruiting list, but I don't get out personally until September."

Dye knew better than to take any business for granted. Larger agencies such as Octagon and SFX had increased their presence in the southeast in recent years. Condon and IMG would swoop in for a high-profile client such as Pollack or Eli Manning, the Ole Miss quarterback taken first the previous year.

But as Dye mapped out his intense fall calendar of recruiting, a more low-profile opponent was taking aim at Dye's home turf of Auburn and Georgia.

Across Lenox Square, Todd France was looking to take his one-year-old sports agency to the next level.

Far beyond the Pat Dye Jr. level.

It had been quiet a year for France and his young agency, FAME (France Athlete Management Enterprises). On August 24, 2003, France resigned from Career Sports Management, the Atlanta agency where he had spent four years building the football division under CSM founder Lonnie Cooper, who represented numerous NBA head coaches, along with Atlanta Braves pitcher John Smoltz.

On September 3, 2003, France's most prominent client, running back Priest Holmes, signed a four-year contract extension with the Kansas City Chiefs worth potentially thirty-six million dollars. The following day, sixteen Career Sports clients faxed termination letters to Cooper's office, hiring France.

Cooper did not let France go quietly. Five weeks later, Career Sports filed suit against France and FAME in Fulton County, Georgia, Superior Court, seeking a judgment that CSM was entitled to all fees from player contracts consummated before September 9, 2003, and unspecified damages against France and FAME.

The saga was a familiar one in the football agent business. A young, aspiring agent goes to work for an established firm to learn the industry. He soon finds he's doing much of the grunt work of recruiting and babysitting clients. Frustrated that the managing partner gets all of the credit, to say nothing of some, if not all, of the commissions, he decides to bolt and start his own agency. The clients, who have grown close to the younger agent, follow.

In 2001, David Dunn left veteran agent Leigh Steinberg, taking fifty clients with him. Steinberg filed suit, and in November of 2002 a jury awarded Steinberg $44.6 million in damages. The NFL Players Association's disciplinary committee voted to suspend Dunn for two years, but Dunn filed for personal bankruptcy, which halted all administrative actions against him. (A federal appeals court overturned the $44.6 million verdict in March of 2005, ruling that mistakes were made by the trial court judge.)

Dunn continued to operate, landing prominent clients for the 2003 and 2004 drafts.

Darrell Wills took a similar route.

Wills worked for IMG, serving as a lead recruiter and agent in the southeast. Shortly before the 2004 draft, he left to form his own agency, taking six clients with him. The NFLPA revoked the agent certification of Wills on the grounds that he violated a non-compete clause in his IMG contract.

Wills reinvented himself as an athlete manager, in the mold of a Hollywood agency. He founded Imagine Sports, partnered with a certified agent and a financial advisor, and began recruiting players for the 2005 NFL Draft.

France's situation was not entirely analogous. Dunn and Wills had joined established football agencies led by two of the NFL's most prominent agents, Steinberg and Tom Condon, respectively. Cooper's background was in representing NBA head coaches and a handful of baseball players. His primary business was creating sports sponsorship deals for companies such as Bell South, the Home Depot, and Keebler.

France, who came to work for Cooper as a marketing employee less than a year out of college, in April of 1994, created the football division virtually from scratch in 1999. Prior to that, the company's only football clients were former University of Georgia quarterback Eric Zeier and another ex-Bulldog, Brandon Tolbert, a linebacker drafted in the seventh round by Jacksonville in 1998.

While Cooper's lawsuit meandered through the courts, France pushed ahead. For the 2004 draft, he landed Georgia Tech linebacker Daryl Smith and Darius Watts, a wide receiver from Marshall University. Both were chosen in the second round.

Now, just a year after leaving Cooper, France had a well-appointed suite of offices not far from Dye, in the shadow of the Ritz-Carlton Buckhead and Emeril's restaurant. There were plenty of blond-wood furnishings and a marketing room full of posters and point-of-sale advertising pieces featuring clients such as Holmes and linebackers Takeo Spikes (Buffalo Bills) and Kendrell Bell (Pittsburgh Steelers).

At thirty-three, France looked younger, despite a few flecks of gray. He kept his otherwise dark hair short, which accentuated protruding ears, and though he possessed a wry, self-deprecating sense of humor, he wore a perpetual look of suspicion. France, who was single, spent much of his time on the road. There were clients to recruit and NFL veterans to service. He often pulled into rest areas to avoid falling asleep at the wheel. On this morning in mid-September, France had made an appearance in the office, though it would be brief. It was Rosh Hashanah.

Tomorrow, it would be back to recruiting. He was lobbying hard for Georgia safety Thomas Davis, Auburn defensive back Carlos Rogers, and Roddy White, a wide receiver from the University of Alabama-Birmingham. France also was on the hunt for Auburn running back Ronnie Brown. Unlike Dye, who was recruiting both Brown and Cadillac Williams, France had decided it best to recruit just one Auburn back.

It was a bold wish list for a young agency, albeit one with established clients such as Holmes, Spikes, and Bell. Already France had heard stories of other agents telling potential clients about the Cooper lawsuit. Besides, his competitors told recruits, France never had represented a first-round pick.

"Can it be that hard?" France asks, sitting at a conference table. "I have eighteen clients. It's not like I just started last year. I did a $36-million contract for Priest Holmes, a $32 million deal for Takeo Spikes. This is all about sales, selling your capabilities, and selling yourself to parents that you can take care of their son and do whatever it is you need to do. And that's not just the contract, that's everything. Someone is going to want the huge agency. You can't win everyone. But you get your foot in the game and you battle away.

"I don't care what you tell me, I'm going to go for it. I know what my capabilities are and what I can deliver, and I'm going to preach it, communicate it, and hope that they agree. There's no exact recipe for any of this, but nobody is going to stop me. I will be relentless."

Jack Scharf was running on adrenaline. His meeting with Ed Hawthorne and Ed Walsh was part of a four-day stint crisscrossing the country, trying to convince the parents that he was the man to represent their sons for the 2005 NFL Draft.

Though it was still mid-September, the draft eight months away, recruiting season was in full swing for "Show Me" Scharf and the rest of the more than 1,300 football agents competing for just 400 or so players who stood any chance at becoming one of the 255 players selected by one of the NFL's thirty-two teams in late April.

At this point, many players with any shot of a pro career had been dealing with agents for at least four months. Many top stars, as freshman and sophomores, begin hearing from agents just hoping to lay the groundwork for when they become draft eligible.

Starting in May of their draft-eligible year, when the NFL's scouting combines release their evaluations of rising seniors, agents begin an all-out blitz on the nation's top talent.

There is a constant barrage of overnight packages, with binders, CD-ROMs, DVDs, and other media from agents touting their skills and experience. Former college teammates, now in the pros, call of on behalf of their reps to recruit. The agents themselves phone players and their parents relentlessly.

Though NCAA regulations prohibit players from committing to agents, even orally, some players make up their minds early, if only to clear the phone lines and make time for girlfriends, parties, and perhaps even a little studying.

To stay within the guidelines, players often do not reveal their choice of agent, sometimes not even to the winning party, until after their final game. Other players deal with the hard sales pitches, spending their fall semesters meeting with agents after classes and practices. Some, like Wisconsin's Anttaj Hawthorne and Georgia's David Pollack, enlisted family members to narrow the field.

That's where Scharf believed he held an advantage. He was not afraid to embark on a grueling travel schedule, like the one this week that took him from his office in San Antonio on Monday to New Haven to visit the Hawthorne camp.

Scharf woke up on Tuesday to fly to Cleveland and meet the family of Justin Geisinger, a left tackle from Vanderbilt, moved on to Fort Lauderdale on Wednesday to charm the family of another Vanderbilt player, defensive end Jovan Haye, before arriving in Tampa to visit with the parents of Louisville wide receiver J. R. Russell.

Now, sitting in the Champions sports bar at Tampa's Westshore Marriott shortly after midnight on Friday, Scharf felt good about the week.

Scharf believed that if he could just get into the home, he could make a successful pitch, using his professional presentation, charm, and even his looks to make a lasting impression. In this way, he was like Tom Cruise's Jerry Maguire, who fancied himself "The Lord of the Living Room."

Jerry Maguire pulled up to the homes of prospective clients in a rented Pontiac Grand Prix or Ford Taurus. Not Scharf, who insisted on a four-door Jaguar XJ8, or even the tan convertible version that Hertz has provided in Tampa at a cost of $129 a day, a bargain compared to rates in many cities.

"It's for that ten-minute period when the player walks you out to the car at the end of a meeting," Scharf said. "Do you want to be seen in a convertible Jag or a Toyota Camry? Obviously, you've got to sell yourself as a skilled negotiator and someone who can market the player to NFL teams and get him ready for the draft. But sometimes it's that ten minutes that makes the difference. Perception is reality.

"I spent six thousand dollars on this trip. Hotel rooms, airfare, four Jaguars that I barely drove. It's crazy that you do all this to visit twenty-one- or twenty-two-year-old kids or parents that sometimes barely have enough money to pay the electric bill. But that's what motivates them, the idea of making their lives better."

Scharf looked at his watch. He had a 7:00 A.M. flight, and his sights were set on about fifteen players, all of whom would require his best efforts. With any luck, he would land five or six, but he knew better than to take anyone for granted. Not after last season, when a cornerback named Dunta Robinson from the University of South Carolina signed at the last moment with Jason Chayut and Brian Mackler of Manhattan-based Sportstars.

The Houston Texans took Robinson with the tenth overall pick and signed him to a deal that included bonuses of $8 million. For Scharf, working on the NFL's standard 3 percent commission, the deal represented a $240,000 loss.

Still, he had five players drafted in the first four rounds in 2004, following a 2003 haul that included Barnett, the linebacker from Oregon State taken in the first round by the Green Bay Packers. In just three years, Scharf and Jeff Griffin, his colleague at Momentum Sports, had become players in the piranha tank of sports agents.

The field still was dominated by major agencies such as International Management Group (IMG) and its football division, run by former NFL players Tom Condon and Ken Kremer, along with SFX and Octagon, which in the late 1990s consolidated several boutique agencies. There were successful, self-promoting individual agents such as Leigh Steinberg and Drew Rosenhaus, who each touted themselves as the inspiration for Jerry Maguire and wrote autobiographies focusing mostly on their negotiating skills.

It was a vicious competition, Scharf knew. Agents often undercut one another on commissions. Stealing clients was commonplace. The business was rampant with reports of agents providing cash and other inducements to college players. Though illegal, the practice rarely was investigated by the NCAA, colleges, or individual states that require agent licensing. The NFL Players Association, which certifies agents and in theory polices them, paid little attention.

Scharf, who says he plays by the rules, never knows quite what he's up against. Still, after departing the bar at the Westshore Marriott, he felt comfortable about his prospects for the 2005 draft, at least the four players whose families he just met.

He even felt confident about Hawthorne, who potentially could become the first blue-chip, consensus first-rounder he ever signed.

"I'm not going to jinx myself and say which guys I'm going to sign," Scharf said. "But there's no way I'm not going to get at least two of the four."

Chapter Two:

THE PRO DEPOT

Tim Ruskell hunched over a laptop computer and pondered how Ronnie Brown could help the Atlanta Falcons. A file provided dozens of details about the running back from Auburn University, from his physical skills to work ethic to intelligence.

The scouting report was one of hundreds that Ruskell, forty-seven, would read over the next seven months. On this afternoon, September 28, 2004, the Falcons were off to a surprising 3-0 start, but Ruskell kept one eye on the distant NFL Draft.

As an assistant general manager in the National Football League, Ruskell's days were spent searching for replacements for injured players and fielding frequent calls from agents and reporters. The day-to-day operation of a NFL franchise is all-consuming, but like his colleagues throughout the league, Ruskell never took his eyes off the next generation of talent. Though he no longer wore the title of scout or director of scouting, he still spent much of his time jetting around the country to watch college football practices, interview coaches, and sometimes hang around for games on Saturdays.

"I don't know how else to do it," Ruskell said. "I can't just look at tape and tell you how this guy is going to be. I have to have the whole package to put together."

During a seventeen-year stint with the Tampa Bay Buccaneers that ended with the 2003 season, Ruskell, along with general manager Rich McKay and player personnel director Jerry Angelo, developed an uncanny knack for discovering guys who were the complete package, even in cases where other teams saw weaknesses. Where some teams focused on a lack of size and speed, the McKay regime noticed leadership and drive. Where other teams noted a lack of raw football talent, they recognized extra doses of heart and hustle.

In 1993, the Buccaneers followed Ruskell's recommendation and took a flyer late in the third round on a safety from Stanford University who was slow, undersized, and playing baseball in the Florida Marlins organization. Ten years later, John Lynch left the Bucs with Hall of Fame credentials and a reputation as one of the game's hardest hitters and one of its most civic-minded players off the field.

In 1995, Tampa Bay used the second of its first-round picks on Derrick Brooks, a promising, if undersized, linebacker from Florida State. Brooks, like Lynch, became a perennial Pro Bowler and Hall of Fame candidate.

In 1997, the Bucs risked the twelfth overall pick on Warrick Dunn, a five-nine Florida State running back who many teams thought was too small to be anything more than a third-down back in the NFL. McKay and his staff viewed Dunn differently, believing he possessed unusual confidence and determination.

Dunn, like Brooks, became a Pro Bowl player and one of the league's most charity-minded players. Brooks took groups of underprivileged children on international vacations. Dunn purchased homes for single mothers, taking care of the down payment and furnishings.

In the third round of the 1997 draft, the Buccaneers thought a slow, skinny cornerback from the University of Virginia possessed the intelligence and leadership intangibles to become an NFL star. Most NFL scouts thought Tiki Barber's twin brother, Ronde, was a midlevel prospect at best.

Tiki, a running back selected in the second round by the New York Giants, became a star in New York. But Ronde, a third-round pick by the Buccaneers, also emerged as a Pro Bowl talent and a key contributor to the team that won the Super Bowl after the 2002 season.

McKay, Ruskell, and Angelo, who became general manager of the Chicago Bears before the 2001 season, quickly realized that a college player's character was as important a variable in predicting future performance as size, speed, and talent. They were willing to overlook a few transgressions only in the case of a phenomenal talent like Warren

Sapp. Even then they made it a point to thoroughly investigate predraft reports of Sapp's drug use themselves.

Character was an umbrella term that the McKay regime divided into "football character" and "personal character." Within each category was a range of traits, but the common denominators were heart, hustle, integrity, citizenship, work ethic, intelligence, leadership, and overachieving on the football field.

The character-first philosophy was not born out of a desire to lead the league in community service. Instead, McKay and Ruskell believed it was simply sound business. So-called "character guys" were less likely to squander their talent, end up on the police blotter, or become troublemakers in the locker room.

In baseball, the Oakland A's and general manager Billy Beane had gained notoriety by using statistical analysis to make draft decisions, dismissing conventional scouting measurements of physiques, potential, and "tools" to assemble low-budget teams that thrived against more well-heeled opponents. The unconventional approach had drawn raves from business leaders, who believed it had applications beyond sports.

Beane's philosophies were chronicled in the best-selling book *Moneyball* by Michael Lewis. McKay enjoyed the work of Lewis, a fellow Princeton graduate, and admired Beane for going against the grain of the rest of the league. At the same time, McKay saw no application to football, and not just because the NFL's economic system created more of a level playing field.

Beane and his disciples placed a huge emphasis on on-base percentage, slugging, and other stats, generally ignoring how a player's personality would affect team chemistry. In baseball, chemistry often was irrelevant. Barry Bonds could cordon himself off from teammates and clash with the media, and nobody cared so long as he kept producing. Teams were forever lining up to acquire high-maintenance, well-traveled players such as Kevin Brown and Gary Sheffield, no matter the baggage they carried.

In the NFL, a problem child such as Keyshawn Johnson or Terrell Owens, no matter how talented, could upset the delicate chemistry of a locker room. The difference, McKay believed, was that NFL schemes were far more interwoven than the game of baseball, where it was easier to isolate a talented malcontent.

Baseball, though a team sport, is essentially a series of isolated matchups. Players were traded in midseason and didn't miss a beat. In football, skills were not always transferable. A player that thrived in one team's offensive or defensive schemes might not fit on a different roster.

"Taking a *Moneyball* concept and trying to apply it to us doesn't work, because there are too many factors," McKay said. "This isn't just about a guy who is going to play left field. The left fielder for the A's is called upon to do the same thing as the left fielders for the Cardinals, Yankees, or Devil Rays. We ask our left corner[back] to do a lot of different things than what the Rams ask of their left corner. The difference with football is that a drafted player has to come in and grow within our schemes."

Just as some baseball people criticized Beane and his moneyballers for looking at players as a collection of stats, McKay believed some NFL teams put too much weight on scouting "measurables" such as size, speed in the forty-yard dash, and the vertical leap. They were important variables, and players needed to reach certain standards across the board, but it was dangerous, McKay felt, to underemphasize the character element.

McKay believed the football scouting process, with its exhaustive background checks and interviews, was analogous to the corporate hiring process.

"It's the reference side of the business taken as far as you can take it. When you hire an employee, you can do the background check, the interview, and call all the references. But until that employee comes on site and works for six months, you really don't know. You can feel better about some than others, but you don't know. What you've got to do is try and eliminate as many of the nonpredicting factors as you can and minimize the risk."

These days, McKay and Ruskell are hardly the only executives that factor character into their evaluation. Speak with a team official at any point in the months leading up to the draft and he's just as likely to reference character as he is a player's physical skills or performance. But no team places such a premium on the intangible as the Falcons do.

"We think character is a pretty good indication of whether you'll live up to your ability," Ruskell said. "It's all about potential. Do you want the guy that has the ability but isn't going to reach that potential? No, because you don't know what you're going to get from day to day. If he's feeling good, he'll give it his all. But if he's not, then you're not going to get that premium player."

Ruskell turned back to the laptop and the Ronnie Brown file. It's what the Falcons call a "College II" report. Falcon scouts visit schools rich with draft talent, like Auburn, three times during the college football season and once during the summer before, when college coaches have more time to chat. During this downtime, scouts build relationships for later in the season. They also file a preliminary "College I" report, which includes physique, medical reports, and basic biographical information.

The College II is more extensive and includes ratings on athletic ability, toughness, instincts, production—all things scouts can glean by watching practice and interviewing. Players are rated 1 to 5 in each category, and Brown, projected as an early first-round pick, had a lot of 4s and 5s.

Ruskell had no idea where the Falcons would be picking. The team was 3-0, but that could mean anything at this point. "I like Ronnie Brown a lot," he said. "You can't eliminate anyone from consideration."

The College II report is mostly complete after a school has played two or three games, though the character report is a work in progress, constantly updated as scouts conduct interviews.

"Nobody wants to tell you flat out if a guy has character issues," Ruskell said. "That's where you have to read between the lines. You pick up hints. Once you've gotten even the hint of a red flag, even if you're not told directly, then you start up the machine."

The Falcons employ a former U.S. Secret Service agent to conduct such investigations, which is hardly unusual. Every team has ex-law-enforcement personnel in similar roles. Then there's the NFL itself, which employs former FBI assistant director Milt Ahlerich as the head of its security. "Not much gets by thirty-two teams looking for information," Ruskell said.

"They dug all the way back to things I did in the eighth grade," said Sapp, now with the Oakland Raiders. "I heard about some of the stuff they found and I thought, 'Damn, how deep can they dig on me?'"

There's no common path to the executive suites of an NFL front office. There are plenty of ex-players, scouts, and coaches. Some have shifted from the college ranks. Ernie Accorsi and Marty Hurney, the general managers of the New York Giants and Carolina Panthers, respectively, began their careers as sportswriters.

Ruskell also logged time in the media business, working as an on-air radio personality in Tampa and Sarasota for five years after graduating in 1978 with a degree in journalism from the University of South Florida. Ruskell played football in high school, but USF did not field a team until two decades later.

He was working at Budget Tapes & Records in Tampa his freshman year when John Herrera, the first scout hired by the expansion Buccaneers, walked in and discovered that the kid behind the register knew a lot about music and football.

Because of that chance meeting, Ruskell worked in 1976 as ball boy for the inaugural Buccaneers team for $1.25 an hour. It wasn't easy duty, shuttling balls from station to station in Tampa's oppressive humidity. During the first practice in franchise history, Ruskell discovered an errant football that was in danger of interrupting a drill. With his hands already full of balls, he kicked it to the sidelines.

Coach John McKay, a stickler for detail and order, decided to send a message to the team by kicking the ball boy out of practice. Ruskell was rehired that night, fired on at least one other occasion, and eventually adapted McKay's attention to detail as his own philosophy. As a ball boy, Ruskell worked alongside McKay's son Rich, then seventeen. Sometimes Ruskell would catch passes from a veteran quarterback named Steve Spurrier.

"I don't know what to say when people ask me how to get into football," Ruskell says. "Don't do it my way. Don't wait for someone to walk through the door and strike up a friendship."

John McKay, who had won four national championships at Southern Cal, proved to be the best man to guide the hapless Bucs, who lost their first twenty-six games and posted just three winning seasons in his nine years in Tampa. The cigar-chomping, floppy-hat-wearing coach always provided the proper perspective with gallows humor and an endless stream of one-liners. In response to a reporter's question about his team's execution following an especially lopsided loss, McKay replied, "I'm in favor of it."

The Buccaneers, undermanned and clad in garish creamsicle orange uniforms, set the standard for personnel mismanagement and poor on-field performance. Owner Hugh Culverhouse, a tax attorney, alienated fans by taking his NFL profits and plowing them into other investments instead of back into the team. The "Yucks" squandered draft choices, despite perennially picking near the top of the first round.

At least McKay had family around. John "J. K." McKay, a former USC Trojan and the older of the two McKay boys, played wide receiver for the Bucs during the first three seasons. Rich's career as a quarterback ended after a freshman season at Princeton—he played four years on the golf team—but he was no less passionate about football.

During the 1979 season, Rich was home from college and suffering from mononucleosis when he stood on the sideline, against doctors' orders, to watch the Buccaneers defeat Kansas City 3–0, to clinch the NFC Central Division title. Two weeks later, the team, led by quarterback Doug Williams, upset Philadelphia in the first round of the playoffs before losing to the Los Angeles Rams in the NFC championship, the highlight of his father's tenure in Tampa.

During those early years, Rich McKay would travel from Princeton into New York in April to sit at the Buccaneers draft table, and he would relay the picks to the podium. He sometimes listened to games in his dorm by telephone by having someone in Tampa prop a radio next to the receiver.

After Princeton, McKay graduated in 1984 from Stetson University law school near St. Petersburg, clerked two years for a Tampa judge, and spent six years serving as the Buccaneers legal counsel, while working at the law firm of Hill, Ward, and Henderson.

Ruskell, meanwhile, got his first scouting gig in 1983 when he was hired by Herrera, who had become the general manager of the Saskatchewan Roughriders of the Canadian Football League (CFL). After two years in Canada, Ruskell scouted for the Tampa Bay Bandits of the United States Football League (USFL) before Angelo hired him in 1987 to be a regional scout for the Buccaneers. Four years later, Ruskell became the director of college scouting.

In 1992, McKay took a paycut and went to work full time for the Buccaneers as vice president of football administration. Unlike Ruskell, who toiled in scouting for second-tier football leagues, McKay's football experience was on the legal side. As general counsel, he had renegotiated the Buccaneers lease at Tampa Stadium in 1990 and put together leases for the teams in the fledgling World League of American Football. At one point, he spent four days at the NFL's New York headquarters sifting through the leases for every NFL franchise.

Culverhouse, who died of lung cancer at age seventy-five on August 25, 1994, taught McKay a lasting lesson in the importance of exhaustive research. With the team for sale following Culverhouse's death, the trustees of the estate, on November 8, 1994, appointed the thirty-five-year-old McKay general manager.

The move generated little media coverage, though Bucs beat writers noted that McKay, and not head coach Sam Wyche, now would have final say on the draft and personnel decisions. It was the first time the Bucs would have a GM with such authority.

Not that it seemed like much of a promotion at the time. With a pending ownership change, McKay had no guarantee of long-term employment. John McKay, now retired, all but discouraged him from taking the gig. Rich told his wife, Terrin, that he might only be GM for seven games, since new owners likely would clean house.

Still, McKay threw himself into the job, knowing full well he needed to overcome the advantages of nepotism and those who viewed him as "John's kid" or "Hugh's boy." While trying his best to assure employees that there was some hope of retaining their jobs under a new regime, he spent two weeks meeting daily with Angelo and Ruskell to figure out why the Buccaneers, in less than two decades, had become what McKay called the "worst franchise in the history of sport." They determined it was because, from the top down, there was no commitment to winning. Secondly, the personnel decisions were horrendous, especially in the first round of the NFL Draft.

After selecting future Hall of Famer Lee Roy Selmon with their first overall pick in 1976, the Bucs in 1977 chose powerful USC running back and McKay family favorite Ricky Bell over Tony Dorsett, the Heisman Trophy–winning back from Pittsburgh. Dorsett became a Dallas Cowboys legend, rushing for more than 12,000 yards. Bell rushed for 1,263 yards in 1979, but his career was derailed by a rare heart disease that killed him in 1984 at age twenty-nine.

In 1986, Auburn running back Bo Jackson turned down Tampa Bay's offer and decided to play baseball, eventually joining the NFL as a Raider. In 1990, the Bucs drafted Alabama linebacker Keith McCants with the fourth overall pick, bypassing the likes of Junior Seau and Emmitt Smith. McCants was a bust, as were other first-round, top-ten picks such as Broderick Thomas (1989), offensive tackle Charles McRae (1991), and defensive end Eric Curry (1993).

In 1987, the Bucs dealt a young quarterback to San Francisco for cash and a pair of draft picks. The players chosen made little impact. Steve Young ended up in the Hall of Fame.

Then there was the time the Bucs literally drafted the wrong guy. In 1982, the team's contingent in New York—McKay notes that it was the one year in his college and law school tenure he did not attend the draft—turned in the wrong card to the podium as a result of a malfunctioning speaker phone back in Tampa. Instead of spending their first-round pick (the number-seventeen choice) on Booker Reese, a defensive end from Bethune-Cookman, they turned in the card for Sean Farrell, a guard from Penn State.

Fortunately for the Buccaneers, the rest of the teams in the first round did not share their high opinion of Reese, and they were able to trade up and draft him in the second round.

"There was too much emphasis put on potential, and not on production," McKay said. "When the word character was used, it was really talking about 'characters,' not character. And so we said we're going to change the way we approach this and go with overachievers. The idea was that, even if we miss on that player and they may not be Pro Bowlers, they're still going to be good players. We need players. We keep having these drafts and you looked at them, and in the first five rounds not one guy was even a starter. That can't happen. You've got to have more than that."

During the 1992 draft, with McKay sitting in as an observer, the Buccaneers had no first-round pick, because former head coach Ray Perkins, acting as personnel director, had traded it nearly two years earlier to the Indianapolis Colts for quarterback Chris Chandler, who had since been cut. Because the Bucs finished 3-13 in 1991, that pick became the number-two choice in the 1992 draft.

"The second pick in the draft was traded for a quarterback who'd been there two years, not played, and was cut," McKay says. "The idea was, 'We're going to have a great year; by then we'll be a great team. This will be a low pick and we'll be happy we did it.' But you just don't know what can happen."

It didn't help that the Buccaneers were forever changing coaching staffs, shifting offensive and defensive schemes, and enduring constant roster turnover. Players drafted to fit one scheme became far less valuable, if not worthless, under a new coordinator.

"We cannot continue to have turnover," McKay told Ruskell and Angelo. "We need to have the same coaches and the same staff, and we need to grow with them because it'll help us from a personnel standpoint."

That sounded good to Malcolm Glazer, who in January of 1995 purchased the Buccaneers from the Culverhouse estate for $192 million, a record price at the time for a sports franchise. In his introductory press conference, Glazer addressed concerns that he would move the team.

"The Bucs stop here," he said. "Tampa is going to have this team forever, as far as the Glazers are concerned."

The community quickly learned the pledge was conditional. Glazer wanted a new stadium to replace the "Big Sombrero," the Bucs antiquated concrete home, which featured aluminum bench seats, no modern amenities, and suites that were quite literally skyboxes, perched high above the top row of seats.

Glazer, a red-bearded, bespectacled Palm Beach resident, originally from Rochester, who made his fortune in trailer parks, nursing homes, restaurants, and TV stations, initially offered to pay for half the new facility. Instead, he spent the first year of his ownership entertaining offers from Baltimore, Los Angeles, Hartford, Connecticut, and Orlando. That gave him the leverage to extract a half-cent sales tax from Hillsborough County that would provide $168 million in financing. Though pitched as a "community investment tax" to finance a wide range of public projects, voters were not fooled. Still, they passed it by a narrow margin rather than risk losing the Buccaneers.

In the end, Glazer did not need to contribute a penny to a state-of-the-art stadium that helped the Buccaneers produce a $40 million profit in 1999. McKay, the league's resident expert on stadium leases, helped negotiate a deal that allowed the Glazers to keep all luxury suite revenue, along with almost all income from tickets, concessions, parking, and advertising. They even received a healthy slice of non-Bucs event revenue. The team did have to pay rent of $3.5 million, along with ticket surcharges of about $1.5 million annually, but that did not even cover the Tampa Stadium Authority's annual operations costs.

While McKay was laying the financial groundwork for Glazer's investment to more than quadruple by 2004, according to *Forbes* magazine, he ensured the football side of the operation measured up.

With a reputation as an administrative guy, McKay hit the road as a general manager in the midnineties, joining Ruskell and Angelo to learn the business of NFL scouting.

"To this day, I don't know what a football guy is, but I knew there were people who thought I wasn't one," McKay says. "I knew I didn't know how area scouts worked, and that's what I wanted to learn. I'd take three-day visits to scout parts of the country and see how scouts did things, what their hours were, how they wrote their reports. I did it from their perspective so I could understand what they do. Going on the road for three weeks, and dealing with the volume of reports that must be written by an area scout, it's not an easy task at all."

McKay, Ruskell, and Angelo looked back on a decade of Buccaneer drafting and saw some common denominators. For starters, the Bucs traded away first-round picks three times, hindering the rebuilding process. As for the players that did not pan out, all of them were college stars that projected as productive NFL players.

Or did they? McKay, with his legal background and lack of NFL scouting experience, wondered if too much emphasis was placed on football skills and potential, and not enough on character, intangibles, and performance. Would they not be better off placing more weight on the nonfootball side of scouting? Wouldn't it make sense to select proven overachievers, albeit ones with perhaps lesser skills, than high-upside guys with raw talent? Were they as thorough as they needed to be when interviewing players? Were they ignoring obvious character red flags?

McKay, Angelo, and Ruskell vowed to avoid players with histories of making bad personal choices off the field. There was no way to completely predict how a player would respond to the dangerous combination of fame, money, and lots of free time. But McKay figured they could increase the odds of avoiding trouble through more extensive character research.

The new philosophy was put to an immediate test for the 1995 draft, McKay's first as general manager. Like the rest of the league, the Bucs were impressed with Sapp, the defensive tackle from the University of Miami. But they figured he would be long gone by the time Tampa Bay picked at number-seven. Instead, the staff wondered how they might grab Derrick Brooks, a promising if undersized linebacker from Florida State who, though of first-round caliber, did not warrant the seventh selection.

The Bucs thoroughly investigated both players, venturing to their colleges and, in the case of Sapp, his hometown of Apopka, Florida, to interview high school coaches, family members, friends—anyone that could provide insight. They believed Brooks made the most of his talents—a mature young man that commanded respect from teammates and opponents. Sapp, though a bit of a handful, was a true talent and a student of the game. He could talk at length about teams that thrived before he entered grade school, especially such dominating defenses as the Pittsburgh Steelers "Steel Curtain," the Minnesota Vikings "Purple People Eaters," or the "Doomsday Defense" of the Dallas Cowboys.

In the weeks before the draft, Sapp's stock began to fall. He acknowledged testing positive for marijuana as a University of Miami freshman and again at the NFL scouting combine. But the *New York Times* reported that Sapp also tested positive for cocaine at the combine. Sapp denied the cocaine charge and the NFL said the report was inaccurate.

Still, the damage was done. McKay and Ruskell flew to Miami to have lunch with Sapp. Having investigated Sapp thoroughly, they were well aware of the drug issues and knew that other teams, with lesser background work, might pass automatically.

"Whatever other issues you may have had, you knew Warren was not going to be unsuccessful," McKay said. "He would not allow it. Some teams weren't paying attention to those issues beforehand. So when they came up, they had to pass since they had not researched them. So he slipped accordingly."

Still, the priority for the Buccaneers was Brooks. McKay dealt his number-seven pick to Philadelphia for the number-twelve choice and two second-round selections. Then he traded two second-round picks to Dallas for the number-twenty-eight pick in the first round. That left Tampa Bay with the number-twelve and number-twenty-eight picks. If Sapp was gone at number-twelve, the Bucs felt they still might get Hugh Douglas, a promising defensive end from Central State in Ohio.

The first ten teams passed on Sapp. That left the Minnesota Vikings. The Bucs knew that head coach Dennis Green and defensive coordinator Tony Dungy liked Sapp.

With the Vikings on the clock, McKay, Ruskell, Angelo, and Bucs head coach Sam Wyche took a stroll on the practice field at One Buc Place.

"Is there any reason we shouldn't take this guy?" Wyche asked. "Do these teams know something we don't?"

The Tampa Bay brass felt comfortable with Sapp. Then they caught a break. Just a few months earlier, the *Minneapolis Star Tribune* had reported that a former employee at Stanford University, where Green previously coached, had threatened to add sexual harassment charges against Green to an employment discrimination suit she had filed against the university. (The suit was settled before any further charges were filed.)

Against this back drop, the Vikings decided they could not afford another public relations crisis, and selected Derrick Alexander, a defensive end from Florida State. The Bucs grabbed Sapp and, sixteen picks later, took Brooks.

When the first day of the 1995 draft ended, McKay and Ruskell rolled a video machine onto the back porch at One Buc Place, the team's cramped, antiquated headquarters. They lit cigars, opened a couple of beers, and watched tapes of the first two players drafted during McKay's tenure as general manager.

"If we were ever going to turn around the fortunes of this franchise," McKay said, "these were going to be the two guys to help us do it."

After twelve straight losing seasons, the turnaround was not immediate. Wyche was fired after a 7-9 season in 1995, replaced with Dungy, the Vikings defensive coordinator. A soft-spoken, deeply religious man who was an undersized defensive back for the Pittsburgh Steelers in the 1970s, Dungy had an affinity for solid citizens who managed to perform beyond their physical capabilities.

"Coach [Chuck] Noll always evaluated the player and the person," Dungy says. "There are a lot of talented football players around, but not everybody is going to make your team better. It's important to have guys who are good teammates, that fit in well, that are going to impact you positively, and character is a big part of that."

Not only was Dungy on the same page, he shared McKay's view of the coach's role in the draft. Around the league, head coaches such as New England's Bill Parcells and Jimmy Johnson, the former Dallas Cowboys coach who had just taken over in Miami, were exerting more control over the draft, seeing themselves as de facto general managers, even at a time when the league's young economic system of free agency and a salary cap made the role of the general manager more complex.

McKay viewed the draft as the domain of the GM and the scouting department. Input from the coaching staff was crucial, solicited at times, but the vast majority of the evaluations needed to come from the scouts. It was impractical to think that coaches could spend eighteen hours a day preparing their teams, from late July through December, if not January, and then take a leading role in evaluating college players.

The Buccaneers had spent much of their first two decades without a strong presence in the personnel department, letting the head coach make draft day decisions. Often, as was the case with Wyche, the head coach also was director of operations.

"With Sam, it was like, 'Let's watch a few plays. Okay, he's our guy,'" Ruskell said. "Rich saw the flaws in the system."

McKay told scouts to think of themselves as writing the draft equivalent of Cliff Notes for the coaching staff.

"We've synthesized this material," McKay would tell the coaching staff. "Now you have to read it and go out and be a cross-checker. This is what we saw, and you tell us we're right or wrong if you see it differently."

The important thing, McKay knew, was that the entire organization had a clear picture of where it wanted to go personnelwise, from the on-field schemes to character issues, and how each new player would add to the chemistry.

"It's no different than when you and your wife bring home the baby," McKay said. "You still have to motivate the player, work him into your schemes. You may find that he can't do this or that, but that's okay. Let him do something else. It's your job as an organization to make him successful. It's too easy to say, 'We may have missed.'"

The Bucs produced a solid draft class in 1996, the first year of the Dungy era, selecting defensive linemen Regan Upshaw (California) and Marcus Jones (North Carolina) in the first round. In the second round, they grabbed Mike Alstott, a bruising fullback from Purdue, and in the third picked up Donnie Abraham, a cornerback out of East Tennessee State, a Division 1-AA program.

Upshaw, Alstott, and Abraham started immediately. Alstott and Abraham would go on to play in Pro Bowls. Alstott, nicknamed the "A Train," became one of the most popular Buccaneers in team history. Jones was slower to develop, but recorded twenty sacks over the 1999 and 2000 seasons.

In 1997, the Bucs hit the jackpot with Dunn and Ronde Barber. They also grabbed offensive linemen Jerry Wunsch (Wisconsin) in the second round and Frank Middleton (Arizona) in the third. Both were starters during the Bucs' late-nineties resurgence. Dunn, Wunsch, and Barber, like Alstott and Brooks, became active in the community.

There were setbacks, to be sure, especially at wide receiver. The Bucs squandered picks on two of Spurrier's Florida wide receivers. Years before Spurrier himself bombed as head coach of the Washington Redskins, Reidel Anthony (a first-round pick after Dunn in 1997) and Jacquez Green (a second-rounder, and the Bucs' first pick in 1998) failed to make an impact. Ditto for Marquise Walker, a Michigan wide receiver taken in the third round in 2002, the Bucs' first overall selection.

Still, unlike previous regimes, the new Buccaneer front office stayed the course with players and philosophy. During training camp before the 1997 season, Barber looked overmatched and struggled to pick up the Buccaneers defensive schemes.

Angelo and Ruskell had lobbied hard to draft Barber, even though Dungy and Herman Edwards, who coached the defensive backs, had reservations. The coaches were impressed with Ronde Barber the person, but not as a potential NFL defensive back.

"He came to camp and was one of the worst players I've ever seen," Ruskell said. "We should have cut him. Jerry and I were backtracking saying, 'You liked him. No, *you* liked him.' He looked like a total bust. You have to give Tony Dungy and Herm Edwards all the credit. They told us, 'You drafted him. You liked him, and we're going to hang in there with him.' And now the guy is one of the best cornerbacks in the league."

Between Dungy's coaching and an influx of players from the draft, the Buccaneers engineered a complete turnaround. After posting a 6-10 record and a fourteenth straight losing season in 1996, the team went 10-6 in 1997. The Bucs finished 8-8 in 1998 before reaching the NFC title game following the 1999 season.

By now, most of the starting lineup on both sides of the ball had come out of McKay drafts. With a strong pipeline of talent, the Bucs were able to release veteran nose tackle Brad Culpepper before the 2000 season and replace him with Anthony McFarland, the first-round pick in 1999. Aging linebacker Hardy Nickerson was let go in favor of Jamie Duncan, a third-round choice in 1998.

In 1999, the *Fort Worth Star-Telegram*, using a complicated draft evaluation formula that included Pro Bowl appearances and player ranking among statistical leaders in various offensive and defensive categories, determined that Tampa Bay had been the best drafting team since 1995.

McKay was quickly reaching his goal of using the draft much like a Major League Baseball team does to stock its farm system. Instead of developing in the minor leagues, they could ease their way into the NFL on special teams or in backup roles.

Not only did the process make the team younger, McKay was better able to allocate valuable money under the salary cap. Instead of re-signing expensive veterans or signing even pricier free agents, he could move second- and third-year players into more prominent roles. With half the roster playing under their relatively modest rookie contracts, it created payroll flexibility.

With a team so close to Super Bowl caliber before the 2000 season, McKay addressed the club's few pressing needs by signing free agent offensive linemen Jeff Christy and Randall McDaniel. For the final piece, McKay dealt the team's two first-round picks in the 2000 draft to the New York Jets for Keyshawn Johnson, the talented but problem child wide receiver. A year later, the Bucs signed quarterback Brad Johnson.

The moves did not push the Bucs over the edge. Instead, the team needed late-season rallies to reach the playoffs in 2000 and 2001, both times losing to the Eagles in Philadelphia. Bryan and Joel Glazer, who oversaw their father's investment, ordered McKay to fire Dungy.

A long, meandering search for Dungy's replacement followed, with unsuccessful flirtations with Parcells and Steve Mariucci. The Glazers rejected McKay's recommendation to hire Marvin Lewis and then traded a pair of first-round picks and two second-round picks to the Oakland Raiders for the right to negotiate with Jon Gruden. During the process, McKay received permission to pursue other employment.

McKay interviewed with Arthur Blank, cofounder of the Home Depot, who had just purchased the Falcons for $545 million. Like the pre-McKay Buccaneers, the Falcons were perennial bottom feeders. Though they reached the Super Bowl after the 1998 season, the Falcons never had posted back-to-back winning seasons.

Blank and McKay clicked immediately, with Blank sharing McKay's vision for building a perennial contender by shrewd use of the NFL draft. Blank, who stressed community service to his Home Depot employees, liked how McKay emphasized character when acquiring players. The men also discovered they shared a passion for long-distance running.

In the end, McKay's ties to Tampa ran too deep. A press conference served as a public reconciliation between McKay and the Glazers, with McKay signing a six-year, $12 million contract extension with Tampa Bay.

Gruden, meanwhile, proved to be just what the Buccaneers needed. Unlike the low-key Dungy, Gruden was not afraid to play the role of fiery motivator. With Dungy's groundwork and a few free agents, Gruden led the Bucs to a 12-4 record and a stunning rout of his former employer, the Raiders, in Super Bowl XXXVII.

The honeymoon didn't last. Two months after the Super Bowl, during owners' meetings in Phoenix, Gruden voiced his feelings that McKay, cochairman of the NFL's competition committee, spent too much time on league issues and not enough on the Bucs. Not only that, Gruden was unimpressed with McKay's recent drafts.

It was inevitable that Gruden's philosophies were going to clash with the McKay regime. Gruden, upon taking the job, planned to overhaul the roster. McKay intervened and added a few pieces to what would become a Super Bowl champion.

Gruden preferred veteran players, though he liked to take an active role in the draft process, too. As for salary cap implications and waiting for draft picks to develop, he'd worry about those matters later. Gruden slept just four hours a night. Patience and long-term planning were not his strong suits.

McKay, with Dungy's backing, avoided players who had run-ins with the law. Gruden lobbied successfully for the Bucs to sign running back Michael Pittman, who was convicted in 2001 for domestic abuse. McKay, unable to match Atlanta's lucrative offer to model citizen Warrick Dunn, went along.

After winning the Super Bowl, Gruden pushed for more control. Every time an aging former star like Junior Seau or Emmitt Smith became available, Gruden expressed interest. He couldn't understand why the Bucs didn't acquire Kyle Turley, a high-maintenance player who didn't fit McKay's character-based system.

McKay, meanwhile, preached building through youth and the draft, and keeping an eye on the long-term salary cap picture—where storm clouds were gathering because of his pre–Super Bowl free agent signings.

Gruden could overlook off-the-field transgressions, even lobbying during the 2003 season for the Bucs to sign Darrell Russell, whose rap sheet included a suspension for violating the league's substance abuse policy and rape charges that were dismissed.

As the 2003 season came to a close, McKay had had enough. He again asked for and received permission to be released from his contract. This time, he and the Falcons' Blank struck a deal. McKay took the high road, thanking everyone in Tampa, including Gruden. Still, even in his opening remarks upon taking the Falcons job, he made it clear where their differences lie.

"We're not in this business to do anything other than win, and I'm one who wants to win the right way. I want to have the right players. I want to have guys that get out in the community. We always said there was a 'Buc player.' And we used to have pictures of Warrick Dunn and Derrick Brooks and John Lynch and we said those are 'Buc players.'"

Now McKay and Ruskell tried to find players to fit the same mold in Atlanta. It's an ambitious formula, to be sure. Rarely does a month pass where an NFL player is not arrested for some crime. In the 1998 book *Pros and Cons: The Criminals Who Play in the NFL,* authors Jeff Benedict and Don Yaeger investigated the criminal records of NFL players and concluded that at least 21 percent of players in the league had been charged with a serious crime.

Many of those players were top stars in the NFL. By eliminating players with criminal backgrounds or character issues from draft consideration, the Falcons could neglect a valuable source of talent.

McKay doesn't think so. "This isn't just a business decision of wanting reliable players. You need to have good guys. It helps fans identify with the football team and it sends the right message in the locker room. When you draft guys, just like when you sign free agents, they have to walk into your locker room. The guys there are thinking, 'Why did they get this guy?' When you bring in the right guys, they'll feel better about it."

McKay believes it's not a stretch to say that the character-first philosophy helped the Buccaneers overcome the fallout from the passing of the unpopular community investment tax that kept the Glazers from moving the team out of Tampa.

"Having good guys was gigantic for us," McKay said. "We had a franchise that not only was disliked but close to hated. People were angered when our players got into trouble with the law. Nobody had a good feel for the franchise from a winning or character standpoint. As we started to win, people began to like the team and wanted to go to games, but also to support the team by wearing shirts and putting flags on cars. That's not just winning, but also having guys that were winning off the field by getting involved in the community."

Not every player turns out to be a choir boy. Dwight Smith, a third-round pick by the Buccaneers under McKay in 2001, pleaded guilty two years later to a misdemeanor charge of brandishing a handgun in an apparent case of road rage. Kenyatta Walker, the team's first-round pick in 2001, was arrested and charged with disorderly conduct in 2003 when he refused to leave a nightclub in the Ybor City section of Tampa. Police needed to use pepper spray to subdue the 300-pound Walker, a chronic underachiever on the field.

"Can you ever be 100 percent right on a guy? Of course not," McKay said. "Some guys will start to hang out with the wrong people. They've never had money and now they're in trouble. That's going to happen. My concern is that we don't go looking for those guys."

McKay and Ruskell, like most NFL executives, do not spend much time grading their draft performances. They try to project where a player is going to be in three years, since by then he will have likely pushed out a veteran and reached his NFL potential. Occasionally they'll look back at a three-year-old draft and grade their thought processes. They find that when they're wrong it's more often because they misjudged a player's football potential, more so than his character.

"What I tell coaches is not to blame the player because we drafted him and he wasn't what we thought he was," McKay says. "Let's blame ourselves and try and make it work. It's like if your child calls from the police station because he's been arrested for DUI. I assume you're going to go down and get them out. You're going to help them out and get them better. It's the same with a player. If a player doesn't work at middle linebacker, move him to outside linebacker, or special teams where he can make you better. Don't just get mad at the player. What happens to all of us is that you get so mad at the player. Why isn't he better than this? He isn't. Sometimes you miss in that regard."

McKay has an additional member of his investigative team. Blank, the Falcons sixty-two-year-old owner, takes an active role in sizing up players the team is considering acquiring, though unlike owners such as Jerry Jones in Dallas and Daniel Snyder of the Washington Redskins, he does not try to be the de facto general manager.

Whether it's joining coaches to meet with free agents over dinner, or sitting in on interviews at the combine, Blank sells the players on Atlanta and his commitment to winning. He also outlines the organization's vast philanthropic endeavors.

Blank, who retired as cochairman of the Home Depot in 2001, believes the same philosophies of customer service and community involvement that built the company into a home improvement juggernaut, translate to the NFL. He cites the 2003 season, when Falcons fans continued to pack the Georgia Dome, even after quarterback Michael Vick broke his leg and the team lost seven straight games.

"At Home Depot, we had tens of thousands of our associates that would spend time in the field doing community work," Blank says. "We created an atmosphere that said giving back is our responsibility, and we made it easy for employees to do so. We got very positive feedback throughout these communities. People felt an alliance, an allegiance with us. That's why, even in 2003, fans still filled up the dome. Fans are going to be loyal to an organization, not just because of wins and losses, but for what it stands for in the community.

"I'm not suggesting every guy on the team is a priest or rabbi. There are degrees of character issues, but you don't want to cross that line because you run a lot of risks. One of the terms I've learned to be sensitive to is risk and reward. Now when I hear it in a character context, I don't want those players on the team."

McKay knows that the character philosophy can come across as holier-than-thou. After all, he tabbed Sapp as the cornerstone in Tampa, and Sapp is in no danger of winning a NFL Man of the Year award. The Falcons have thrived behind Vick, who though not drafted by McKay, has endured a couple of embarrassing off-the-field episodes.

"Nobody says that they're all going to be perfect," McKay said. "You have to bring in guys that come from all different walks of life and backgrounds. You're going to have guys that don't exactly fit the mold as far as being team players and treating others with respect. You can't draft all *A*s in character, and if you did you'd probably lose every game."

On the afternoon of September 28, 2004, McKay was sitting on bleachers overlooking the practice fields at the Falcons training center in Flowery Branch, a rural but growing suburb forty miles northeast of Atlanta. It's the Taj Mahal of NFL facilities, with a seventy-five thousand-square-foot corporate headquarters, an indoor turf field, a massive locker room, palatial executive offices—even an interactive Falcons museum and gift shop. Soon construction will begin on luxury garden apartments for players to live in during training camp in 2005, a first in the NFL.

At forty-five, McKay's age finally has caught up with him. With thinning, prematurely gray hair, he never quite looked the part of boy wonder, even as a thin thirty-five-year-old general manager who often could be found around the Buccaneers training complex wearing workout clothes following a lunchtime run. Recent laser surgery has allowed him to discard eyeglasses he wore for years.

It also could be that McKay always seemed older because of a long football background, from a childhood spent around championship teams at Southern Cal, to high school years as a Buccaneers ball boy, to nearly two decades in NFL front offices. He's served on several league committees, most notably the competition committee, which he's cochaired since 1998.

Throw in a Princeton diploma, a law degree, stadium lease experience, and public relations savvy, and it's the type of resume that would seem perfect for the role of NFL commissioner. McKay long has been mentioned as a successor to Paul Tagliabue, though the topic is perhaps the only question that can make the usually unflappable general manager squirm.

"It makes me very uncomfortable. You're taking about an existing guy that has done a fantastic job and has been very nice to me. If he said tomorrow, 'Okay, I want out,' then I wouldn't mind anybody asking me—although there are a lot of people in the line way ahead of me."

First, McKay wants to put together back-to-back winning seasons for the first time in Atlanta Falcons history. Like the dozens of agents that work out of Atlanta because it provides for easy access to many of the schools in the football-rich ACC and SEC, McKay is able to see a lot of college football during the busy NFL season. It helps that the University of Georgia, which does not have an indoor practice field, occasionally buses the team an hour, from Athens to Flowery Branch, to use the Falcons' facilities during bad weather. On those days, McKay and his staff got an exclusive look at the Bulldogs.

Athens had been a popular destination for NFL scouts and agents this fall. Defensive end David Pollack was projected as an early first-round pick. Quarterback David Greene, wide receivers Reggie Brown and Fred Gibson, and free safety Thomas Davis, a junior leaning toward going pro, also figured to be early draft selections.

Not that the Falcons president, once dubbed a "nonfootball guy," was going to wait for the talent to come to him. He would take an annual trip to the West Coast, where his father once coached at the University of Southern California and played at the University of Oregon. He would fit in as many scouting trips as possible around the Falcons' season and make sure to interview his younger players about former college teammates eligible for this year's draft.

"The thing I learned from law and trial work is that those that are the most prepared win," McKay said. "Not the most talented lawyer. You don't have to give the best closing argument or have the prettiest exhibits or the most impressive witnesses. It's the most prepared that tends to win. Same thing with the draft. Draft day itself should be easy, a nice fun day that unfolds the way you thought it should. Do we have the most talented staff? I think we have one of the best, but that's open to debate. I do know that nobody is going to outwork us."

McKay and his staff, like those of other NFL teams, generally have little trouble getting access to college football departments. College coaches recognize that the higher their players are drafted, the easier it will be to recruit high school kids dreaming of NFL careers.

Some coaches limit access, fearing that the presence of NFL scouts might influence their underclassmen to leave school early, or at the very least distract them from preparations for the upcoming game. Either way, there's a sometimes uneasy alliance between college football programs and the NFL that goes back nearly a century. It was this very conflict that led to the creation of the NFL Draft.

Chapter Three:

THE DRAFT—
THEN AND NOW

As early as 1920, professional football faced the problems of rapidly escalating salaries, players leaving teams for better financial offers, and the use of college players still enrolled in school.

On January 28, 1922, five months before the American Professional Football Association changed its name to the National Football League, John Clair of the Acme Packing Company admitted to using players who had college eligibility remaining during the 1921 season for the Green Bay Packers. Clair and the Green Bay management withdrew from the league.

Curly Lambeau promised to obey league rules and bought back the Packers franchise, but the issue of using college players did not go away. In 1925, Red Grange took off his University of Illinois uniform on a Saturday in late November and made his professional debut for the Chicago Bears the following Thursday, Thanksgiving Day.

George Halas, the player-coach-owner of the Bears, decided to put a stop to the practice, or at least keep others from following his lead. During a league meeting in 1926, he proposed a rule prohibiting teams from acquiring players whose classes had not yet graduated.

Halas violated his own rule in 1930, signing Notre Dame running back Joe Savoldi. In 1931, league president Joe Carr fined the Bears,

Packers, and Portsmouth (Ohio) Spartans one thousand dollars each for using college players whose classes had not graduated, and over the next few years more tension arose between the league and college coaches.

During a meeting of the nine league owners on May 19, 1935, Bert Bell, the owner of the struggling Philadelphia Eagles, proposed a draft. Teams would pick, in reverse order of finish, from among the players whose college eligibility was ending.

It was a simple concept, one not yet employed by any other professional sports league, and one that would become a cornerstone of the NFL's competitive balance.

Bell, whose Eagles had finished the 1934 season 2-9 and had not posted a winning record in their first three years in the league, had a vested interest in the draft. Teams such as the Bears and New York Giants, which dominated the league in its early years, had little to gain.

Still, Halas and Giants owner Tim Mara embraced the plan, recognizing that competitive balance was essential to draw fans to games during the Depression. Others would suggest the draft had less to do with leveling the playing field than it did with holding down salaries. After all, a drafted player could negotiate with just one team.

"There is some truth to that argument," Halas said in his autobiography. "But time proved that by leveling the clubs, the draft system heightened the attractiveness of the sport. It created bigger audiences, which brought bigger revenue, which brought higher salaries for all players."

When NFL owners met at the Ritz Carlton Hotel in Philadelphia for the inaugural NFL Draft on February 8, 1936, the setting was less formal than that of a modern-day fantasy football gathering.

The group included league pioneers Halas, Mara, Art Rooney of the Pittsburgh Pirates, George Preston Marshall of the Boston Redskins, Curly Lambeau of the Green Bay Packers, Charles Bidwill of the Chicago Cardinals, Dan Topping of the Brooklyn Dodgers, George Richards of the Detroit Lions and, of course, Bell, representing the Philadelphia Eagles.

None of the owners arrived wielding scouting reports, three-ring binders, or anything that could constitute formal research. On a wall was posted a list of ninety players whose eligibility had expired, culled from various All-America and all-conference teams.

Bell, a onetime University of Pennsylvania quarterback, who in 1946 would become the NFL's second commissioner, kicked off the draft by selecting Jay Berwanger, a halfback from the University of Chicago who had captured the inaugural Heisman Trophy.

Berwanger greeted the news of his historic selection with indifference. At a time when star players such as Bronco Nagurski of the Bears made just four hundred dollars a game, Berwanger didn't view professional football as an attractive career path. He planned to become a sports writer, of all things, and covered football for the *Chicago Daily News* before moving on to a more lucrative business career.

Bell, who would sign none of his nine draft picks, dealt Berwanger to Halas, who would have no better luck signing him. The low salaries scared off all but thirty-one of the eighty-one players from the 1936 draft. Among those not to sign were Notre Dame halfback Bill Shakespeare, selected third overall by the Pittsburgh Pirates; and an end from Alabama, taken in the fourth round by the Brooklyn Dodgers, by the name of Paul "Bear" Bryant.

The draft generated no media coverage, just a three-paragraph mention buried in the *New York Times* sports section several days later.

In 1937, with the addition of the Cleveland Rams, the draft grew from nine rounds to ten. The process expanded several more times until it reached thirty rounds in 1943. Most players drafted that year reported for military service, not the NFL.

There were other wrinkles, all in the name of promoting parity. From 1938–1948, the NFL allowed only the teams with the five worst records to draft in the second and fourth rounds.

In 1947, the NFL introduced the "bonus selection." One randomly selected team received an extra pick, a predraft choice. Once a team was selected, it was disqualified from future lotteries, a system that lasted through 1958. The bonus selections included future Hall of Famers Chuck Bednarik (Philadelphia, 1949) and Paul Hornung (Green Bay, 1957).

The early drafts were jovial, free-flowing affairs. Cigarette smoke hung over the room. Bell served as master of ceremonies, establishing a precedent for future commissioners throughout sports on draft day, announcing the picks himself and mangling difficult surnames.

After World War II, NFL teams continued to struggle to convince many of their draft picks to play in the league. The draft had effectively stopped the escalation of salaries by restricting players to one potential employer.

The All-American Football Conference changed that in 1946. Unlike a pair of short-lived operations both known as the American Football League, the AAFC represented a legitimate threat. The inaugural AAFC included the Cleveland Browns, San Francisco 49ers, and Miami Seahawks, who were replaced the following year by the Baltimore Colts.

The Browns were especially adept at acquiring talent, including quarterback Otto Graham, fullback Marion Motley, guard Bill Willis, center Frank Gatski, tackle/kicker Lou Groza, and end Dante Lavelli—all future members of the Pro Football Hall of Fame.

The AAFC didn't bother with a draft its first year. With so much talent coming home from the war and only ten NFL teams, there was no need. The NFL, taking no chances on revealing its players, held its draft in secret.

In a harbinger of the AFL–NFL conflict to come in the 1960s, separate leagues caused salaries to escalate. Dan Topping, who owned the baseball and NFL Yankees, offered two-sport Georgia star Charley Trippi a two-year baseball deal for $200,000, along with a football contract. Charles Bidwill, owner of the AAFC's Chicago Cardinals, countered with a four-year deal for $100,000 and a tryout with the Cubs. Trippi, who had spoken to Bidwill first, signed with Chicago.

The Trippi signing accelerated talks for a common draft, if not a merger. With teams in both leagues struggling financially, especially in the AAFC, the leagues merged on December 9, 1949. Only the Browns, 49ers, and Colts entered the NFL intact.

Competition from the AAFC did not inspire NFL teams to assemble scouting staffs and devote significant resources to scouting. Throughout the 1940s, some team executives would prepare for their next pick by perusing the pages of *Street & Smith's Football Year Book* or other college football magazines.

A few teams set up informal scouting networks of college coaches and former players, but the Los Angeles Rams, under owner Dan Reeves, were the first to assemble what could be called a scouting department.

Reeves, who purchased the Cleveland Rams in 1941 and moved them to Los Angeles in 1946, believed the key to football success was finding overlooked talent. Among his first hires was Eddie Kotal, a former Green Bay Packers player and small-college coach.

The scouting lifestyle Kotal created remains pretty much intact today. He spent two hundred days a year on the road, traveling from campus to campus to watch players and interview coaches. He'd start by hitting most of the major schools in the spring and then crisscross the country from the beginning of August practices through the final games. Kotal would visit as many as ten schools a week, following a familiar pattern of watching game films and interviewing coaches. After dinner, he'd retire to his hotel room to write reports.

Kotal also timed players in the forty-yard dash. Paul Brown, who began his professional coaching career in Cleveland in 1946, figured it was an accurate measure of football speed, since it was the approximate distance a player would cover on a punt. (Brown also measured the cognitive abilities of his players by giving them a twelve-minute, fifty-question test similar to the Wonderlic, the fifty-question aptitude test players now take during the NFL Scouting combine.)

Kotal built vast networks of contacts throughout the country and filed his reports in dozens of notebooks. Reeves and Kotal assembled files on every senior in the country, rolling into the drafts throughout the 1950s with trunks full of information. Other teams shook their heads in amazement, many still drafting out of *Street & Smith's* or by phoning college contacts between selections.

There were no phones in the draft room back then, and team officials sometimes disappeared for a half hour or more, there being no time limits on picks. The Rams were ahead of the game in this area, too. Under the direction of a savvy public relations director and future general manager named Pete Rozelle, they set up shop at the 1956 draft with a phone at their table.

The Rams, with a huge advantage in scouting, posted winning records in nine of their first ten seasons in Los Angeles, reaching the championship game three straight years (1949–51) and winning in 1951.

In scouting, the Rams left no stone unturned. In 1946, they broke the league's color barrier by signing UCLA halfback Kenny Washington and end Woody Strode, who became the first African Americans to play in the NFL in the modern era. In 1949, the Rams acquired Paul "Tank" Younger out of Grambling as a free agent, making the running back the first player in the NFL to come from an all-black college.

Reeves and Kotal specialized in the overlooked small-school player, believing other teams placed too much emphasis on level of competition. In 1951, they spent a nineteenth-round choice on a defensive end from tiny Arnold College. Andy Robustelli ended up in the Pro Football Hall of Fame.

Some small college players were not even in school when the Rams discovered them. Future Hall of Famer Dick "Night Train" Lane, who had played at Scottsbluff Junior College, wandered into the Rams office after a four-year stint in the army and was given a tryout. In 1953, the Rams discovered defensive tackle Gene "Big Daddy" Lipscomb, who did not play college ball, playing football in the military.

The Rams did not limit their college scouting to football. Before the 1950 season, the Rams signed Bob Boyd, a track star from Loyola of Los

Angeles who played seven years at wide receiver. In 1955, they spent a thirtieth-round pick on K. C. Jones, a member of the San Francisco University national championship basketball team. Jones reported to training camp before opting for a career with the Boston Celtics.

The Rams were the first team to understand the value of hoarding draft picks. Six times between 1952 and 1959 they had two first-round picks. In 1955, they drafted four times in the second round.

Sid Gillman, the Rams head coach from 1955 to 1959, inspired future generations of NFL scouts by separating game film into offensive and defensive reels, cutting the film further to isolate specific plays and situations.

Still, it's not as though the Rams or any other team had a crystal ball. In 1955, the Pittsburgh Steelers spent a ninth-round draft pick on a former walk-on quarterback from Louisville. The Steelers cut the kid, who had gone to high school in Pittsburgh, and Johnny Unitas signed with the Baltimore Colts, becoming one of the best quarterbacks ever.

The 1957 draft, held on November 27, 1956, featured another accidental find. The Cleveland Browns were desperate for a quarterback, but Notre Dame's Paul Hornung, Stanford's John Brodie, and Purdue's Len Dawson were gone by the time the Browns picked sixth. So the Browns "settled" for Jim Brown, the All-America running back from Syracuse.

The Green Bay Packers, meanwhile, were laying the groundwork for their success in the 1960s. Jack Vainisi began scouting for the Packers in 1950, and, like Eddie Kotal, developed a network of high school and college coaches around the country. Vainisi traveled constantly, even spending much of his honeymoon in 1952 driving through Texas and Oklahoma looking at players.

Vainisi scouted and recommended seven future Hall of Famers, including Hornung and Alabama quarterback Bart Starr (nineteenth round, 1956). In 1958, he drafted a pair of future Canton enshrinees, taking Louisiana State fullback Jim Taylor in the second round and Illinois linebacker Ray Nitschke in the fourth.

Vainisi worked like a man with little time; he suffered from a heart condition that killed him in 1960 at the age of thirty-three, but not before he convinced the Packers board to hire a New York Giants assistant coach named Vince Lombardi as head coach.

The draft still remained a low-key affair, held late in the year and staged at various points in hotels in Chicago, Milwaukee, and Philadelphia. Many players learned of their selections in the newspapers, receiving calls days later from team officials. By the time they reported to a postseason all-star game such as the Senior Bowl or East–West Shrine Game, they already were drafted.

"I got the call at my fraternity house maybe a week later," says Boyd Dowler, the Packers third-round pick out of Colorado in 1959, who would become a standout wide receiver. "It's not like anyone was calling a press conference."

Still, there were signs that scouting and the draft process were becoming more formalized. In the late 1950s, Austin Gunsel, a former FBI agent, joined the NFL's finance department, eventually working as treasurer and unofficial director of security. Gunsel implemented a policy of hiring an ex-FBI agent in each NFL city, a role that would evolve to include background screening of NFL draft picks.

The defining year that transformed the NFL Draft from a backroom gathering into a high-stakes, competitive affair was 1960, the year the American Football League and the NFL's Dallas Cowboys began play and Rozelle was elected NFL commissioner.

Unlike the AAFC and previous incarnations of the AFL, the new American Football League appeared to have financial staying power. Its ringleader was twenty-seven-year-old Lamar Hunt, the son of oil millionaire H. L. Hunt. The younger Hunt, unable to land a stake in an NFL team, formed a new AFL, with franchises in eight cities: Boston, Buffalo, New York, Houston, Dallas, Denver, Oakland, and Los Angeles.

The AFL held its first draft on November 23, 1959, and it quickly became apparent that the new league was willing to battle the NFL for every top college star. The fight reached a crescendo after the 1964 college football season when the AFL's New York Jets signed Joe Namath, the promising quarterback from the University of Alabama, to a three-year deal for more than four hundred thousand dollars.

The NFL, suffering defections among veteran players as well, hoped to put an end to its pesky competitor, or at least banish it to minor league status. Using levels of secrecy and scope that would have made the CIA proud, the NFL essentially kidnapped the draft class in November of 1965.

Commissioner Rozelle had been inspired more than a year earlier by his former boss, Rams owner Dan Reeves, to put together "Operation Hand-holding," more commonly known as the NFL's baby-sitting program. Reeves believed that the key to preventing college players from signing with the AFL was to establish relationships early on in the process. By employing businessmen skilled in the art of sales to serve as recruiters of sorts, they could get a head up on the AFL.

Reeves intended to implement his plan in Los Angeles, but Rozelle realized it could be done leaguewide. He borrowed Bert Rose, the former Rams public relations director, who was to direct the Los Angeles babysitting operation, and assigned him the entire league.

The operation was unveiled on a limited scale for the draft in November of 1964. By the following year, after the Namath signing, it was a well-oiled machine.

The NFL assigned 125 babysitters, officially called "representatives," to fan out across the country and attach themselves to top prospects in the two weeks leading up to the draft. Some babysitters were scouts, but many were selected from the front offices of various teams. Others were local salesmen. It was the babysitter's job to sell the NFL. On draft day, a call center was set up in New York and teams were patched through to players and their supervisors, who helped negotiate terms. Armed with a partial list of selections from the AFL's draft three weeks earlier, the NFL quickly was able to sign the vast majority of draft talent.

By January, 75 percent of the 232 players drafted by the fourteen NFL teams had signed contracts. Only 40 were lost to the AFL. The AFL signed 46 percent of its 181 draftees. Of the 111 players drafted in both leagues, 79 signed with the NFL, 28 with the AFL, and 4 went unsigned.

With the leagues spending a combined $7 million to sign their 1966 draft choices, it was becoming clear that neither side was winning. Following a series of secret merger meetings between the AFL's Hunt and Tex Schramm of the Dallas Cowboys, Rozelle announced a merger on June 8, 1966.

By then the Cowboys had taken the lead in scouting and dominating the draft. Schramm, the former Rams general manager who had taken a similar role with the Cowboys, longed for a way to streamline and organize the mountains of data collected on college seniors. While working for CBS Sports during a brief interlude between NFL jobs, Schramm covered the 1960 winter Olympics in Squaw Valley, California, and was impressed by the power of an IBM computer used to calculate stats and times.

Since the cost of a computer was too much for one team to bear, Schramm enlisted the Rams and 49ers, both friendly competitors, to share the investment. Over the next four years, the teams created a computer model to evaluate players. They called their three-team combine "Troika."

It took more than four years to develop a computer system that could quantify the subjective elements of scouting. The result was a standard scouting form that graded players in five areas: character, quickness, competitiveness, strength, and mental alertness. Each player was ranked in each category from one to nine, with nine being the highest.

The first computer rankings, produced before the 1965 draft, listed Namath, the Alabama quarterback, at the top of the list. Even cynics could not argue with the computer's results.

The Cowboys' pioneering use of computers fostered a stereotype of the team relying on technology to draft. Fans envisioned Tom Landry, the team's stoic head coach, waiting as a massive machine beeped and chirped, finally belching out a slip with a name.

In reality, the computer was just a tool for the Cowboys' thorough scouting system led by Schramm and Gil Brandt, a former hospital baby photographer and part-time Rams employee who became the Cowboys' first personnel director.

Brandt attended the University of Wisconsin, but instead of playing football he became one of the first self-taught draft experts or "draftniks," writing to college athletic departments to borrow game films. By reuniting in Dallas, Schramm and Brandt continued the pioneering scouting legacy of the Rams.

The Cowboys drafted wisely with their first-ever pick, selecting defensive tackle and future Hall of Famer Bob Lilly from Texas Christian with the thirteenth overall pick in 1961. But the Cowboys would become better known for mining the ranks of undiscovered talent.

Brandt, like Eddie Kotal, was a tireless worker, building a deep network of contacts in college football offices, right down to secretaries and trainers. He sent gifts to sources and peppered prospects with Cowboys information. In Brandt's first months on the job, he signed two dozen free agents, a trend he would continue throughout his career, even when the Cowboys were well stocked.

Like the 1950s Rams, the Cowboys focused on small schools, going where other teams did not. Brandt wrote college coaches in other sports for recommendations on athletes that might make good football players, and gambled on them with low draft picks or free agent contracts.

Basketball players Cornell Green (Utah State) and Pete Gent (Michigan State) became productive NFL players at cornerback and wide receiver, respectively. (Kentucky's Pat Riley stuck with the NBA route.)

Bob Hayes, best known as a gold medal sprinter at the 1964 Olympics, became a star wide receiver, though Carl Lewis never took the Cowboys up on their offer.

Then there was Naval Academy quarterback Roger Staubach, whom the Cowboys drafted in the tenth round in 1964 and waited for while he fulfilled a five-year service commitment.

The Cowboys were the first team to scout for "character" in terms of citizenship. Landry, the no-nonsense coach, wanted clean-cut, God-fearing, family men. He figured hard-partying players were less likely to make the most of their talents and more likely to embarrass the franchise. It was an ambitious goal, though the Cowboys benefited from players in both categories.

Brandt began interviewing players whenever possible. He asked them what they thought of the Dallas Cowboys, to gauge their passion for playing for the franchise. Not that it was a tough sell. In 1966, the Cowboys began a stretch of twenty consecutive winning seasons.

"We'd ask a lot of stupid questions," Brandt said. "We'd say, 'Just out of curiosity, did you play Little League baseball? Yeah? What position did you play?' If the kid said second base, you'd think, 'Uh-oh. He must not have been a very good athlete. Otherwise he would have been playing shortstop.'"

By the early 1970s, Schramm and Brandt feared the rest of the league had caught up with the Dallas scouting juggernaut. No longer were teams ignoring small schools and other popular Cowboys' fishing holes.

"Our scouts have seen it coming," Schramm told the *Fort Worth Press* in 1973. "They say it's like a jungle out there. Every place they go to look at a player they run over half a dozen scouts from other teams."

The gap between the Cowboys and everyone else closed in part because of the creation of combines, like the early Troika, where teams pooled scouting resources and shared basic information to save time and money. In 1963, three teams formed LESTO (Lions-Eagles-Steelers Talent Organization). The Bears came on board the following year to make it BLESTO. CEPO (Central Eastern Personnel Organization), formed in 1964, was made up of the Colts, Browns, Packers, and St. Louis Cardinals.

The Dallas run wasn't quite over, in part because the Cowboys, like the earlier Rams, believed in stockpiling draft picks. With selections obtained from other teams, they drafted defensive end Ed "Too Tall" Jones with the first overall pick in 1974. The following year, Dallas selected defensive tackle Randy White with the second pick, obtained from the New York Giants in exchange for quarterback Craig Morton.

Then there was Tony Dorsett. The Tampa Bay Buccaneers, who drafted future Hall of Famer Lee Roy Selmon with their first-ever pick in 1976, kicked off the 1977 draft by taking running back Ricky Bell, who had played for Bucs head coach John McKay at Southern Cal.

Dallas then traded four picks to Seattle for the rights to the number-two selection, which they used on Dorsett, the Heisman Trophy winner at Pittsburgh and the first college running back to rush for more than 6,000 yards. Dorsett would rush for 12,739 yards in the NFL, nearly 10,000 more than Bell.

Still, Schramm's prediction of a more level scouting playing field was coming true. From 1971 through the 1981 season, four teams won all of the Super Bowls, and the common denominator between Dallas, the Pittsburgh Steelers, Miami Dolphins, and Oakland Raiders was an ability to take advantage of scouting and the draft.

The Steelers drafted at least one Hall of Famer each year between 1969 and 1972. After a forgettable 1973 draft, they put together the best class of all time in 1974. Despite picking late each round because of a 10-4 record in 1973, the Steelers chose future Hall of Famers with four of their first five picks: wide receiver Lynn Swann in the first, linebacker Jack Lambert in the second, wide receiver John Stallworth in the fourth, and center Mike Webster in the fifth. No other team ever has selected more than two future Canton enshrinees in one draft.

By the late 1970s, the draft had been moved ahead from November to January to April, allowing teams a full four months from the end of the college bowl schedule to further analyze players.

In 1971, Dallas, San Francisco, and Buffalo, descendants of the original "Troika" combine, staged the first scouting combine event. Fifty players showed up to be measured, poked, and physically tested. Over the next twelve years, as many as three combines were staged over separate weekends following the Super Bowl. BLESTO brought its players to the Pontiac Silverdome for a few years. The National Football Scouting combine, a descendant of CEPO, held its event in Tampa, while a third group, which included Dallas and Seattle, used the Seattle Kingdome.

In 1984, the NFL brought some sanity to the process, establishing one leaguewide combine, held at the New Orleans Superdome. Only five teams did not participate. All twenty-eight clubs showed up in 1985, when the combine took place in Tempe, Arizona, and was marred by rain. The combine returned indoors to New Orleans for a year before finding a permanent home in Indianapolis and the Hoosier Dome (now the RCA Dome).

The crumbling of the Schramm-Brandt-Landry dynasty in Dallas began with a series of bad drafts in the late '70s and early '80s. With Staubach's career winding down, Dallas passed on Notre Dame quarterback Joe Montana, selected by the 49ers in the third round in 1979. With Montana at the helm, the 49ers won four Super Bowls. His favorite target, wide receiver Jerry Rice, came out of tiny Mississippi Valley State in 1985, and became the scouting poster child for small-school players.

A new wave of talent became available in 1990 when underclassmen became eligible for the draft. A year earlier, Oklahoma State running back Barry Sanders challenged the NFL's rule that a player needed to be four seasons removed from high school to be draft eligible. The NFL made an exception for Sanders, and a year later the rule was rewritten to require the passage of just three college seasons after the player's high school graduation for eligibility.

Dallas, coming off a 1-15 season and under the new management of owner Jerry Jones and head coach Jimmy Johnson, spent the first pick of the new underclassman era in 1990 on Emmitt Smith, a junior running back from the University of Florida. Along with Troy Aikman, the team's number-one pick from the year before, Smith would build a new Cowboys powerhouse.

After the 1992 season, players with four years of experience were granted unrestricted free agency in a settlement of a lawsuit filed in 1987 by the NFL Players Association. In 1993, a new collective bargaining agreement between the union and the NFL created a salary cap. Free agency seemed, on the surface, to lessen the importance of the draft. Teams now could plug gaps with free agents.

In reality, the draft became more important. A good draft, especially at the lower rounds, could provide talent at a bargain price, locked in for years. On the flip side, a high-priced bust selected in the first round could wreck a team's salary cap flexibility to sign talent in the years to come. Now more than ever, a team's scouting efforts needed to focus on whether a player had the physical skills, mental makeup, and character to cut it in the NFL.

The Indianapolis Colts and San Diego Chargers came to know this better than anyone. In 1998, the Colts held the first pick in the draft and were torn between two quarterbacks: Peyton Manning of Tennessee and Ryan Leaf of Washington State.

Both were big, strong-armed passers with undeniable talent. Manning, the son of former Saints quarterback Archie, lived in the film room and grew up with the idea of following his dad into the NFL. Leaf was less polished, but many scouts believed he had a higher "upside."

With millions of dollars on the line, the Colts and Chargers spent the months leading up to the draft getting inside the heads of both. The Chargers turned to Jonathan Niednagel, a researcher at the Brain Type Institute in Missouri, who believed there were sixteen distinct "brain types." That explained why some people are better suited to be quarterbacks or CEOs than others.

A year earlier, Niednagel's stock rose when he gave the Orlando Magic a glowing review on prep star Tracy McGrady before the NBA Draft. He warned the Chargers that Leaf did not have the brain type to handle the pressures of leading a rebuilding team. Manning, Niednagel believed, would be a star.

The Chargers didn't listen and handed Leaf a bonus of $11.25 million. From the beginning, Leaf established a pattern of poor play and immature behavior. The Chargers released him after three horrific seasons and he was out of football two years after that, arguably the biggest bust in draft history.

With the dawn of the new millennium, scouting and success in the draft continued to separate the most successful franchises from everyone else. The New England Patriots, under head coach Bill Belichick and general manager Scott Pioli, built a dynasty through the draft, led by quarterback Tom Brady, a sixth-round pick in 2000.

By the time the Manning–Leaf debate heated up in the spring of 1998, the NFL Draft had become a multimedia extravaganza. Sports radio, which exploded in the 1990s, became a twenty-four hour barroom for endless speculation. Draft talk could be found every day of the year. It was the perfect never-ending debate, since nobody, with the possible exception of Niednagel, could truly predict the success or failure of a player.

The emergence of the Internet in the late 1990s created an additional outlet for draft discussion. Suddenly every self-proclaimed draft expert needed to have a Web site, complete with player information and a regularly updated mock draft.

Then there was ESPN, which turned a smoky backroom business meeting into must-see TV.

When ESPN asked the NFL to broadcast its annual "selection meeting" in 1980, it was not because network officials envisioned millions of viewers or a cult following for year-round draft coverage. The year-old, fledgling cable sports station in Bristol, Connecticut, merely was looking for some much needed programming. Anything featuring the NFL shield seemed like a good bet.

The future "worldwide leader of sports" was in just seven million homes at the time, and had not yet landed contracts to televise major sports leagues. When ESPN's president Chet Simmons approached Rozelle about televising the draft, the commissioner all but laughed.

Even a marketing visionary like Rozelle found it difficult to see the allure of watching a bunch of guys sitting around tables shouting out names. That didn't sound like riveting television, especially not on Tuesday and Wednesday afternoons, which was when the draft was held until 1988.

The move to weekends that year was not one of Rozelle's shrewd marketing decisions, but merely a concession to New York's Marriott Marquis hotel, which began hosting the draft in 1985 to boost business. Three years later, Marriott needed the space to handle the lucrative midweek banquet circuit.

Instead of paying more for the weekday space, Rozelle shifted the draft to Saturday and Sunday, much to the chagrin of team officials, who didn't want to give up a weekend in the off-season.

They would never get it back. The league and the network quickly discovered that there were millions of football-starved fans across the nation just like the crazy young men who showed up at the draft site to boo the New York Jets' selections in person. The Marriott Marquis would be the last of a long series of hotels to host the event, giving way to a theater at Madison Square Garden.

ESPN drew nearly 1.7 million viewers in 1988 to view the draft. By 1993, the audience had grown to 2.5 million. In 2004, a staggering 31 million viewers tuned in over what had become a marathon, two-day affair to hear that their team was "on the clock."

ESPN is now in more than ninety million homes and is the only network to have broadcast the four major team sports during the same year. But even with multiple channels and thousands of hours of live coverage, the draft arguably is its signature event—or rather pseudo-event.

For all of ESPN's multiple sets, prepackaged features, and glitzy introductions, the draft, at its essence, is nothing more than a business meeting conducted in painfully slow fashion, at least in the first round. Still, each spring the network manages to grab attention away from athletes competing in actual contests.

Nothing is more suited to ESPN, its army of analysts, and its self-promotional engine, than the NFL Draft. There's a five-month calendar of preliminary events, beginning with college bowl games, many of which appear on ESPN. There's the Senior Bowl, held in late January and heavily covered by ESPN, and the late-February NFL combine, which is broadcast exclusively on the NFL's own network, but is covered extensively by ESPN. That leaves two months for ESPN to scrutinize the volatile draft "stocks" of every position and player, which it does to some degree all year.

The draft has become the NFL's off-season marketing platform, stealing attention from the first month of the Major League Baseball schedule and the end of the NBA and NHL regular seasons, and keeping the NFL in the forefront.

That's significant because the NFL, among the four major sports leagues, has the longest stretch between its championship game and first regular season contest. The draft, held in late April, falls almost in the middle of the hiatus. Unlike baseball, with its unknown cast of high school and college draftees, or the NBA's increasingly European contingent of draft picks, NFL selections are college stars and familiar faces to fans, especially in the early rounds.

Because of parity in the NFL, fans believe their teams are just one young player away from the Super Bowl, even though few NFL draft picks make an impact as rookies. Still, most at least play special teams and contribute in backup roles. They certainly don't disappear for years in the minor leagues like their counterparts in baseball and hockey.

Then there's the unbridled popularity of the NFL itself, fueled by lasting labor peace and competitive balance, to say nothing of undertones of sex (cheerleaders) and violence, along with a weekly episode format that's ideal for television and the short attention spans of the technological age. Most teams compete in new, publicly funded stadiums, and have waiting lists of thousands of fans willing to purchase tickets.

The NFL has become a runaway cash machine. In September of 2004, *Forbes* Magazine, in its annual listing of franchise values, valued nineteen NFL clubs at $700 million or more. The only sports team ranked ahead of the lowest-valued NFL franchise (Arizona Cardinals,

$552 million and climbing, with a new stadium under construction) was the New York Yankees.

No sport, with the possible exception of NASCAR, approaches the NFL's popularity.

"Baseball is America's pastime," Howie Long said during his Pro Football Hall of Fame induction speech in 2000. "But football is truly America's passion."

That passion is channeled by thousands of draftniks, who, through the Internet, follow the ups and downs of a player in the months leading up to the draft with the intensity of day traders. The draftniks mock-draft endlessly and collect information obsessively.

No draftnik rivals the legendary Joel Buchsbaum, a reclusive, self-taught football analyst who for more than two decades watched film and worked a network of sources as vast as any NFL scout or executive, al-most exclusively by phone from his Brooklyn apartment. His *Pro Football Weekly* columns and draft books were considered must-reading for fans and NFL executives, many of whom turned to *him* for information. New England Patriots head coach Bill Belichick and Ernie Accorsi, the general manager of the New York Giants, were among those that at-tended Buchsbaum's funeral in 2002.

Buchsbaum, with a gaunt physique and nasal voice, never was a good fit for television, though he appeared regularly on radio. The TV void was filled by Mel Kiper Jr., who, as an eighteen-year-old in 1979, assem-bled his own draft guide and distributed it to NFL executives and media.

Accorsi, then the general manager of the Colts, was among those that sent words of encouragement. By 1984, Kiper was on ESPN and becom-ing the face of the draft, with his signature pompadour hair and endless stream of player information.

In his early ESPN days, Kiper was more likely to take teams to task for what he viewed as bad selections, famously calling out the Jets in 1989 for drafting linebacker Jeff Lageman from the University of Vir-ginia in the first round.

"It's obvious to me the Jets don't know what the draft's all about," Kiper said.

Kiper knew exactly what the draft was about, and what it was becom-ing, a year-round process that blurred college and professional football and channeled the passions of fans of both. From one draft report in 1979, he built an empire of draft publications. He parlayed a one-weekend ESPN gig into yearlong employment that included regular draft projections online and on television and a college football–themed radio show in the fall.

"When you say Mel Kiper you think of the NFL draft," Kiper has said. "That's something I've always been very proud of."

As for Lageman, he enjoyed a productive, decade-long career with the Jets and Jacksonville Jaguars. Perhaps Kiper could be forgiven for undervaluing the linebacker. After 1942, when Pittsburgh drafted halfback Bill Dudley first overall, the University of Virginia generated just three first-round picks in the next forty-six years.

After Lageman, the Cavaliers produced five first-round selections in the next decade, most notably Herman Moore of the Detroit Lions in 1991. But entering the 2004 season, no Cavalier had been selected before the third round since the 2000 draft.

That was bad for recruiting, since it did not speak highly of Virginia's ability to prepare players for the NFL. Nobody knew that better than Al Groh, the longtime former NFL assistant now at the helm of his alma mater, who ran his ship like a pro franchise and was determined to make Virginia the top NFL prep school.

Chapter Four:

PRO COLLEGE
FOOTBALL

The Virginia Cavaliers were 4-0 and ranked tenth in the country when they took the field at home against Clemson on October 7, 2004. Al Groh, the longtime Bill Parcells disciple who had resigned as head coach of the New York Jets after a one-year stint four years earlier, had transformed a Virginia program with a recent history of good, but not great squads into a national title contender.

Across the sideline, Tommy Bowden paced anxiously. Son of Bobby Bowden, the veteran Florida State head coach, Tommy saved his job at Clemson with a strong finish in 2003. That mattered little now, what with the Tigers off to a 1-3 start and fans again calling for his head.

Clemson defeated Virginia twenty-nine straight times before the Cavaliers stopped the streak in 1990. The teams had split the series since, with Virginia holding a slight advantage, but the Cavaliers fans still remembered the streak and took great joy in Clemson's downfall.

With so many subplots, ESPN officials were thrilled with their decision months earlier to schedule the upstart Cavaliers and struggling Tigers as one of their two Thursday night matchups. The national media had not converged on Charlottesville, though Virginia's spacious press box had a larger-than-average crowd on hand.

For a group of eleven National Football League scouts and executives patrolling the sidelines before the game, the contest was meaningless;

they planned to depart long before the finish to beat traffic. They were on hand to get a close look at about a dozen of Groh's players with serious NFL potential, along with a lesser number of Clemson standouts.

The Cavaliers stormed out of a tunnel pumped full of smoke by a fog machine, to the delight of a sellout crowd of 61,833. Groh jogged over to the sidelines and greeted three friends from his NFL days.

There was Tom Donahoe, the president and general manager of the Buffalo Bills, whom Groh met when Donahoe was an area scout with the Pittsburgh Steelers and Groh was head coach at Wake Forest in the early 1980s. There was Terry Bradway, who took over as general manager of the New York Jets after Groh departed, and Charlie Casserly, the Houston Texans general manager, who never worked with Groh but shares a mutual respect based on their years of NFL experience.

The NFL officials, or at least their scouting staffs, had watched videotapes of Groh's players and were impressed with their size, speed, and playing ability. The executives had spent the previous hour roaming the sidelines as players warmed up, analyzing "body types." They took notes on whether bodies were chiseled or soft, whether arms were long or short, and whether calves were skinny or tight.

Now they turned to Groh to help fill in the gaps that videotape or medical evaluations could not provide. Were there any discipline problems? Did a particular player lack heart or motivation? How passionate was a certain player about football? The line of questioning was not nearly as deep as it might be back at the Virginia football facility, without a game on the line, but it was valuable nonetheless.

They expressed interest in Elton Brown, the massive, six-six, 338-pound offensive guard considered among the best in the country at his position. They asked about Alvin Pearman, who technically was the backup tailback, but saw significant playing time, thrived on special teams, and showed flashes of NFL potential. The scouts were curious about defensive end Chris Canty, who was projected as a first-round pick in the 2005 draft as recently as two weeks ago, before a devastating knee injury against Syracuse sidelined him for the rest of the season.

Brown, Pearman, and Canty were seniors, along with a half dozen other players with lesser NFL prospects. They were hardly the only Virginia players eligible for the 2005 NFL Draft, though the scouts knew better than to ask Groh—or any other college coach—about underclassmen.

Players that are at least three seasons removed from high school are eligible for the draft. Juniors can leave early. So can a sophomore, if he spent a year in prep school following high school graduation or was "redshirted," not playing as a college freshman in order to develop further.

Groh, like most college coaches, believes there is almost never a reason for a player to leave school for the NFL with eligibility remaining. After all, he could benefit from another year of development at the college level.

That's usually true—less than half of underclassmen who declare early for the draft are selected in the first three rounds—but it's *definitely* true that college football coaches win more games when their best players complete their college eligibility, rather than leaving early for the NFL.

It's a sometimes uneasy alliance between the NFL and the colleges. The college coaches stress that they're serving student-athletes, and don't want players looking beyond the next game, let alone to the next level. At the same time, they realize the best way to recruit high school kids to their school is to produce a steady parade of players to the NFL.

So the college coaches throw open their office doors during the season, allowing NFL scouts to arrive early on weekday mornings and watch videotape of players. The scouts, always clad in golf shirts or jackets bearing their NFL team logos, can spend much of the morning chatting with trainers, assistant coaches, tutors, and the head coach himself about players. After lunch they can watch practice.

On game days, they receive press-box credentials and can wander the field before the game. In exchange for such carte blanche access, they agree not to ask about or express interest in underclassmen, even those widely considered to be leaving early.

Sometimes college coaches will let NFL friends know if players are coming out early, if only to give them a head start on scouting. Like character evaluation, it's one area where scouts must have a strong network of sources to provide them with inside information.

"It's imperative that scouts dig deeper," says Donahoe, the Bills president. "You need guys you can trust that will tell you if someone is a good character guy or not. If you have developed those right relationships, you'll get an honest evaluation."

By now, many scouts had been clued in about Heath Miller, who was in his fourth season at Virgina but was just a junior because of a redshirt season in 2001. As a sophomore, Miller led all tight ends in the nation with seventy receptions for 835 yards. Like many draft prospects, he already was dealing with agents, which was allowed under the guidelines of the National Collegiate Athletic Association (NCAA), so long as the player receives nothing of value, not even a can of soda.

Scouts viewed Miller as the prototype tight end for the increasingly popular West Coast offense, which emphasizes short passes and places a premium on catching over blocking when it comes to tight ends.

Miller kept in close contact with Matt Schaub, the Virginia quarterback the previous season, who now was a rookie with the Atlanta Falcons, for advice about choosing an agent. David Dunn, Schaub's representative, was lobbying hard through Schaub and directly to represent Miller for the NFL Draft.

As a student, Miller was a senior. But he was a junior by NCAA guidelines, which technically made him off limits to NFL scouts, though most knew to treat him like a senior and scout accordingly.

Three other players were *definitely* off limits. Ahmad Brooks and Darryl Blackstock were NFL prototype linebackers and represented Groh's finest work as a talent developer since returning to the college ranks. D'Brickashaw Ferguson quietly had emerged as one of the nation's top left tackles.

Brooks and Blackstock, standing six-four and weighing between 240 and 260 pounds, delivered bone-crunching tackles and ran much faster than other players their size. Nobody knew that better than Groh, who as a linebackers coach under Parcells for the Jets, New York Giants, and New England Patriots had worked closely with the likes of Hall of Famer Lawrence Taylor and Pro Bowlers Carl Banks, Mo Lewis, Chris Slade, and Willie McGinest.

Blackstock and Ferguson were juniors, Brooks a sophomore, but all three were eligible for the draft, Brooks by virtue of a season spent in prep school.

Few players in college football in 2004 had as much upside as Brooks, named by USA Today the 2001 High School Defensive Player of the Year. Ahmad ran so fast, hit with so much force, and possessed so much raw athletic ability that Groh had at times lined him up as a kickoff returner, wide receiver, and safety.

Brooks, like every other college football player with pro potential, was getting bombarded with letters and phone calls from many of the one thousand three hundred agents registered by the NFL Players Association, all hoping to earn a 3 percent commission on the career earnings of the next Lawrence Taylor.

The agents had their work cut out for them, and not just because Brooks was so coveted and unsure of whether he was coming out. His father, Perry, played eight seasons at defensive tackle for the Washington Redskins and knew all about dealing with agents. Having grown up in a two-parent household with the financial comfort that comes from an NFL career, Brooks did not need to leave early for pro football riches.

Blackstock was a different story. When he was a freshman, his then-girlfriend became pregnant, and he now had a thirteen-month-old son, Savion, to support.

The agents would try their best to get close to Blackstock, Brooks, and Ferguson. As for the scouts and NFL executives, they knew to keep their distance.

Chris Canty tried to get comfortable as he watched ESPN's coverage of the Virginia–Clemson game. Lying in a hospital bed in Birmingham, Alabama, amid a fog of painkillers, he surveyed the wreckage of his left knee and, he feared, his football career.

Al Groh, ever wary of the media, had refused to disclose much about Canty's injury, even though there was no chance of the senior defensive end returning to play college football. The only thing Groh told the press was that Canty had suffered a season-ending, "severe left knee injury."

Severe? Canty's lower leg had essentially been ripped from his body at the knee. It was still in one piece, but the posterior cruciate ligament (PCL), lateral collateral ligament (LCL), and anterior cruciate ligaments (ACL) were shredded. Only the medial collateral ligament (MCL) remained intact.

The first thought Canty had upon being helped from the football field in agony twelve days earlier was not when he'd play football again, but whether he would ever *walk* again.

It was a routine play. Canty chased down Syracuse tailback Damien Rhodes from behind. Two players—one from each team—converged and Canty's left knee buckled from the weight of the pile.

Canty, like the rest of his teammates, knew the story of Anthony Poindexter, the team's running backs coach who, as a hard-hitting safety for the Cavaliers in 1998, saw a once-promising NFL career crumble amid a similar pile of bodies. Poindexter had returned for a senior season, turning down an early entrance to the NFL.

After the 2003 season, Canty requested a rating from an NFL advisory committee that evaluates the draft prospects of juniors and other players three years removed from high school. It's a notoriously conservative bunch, and the information it provides to juniors all but discourages players from going pro early. The letter begins with, "Since 1990, when the National Football League reluctantly concluded that a change in its eligibility standards was necessary . . ." as if the NFL made the decision unilaterally, not in the face of litigation.

The committee, which is made up of twelve NFL scouts and executives, along with representatives from BLESTO and National Football Scouting, "serves in a limited advisory capacity for players faced with the decision of whether to make such a declaration" for the NFL Draft. The committee provides one of five assessments. The player either:

- will be drafted in round one
- will not be drafted higher than the second round
- will not be drafted higher than the fourth round
- will not be drafted higher than the sixth round
- will not be drafted

The committee stresses that the rating is merely a "good faith opinion" and is "in no way a commitment or guarantee of any player's selection." Despite the explicit instructions and qualified language of the rating, players often interpret the rating of "will not be drafted higher than the second round" as "will likely be drafted in the second round."

That's sufficient reason for many players to go pro. But not for Canty, who did not play football until his junior year of high school in Charlotte, North Carolina, and received only two Division 1 scholarship offers, from Virginia and Boston College.

He arrived in Charlottesville in the fall of 2000, a gangly six-seven, 215 pounds, with decent potential. A "project," in coach-speak. Canty immediately set up shop in the weight room and steadily put on weight. By 2002, he was a well-chiseled 280 pounds and led ACC defensive linemen in tackles. On pace to graduate after the 2003 season, there seemed little reason to return.

Instead, Canty purchased disability insurance, enrolled in graduate school and, like Poindexter six years earlier, shredded three of the four ligaments in a knee on a similar play.

As Canty underwent an examination in the training room the morning after the injury, Groh was among his first visitors.

"You can't control what happened, but you can control how you react to it," Groh said. "Now you just have to be the fastest guy to come off this kind of injury."

Canty nodded and forced a smile, even as he winced in pain. Virginia players marveled at how Groh could compartmentalize any setback, no matter how serious. Just another minor obstacle to overcome, he made it seem.

There was precedent. Running back Willis McGahee endured the same injury at the University of Miami and now was thriving for the Buffalo Bills.

I can do this, Canty told himself.

The next visitor was Poindexter. Unlike Groh, his expression was not one of compassion or encouragement, but urgency.

"Listen to me, you've got to get out of here as fast as you can and have the surgery," Poindexter said. "I waited three weeks to get it done. Scar tissue sets in. You want to give this the best shot possible."

Within days, Canty was stretched out uncomfortably on a plane to Birmingham, where James Andrews, the orthopedist who had put hundreds of pro athletes back together, operated on the knee.

Now Canty watched from the hospital bed as the Cavaliers moved on without him. Faith, he reminded himself, would be his guide. Shirley Canty, the pastor of the Calvary United Methodist Church in Charlotte, and her congregation were praying hard on behalf of her injured son.

Yes, Chris Canty told himself, he would make it back in time for the NFL Draft, now just six and a half months away. He would become the fastest guy to return from the surgery and would have the pro career NFL scouts had envisioned nine months earlier. That much, he knew, was certain.

First, he had to figure out how to walk again.

As Canty settled in to watch the second half, the NFL scouts and executives quietly observed the game from the press box. They were assigned seats in two rows on the far end of the box, far away from the media, and with plenty of space between one another.

It's not that scouts worry about competitors peeking at their notes; given the grueling travel and marathon hours, many of them become good friends. Besides, they glean most of their information from watching film, practice, and interviewing coaches, and they take few notes during games. Virginia's media relations department, following Groh's lead, just wanted to make sure the NFL representatives felt comfortable.

It was an impressive gathering of NFL brass, who were on hand not only because of the volume of draft-eligible talent in the game, but because Thursday night is a good time for a general manager or personnel director to duck out and see a game.

During the season, a NFL general manager is immersed in the day-to-day running of a team. There are injured players to replace, constant meetings with team owners, coaches, and agents, and a daily barrage of interview requests from reporters.

The bulk of scouting is handled by a staff of "area scouts" spread out across the country, like the ones on hand that evening representing the Carolina Panthers and Dallas Cowboys. Over the course of the college football season, they file hundreds of reports, which in January become the basis for a more thorough evaluation that includes the general manager and coaching staff.

Still, most GMs try to find the time during the season to see at least three college games a month, usually not far from home. When the team is playing on the road on Sunday, the executives will visit a nearby school on Friday and Saturday. The idea is to build a working knowledge of college players in the fall so they'll be up to speed when draft meetings begin in earnest in December and January.

For Vinny Cerrato, the vice president of football operations for the Washington Redskins, attending the Virginia–Clemson game was a no-brainer. He made the two-hour drive from his northern Virginia home and would be back in the office early the following morning.

Like other NFL executives, Cerrato relies heavily on a vast network of college coaches he knows from previous jobs, first as recruiting coordinator at Notre Dame from 1986–1990 and from nine seasons spent in scouting with the San Francisco 49ers.

Before the game, while his competitors from other teams chatted up Al Groh, Cerrato checked in with Clemson offensive line coach Brad Scott and Mark D'Onofrio, Virginia's tight ends and special teams coach.

Cerrato had never worked with either, though he sometimes recruited head-to-head against Scott when Scott was Florida State's recruiting coordinator in the late '80s. Cerrato also tried unsuccessfully to recruit D'Onofrio to Notre Dame (D'Onofrio chose Penn State). Still, those are significant enough connections, so that Cerrato feels comfortable turning to the two assistants for insight into players.

Then again, Cerrato is blessed with the ability to build lasting relationships, even with unlikely people. He was among the first employees hired when Daniel Snyder purchased the Redskins in 1999, and aside from spending the 2001 season as an analyst for ESPN, he has stayed in the good graces of the notorious taskmaster. Cerrato counts sports agent Gary Wichard among his closest friends, even serving in his wedding party.

Building a network of people for draft scouting purposes was no different.

"When you want to know about a player, you start with the friends you have on the coaching staff," Cerrato says. "From there, you go to the strength coach, trainer, graduate assistants—regardless of whether you have previous relationships or not. You learn in this business how to build relationships quickly."

Cerrato had a national championship ring from his stint under Lou Holtz at Notre Dame and a Super Bowl ring from the 49ers from 1994. But the Redskins had struggled under Snyder's ownership. Even Joe Gibbs, the Hall of Fame coach who came out of retirement nine months earlier, had made little difference over the first month of the 2004 NFL season.

The 2005 draft would be the second since Gibbs's return. Gibbs always has been a fan of using multiple tight ends, retaining as many as five on the roster, and Cerrato was keeping an eye on Heath Miller, Virginia's All-American.

Early in the second half, with Virginia just ten yards from the end zone, Miller ran a perfect pattern to his left and reached over his shoulder for the ball. But quarterback Marcus Hagans overthrew him.

"We ran that same play against Dallas last week," Cerrato says.

NFL rules prohibit team employees from commenting on underclassmen. Cerrato did not speak directly about Miller, though he almost certainly knew the tight end was likely to go pro.

"A lot of times, the school will tell you if a guy is coming out," Cerrato said, not referring to Miller specifically.

At halftime, Cerrato departed to beat the traffic. Most of his colleagues followed shortly. For NFL scouts, the game is far less important than information gleaned beforehand.

Two seats over from Cerrato's empty chair, Tom Donahoe scribbled down notes and chatted with Bill Rees, the director of player personnel for the San Francisco 49ers. Donahoe shuffled scouting reports on Clemson and Virginia players provided by BLESTO, one of the two scouting services most NFL teams subscribe to.

For Donahoe, the president and general manager of the Buffalo Bills, the trip to Charlottesville was a welcome respite from the day-to-day running of a struggling franchise.

A former high school football and basketball coach, Donahoe rose through the ranks of the Pittsburgh Steelers scouting department and spent most of the 1990s running one of the decade's most successful teams. After losing a power struggle with head coach Bill Cowher and getting fired, Donahoe spent a year working for ESPN before being hired by the Buffalo Bills, another team of the '90s.

Unfortunately for Donahoe, the Bills were light years removed from the team that appeared in four consecutive Super Bowls (losing all four) under head coach Marv Levy and quarterback Jim Kelly. Though the Bills finished 11-5 as recently as 1999, and 8-8 the season before his hiring, Donahoe inherited an aging roster with contracts that provided him little flexibility under the salary cap. Some twenty-three million dollars of cap money already had been spent on players long gone.

Donahoe did what he could, shipping a first-round pick to New England for Drew Bledsoe, who resurrected his career in Buffalo. Before the 2003 season, Donahoe carved enough room under the salary cap to sign star safety Lawyer Milloy, a victim of the cap in New England.

Still, the turnaround had been slow. Under Donahoe, the Bills went 3-13 in 2001, 8-8 in 2002, and 6-10 in 2003. They were 0-3 when Donahoe boarded team owner Ralph Wilson Jr.'s private jet to Charlottesville.

"We've had so many problems the first couple of years in Buffalo because of cap problems and a roster that badly needed to be turned over," Donahoe said. "Our roster was terrible three years ago, just pathetic."

Like his colleagues around the league, Donahoe faced the challenge of managing the salary cap. Successful franchises create a pipeline of young, relatively inexpensive players through the draft. As established players grow older and gain the leverage to demand more lucrative contracts, teams can release them, confident that the younger players can step into expanded roles.

The problem occurs when draft picks don't pan out, forcing teams to re-sign the veteran or acquire a comparable free agent to fill in the gap. That results in a bigger hit to the salary cap, especially if the veteran player gets hurt or his skills deteriorate quickly.

"You always have to be looking ahead with the cap and contracts," Donahoe says. "Sometimes you're forced with the cap to make decisions, and some guys you just can't keep. Ideally, you want to have a roster where you have guys from the draft you can plug in. But we've got so many holes right now, we're just trying to get players anywhere we can get them."

With a five-year contract through 2005, Donahoe's future in Buffalo hinged in part on having a successful draft in 2005. That was what made out-of-the-way trips to places like Charlottesville so important. Of course, as his NFL competitors in the press box reminded him as he packed up to leave, it's a lot easier with a private jet at your disposal.

"My travel isn't nearly as tough as what these guys face," said Donahoe, who logged thousands of hard scouting miles working for the Steelers. "Plus, this is the best part of the job. You can take a lot of the other stuff and you can have it, but going out and evaluating players, that's the fun aspect of what I do."

Anthony Poindexter huddled on the sidelines with Virginia's running backs, barking instructions and imploring his troops to raise their level of play even higher. It was late in the third quarter and the Cavaliers were well on their way to rushing for 257 yards against Clemson.

Poindexter never figured on working as a college football assistant coach, at least not at the age of twenty-eight. With a shaved head, confident swagger, and a powerful six-one build, he looked like he belonged in the NFL. Most figured the former All-American safety, known as one of the game's most ferocious hitters during his college years, would spend at least a decade in the league.

Instead, Poindexter lasted just parts of three seasons with the Baltimore Ravens and Cleveland Browns, though not for a lack of talent or worth ethic. Now his name was synonymous not with hitting but with injuries and unfulfilled dreams.

In 1998, Poindexter turned down a shot at the NFL and returned for his fifth and final year of eligibility at Virginia. Considered a "not higher than the second round" prospect by the NFL advisory committee that provides ratings for draft-eligible underclassmen, Poindexter opted to improve his stock with a fifth season.

The decision looked like a wise one early in the fall, when Poindexter continued to terrorize opposing running backs and wide receivers. Then, in a four-player scrum against North Carolina State in the seventh game of the season, he shredded three of the four ligaments in his left knee, jeopardizing his career.

Like many top college players, Poindexter had taken out a $1 million disability insurance policy that he could collect only if he did not play in a NFL regular season game. He kept his options open as long as possible, rebuilding the injured knee with the help of a trainer who had worked with All-Pro wide receiver Jerry Rice.

Drafted by the Baltimore Ravens in the seventh round in 1999—a far cry from his potential second round projection before the injury—Poindexter spent the 1999 season on the Ravens inactive squad and then voided the policy by playing in 2000. He played sparingly but earned a Super Bowl ring, even though he did not actually see action in Super Bowl XXXV against the New York Giants in Tampa, Florida.

"It was a risk, but I figured I was a young guy with a college degree to fall back on," Poindexter said. "I didn't want to look back years from now and wonder, 'What if I had pursued it?' Hopefully, I'll make things up financially."

Poindexter's comments were made at the Super Bowl in 2001 and his career ended the following fall when he was released by the Cleveland Browns with career earnings below a million dollars. Groh, who as an assistant under Bill Parcells was not allowed to speak to the media, imposed the same gag order on his assistants.

"Anthony is the saddest story I've had representing pro athletes," said Ben Dogra, an agent for SFX Sports who served as Poindexter's agent, and at the moment was recruiting Virginia linebacker Darryl Blackstock. "Anthony was never a great athlete. He was a great football player who made it on instincts. The injury cost him a half-step. If Barry Sanders or Deion Sanders loses a half-step, they're okay. Willis McGahee was a 4.3 guy (in the forty). Now he's 4.4 and that's still pretty good. But Anthony has never complained to me, never once saying 'I should have gone pro.'"

By hiring Poindexter as a graduate assistant for the 2003 season and promoting him to running backs coach for 2004, Groh created a highly visible cautionary tale for players weighing a decision to go pro early.

Though Groh hoped to keep his raw-but-promising linebackers from departing for the NFL as underclassmen, there were strong counterarguments in their midst in Poindexter and now defensive end Chris Canty, who turned down NFL money to return for a fifth season only to suffer a season-ending knee injury twelve days earlier against Syracuse.

Poindexter had become such a strong argument for going pro that players from other schools invoked his name when considering their options. Agents hoping to convince underclassmen to turn pro early mention Poindexter as Exhibit A. Michael Vick cited Poindexter when he left Virginia Tech early in 2001, becoming the draft's top overall pick when he was selected by the Atlanta Falcons.

"I had to look at it from a lot of different aspects," Vick said. "Maybe I would have had an injury that was career-ending. Maybe I would have had an injury that would have hampered me for two or three games and caused my stock to drop."

Of course, no coach would begrudge a consensus top pick like Vick from leaving early, regardless of reason. Groh was correct when he noted that, "If you go to the NFL (early), you might get hurt. If you play football at any level, you might get hurt. If you get scared of getting injured in college and go to a NFL team unprepared to deliver, you might get cut. Where does that leave you?"

Perhaps in a situation a lot like that of Anthony Poindexter.

Al Groh's office at the University of Virginia is a shrine to his thirteen years of NFL coaching experience, mostly as a linebackers coach under Bill Parcells. There are autographed photos from former players such as Clay Matthews, Mo Lewis, and Curtis Martin, a framed letter from Lawrence Taylor on the occasion of his Hall of Fame induction, thanking Groh for "making me into the best player I could be," and game plans from Groh's NFL days in binders color-coded green (New York Jets), blue (New York Giants), and red (New England Patriots).

The décor is less of an ego wall than it is a reminder to current and prospective players that Groh is in the business of acquiring and developing NFL-caliber talent. Like every college coach, he preaches that his primary focus is to educate young men and win national championships. In the competitive world of college football recruiting, where every high school star is convinced he's just four years—if not three— away from a career in the NFL, Groh makes full use of his program's vast NFL pedigree.

"We're used to coaching NFL players and we want to continue to coach NFL players," Groh says. "We just want to do it before they get to the NFL instead of after."

During the 2004 season, Groh was one of only eight head coaches in Division 1-A with NFL head coaching experience. Groh spent just one year as a head coach, leading the Jets to a 9-7 record in 2000 after taking over for Parcells. Like Parcells, his longtime mentor, he micromanaged everything and clashed with the media. Unlike Parcells, Groh did not have the track record of winning as a head coach or the larger-than-life personality to pull off such a style effectively. When Groh resigned to become head coach at his alma mater, few tears were shed.

"Yeah, we were 6-1 at one point, but a lot of that was despite the fact that Al was the coach," Kevin Mawae, the Jets Pro Bowl center, told the

New York Daily News upon Groh's departure. "He tried to micromanage, and a lot of guys tuned him out a long time ago. I don't think there's much heartache about Al leaving. Guys aren't hurt that he's gone. For the most part, guys weren't happy. It's hard to play for a guy when you're not happy."

Back at the college level, where he coached at Wake Forest from 1981 to 1986, Groh had not needed to worry about the happiness and feelings of handsomely compensated professional athletes. If players did not like Groh's system, well, they must not be cut out for playing at the highest level. Quotes posted on the door to Groh's office all but served as warnings.

From Ray Lewis, the Baltimore Ravens All-Pro linebacker: "Pain is only temporary, no matter how long it lasts. Don't use pain as an excuse. It's not important."

From Parcells: "I'm looking for big, fast guys who can play football, are aggressive, and have a passion for the game. I really don't like guys who don't like football and are not willing to do what it takes."

George Welsh, Groh's predecessor at Virginia, left the program in good shape when he retired after the 2000 season. Before Welsh took over in 1982, Virginia had produced just two winning seasons in twenty-nine years. Under Welsh, the Cavaliers became a perennial bowl game participant and put together a string of consecutive winning seasons from 1987 through 1999.

But Welsh, a graduate of the U.S. Naval Academy, who served as an assistant under Joe Paterno at Penn State before returning to Navy as head coach, never was comfortable having pro scouts around. NFL officials were allowed into practices, but Welsh made it clear he wasn't happy about it. The old salt was old school. The Cavaliers did not have their names on the backs of their uniforms and for much of Welsh's tenure wore white helmets without logos.

Welsh's staff usually consisted of career college coaches in their forties and fifties. Unlike Groh, Welsh did not have a vast network of NFL friends and acquaintances. He viewed sports agents with disdain.

If his program was not viewed as NFL preparatory, Welsh didn't care. He was pleased when players like Herman Moore, Aaron Brooks, and Tiki and Ronde Barber achieved stardom in the NFL, but he was more proud of their accomplishments at Virginia.

When Groh took over for the retiring Welsh in 2001, the first thing he did was put a professional stamp on the program. He slapped names on the uniforms and hired assistant coaches in their early 30s, most with NFL playing, coaching, or scouting experience. He fielded calls from agents and even brought them in for an "NFL Agents Meeting" to speak with players and their parents each summer. Groh hired a strength coach, Evan Marcus, who previously worked for the New Orleans Saints.

Ever the micromanager, Groh even took an active role in the production of the media guide, which no longer read "media guide" on the cover, but instead served as more of a glossy, high-end recruiting tool. The book had doubled in size and become a tribute to the NFL background of Groh and his staff.

The 296-page 2004 edition included hundreds of references to the NFL, including a page on the NFL Agents Meeting. Groh had invited a handful of agents that he respected to talk to his players. The group included Jimmy Sexton, the agent for Parcells and a number of NFL veterans; Brad Blank, who represented a long line of Cavaliers, including Moore and Slade; and Anthony Agnone, whose clients included Patrick Kerney, the former Virginia defensive end now with the Atlanta Falcons.

After the table of contents and two pages on the football stadium came the first of many references to Groh's NFL background:

When Virginia head coach Al Groh and his staff talk about what it takes to be the best in college and pro football, players listen. As a former NFL coach who has been to two Super Bowls, Al Groh is an expert at evaluating and developing exceptional talent.

Through his first three seasons, Groh had yet to take his alma mater beyond the level of the Welsh regime. In 2001, Groh's first year, the Cavaliers posted their first losing season since 1986 before winning nine games in 2002 and eight in 2003. Still, Groh had managed to raise the profile of the program. He convinced students to scrap the century-old tradition of wearing semiformal attire to games and wear orange T-shirts instead. A marching band replaced a ragtag pep group. Using his staff's NFL experience as a recruiting tool, he began landing blue-chip recruits such as Brooks and Ferguson.

Unlike many college coaches who restrict access to practice for fear of compromising game plans, Groh maintains an open-door policy all season long, except on Thursdays. The scouting reports his coaches file on Virginia's high school recruits are modeled after the NFL. During recruiting season, the coaches rank prep players on a board in a conference room just like NFL teams create a draft board.

The afternoon after Virginia defeated Clemson 30–10, to improve to 5-0, Groh pulled out a laminated scouting report. There were spaces for coaches to fill in remarks on objective information such as height, weight, and years as a starter. There were areas to note more subjective evaluations such as personality, character, work ethic, and competitiveness.

"All we've done is substitute the word recruit for draft," Groh said. "You have the same two categories as the NFL: tools and makeup. Tools are physical skills. The makeup category, that's the part that's going to help a player take advantage of the tools or the deficiency that doesn't let him take advantage. Each category is just as important in recruiting."

As if on cue, Groh's cell phone rang. He glanced at the caller ID and saw that it was Eugene Monroe, who ranked as the top prep offensive lineman in the country. Monroe had verbally committed to Virginia, but until he signed in February Groh and his staff needed to continue the strong sales pitch.

"Eugene, did you see the game last night?" Groh asked. "Did you see number sixty-six, D'Brickashaw Ferguson? That's your position, Eugene. We're like the Holiday Inn. We have a reservation in your name. . . . So how was practice? . . . Yeah, it was a big win. We played well, but we have a real challenge on our hands this weekend against Florida State."

Groh did not mean to suggest that Ferguson was leaving a year early, but that Monroe, too, eventually would play left tackle, the most valuable spot on the offensive line, because it protects the blind side of a right-handed quarterback.

Five minutes later, Groh said good-bye to Monroe. Groh's pro background did not come up during the conversation, though it often does during recruiting chats. It's a valuable card to play.

"If you were going to school, would you rather be taught by a teaching assistant or a full professor?" Groh asked. "Who would you rather be taught by?

"Look, evaluating talent is really the same at any level. I'm doing the same thing now that I was in the NFL. The only difference is that now I'm also the general manager and the player personnel director."

Like a NFL general manager, Groh spoke frequently to agents. Some college coaches all but unleash dogs on what the NFL Players Association calls "certified contract advisors." Not Groh. He uses his NFL experience to screen potential representatives for players, setting up the agents meeting himself and even arranging meetings between players and agents during the season. Some, like the ones he invited to the agents meeting, play by his rules and communicate through Groh. The rest contact players directly.

"Agents are going to talk to players, so you can pretend it doesn't happen or be part of the process," Groh says. "That doesn't mean you're controlling the process. I don't know if it can be controlled. It's going to go on. You can't tell the players not to have contact with agents, because the agents are going to contact them."

Some schools downplay the pro preparatory process. After all, student-athletes are enrolled to graduate and win college football games. Nobody is supposed to be thinking of going pro, right?

"I don't know if this is a progressive philosophy, but we're not having our heads stuck in the sand," Groh says. "We try to be a full-service organization. Whether it's academic or career counseling, within the NFL or out, agent selection and getting ready for the next level, we try and provide the best counseling based on our experience.

"When [NFL] draftable players are a big factor in your winning, you're going to get the attention of the next generation of players. That generation, besides wanting to win, wants to go to the NFL. They can look at us and say this is the place that knows how to train them."

Groh turned his attention to a television screen perched near his desk. There was game film to watch of Florida State, but his thoughts were never far from the pro game. Not that he was looking to get back to the NFL. It's just that when you're sixty years old and had spent thirteen of the previous seventeen years working for five different NFL teams, your network of friends in the league is enormous. He heard from many of them, perhaps a little more so this fall because of the NFL potential of many of his players.

Besides Parcells, Groh worked with Bill Belichick, the head coach of the New England Patriots, and New York Giants head coach Tom Coughlin. He coached alongside up-and-coming head coaching prospects such as Romeo Crennel of the Patriots and Mike Nolan of the Baltimore Ravens. Front offices around the league were full of former Groh colleagues, from scouts to strength coaches to guys like Giants general manager Ernie Accorsi, Baltimore GM Ozzie Newsome, and Scott Pioli, the general manager of the Patriots.

Groh also has sent several of his Virginia assistants to the NFL. The Jacksonville Jaguars staff included Bill Musgrave, Groh's offensive coordinator in 2001–2002; and Andy Heck, most recently Virginia's tight ends coach in 2003. Corwin Brown was in his first season with the Jets after three years as Virginia's special teams coach.

The University of Virgina's season was not even half over, the 2005 NFL Draft was nearly seven months away, but Groh knew the scouts and agents already had spent the last six months evaluating his players.

Chapter Five:

BIRDS OF PREY

N early two months before Eli Manning, Robert Gallery, and Larry Fitzgerald became the first three selections in the 2004 NFL Draft, preparations for the 2005 event got underway.

In March of 2004, NFL scouts and executives traveled around the country to college campuses for pro timing days, a sequel to the NFL scouting combine. At these events, referred to simply as "pro days," prospects for the 2004 draft were weighed, measured, and put through the familiar battery of tests designed to measure strength, speed, flexibility, agility, and quickness that they underwent at the combine.

With scouts already on campus, and with athletic department officials testing players anyway, many schools worked out their juniors immediately following the workout. Other schools waited a few weeks, but by the time the San Diego Chargers selected Manning on April 23, 2004, trading him immediately to the New York Giants, most every rising senior had been tested and initial reports filed.

Not that every team had to produce their own. Scouting is a grueling job. After spending most of the months between August and April on the road, scouts have their eye on vacations in May, June, and July, not the

2005 Draft. Thankfully, two national scouting services—BLESTO and National Football Scouting, Inc.—handle the heavy lifting.

BLESTO, based in Pittsburgh, formed in 1963 as a way for four teams—the Bears, Lions, Eagles, and Steelers—to share scouting expenses. National Football Scouting, or "National," is the other surviving combine of the 1970s. For the 2005 draft season, it had fifteen members, including BLESTO founder Philadelphia. BLESTO had a roster of twelve teams, including the Atlanta Falcons.

Five teams—Baltimore, Indianapolis, New England, Oakland, and Washington—were unaffiliated in 2004, preferring to do their own scouting. Though it might seem like these teams were being frugal—membership costs just one hundred thousand or so annually, along with, in many cases, the contribution of an entry-level scout—the teams are not at much of a disadvantage. Given the exhaustive nature of scouting, it's not difficult to assemble this early-stage information. Not only that, but unaffiliated teams end up acquiring the reports.

So, too, do agents, who use them for recruiting, as do a number of Internet draft gurus. For agents, the information is most useful because it includes player telephone numbers.

In mid-May of 2004, three weeks after the draft and following rookie minicamps, scouts from teams belonging to BLESTO and National convened in Florida. The BLESTO gang met in Orlando, the National contingent in Longboat Key, near Sarasota.

The scout or scouts who were in attendance at the junior days presents a report and a grade is assigned. BLESTO rates its players on a 1.00–5.00 scale, with the lower the score the better. National uses a 1.00–8.00 scale. The higher the number, the higher the rating.

Though the reports are anything but exhaustive, and don't begin to account for all of the character research teams will undergo over the next eleven months, they at least provide a starting point. They also, for the most part, provide a pretty good barometer of where many players will be drafted, barring a major injury or arrest, and not accounting for underclassmen that may enter the draft.

Here's a look at the top-rated rising seniors by position by BLESTO and National in June of 2004. BLESTO is on the left, National on the right. Draft-eligible underclassmen are not included in the ratings.

BLESTO AND NATIONAL RATINGS FOR THE 2005 DRAFT AS OF SPRING 2004

QUARTERBACKS

BLESTO	National
Dan Orlovsky—Connecticut—1.25	Charlie Frye—Akron—6.1
Charlie Frye—Akron—1.27	Dan Orlovsky—Connecticut—6.0
Andrew Walter—Arizona State—1.45	David Greene—Georgia—5.7
David Greene—Georgia—1.49	Andrew Walter—Arizona State—5.5
Ryan Fitzpatrick—Harvard—1.51	Jason White—Oklahoma—5.5
Matt Jones—Arkansas—1.55	Ryan Fitzpatrick—Harvard—5.4
Derek Anderson—Oregon State—1.57	Kyle Orton—Purdue—5.4
Timmy Chang—Hawaii—1.60	Derek Anderson—Oregon State—5.3
Jason White—Oklahoma—1.63	James Kilian—Tulsa—5.1
Darian Durant—North Carolina—1.68	Matt Jones—Arkansas—5.0

RUNNING BACKS

BLESTO	National
Carnell Williams—Auburn—1.16	Carnell Williams—Auburn—7.0
Cedric Benson—Texas—1.24	Ronnie Brown—Auburn—6.3
Ronnie Brown—Auburn—1.34	Cedric Williams—Texas—6.0
Walter Reyes—Syracuse—1.44	Kay-Jay Harris—West Virginia—5.8
Marvin Townes—East Carolina—1.44	Walter Reyes—Syracuse—5.6
Kay-Jay Harris—West Virginia—1.47	Anthony Davis—Wisconsin—5.5
Cedric Houston—Tennessee—1.53	Lydell Ross—Ohio State—5.5
William Brown—East Carolina—1.54	Marvin Townes—East Carolina—5.5
Anthony Davis—Wisconsin—1.57	Brandon Jacobs—Southern Illinois—5.4
Lionel Gates—Louisville—1.60	Jermelle Lewis—Iowa—5.4

FULLBACKS

BLESTO	National
Paul Jefferson—Penn State—1.45	Paul Jefferson—Penn State—5.3
Manuel White Jr.—UCLA—1.55	Manuel White Jr.—UCLA—5.0
Zach Tuiasosopo—Washington—1.57	Zach Tuiasosopo—Washington—4.9
Issa Banna—Northwestern State (LA)—1.8	Matt Phillips—Edinboro—4.7
Kevin Dudley—Michigan—1.8	Jeremy Thomas—Georgia—4.7

WIDE RECEIVERS

BLESTO	National
Craphonso Thorpe—Florida State—1.22	Braylon Edwards—Michigan—6.7
Terrence Murphy—Texas A&M—1.23	Mark Clayton—Oklahoma—6.4
Mark Clayton—Oklahoma—1.29	Terrence Murphy—Texas A&M—6.3
Braylon Edwards—Michigan—1.35	Craphonso Thorpe—Florida State—5.7
Josh Davis—Marshall—1.41	Josh Davis—Marshall—5.7
Fred Gibson—Georgia—1.41	Fred Gibson—Georgia—5.7
Craig Bragg—UCLA—1.43	Charles Frederick—Washington—5.7
Charles Frederick—Washington—1.47	J. R. Russell—Louisville—5.5
Brandon Jones—Oklahoma—1.47	Roddy White—Alabama-Birmingham—5.5
Courtney Roby—Indiana—1.47	Reggie Brown—Georgia—5.4

TIGHT ENDS

BLESTO	National
Alex Smith—Stanford—1.37	Alex Smith—Stanford—5.7
Vincent Jackson—Northern Colorado—1.49	Kevin Everett—Miami—5.5
Dave Kashetta—Boston College—1.53	Dave Kashetta—Boston College—5.4
Anthony Curtis—Portland State—1.63	Andrew Clark—Toledo—5.2
Kevin Everett—Miami—1.68	Anthony Curtis—Portland State—5.2
Billy Bajema—Oklahoma State—1.7	Gary Godsey—Notre Dame—5.2
Adam Bergen—Lehigh—1.72	Adam Bergen—Lehigh—5.1
Joel Dreessen—Colorado State—1.72	Alex Holmes—USC—5.0
Gary Godsey—Notre Dame—1.72	Steve Fleming—Arizona—4.9
Greg Estandia—UNLV—1.73	Eric Knott—Michigan State—4.7

OFFENSIVE TACKLES

BLESTO	National
Chris Colmer—North Carolina State—1.2	Alex Barron—Florida State—6.7
Alex Barron—Florida State—1.21	Ray Willis—Florida State—5.9
Khalif Barnes—Washington—1.28	Jeremy Parquet—Southern Mississippi—5.8
Adam Snyder—Oregon—1.32	Calvin Armstrong—Washington State—5.7
Adam Terry—Syracuse—1.36	Khalif Barnes—Washington—5.7
Ray Willis—Florida State—1.39	Michael Munoz—Tennessee—5.7
Jammal Brown—Oklahoma—1.42	Morgan Davis—Wisconsin—5.6
Michael Munoz—Tennessee—1.42	Wesley Britt—Alabama—5.5
Jeremy Parquet—Southern Mississippi—1.45	Jammal Brown—Oklahoma—5.4
Rob Petitti—Pittsburgh—1.45	Chris Colmer—North Carolina State—5.4

OFFENSIVE GUARDS

BLESTO	National
Chris Kemoeatu—Utah—1.34	Adam Snyder—Oregon—6.1
Marcus Johnson—Mississippi—1.36	Elton Brown—Virginia—6.0
David Baas—Michigan—1.46	Dylan Gandy—Texas Tech—5.7
Doug Buckles—Mississippi—1.47	Marcus Johnson—Mississippi—5.7
Elton Brown—Virginia—1.53	Claude Terrell—New Mexico—5.7
Dan Buenning—Wisconsin—1.54	Doug Buckles—Mississippi—5.5
Doug Nienhuis—Oregon State—1.57	Dan Buenning—Wisconsin—5.5
Dan Connolly—Southeast Missouri State—1.60	Chris Kemoeatu—Utah—5.5
Jonathan Clinkscale—Wisconsin—1.61	David Baas—Michigan—5.4
C. J. Brooks—Maryland—1.63	Cody Campbell—Texas Tech—5.4

CENTERS

BLESTO	National
Jason Brown—North Carolina—1.43	Vince Carter—Oklahoma—5.9
Ben Wilkerson—LSU—1.45	Ben Wilkerson—LSU—5.7
Raymond Preston—Illinois—1.59	Jason Brown—North Carolina—5.5
Matt Brock—Oregon State—1.68	Junius Coston—North Carolina A&T—5.4
Junius Coston—North Carolina A&T—1.73	Raymond Preston—Illinois—5.4

DEFENSIVE TACKLES

BLESTO	National
Shaun Cody—USC—1.25	Shaun Cody—USC—6.5
Mike Patterson—USC—1.32	Anttaj Hawthorne—Wisconsin—6.3
Lorenzo Alexander—California—1.40	Jonathan Babineaux—Iowa—6.0
Jonathan Babineaux—Iowa—1.44	Atiyyah Ellison—Missouri—5.5
Anttaj Hawthorne—Wisconsin—1.47	Ronald Fields—Mississippi State—5.4
Dusty Dvoracek—Oklahoma—1.50	Larry Burt—Miami (OH)—5.2
Atiyyah Ellison—Missouri—1.53	Jason Jefferson—Wisconsin—5.2
Ronald Fields—Mississippi State—1.60	Anthony Bryant—Alabama—5.1
Jason Jefferson—Wisconsin—1.62	Tim Bulman—Boston College—5.0
Tom Sverchek—California—1.63	Mike Patterson—USC—5.0

DEFENSIVE ENDS

BLESTO	National
David Pollack—Georgia—1.15	David Pollack—Georgia—7.0
Dan Cody—Oklahoma—1.26	Marcus Spears—LSU—6.0
Demarcus Ware—Tory State—1.33	Matt Roth—Iowa—5.7
Bill Swancutt—Oregon State—1.36	Demarcus Ware—Tory State—5.6
Matt Roth—Iowa—1.38	Kevin Huntley—Kansas State—5.5
Marcus Spears—LSU—1.38	Eric Moore—Florida State—5.5
Jimmy Verdon—Arizona State—1.41	Jimmy Verdon—Arizona State—5.5
Jonathan Jackson—Oklahoma—1.45	Vincent Burns—Kentucky—5.4
Chris Canty—Virginia—1.48	Dan Cody—Oklahoma—5.4
Eric Moore—Florida State—1.49	Jim Davis—Virginia Tech—5.4

MIDDLE LINEBACKERS

BLESTO	National
Roger Cooper—Montana State—1.45	Marcus Lawrence—South Carolina—5.8
Barrett Ruud—Nebraska—1.50	Robert McCune—Louisville—5.6
Robert McCune—Louisville—1.66	Adam Seward—UNLV—5.4
Kirk Morrison—San Diego State—1.68	Ronald Stanley—Michigan State—5.4
Nigel Eldridge—Alabama-Birmingham—1.69	Mike Goolsby—Notre Dame—5.3

OUTSIDE LINEBACKERS

BLESTO	National
Derrick Johnson—Texas—1.23	Barrett Ruud—Nebraska—6.5
Kevin Burnett—Tennessee—1.31	Kevin Burnett—Tennessee—6.0
Jared Newberry—Stanford—1.38	Derrick Johnson—Texas—6.0
Lance Mitchell—Oklahoma—1.40	Paul Walkenhorst—BYU—5.4
Jonathan Pollard—Oregon State—1.46	Jared Newberry—Stanford—5.3
Adam Seward—UNLV—1.47	Danny Triplett—Northern Iowa—5.3
Matt Grootegoed—USC—1.49	Roger Cooper—Montana State—5.2
Boomer Grigsby—Illinois State—1.51	Michael Boley—Southern Mississippi—5.0
Ryan Claridge—UNLV—1.52	Ryan Claridge—UNLV—5.0
Trent Cole—Cincinnati—1.59	Sarth Benoit—Southern Connecticut—5.0

CORNERBACKS

BLESTO	National
Antrel Rolle—Miami—1.17	Antrel Rolle—Miami—7.0
Corey Webster—LSU—1.21	Marlin Jackson—Michigan—6.3
Ronald Bartell—Howard—1.28	Ronald Bartell—Howard—6.1
Marlin Jackson—Michigan—1.32	Antonio Perkins—Oklahoma—6.0
Antonio Perkins—Oklahoma—1.46	Corey Webster—LSU—6.0
Abraham Elimimian—Hawaii—1.50	Karl Paymah—Washington State—5.6
Derrick Johnson—Washington—1.50	Cedrick Williams—Kansas State—5.6
Dustin Fox—Ohio State—1.52	Markus Curry—Michigan—5.5
Cedrick Williams—Kansas State—1.55	Vince Fuller—Virginia Tech—5.5
Karl Paymah—Washington State—1.58	Alphonso Hodge—Miami (OH)—5.5

SAFETIES

BLESTO	National
Jamaal Brimmer—UNLV—1.42	Jermaine Harris—South Carolina—5.5
James Butler—Georgia Tech—1.43	Jamaal Brimmer—UNLV—5.4
Aaron Francisco—BYU—1.43	Dustin Fox—Ohio State—5.4
Oshiomogho Atogwe—Stanford—1.49	Chris Harrell—Penn State—5.3
Jason Leach—USC—1.5	James Butler—Georgia Tech—5.2
Riccardo Stewart—Arizona State—1.5	Sean Considine—Iowa—5.2
Travis Daniels—LSU—1.56	Justin Fraley—Minnesota—5.2
Donte Nicholson—Oklahoma—1.57	Terry Holley—Rice—5.2
Sean Considine—Iowa—1.58	Jamacia Jackson—South Carolina—5.2
Marviel Underwood—San Diego State—1.59	Jason Leach—USC—5.0

Note: The author acquired copies of the BLESTO and National reports, but this grouping was assembled by Rob Rang for NFLDraftScout.com.

Here's a look at rankings of players at several schools with significant prospects for the 2005 draft:

AUBURN
Carnell Williams, RB, 7.0, 1.16
Ronnie Brown, RB, 6.3, 1.34
Carlos Rogers, CB, 5.0, 1.76
Jason Campbell, QB, 4.6, 1.85

FLORIDA STATE
Alex Barron, OT, 6.7, 1.20
Craphonso Thorpe, WR, 6.3, 1.22
Ray Willis, OT, 5.9, 1.39
Eric Moore, DE, 5.5, 1.49
Bryant McFadden, CB, 5.4, 1.64
Chauncey Davis, DE, 5.1, 1.75
B.J. Ward, FS, 5.0, 1.79
Chris Rix, QB, 4.9, 1.72
Jerome Carter, SS, 4.7, 1.85
Kylar Hall, FS, 4.4, 1.90
Travis Johnson, DT, 4.4, 1.85

GEORGIA
David Pollack, DE, 7.0, 1.15
Fred Gibson, WR, 5.7, 1.41
David Greene, QB, 5.7, 1.49
Reggie Brown, WR, 5.4, 1.51

VIRGINIA
Elton Brown, OG, 6.0, 1.53
Chris Canty, DE, 5.3, 1.48
Alvin Pearman, RB, 4.5, 1.80
Patrick Estes, TE, 4.4, 1.90
Jermaine Hardy, SS, 4.4, 1.88

The Atlanta Falcons college scouting staff is headed by Phil Emery, who joined the team on May 18, 2004 after a six-year stint with the Chicago Bears. He received a strong recommendation from Bears general manager Jerry Angelo, who had worked for more than a decade in Tampa with Falcons general manager Rich McKay and assistant GM Tim Ruskell.

Emery was one of several replacements in the scouting staff McKay and Ruskell had made since the 2004 draft. Compared to some new regimes, there was modest turnover on the seven-member scouting staff, with openings filled from within.

The group ranged in age from young Matt Berry, a former Falcons intern working his first year as an area scout, to sixty-seven-year-old Boyd Dowler, who played twelve seasons as a wide receiver in the NFL (1959–1971), mostly for the Green Bay Packers under Vince Lombardi.

In between, there was Billy Campfield, who spent most of his six-year NFL career with the Philadelphia Eagles; Bob Harrison, a veteran of thirty-three years of pro, college, and high school coaching; Taylor Morton, a former college assistant at Southern Miss and Auburn; Mark Olson, a former NFL advance scout, in his first year scouting the draft; and Bruce Plummer, a five-year NFL veteran who serves as the Falcons' BLESTO scout.

Dowler is the Dick Clark of NFL personnel, a man who could pass for his early fifties. At six-five, with thick gray hair, he's a testament to clean living, exercise, and good genes. He led the Packers in receptions seven times and still ranks among the franchise's all-time leaders with 448 catches for 6,918 yards.

Having played a key role on Lombardi's legendary teams, Dowler could be forgiven for being one of those crotchety ex-players forever bemoaning today's spoiled NFL stars. Instead, he has an uncanny knack of relating to the younger generations.

"He's just one of the guys," says Morton, who is three decades younger. "You forget how old he is until he starts telling some story about Bart Starr and Vince Lombardi."

Scouting is a thankless job. Starting in August, the area scouts visit college campuses, spending the bulk of the next eight months on the road, an average of about twenty nights a month.

Not all schools are created equal. Emery and Ruskell took the BLESTO reports and used them to narrow the field. A school chock-full of draft talent will receive three visits from an area scout, with Ruskell, Emery, and even McKay visiting key schools. For the 2005 draft, that group includes Auburn, Georgia, Oklahoma, Florida State, Miami, Southern Cal, LSU, and Virginia. A smaller school, such as Troy State, would get more attention than usual because of promising defensive end Demarcus Ware. The same was true of the University of Alabama-Birmingham, which featured wide receiver Roddy White.

Other schools, especially those not in Division 1-A, would receive one or two visits. Some perennial powers would get less attention, either because they were struggling or because the bulk of their talent was freshman and sophomores in 2004. That group included Arizona, Notre Dame, Penn State, and Pittsburgh.

When McKay and Ruskell arrived in Atlanta, they added another requirement to the scouts' workload. During the slower months of June and July scouts are to visit the top ten schools in their areas. It could be low-key. Take the wife and kids. Call it a mini-vacation. Most college towns are fun to visit in the summer. This way, the Falcons scouts get the first crack at coaches, before they've told the stories of players for the fiftieth time. Unlike during the season, when college coaches are distracted by game preparations and the intensity level is high, especially when a team is losing, coaches are more accessible.

"Schools actually liked seeing our guys," Ruskell said. "Someone from the outside world was actually visiting. There's not much to do during those periods, and it was a treat to have someone come in and visit. It got to the point where our guys were saying, 'Okay coach, I have enough here.' You couldn't shut them up."

In the fall, days typically begin at 7:00 A.M., with scouts rolling into a college football office armed with donuts or bagels for the coaching staffs. Scouts wear team-logo clothing, in part to help jog the memories of assistant coaches who don't always recognize the legions of visitors parading through the offices.

Much of the morning is spent watching film. Unlike video from actual broadcasts, the film is broken down by offense and defense. The first scout into the room gets control of the remote control. Getting the clicker means arriving no later than seven.

The goal is to watch film of the most recent game, plus that of the two toughest opponents. That's especially important with Division 1-AA schools, which might have only faced two Division 1-A foes.

Throughout the morning scouts check in with assistant coaches, strength coaches, academic advisors, NCAA compliance directors, graduate assistants, resident advisors in the dorm, tutors, secretaries, cops, and anyone else that can provide details on a player's work ethic, drive, personality, family background, academic performance, and disciplinary problems, if any. A scout's job is as much that of detective or investigative reporter as it is football expert.

"It's not enough to say, 'This is a good kid, he works hard and has no problems off the field,'" McKay says. "Not good enough. We want to know where he came from, what his parental situation was. We want to make sure the scouts have talked to the high school coach. We want to know about his education, so we talk to the academic advisor about every player. We want to hear from the position coach, the head coach, teammates, and ask their views of the player. Then obviously we want to know all the off-the-field issues. You're developing a whole picture and it takes a lot of time."

Sometimes a scout's investigation reveals that a player has been taking money from boosters or from agents, cardinal sins to the NCAA. The Falcons factor that in to their character evaluations.

"If this guy is that easily corruptible, it probably shows up elsewhere," Ruskell says. "Does he skip workouts? Does he come late to meetings? Has he gotten in trouble? It's a red flag that maybe this guy is a follower, that he's not his own man and doesn't have leadership skills. We're not going to just brush that off under the rug."

Scouts could watch film back at their team offices or at home, since many scouts live in the areas they cover. Falcon scouts do that in June and July to get an early look at players, and often as the season progresses. But it's tough to get a true read on a player's physique on television. Plus, there's a lag time between the end of a game and when the film is available for view outside of school. Colleges send the film to a dubbing center, where it's mass-produced for all NFL teams, but sometimes more than a month can go by before it's widely distributed.

If nothing else, by watching film on the same day they watch practice and interview school officials, they're able to write reports with all of the information fresh.

In the afternoon, scouts attend practice—a good indicator of how hard players work, though not as valuable as the two-a-day preseason practices in August, when players wear full pads all week long and are fighting to win jobs.

Access to practice, and to the football department in general, varies from school to school. Some old-school coaches, such as Penn State's Joe Paterno, restrict availability. Others, like Florida State's Bobby Bowden and Miami's Larry Coker, open the offices for part of the season. Some let scouts watch just the first part of practices, fearful that their game plans might be compromised. Others change their policies during the season, wreaking havoc on a scout's travel plans. Then there are coaches like Virginia's Al Groh, who provides unlimited access to scouts all season long, with the exception of Thursdays.

"I don't see how their doing their job hinders us from doing ours," Groh says. "The players are trying hard to prove themselves and we should give them an opportunity to showcase that."

In many respects, the job of a scout is similar to that of a sportswriter. Both groups spend their days interviewing sources and many nights writing. They endure marathon travel, preferring to stay at Marriott properties because of the company's attractive frequent traveler program. They spend many weekends in press boxes watching games, grabbing food on the go. Camaraderie develops among competitors in both fields.

Few are going to get rich in either profession. Though some veteran scouts can command $100,000 salaries, most earn less. The starting salary for young scouts is so low, there's even a name for it: "25 for 25"—referring to a twenty-five-year-old making $25,000.

Both groups rely on networks of reliable sources to provide off-the-record information. Scouts, many of which coached or played in the college ranks, turn to ex-colleagues first, gradually developing new sources. College coaches, working in a high-turnover profession, tend to be receptive to the scouts. Today's aggravation could be tomorrow's job lead, especially when an NFL general manager or scouting director rolls through the office.

Still, there's a fine line to walk. A college coach's recruiting of high school players depends in part on producing NFL players. An honest assessment of a college player to a NFL scout might hurt the kid's chances.

"They make their living on these decisions, so I'm not going to lie to them," says Florida State's Bowden. "I know I expect the high school coaches to be just as forthright with me. We all want to know the same things. What kind of kid is he? Is he dependable? Is he a slacker? Can you count on him? Is he an overachiever or an underachiever? If you sell a scout on a player and he's a complete flop, you lose all credibility."

"They're looking to invest millions of dollars in a guy and they want stability," says Georgia Tech head coach Chan Gailey, a former Dallas Cowboys head coach.

College coaches spend a lot of time talking about their "student athletes" and how they never want them looking beyond Saturday's game, let alone to a career in the NFL. Having logo-clad NFL employees roaming the halls of the football offices and standing on the sidelines during practice doesn't exactly reenforce the message.

Then again, scouts generally are expected to leave the offices before lunchtime, when players begin arriving. Scouts are forbidden from speaking to players beyond a friendly hello. Coaches figure that if players happen to notice scouts on the sidelines, they're more likely to work harder. At Florida State, Bowden has gone so far as to have a NFL scout speak to a talented underachiever.

"We'll have the scout tell the player what he's throwing away," Bowden says. "When we can't get him going, sometimes it helps for the kid to hear it from a guy wearing a shirt with an NFL logo."

The Falcons ask scouts to speak to a minimum of three solid sources, preferably five. If the first three say the same thing, that's enough to constitute a consensus. McKay and Ruskell urge scouts to step out of the familiar ring of the football staff and seek out those without a vested interest.

At Florida State, Ruskell turns to Brian Battle, the director of compliance. In that role, Battle helps players obtain disability insurance, assists juniors considering going pro by applying for a predraft rating from the NFL advisory committee, organizes an annual "Agent Day" meeting between Seminoles and agents, and even teaches a class called "A Career in Professional Sports," that's popular among players.

Battle, in many respects, gets to know more about the players than the coaching staff does. Since a player's success in the NFL depends in part on how fast he can process intricate schemes, the Falcons turn to people like Battle to find out how a player thinks. They prefer to do that than rely on the Wonderlic, the notorious, fifty-question aptitude test players take during the NFL scouting combine in February.

"You have to get outside the protective zone of the coaching circle," Ruskell says. "They protect the players, and you would too if you were a coach. After all, these are the guys that help me keep my job and make me look good and keep the winning tradition. A guy like Brian has a great perspective because he can speak to the intelligence level. Does the kid just sit there or does he participate in class? You want to know that because it eliminates the guess work. You don't have to rely on the Wonderlic."

After practice and dinner, scouts must translate a day's worth of information into reports. With scouts often hitting one school a day, the only way to keep up with the workload is to write at night in a hotel room, either in the same town or after driving to the next day's school.

"You have to get the reports done while it's all fresh in your mind," says Ruston Webster, the director of college scouting for the Tampa Bay Buccaneers, a holdover from the McKay-Ruskell regime. "You've worked all day, driven maybe three or four hours, and now you've got reports to write. It's tough."

It's not unusual for a scout to spend twenty nights a month on the road in the fall. There are long stretches in December, February, and April, where they work out of team headquarters, but that's the road, too, for most scouts, who live where they scout. The biggest grind is January and March, when the schedule of postseason all-star games and college "pro day" workouts is relentless.

"It takes a toll on you," says Ruskell, who paid his dues as an area scout in the CFL, USFL, and for the Buccaneers. "There's the stress of being away from the family and not being part of the office environment. You don't always feel like you're part of what's happening."

Falcons scout Taylor Morton, whose area in the fall of 2004 included Texas, Oklahoma, Kansas, Louisiana, and Arkansas, typically logs more than six thousand miles driving each fall. He hits the road four times for ten-day stretches, flying from his home near Atlanta to Dallas.

Boyd Dowler, who lives in Tampa, drives loops through his territory, which includes Florida, Mississippi, and Alabama, a fertile area for the 2005 draft, with schools such as Florida State, Ole Miss, and Auburn. Though Georgia belongs to Athens-based scout Bob Harrison, the state is thoroughly covered by the entire Falcons staff.

Dowler hits Georgia Tech and Georgia twice. When bad weather forces the Bulldogs to use the Falcons' indoor facility at Flowery Branch, any Falcons scout nearby is able to watch practice.

Tech attracts little attention, though that has less to do with the overall talent of Gailey's team as it does the lack of draft-eligible players. Five Yellow Jackets were drafted in the 2004 NFL Draft, the most in twelve years, and most of Gailey's talent is in the freshman and sophomore classes. If nothing else, Georgia Tech's downtown Atlanta campus is a popular destination for Falcons scouts—and the numerous agents that call the city home—because of home games against Miami, Virginia Tech, and Virginia.

Ironically, most scouts rarely see their own team play in person, since they're driving around the country visiting college campuses. At least they're able to listen to the games through Sirius satellite radio, which paid the NFL $220 million to broadcast all of its games for seven years, beginning in 2004.

The Falcons keep their scouts in the loop by assigning each one a position before the start of training camp. During the first two weeks of camp the scouts follow those players and coaches around to get a better feel for the scheme, existing personnel, and the team's needs at the position. Midway through camp they begin their tour of preseason college football practices.

During the fall, the seven scouts combine to write reports on more than twelve hundred players. They reconvene at Flowery Branch in December to make an initial cutdown of players, eliminating those that did not fit the Falcons offensive or defensive schemes and those that didn't pass the character filter.

Beginning in January, the scouts serve as cross-checkers. They go to bowl games, along with postseason all-star games such as the Senior Bowl, East–West Shrine Game, and Gridiron Classic—and concentrate on evaluating players at the position they focused on during training camp.

The area scout's grade and the cross-checker scout's rating form the basis of the first draft board, which is put in place prior to the NFL combine in February. The Falcons coaching staff serve as cross-checkers at the combine and during March pro days back at campus, but the idea is not to tweak the grade significantly. It's a lesson McKay learned from George Young, the late New York Giants executive.

"Be as loyal as you can to that first board," McKay says. "If you let it become too modified, then you've taken the art of scouting out of it and it becomes more of a groupthink process, and sometimes that's not a good thing."

The Falcons, in just one calendar year under McKay, have undergone a thorough remodeling. When Arthur Blank purchased the team early in 2002, head coach Dan Reeves ran the personnel department. Defensively, the team was a mess. Wade Phillips, the defensive coordinator, employed a 3-4 scheme (three down linemen, four linebackers), an effective setup for some teams, but not for the Falcons' smaller linemen. Defensive end Patrick Kerney, matching up against linemen forty pounds heavier, got pounded on a weekly basis. In 2003, the Falcons finished last in the league in passing defense and total defense and twenty-ninth against the run.

When Blank hired McKay, it was clear who ran the personnel department, especially since McKay would get to choose the head coach. The men agreed on the philosophy of the general manager, not the head coach, being in charge of the organization. Blank referred to the process as "looking for a GM or coach, not a king."

Just as McKay selected a former defensive coordinator, Tony Dungy, to rebuild the Buccaneers in 1996, McKay hired Jim Mora, who had spent five years in the role in San Francisco. Mora's father, also named Jim, was a longtime NFL head coach.

McKay's defense in Tampa had ranked among the league's best by using speedy defenders that some viewed as undersized. Mora and new defensive coordinator Ed Donatell scrapped the 3-4 scheme and installed a 4-3. Kerney benefited immediately, recording seven sacks in the Falcons' first four games in 2004.

Before the season, Mora and Donatell identified free agent Rod Coleman of the Raiders as the ideal fit at undertackle, the penetrating, pass-rushing position that was the key to an effective 4-3 scheme, a position Warren Sapp had filled in Tampa.

With a guy like Sapp or Coleman, it was possible to get by with almost anyone at nose tackle. In Tampa, Sapp's running mates included twelfth-round draft pick Brad Culpepper and Chartric Darby, an undrafted free agent.

"We could even play with Reggie," McKay would say, referring to Reggie Roberts, a burly man but more suited to his role as the Falcons public relations director.

Pat Dye Jr., Coleman's agent, knew things were changing in Atlanta when he took his reluctant client to meet with the Falcons. Coleman grew up a Giants fan in Philadelphia and wanted to sign with New York. There he met with a Giants position coach over dinner.

In Atlanta, Coleman broke bread with a fourteen-person Falcons contingent that included Blank, McKay, Mora, and Ruskell. Coleman signed a six-year, $27.8 million deal with the Falcons.

McKay preached speed to his scouting staff and spent his first Falcons draft pick on DeAngelo Hall, a cornerback from Virginia Tech who posted one of the fastest times in the forty-yard dash at the 2004 combine. Alex Gibbs, the new offensive line coach, wanted fast, athletic linemen modeled after those that played under him in Denver during their two Super Bowl–title seasons.

The most ambitious part of the makeover was the installation of a West Coast offense, which relies on finesse linemen in the Gibbs mold, but also a ball-control, precision passing game that didn't quite fit the talents of Michael Vick, the NFL's best running quarterback.

That was a work in progress. Tight end Alge Crumpler, a sure-handed tight end, fit the West Coast well. So did Warrick Dunn, a reliable receiver out of the backfield. Unfortunately, the Falcons did not have a big target at wide receiver. Vick, a fan of former 49ers quarterback and West Coast master Steve Young, was a willing pupil. Mora figured it would take a season or two to be fully implemented.

With the transition complete and the Falcons off to a 6-2 start in 2004 through October, Falcons scouts were well aware of what they were expected to locate for McKay. They were looking for smaller, aggressive, athletic linemen on both sides of the ball. They needed linebackers and defensive backs to bolster an improving defense. They needed a big wide receiver to help the West Coast offense. Above all, they needed fast, high-character players that were leaders, quick studies, overachievers, and solid citizens.

With all that in mind, it would be easy to narrow the field. By the time the Falcons scouting department convened in February, before the combine, they would have extensive reports. The area scout would have seen players three times: in August during two-a-day practices, after three games, and after the sixth or seventh game. Emery, the director of college scouting, would hit as many of the major schools as possible. Scouts would have cross-checked throughout January at the bowl and all-star games.

Ruskell and McKay would try to see as many games as possible, piggybacking trips to college games onto Falcons road trips. Before the Falcons played at San Francisco on September 12, Ruskell and McKay attended the California–New Mexico State game. When the team was home, they would watch games at Auburn, Georgia, or Georgia Tech.

Some scouting was as easy as walking downstairs from the Falcons second-floor executive offices to the locker room below. Though NFL players hesitate to reveal dirt on former college teammates, they also realize the potential impact the players could have.

Before the 2004 draft, the Falcons brass made it a point to ask Vick about Hall, a fellow ex-Virginia Tech Hokie. This year, the Falcons turned to young players such as rookie quarterback Matt Schaub, who as a University of Virginia senior during the 2003–2004 school year played with the members of the draft class of 2005.

"They want to make sure they're getting what they're paying for," Schaub said. "They'll ask about personality and character because that's such a big part of it. A guy can be a great player, but he might be lacking off the field and could hurt the team."

By the time scouts met before the combine, they would have a thorough understanding of a player's personality, family background, work ethic, drive, and integrity. The Falcons assign each player a double-letter grade that represents football character and personal character.

Football character refers to a player's ability to maximize his potential. A grade of A or B means the player works hard on the practice field, shows leadership qualities, learns quickly, plays through pain, commands respect from teammates, and instills fear in opponents. Personal character takes into account a player's history of criminal or disciplinary problems, if any. High-maintenance, diva players, no matter how talented, will score low in this area.

"We're looking for great character guys," Ruskell says. "If a guy is rated a D or below in that area, there's a possibility he's going to embarrass the franchise. At the very least, he's a guy who might just be too tough to get going."

Draft-eligible players that rate highly in football talent, character, and intangibles such as leadership are given a special "Falcon Filter" rating by Ruskell, a carryover from the "Buccaneer Filter" used in Tampa. When that player's card is posted on the "war room" ranking board, it's stamped with a team logo.

"You see five, maybe seven players a year where everything is so good we'll put the bird on the card," Ruskell says. "Those are exceptional guys, very rare. They lift the level of play of those around them. We make it hard to get. They might not be the greatest players, but they have exceptional intangibles."

Before the 2004 draft, Ruskell and his staff placed a Falcon Filter on Philip Rivers, the North Carolina State quarterback who was picked fourth overall, and Jonathan Vilma, the Miami linebacker picked twelfth by the New York Jets. In Tampa, Derrick Brooks and John Lynch earned Buccaneer Filters before their drafts.

"We're talking about the guy who everyone agrees is the leader of the team," Ruskell says. "Everyone rallies around him. He's the guy that organized off-season workouts. He's the guy that calls you when you're late. He's a natural leader and he lifts the level of play of everyone around him. You don't want to make him mad by showing a lack of effort, because he'll be right in your face. That's the guy you're looking for."

Chapter Six:

THE CHALLENGER

On the afternoon of November 13, 2004, Frank Dorazio walked the sidelines before the University of Miami's game against the University of Virginia in Charlottesville. As an area scout for the Tampa Bay Buccaneers based in Cleveland, it's Dorazio's job to cover the northeast.

It had been a grueling week for Dorazio, in his fourth season with the Buccaneers. He left home on Monday and drove to nearby Akron University. The following day, he visited Columbus and Ohio State, just as *ESPN the Magazine* published an article where former running back Maurice Clarett alleged that Buckeye football players were paid by boosters, provided with improper academic help, and given high-paying, no-show summer jobs. Ohio State officials denied the allegations.

After a tense day in Columbus, Dorazio traveled to West Virginia University on Wednesday and stopped at the University of Maryland on Thursday before arriving in Charlottesville on Friday.

Dorazio, forty-one, figures he drives between 20,000 and 30,000 miles over the course of a season, somewhere between 1,000 and 1,500 clicks a week. He was scheduled to spend 186 nights on the road in 2004. Like most scouts, he's put together a vast network of contacts from his previous gigs, and the one consolation for spending so much time on the road is getting to catch up with old friends.

A 1985 graduate of Ohio State, where he served as a manager for the football team, Dorazio worked briefly for the Cleveland Indians and Cleveland Browns before beginning a nine-year stint at Purdue University, working mostly on football recruiting. After that, he spent three years at Southern Cal as director of football operations before joining the Buccaneers before the 2001 season.

With such a journeyman resume, Dorazio runs into former colleagues almost everywhere. In Charlottesville, he visited with Luke Goldstein, his former roommate at USC, who now served as the Cavaliers' video coordinator.

Dorazio dutifully brings donuts or bagels wherever he goes, though he wonders if that tradition is waning. "So many coaches are on low-carb health kicks," he said. "I'm going to start bringing a fruit basket or something."

As the Cavaliers and Hurricanes underwent pregame drills, Dorazio searched for familiar coaches and kept an eye on players, making notes of body types. A chiseled guy is said to have a "beach body." Scouts obsess over hips and how loose or tight they are, since that will largely determine his agility and ability to generate power. Then there's a guy's butt or "bubble." Linemen need to have a big bubble.

"It's sometimes harder to get a read on guys at practice," Dorazio says. "Their jerseys are hanging out. Practice pants sometimes are baggier. This is more of a true read."

Al Groh and his Cavaliers still were in the hunt for the ACC championship. After an embarrassing, 36–3, loss at Florida State on October 16, Virginia rebounded to defeat Duke and Maryland to improve to 7-1. Elton Brown, the team's massive offensive guard, remained one of the top NFL prospects at his position. Scouts continued to keep an eye on Groh's talented underclassmen: linebackers Darryl Blackstock and Ahmad Brooks, tight end Heath Miller, and offensive tackle D'Brickashaw Ferguson. Senior Alvin Pearman, already a talented special teams player, had unseated Wali Lundy as the starting tailback and was drawing interest from NFL scouts.

Since Rich McKay and Tim Ruskell left the Buccaneers, things had changed in the scouting department under new general manager Bruce Allen. Ruskell's rating system had been streamlined. Unlike the Falcons, the Buccaneers do not have scouts serve as cross-checkers. With Ruskell's position still open, Ruston Webster, the director of college scouting, cross-checked the entire country.

Tampa Bay had a full arsenal of draft picks for the first time since

1999, having surrendered premium selections to acquire wide receiver Keyshawn Johnson in 2000 and head coach Jon Gruden in 2002. The Bucs acquired five more through trade, giving them a pair of picks in the third and fifth rounds, and four in the seventh, for 2005.

That made this year's draft especially important for the Buccaneers, who had gotten off to a 3-5 start after finishing the 2003 season 7-9. The glow of the 2002 Super Bowl victory had faded quickly. The following day, the Buccaneers would face the surprising Falcons, who were 6-1, in Atlanta.

Dorazio wouldn't be there. He planned to visit with Goldstein after the game and go into the football office on Sunday to watch film. Like most scouts, Dorazio had learned to root for the teams he had to visit the following week.

"Otherwise everyone is quiet and depressed—the coaches, secretaries, everybody," Dorazio says. "It's a bad atmosphere."

Chris Canty spent little time in the bad atmosphere of Virginia's postgame locker room. The Cavaliers, trailing just 17–14 heading into the fourth quarter, surrendered fourteen points and essentially were eliminated from ACC title contention by Miami.

Two Hurricanes juniors, both expected to turn pro early, did most of the damage. Frank Gore, enjoying a strong comeback season after enduring major surgeries on both knees, rushed twenty-eight times for 195 yards. Roscoe Parrish, a speedy five-ten wide receiver, scored twice in the fourth quarter, returning a punt sixty-two yards and hauling in a twenty-five-yard pass from quarterback Brock Berlin.

Canty, two months removed from knee surgery, watched the game on the sidelines, clad in the same orange-and-blue nylon running suits the Cavaliers wore to and from games. Technically, he still was a member of the team, though this was his first time back in Charlottesville since the injury. Sitting outside a reception for Cavalier football alumni afterward, he felt more like a returning graduate than an active player.

Canty was, after all, a graduate of the University of Virginia, having received his degree in May. After the injury, he dropped out of graduate school to undergo rehabilitation, first in Birmingham and then in Charlotte. Unlike other Cavaliers eligible for the 2005 NFL Draft, he was free to sign with an agent at any time, and had narrowed the field to four.

During the previous three weeks, the agents traveled to Charlotte and found their way to the Canty residence, a two-story brick home not far from downtown, in a tree-lined subdivision of houses built in the late 1980s. New homes in nearby communities began at four hundred and fifty thousand dollars.

Joseph Canty, Chris's father, works as a general contractor. His mother, the Reverend Shirley Canty, is pastor of the Calvary United Methodist Church.

Chris Canty had heard all of the stories of agents offering illegal inducements to players to sign, especially those players from modest backgrounds. Cars or cash in the form of "marketing guarantees," an advance against future endorsement earnings, income that only highly-drafted quarterbacks, running backs, and wide receivers ever see.

Canty said he did not receive those pitches, in part because he had his parents handle agents, and also because, unlike some NFL hopefuls, he does not come from modest financial means.

"Look around," Canty said during a visit to his home. "We've been blessed. My parents do very well making a living. By no means are we rich, but we're comfortable. Money, thank God, is not an issue for my parents anymore."

It wasn't always that way. The second of three sons, Chris was born on November 10, 1982, in the Bronx and raised in a part of the borough that Chris describes as "not right in the tough part of the Bronx, but right down the street from there."

Joe Canty worked for the city of New York Health Department, while Shirley served Methodist churches, first in Harlem and then in Queens. One afternoon in 1993, Shirley went to pick up the boys from school and returned to find their home had been robbed.

The family moved to Raleigh, North Carolina, soon after, settling in Charlotte three years later. With Charlotte booming, Joe's business blossomed in the late 1990s. Chris enrolled in the prestigious Charlotte Latin School, a private, 122-acre campus that passersby sometimes mistake for a small college.

Chris was more of a basketball player in high school, not even playing football until his junior year. Standing six-seven and at 215 pounds, he was too small to play power forward for big-time college programs. Still raw as a defensive end/tight end, he attracted little interest from Division 1-A programs, choosing Virginia over Boston College. Canty arrived in Charlottesville in the summer of 2000 with no aspirations of a career in the NFL, figuring he'd get a solid education and maybe contribute on the football field.

His first two years did nothing to change that view. George Welsh, in what would be his final year at Virginia, redshirted Canty as a freshman. Canty played as a backup in 2001, broke his leg during spring drills, missed the first two games of the 2002 season, and was not at full strength to start until the sixth game of the year.

By then, offensive linemen were struggling with the tall lineman with the huge wingspan and unlikely speed. He led ACC defensive linemen in tackles for the season, capturing second-team all-conference honors. By the end of the year he was getting mail from agents. Three seasons removed from high school, he was eligible for the 2003 NFL Draft.

Canty never considered it, returning as a redshirt junior in 2003, again leading the ACC linemen in tackles. By then, agents were swarming. Ethan Lock, the Arizona-based agent for former Cavaliers Tiki and Ronde Barber, was a frequent caller. So too was Brad Blank, who represented a long line of Virginia players, including Jeff Lageman, Herman Moore, and Chris Slade.

Canty let his parents deal with the agents. After the 2003 season, now weighing around 280, he applied for a predraft rating from the NFL's advisory committee and received an encouraging result: "not higher than the second round," the committee's second-highest rating. Canty considered signing with Blank and going pro, but again opted to stay in school. He already had disability insurance and re-upped for the 2004 season.

"I didn't think my skill level was as high as I wanted it to be," Canty said. "More importantly, I wasn't ready for that kind of lifestyle, being on my own and making financial decisions for myself. I was always a pretty responsible young man, but felt like I wasn't ready for that opportunity. Plus, Charlottesville is not a bad place to be. You can never get back that last year of college."

Lock and his Atlanta-based colleague Michael Brown told Canty about a training center in Arizona called Athletes' Performance, where the agency sent its clients to work out in the weeks before the NFL combine. During the summer of 2004, Canty and his parents traveled to Phoenix at their own expense and paid for Chris to train for a week.

By the time the 2004 season began, Lock was the front-runner to land Canty, now projected as a first-round pick for the 2005 draft. Lock was in the stands in Charlottesville when Canty blew out his knee against Syracuse on September 25, 2004, but like many who watched Canty helped off the field, he figured it was just a sprained ankle or knee.

Even when agents learned of the extent of the injury, few backed away, and the Cantys welcomed a parade of agents into their home in late October and November. There was IMG's Tom Condon. Brown and

Lock made a presentation. David Joseph, a Greensboro, North Carolina, agent who at the time represented Eagles wide receiver Terrell Owens, also came. Cary Fabrikant, a South Florida agent whose company represents twenty NFL veterans, rounded out the group.

The agents typically arrived after dinner and each spent the better part of three hours running through their qualifications, skills in negotiations, services, and how they would best prepare Chris for the NFL Draft. Some brought DVDs of their company, and Chris and his parents aired them on their big-screen TV, nestled in a corner across the room from Chris's diploma from the University of Virginia and several framed press clippings.

"There's always one key element that an agent says he can do better than anyone else in the world, whether that be financial advice, marketing, you name it," Canty says. "They all have an angle. The only thing you can do is pick the guy who best fits you, your personality. You've got to figure out what you need from them, whether it's a lot of attention or a little. It's who you feel comfortable with."

Canty said he managed to avoid the seamier side of recruiting. Many agencies send intermediaries, more commonly called "runners," to do the legwork. They set up shop in a college town, attach themselves to players, and, using whatever means necessary, deliver clients to agencies. Some runners are paid covertly, their relationships secret. Others are full-fledged agency employees, paying their dues until they became licensed agents themselves.

The NFL Players Association, which oversees the certification and regulation of agents, prohibits its "certified contract advisors" from offering financial inducements to lure players, but it's nearly impossible for the union to catch violators, since agents are permitted to loan or give money to players *after* signing them as clients. Proving when an inducement was made is difficult, especially with neither agents nor players serving as whistle-blowers.

At Virginia, head coach Al Groh tried to keep runners away from his players. He brought agents he believed acted aboveboard to his summer agent day to meet with players and parents. He installed security officers in the stairwells outside the parking garage at Scott Stadium. They checked that everyone entering the area outside the Virginia locker room—parents, alumni, friends—wore the appropriate wristband. Still, Groh knew, there was no deterrent any college coach could employ to keep runners and agents away from players, including talented underclassmen.

One floor above the garage, anyone could walk into the lobby, where Virginia football alumni had gathered following the Miami loss. Sitting alongside a check-in table, Canty felt ready to become one of the first members of the 2005 draft class to sign with an agent. All around him were former Cavaliers, most of whom never played a down in the NFL.

The decision looked like a lock. Ethan Lock.

While the Atlanta Falcons headed north on Saturday, November 20, 2004, to face the New York Giants the following day, assistant general manager Tim Ruskell opted to take a later flight so he could watch eighteenth-ranked Virginia face Georgia Tech in midtown Atlanta.

Ruskell arrived nearly two hours early at Bobby Dodd Stadium, located right on campus not far from Coca-Cola world headquarters. He met up in the press box with Falcons scout Bob Harrison, who is based in Athens and scouts the state of Virginia as part of a mid-Atlantic coverage area.

Ruskell and Harrison took the elevator down to the field, where they watched Virginia go through its pregame routine. They spent little time on Georgia Tech, partly because they see a lot of the hometown team, but also because Chan Gailey's roster did not have much draft-eligible talent for 2005. The Yellow Jackets draft prospects for 2006 and beyond looked promising, especially freshman wide receiver Calvin Johnson.

James Butler, Tech's senior safety, was rated highly by BLESTO and National before the season. ESPN's Mel Kiper Jr. ranked Butler as his top safety and number twenty-five prospect overall, but thus far, scouts had failed to see early-round talent in film and in person during his senior season.

Ruskell walked the sidelines, searching for familiar faces. Having scouted for nearly two decades, he knows at least a few people on every major coaching staff. Ruskell stopped to talk to John Garrett, Virginia's wide receivers coach, who spent three seasons in Tampa Bay's personnel department during Ruskell's early years with the Buccaneers.

Next Ruskell chatted with Tom Sherman, a longtime Virginia assistant coach who now worked in an administrative role for Al Groh's program. Before heading up to the press box, Ruskell spoke to Lynn Swann, the Hall of Fame wide receiver and ABC Television commentator.

Upstairs, Ruskell found his assigned seat in the scouts section of the press box. Few NFL team employees were on hand. Scouts generally prefer to watch games with draft-eligible talent on both sides of the field, though a game like this had its advantages, because scouts could focus on fewer players.

Unlike fans, who follow the ball as they watch the game, scouts concentrate on players. If a scout is watching, say, a group of defensive backs, he's unlikely to have much of a feel for how the offensive line is performing.

"You miss a lot of the game this way," Ruskell says.

Ruskell was making comments on a chart that had a dozen or so Virginia players listed. There was not a whole lot of space.

"You know those hard-boiled Easter eggs with all the tiny words written on them?" he says. "If this gig doesn't work out, I might look into that. I've gotten pretty good at writing small."

By now, nine games into the college football season, Ruskell had detailed reports from the Falcons' area scouts. The scouts had studied film and watched practices and games. They had visited each campus with significant draft talent multiple times, interviewing three to five people at each school for every player. On December 11, they would reconvene at Falcon headquarters in Flowery Branch to begin narrowing the field of scouted players.

Ruskell was not gung-ho about Elton Brown, Virginia's 330-pound, All-American guard who was projected as a first-round pick in the draft. The Falcons offensive coordinator, Alex Gibbs, preferred smaller, athletic linemen who could get off the line quickly and adjust on the fly with guys coming at them.

"Brown does not move well laterally," Ruskell says. "He's not a bender, which is to say he has tight hips. He doesn't drop his hips, and that keeps him from going side to side and changing direction well. It's more physical than a technique thing. He's going to be a quality player in the league, but probably not for us."

Ruskell, like a lot of NFL personnel, was bullish on Alvin Pearman, Virginia's five-nine running back. Pearman began the season as the backup to Wali Lundy, a junior, but seized the starting role after Lundy struggled in a loss to Florida State.

Scouts loved Pearman's versatility. He caught balls out of the backfield, played special teams, and even occasionally lined up as a wide receiver. Ruskell watched Pearman as he swung out to the right, hesitated, and then burst upfield.

"I'm becoming a big Alvin Pearman fan," Ruskell says. "He lets the play develop in front of him and lets his blockers do the work. He's slightly slower and smaller, so that helps. The problem is that he doesn't have that huge burst of speed once the play develops. You hear great things about his work ethic and character."

Ruskell also liked Marquis Weeks, a star running back in high school, who played sparingly at the position his first three seasons at Virginia behind Pearman and Lundy. Weeks now was lining up as a safety, but continued to thrive as a kickoff returner.

From watching film and talking to his Virginia sources, Ruskell learned that Weeks had the vision and cutback skills to thrive at the next level. Chiseled, with washboard abs, Weeks had a "beach body," along with speed.

In September, Weeks returned a kickoff one hundred yards for a touchdown against North Carolina. When asked about the play by reporters, he delivered one of the year's more memorable quotes.

"That was just instinct," he said, "kind of like running from the cops."

Weeks, at five-ten, was undersized, just like the five-nine Pearman. Just like Tiki Barber, the five-ten ex-Virginia back now playing with the Giants. Just like Warrick Dunn, Ruskell's own five-nine starter with the Falcons.

Barber and Dunn would square off the following day at Giants Stadium. Both were drafted in 1997, Dunn out of Florida State with the twelfth overall pick to Ruskell and the Buccaneers, Barber early in the second round to the Giants.

"Dunn showed a little more burst," Ruskell said. "He had the strength of a bigger man in a larger body. Tiki was a little undersized and looked slower. But it was pretty even. That might have been an example of with everything else being equal we went with the [local] Florida State guy."

Ruskell glanced up at a television to catch a replay. Since TV cameras follow the ball, broadcasts are of little help in scouting defenses, though replays help. For all of the talk about how the wider, HDTV technology would broaden the viewer's perspective, Ruskell hasn't found it to be much of an improvement, at least in scouting.

"There's no substitute for live games," he says.

ABC runs a note on Virginia center Zac Yarborough not allowing any sacks. "It means nothing," Ruskell says. "Nor do I believe it."

Yarborough was a prime example of how it's possible to be an outstanding college player and have little NFL potential. A three-year starter, he was under consideration for the Rimington Award, given to the nation's top center. At six-four, he had the size, though he needed some more bulk on his 276-pound frame. He had the bloodlines; his father Jim played ten years at offensive tackle for the Detroit Lions. Zach even served as Virginia's long-snapper on special teams, always a valuable skill in the NFL.

Like Elton Brown, Yarborough had stiff hips. Unlike Brown, he did not possess the raw skills to compensate for a lack of athleticism and mobility. If he got a shot at the NFL, it would come as an undrafted free agent.

Ruskell was thankful that all of the kickers and punters in the game were underclassmen. Teams rarely spend draft picks on kickers—the blanket term used for both positions—and scouts hate wasting energy writing reports on kickers. Unless a kicker has phenomenal leg strength or uncanny accuracy, most teams are content to sign free agent kickers.

Virginia led Georgia Tech 10–0 at halftime. Pearman provided a six-yard touchdown run. Connor Hughes, a junior already projected as one of the better kickers for the 2006 draft, chipped in with a thirty-three-yard field goal. As usual, junior linebackers Ahmad Brooks and Darryl Blackstock had dominated the opposition.

As a NFL executive, Ruskell faces fines for commenting specifically on juniors to the media, though he was keeping an eye on Virginia's talented cast of draft-eligible underclassmen, for future reference if nothing else.

"I'll say this," Ruskell said. "It's a very talented group."

Ruskell and Harrison departed in the third quarter with the rest of the modest scout contingent. Down on the field, Blackstock was enjoying himself, in the midst of a three-sack performance.

After each sack, Blackstock pointed to the sidelines and Chris Slade, the former New England Patriot who held Virginia's all-time sack record with forty. Slade, now retired at thirty-three and living in Atlanta, was one of Groh's all-time favorite players. Though Groh never asked Slade to lobby Blackstock to stay for a senior season, Slade made it a point to present the pros and cons.

"The NFL will always be there," Slade said on the sidelines as the final seconds ticked off on a 30–10 Virginia win. "But it's a personal thing. Nobody can make that decision for him."

After Groh met with the media and the players showered, they made their way to a bus parked alongside a plaza on the north side of the stadium. A small gathering of Virginia parents and fans offered congratulations.

There were no agents, even though Atlanta was a hotbed of "certified contract advisors," as they were referred to by the NFL Players Association. There was little interest in Georgia Tech's players, and plenty of more prestigious games going on throughout the country.

Atlanta-based Todd France, who a year earlier signed Tech linebacker Daryl Smith, was not at the game. But with the college season winding down, the young agent was getting into position to have a blockbuster 2005 draft.

By late November France was well on his way to taking his fifteen-month-old France Athlete Management Enterprises (FAME) company into the upper echelons of football agencies.

Like his competitors, France did not know for sure which players would sign with him. In four and a half years as an NFLPA certified contract advisor, he had learned not to consider a client his own until the signature was on the dotted line.

Nat Dorsey reminded him of that. In the fall of 2003, Dorsey was a promising junior offensive tackle at Georgia Tech who was considering going pro early. France thought he had him, at least until he signed with SFX agent Ben Dogra.

Dorsey should have stayed in school. He failed to impress NFL scouts prior to the draft, and lasted until midway through the fourth round, when the Minnesota Vikings took him. He received a signing bonus of $308,000. Combined with his 2004 salary of $230,000, he generated just $16,140 in commissions for Dogra and SFX Sports, which paid more than that for Dorsey's precombine training and lodging in Arizona.

The draft is funny that way. A player rated high by scouts and the media in the fall can see his stock plunge by April, even without an injury, arrest, or failed drug test. Sometimes, as in the case of Nat Dorsey, scouts get scared when a kid's motivation and drive do not seem to match the level of raw talent.

It still was a good draft for France. With the seventh pick in the second round, the Jacksonville Jaguars selected linebacker Daryl Smith, Dorsey's Georgia Tech teammate, and France negotiated a signing bonus of $1,872,000. Later in the round, the Denver Broncos drafted Darius Watts, a wide receiver from Marshall University. He received a signing bonus of $1,265,000. Along with their 2004 salaries, France would earn commissions of $107,910.

Still, France knew rival agents would use his lack of first-round representation against him, to say nothing of a pending lawsuit filed by his former employer, Career Sports Management, for resigning in 2003 and taking sixteen clients with him.

That does not stop France from aiming high. His four main targets were potential first-rounders: Auburn running back Ronnie Brown and cornerback Carlos Rogers; Roddy White, a wide receiver at Alabama-Birmingham; and Georgia safety Thomas Davis, a junior who seemed likely to leave school early. Though Auburn and Georgia had other promising players for the 2005 draft, France had made a presentation to just one other prospect, pitching Georgia's Fred Gibson a year earlier when the wide receiver was considering leaving school early.

France knows the key to getting considered by a client is to get in the door. The ultimate sales pitch is vital, and France has developed a reputation for having one of the most high-tech, DVD presentations of anyone in the industry, along with the requisite information on his success negotiating for clients.

He's at his best translating the glossary of NFL signing terms for players and family members. Phrases such as "option bonuses," "voidable years," and "escalators," quickly become simplified. France spent nearly a decade cutting big-time sports-marketing deals for Atlanta-based Career Sports Management, and his presentation includes the highlights of the deals he's done for clients.

Pat Dye Jr., the rival Atlanta agent, takes a preemptive strike against agents like France during his presentations. "Let's separate the sizzle from the steak," he tells parents and recruits, usually before detailing his seventeen-year track record.

France has learned quickly to tailor his presentations.

"You're selling your capabilities and establishing a comfort factor with the parents that you can take care of their son and do whatever it is you need to do. And that's not just the contract, that's everything. On field, off field, contract, someone they can trust—everything. Sometimes you're viewed as not having enough clients. Sometimes you have too many."

First, France needs help opening the gates, and that's where existing clients prove useful. Takeo Spikes, a linebacker from Auburn, is in the midst of a six-year deal worth $32 million. France's clients from Georgia include Bills left tackle Jonas Jennings and Kendrell Bell, a linebacker for the Pittsburgh Steelers. Both can become free agents at the end of the season.

If, say, Ronnie Brown is wondering what kind of marketing deals France could swing for him, he need only step into a wing of France's Atlanta office suites devoted largely to the many endorsement deals

Spikes, Bell, and Priest Holmes have landed, despite playing in small-market NFL cities.

Then there's the issue of finding the gatekeeper. Some kids delegate their parents to deal with agents and narrow the field. Others handle it themselves or enlist the help of a high school coach or friend.

"Sometimes the dad says everything is run through him, and meanwhile you find out he's not involved at all," France says.

In some cases, the college coach has his own agent and provides a point of entry to his representative. Jimmy Sexton has had good luck with client Nick Saban's players at LSU. More often that not, that connection proves irrelevant.

France spends most of the fall on the road. If he's not visiting recruits and families, he's flying off to tend to his current roster. He'll travel to an NFL city and visit clients on the home team on Friday and check in with any visiting clients at their hotel on Saturday. After the game on Sunday, he'll see the visiting team off on the bus before they fly out, have dinner with family members still in town, and then fly out on Monday morning.

"Nothing is easy," France says. "I won't be outworked and I just take care of my guys because it's a very nonloyal business. The famous agent line is 'Where's your agent?' implying that you're there and the agent is not. I've never said that to anyone, but I can see it happening. If you keep in touch and have a relationship, you can't worry about it."

Though France is a relative newcomer to the NFL agent business, the seeds of his involvement were planted nearly two decades ago. In 1986, Lonnie Cooper founded Career Sports Management, an Atlanta sports-marketing company that arranged appearances and endorsements for a small but growing client list of NBA coaches and players, including Atlanta Hawks head coach Mike Fratello, pint-sized guard Spud Webb, and power forward Cliff Levingston.

One afternoon, Levingston wandered into Marietta Toyota looking to purchase a 4Runner. Bob Pressley, the general sales manager, said he ran a credit check on Levingston and discovered all sorts of red flags. Levingston, like many generous pro athletes, had co-signed loans for others, some of whom never held up their end of the deals.

Cooper was summoned to straighten things out and Levingston was able to purchase the 4Runner. Cooper and Pressley also began discussions on what later would become a three-year deal for Fratello to serve as spokesman for Marietta Toyota.

In those days, long before seven-figure NBA coaching salaries became commonplace, Cooper realized that the marketing and endorsement side of the business could be every bit as lucrative as contract negotiations.

As Cooper's business grew, he kept things lean, but realized in 1990 that he needed help. He hired a young, aspiring sports marketer named Reed Bergman to shoulder some of the load.

France, born July 8, 1971, was enrolled at the University of Alabama, with a vague goal of working in sports. His family moved from Chicago to Atlanta in 1987, shortly before his junior year of high school, when his father was promoted from senior vice president to president of an Atlanta-based publishing business. Todd France graduated from Alabama in 1993 with a degree in communications, with a focus on advertising.

France paid his dues at the lowest rungs of sports. After graduation, he went to work for the Atlanta Knights, a minor league hockey team that performed downtown to sparse crowds at the Omni, and was best known for playing female goaltender Manon Rheaume for two games during the previous season.

Like most minor league sports employees, France did a little bit of everything. He sold sponsorships and advertising, hawked tickets, and pitched in whenever. He worked briefly for the Atlanta Fireants, a professional roller hockey team that played one season in Atlanta (1994) before moving to Oklahoma.

In April of 1994, Bergman hired the twenty-two-year-old France to work with him in the marketing department at Career Sports for seventeen thousand dollars a year. France threw himself into the job, working eighteen-hour days and immersing himself in the world of sports marketing. His specialty was consumer products deals, and he built relationships with companies such as The Keebler Company, Nestle, and SmithKline Beecham, makers of products such as Aquafresh and Tums.

France would approach the companies, ascertain their sports marketing goals, and put the deals together. Keebler's Cheez-It crackers became a sponsor of young NASCAR drivers Tony Stewart and Buckshot Jones. France negotiated the title sponsorship of the Cheez-It 250, a NASCAR race in Bristol, Tennessee. There were dozens of contests involving consumer products and sports-related prizes and CSM did everything from getting the point-of-sales materials designed to being on site to make sure the winners received everything. Typical was a trip France made to Disney World to greet three winners of a lunch with Jay Novacek, the former Dallas Cowboys tight end.

France helped negotiate a contract for ex-Georgia quarterback Eric Zeier to become a broadcaster at his alma mater. Zeier, who played six seasons in the NFL as a backup, was the closest thing Career Sports had to a legitimate football client when France approached Cooper in the fall of 1999 with the idea of starting a football agency division.

Cooper's practice still was dominated by NBA and college basketball coaches, along with a handful of baseball players, most notably Atlanta Braves pitcher John Smoltz.

After Bergman left in 1997 to form a marketing company with baseball agent Scott Boras, France was promoted to senior vice president of sales and marketing. Cooper continued to run the representation side of the business, though France was becoming increasingly interested in working as an agent.

He considered basketball and its eye-popping salaries, but NBA rosters were small and increasingly composed of players from all over the world, which made recruiting difficult and expensive. Plus, a handful of NBA agents held a virtual stranglehold on the league.

Baseball showed potential, and France was familiar with the field through Cooper, having made marketing-related presentations to potential CSM clients. With guaranteed contracts and commissions as high as 5 percent, baseball has made several agents multi-millionaires. There are few barriers to entry. As long as the aspiring agent has no felony convictions, and one client on a team's forty-man roster, he can be licensed by the Major League Baseball Players Association.

The NFL offers no guaranteed contracts, commissions of no more than 3 percent, and player careers that last an average of just three and a half years. To become a registered contract advisor, a would-be agent needs to possess a four-year degree from an accredited college or university, pass a background check, attend a two-day seminar, pass an exam, and fork over one thousand six hundred dollars. Then there's a dizzying array of licenses and fees agents face in order to operate legally in most states, though enforcement of such regulations often is spotty.

But the reason the number of football agents outweigh baseball representatives by nearly a four-to-one margin is because of the shorter gestation period between the time a player is drafted and when he reaches the big time.

Few baseball players ever have gone straight from draft day into the major leagues. Most spend four or five years toiling in the minors, during which time they make little money but expect their agents to provide them with equipment, shoes, and all manner of financial and moral support. Once they reach the majors, they're not eligible for a huge payday through salary arbitration until they've played three years. That's when more experienced agents swoop in and sign them, negating any work and investment the entry-level agents have made for years.

In football, players go right from draft day to a NFL minicamp, sometimes within a week, though contract negotiations last three months, until the start of preseason camp, and often beyond. Signing bonuses after the second round are modest, but there's an immediate commission, along with one off the rookie salary.

No wonder the ranks of football agents, or at least wannabe agents, had swelled. In the fall of 2004, there were more than thirteen hundred NFLPA-certified agents. More than two-thirds of them did not have a single client in the league.

The sudden paydays and soaring salaries have unleashed another agent subcategory on college campuses: financial advisors. Though most players will not earn enough money to make it worthwhile for investment managers, even at a management fee of 1 to 2 percent, to handle their portfolios, the financial gurus still recruit potential NFL clients with gusto. Like their agent counterparts, they see the route to riches beginning with one client.

"An agent's work is done pretty much when the career is over," says Bruce Smith, an Atlanta-based financial advisor. "A financial advisor relationship can go on for decades."

For football agents, the rising salaries come with a price. Greater competition among agents makes it possible for potential clients to ask for the world. NFL hopefuls now expect a full slate of predraft training services, and the poaching of clients is even more rampant than in baseball. Still, it's a heck of a lot easier for an agent to break into football than baseball.

Major League Baseball increasingly has become the domain of players from Latin America, requiring agents to foot the bill for expensive travel and assemble a bilingual staff. A football agent can set up shop in Georgia or Florida and recruit mostly out of his car. Agencies don't need Spanish-speaking employees, though most firms include both white and African-American agents.

"All Caucasian agents have that," says Darrell Wills, who worked for IMG until 2004, when the NFLPA revoked his certification when he tried to take six IMG clients with him and start a new firm. "They hire a guy to get them into the living room, but they never want him to get to the point of doing the contract."

Wills's claim is open to debate, though the issue of race permeates any discussion of draft recruiting. With the vast majority of NFL players African-American, it's perhaps not surprising that some of the more prominent agents—such as Carl and Kevin Poston, Roosevelt Barnes, and Eugene Parker—also are black. In Major League Baseball, where African-American players have become an even smaller minority over the last two decades, white agents dominate the field.

Not long after Wills left IMG, longtime football operations employee Chris Singletary, who is black, earned his agent certification and took a prominent role in recruiting for the 2005 draft, joining veteran agents Tom Condon and Ken Kremer, who are white.

At Momentum Sports, based in San Antonio, Jack Scharf and Jeff Griffin work in tandem. Scharf, who is white, and Griffin, who is black, received their agent certifications on the same day in 2002.

"The race card gets played by some agents, but most families, whether they're African American or white, see right through that," Scharf says. "I don't think it's nearly the factor some agents make it out to be, nor should it be."

Patrick Kerney, the defensive end for the Atlanta Falcons, recalls an amusing case of racial misidentification. Kerney was a relative unknown entering his senior season at the University of Virginia in 1998, projected as perhaps a fifth-round draft pick, but his stock rose with a solid senior campaign, and a flurry of communication from agents ensued.

"This one agency sent me a letter that read, 'Dear Patrick, we pride ourselves on providing the utmost service to you, the African-American athlete,'" Kerney says.

The same agent called one of Kerney's black teammates, defensive tackle Antonio Dingle, and suggested that the three of them meet in Charlottesville for a get-acquainted session. Dingle, having received a similar letter, knew the agent's angle.

"There's something about Kerney you might not understand," said Dingle, who went on to a brief NFL career.

"Oh, is he on the take?" the agent asked. "Has he signed with an agent already?"

"No," Dingle said. "Kerney is white."

Kerney, who signed with Maryland-based agent Anthony Agnone, shakes his head at the story. "I guess some people don't bother to look at the media guide."

France is a one-agent show, though he has an office staff of four to provide the level of concierge service that NFL players demand, including the negotiation of home and auto deals, travel arrangements, marketing and endorsements, everything down to wedding planning and wardrobe assistance.

Compared to that, the actual negotiation of contracts is easy and straightforward. Anyone armed with the pick-by-pick contract results from the previous year's NFL Draft can do a reliable job predicting what a team is willing to pay the following season, though that doesn't stop agents from trumpeting any tweaks they manage to negotiate to potential clients.

"I don't think it's brain surgery doing that structured thing that goes on in the NFL Draft," says Boras, who through loopholes and hard-line negotiating has fueled the escalation of baseball draft bonuses over the last two decades.

Boras has become such a powerbroker in baseball that teams sometimes pass up his clients in the draft rather than risk a protracted negotiation. In the NFL, where salary caps and slotting prevail, teams put far less weight on a player's representative.

"Any holdout that occurs after the first fifteen picks, you really have to ask yourself why," says Atlanta Falcons president Rich McKay. "These are pretty easy deals to do, especially after the second round."

France thought so, especially after nearly six years of negotiating sports marketing contracts. In February of 2000, at the age of twenty-eight, he became a certified contract advisor. His first client was Mareno Philyaw, a wide receiver from Troy State selected in the sixth round of the 2000 draft by Atlanta. Philyaw played only briefly in the NFL, but left a lasting legacy to France by introducing him to Falcons teammate Darrick Vaughn.

Vaughn, a cornerback drafted out of Southwest Texas in the seventh-round that year, was no more likely than Philyaw to enjoy a lengthy, high-paying NFL career. But in early 2001, Vaughn mentioned that a friend of his from Texas was getting out of college and was interested in pursuing a career in sports marketing.

France met with Vaughn's friend and, even though he could not offer him a job, tried to be encouraging. That might have been the end of it, if not for a phone call in early 2002. The kid had a buddy employed in the NFL, who was looking for new representation.

His name was Priest Holmes.

Holmes wasn't even drafted coming out of Texas in 1997. Back then, at five-nine and two years removed from a torn ACL, he was less of a prospect than Philyaw or Vaughn. After four seasons in Baltimore, he found the perfect home in Kansas City, which employed a zone-blocking scheme that showcased his patient running style. In 2001, Holmes led the NFL in rushing with 1,555 yards in his first season with the Kansas City Chiefs. With little notice, France met Holmes in Atlanta on a Saturday and after a brief presentation handed him a standard player representation agreement and a preaddressed FedEx envelope.

France knew only that CSM was one of four agencies Holmes was considering, and he wasn't especially confident of his chances. After all, it was rare to sign a client after just one meeting. But four days later, France received the signed contract back via FedEx.

No longer was France just another one of the dozens of faceless agents with a small stable of fringe NFL players. He now represented arguably the NFL's best rusher, a twenty-seven-year-old with high-earning years ahead of him. Holmes was signed through 2005, with his commissions going to a previous agent, but France was free to negotiate marketing deals.

The Holmes signing, via Vaughn and Philyaw, on July 26, 2002, reenforced France's belief in the power of the existing client network. Earlier that year, he signed Spikes, who had just finished his fifth season with the Cincinnati Bengals and was one of the more prominent free agent linebackers. Those two clients gave France credibility when he recruited college players for the draft. Until this point, his only significant draftee had been Kendrell Bell, drafted by Pittsburgh out of Georgia in the second round in 2001.

During the next two years, France built a client list of sixteen players, many from Auburn, Alabama, Georgia, and Georgia Tech. He kept a low profile, staying out of the media spotlight, and joked that he was not even the most prominent Todd France working in football. In 2002, a kicker from the University of Toledo with the same name entered the league as an undrafted free agent, signing with the Minnesota Vikings.

Still, by the summer of 2003, agent Todd France, former Atlanta Fireants salesman, had grown too big for Career Sports Management. On August 24, France declared his independence from Cooper, taking his football clients with him.

Cooper did not let France go quietly. On October 10, 2003, he filed a lawsuit in Fulton County, Georgia, Superior Court, against France. The suit claimed that Career Sports was entitled to all of the fees from the sixteen players for contracts consummated before September 9, 2003, and unspecified damages against France and his new company, France Athlete Management Enterprises (FAME).

Career Sports received sixteen faxed termination letters from NFL player clients, including Holmes, on September 4, 2003, the day after the Chiefs announced a four-year contract extension worth as much as $36 million.

Cooper, through Career Sports vice president of public relations Jamie

Sims, declined comment for this book. With the suit still unresolved as this book went to press, France had little to say, but hinted that his departure was due in part to wanting a bigger piece of the action at Career Sports.

"My preference was to stay where I was and keep doing things, but there comes a time where things need to be handled a certain way and you need certain securities with your job. If that's going to happen, great. If it's not, you consider alternatives. I don't know how much more I can say. I never envisioned myself doing this, but when it came down to it, when push came to shove, you've got to do what's best for you."

The affidavits and depositions filed as part of the suit provide conflicting accounts of France's role and the events leading up to his departure. The sides agreed that France proposed that CSM start a football representation arm of the agency in the fall of 1999. France and Cooper were agents of record for each player signed, though all commissions went to CSM. France, at the time of his resignation in 2003, earned a salary of approximately one hundred and seventy-five thousand dollars plus benefits, including a country club membership.

Beth Brandon, CSM's chief operating officer, said in an affidavit that when France proposed the football division, he asked that Cooper act as his "trainer and mentor until he was properly trained." Brandon said CSM agreed to the proposal with the understanding that France not neglect his sales duties in other divisions.

CSM paid all of the start-up costs of the NFL division, including salaries and benefits of other employees working with France, as well as all costs involved with France becoming a certified agent by the NFL Players Association, along with the various states that require licensing.

In July of 2003, according to Brandon, France asked for a new compensation package that included a doubling of his salary and half of the NFL player commissions. He also requested CSM pick up the lease payments, maintenance, and insurance on his Mercedes. The new salary alone, Brandon said, "would have come close to matching CSM's expected gross revenues in its NFL division for 2003 and would have exceeded the expected gross revenues for 2004."

Brandon also said in her affidavit that France neglected his other sales activities and focused almost exclusively on the NFL division. France's work on the NFL endeavor, Brandon said, "failed to produce any net profit for CSM for a substantial period," and his "neglect of his other duties and his initial failure to generate significant new NFL business" caused CSM revenues to drop and costs to escalate.

France, in his affidavit, said he continued to fulfill his sales and marketing responsibilities while creating the NFL division. He opened CSM sales offices in Los Angeles and Chicago. The bulk of the time he spent on the NFL division was on nights and weekends. France acknowledged that in lieu of receiving the fifty percent share of fees to which he was entitled under the NFLPA's standard representation agreement, he would be paid a salary by CSM.

But, France said in the affidavit, "At no time during my employment did I agree that this arrangement would continue upon the termination of my employment with CSM." France said he had not received a pay raise in more than five and a half years. France said that during a meeting on July 21, 2003, Cooper asked him to make a compensation proposal, but that France, not being privy to CSM's financials, was "not in position to fairly determine an appropriate salary increase."

A month later, France departed. Bergman, who says he reached his own settlement with Cooper after splitting in 1997, remains friends with France. "Lonnie took a chance that Todd could help him, and he clearly did," Bergman says. "Todd built an athlete representation practice for Lonnie and made him an awful lot of money."

Rival agents aren't so quick to paint France as a victim. "He was able to use Cooper's resources to build himself a nice little business, and once he got a foothold, he took off," says an agent with comparable experience in the field. "Most of us have to find a way to foot the start-up costs ourselves."

France's departure had overtones of *Jerry Maguire*, though unlike Maguire, who left with just one client, the entire football division joined France at FAME. France resigned on a Sunday night and one of his first calls was to Jennifer Krompass, who worked with France as CSM's new business coordinator. She resigned Monday morning and showed up at France's townhouse ready to work.

Realizing France had little more than a cell phone, pen, and paper, she took him to a Staples outlet to buy office supplies. As Krompass began loading a cart with supplies, France took stock of his pending start-up costs and put several items back on the shelves.

They operated out of France's home for six months as the agent incorporated, recruited for the 2004 draft, serviced his existing clients, located office space, and supervised the decoration. He settled on a black-and-silver motif for the FAME logo, ordered large images of his clients from various NFL photographers, and set up a marketing room that was part memorabilia gallery, part convenience store. The furniture was black leather and silver metal, the floors light hardwood.

When it was done, shortly before the 2004 draft, someone gave FAME a goldfish bowl for the entryway, a tribute to the one Jerry Maguire took from his previous employer on the way out the door. France and Krompass didn't fall in love like Maguire and his accountant, but oversaw a rapid start-up operation. France would be the only one involved in athlete recruiting.

"It's all me," France said. "Would I like to have help? It would ease the workload. Say I'm at a Georgia-Auburn game. I'll see agents from the same company planted on both sides in the stands. I'm on one side saying hello to whomever, then I have to sprint around to the other side and casually walk up to the other group. But I wouldn't have it any other way."

The CSM lawsuit seems to have no impact on France as he recruits clients for the 2005 draft. As usual, he must navigate the murky waters of state and university regulations regarding contact with players.

"Some schools don't want you talking to kids until after the end of the season," France says. "You can follow that rule, but you're not going to sign a kid ever. You'll be the only one following that rule. Why else would kids be signing right after their bowl games? You do the best you can to play by the rules.

"Different schools go different ways. Alabama used to have a rule that if you signed up as a registered agent, you can't talk to kids. I told the compliance guy that if your goal is to have agents sign up, it's not going to work. They'd rather not sign up, and talk to your players. Now you sign up and it doesn't say you can't talk to players. An agent list is just something they can provide to players, saying these agents have at least followed state and school rules. We're not recommending them, but they've registered."

Schools walk a fine line with agents. Be too strict and risk nobody following rules and protocol. Be too loose and risk agents plying players with illegal incentives.

Instead, most schools strike a happy medium. Instead of banishing agents from campus, which is impossible, school officials try to make them part of the process. That strikes some as letting the fox into the henhouse. But for schools like Florida State University, who have been embarrassed by agent scandals, it's a worthwhile tactic.

For most of the year, FSU and other schools try to keep agents away from campus. But for one day a year they throw open the doors and invite them to make their pitches.

They call it "agent day."

Chapter Seven:

AGENT DAY

P at Dye Jr. and Bill Johnson sat in desk chairs and smiled at Ray Willis, his wife Kimberly, and a roomful of Ray's relatives. It was November 21, 2004, and Dye and Johnson had thirty minutes to make their sales pitch to Willis, a Florida State offensive tackle considered a possible second or third-round pick.

The Willis camp sat in deep-cushioned garnet-red theater chairs with flip-up desktops, in Room 2302 of Florida State's massive football complex, a shrine to the big business of college football. During the season, the room was used for position meetings. Motivational signs were posted throughout. (YOU CAN'T LIVE SOFT AND FIGHT TOUGH.)

On this Sunday afternoon, the school had invited agents to sit down one-on-one with the school's draft-eligible players. It was the one day of the year that Florida State, like every other major football program, did not try to keep agents off campus and away from players.

"Agents drive us nuts," said Bobby Bowden, the school's longtime head coach. "They're probably the number-one problem in college coaching."

Bowden should know. A decade earlier, recruiters working for agents provided several of his top players with a free shopping spree at a sporting goods store. "The Foot Locker Incident" prompted a NCAA investigation that landed FSU on probation for one year. Steve Spurrier, head coach at rival Florida at the time, labeled FSU "Free Shoes University."

As part of Florida State's penance, it cracked down on agents and set up its agent day, where football representatives registered with the school and licensed by both the NFL Players Association and the state of Florida are allowed to submit names of players they wished to meet. The players then were asked to submit a list of agents they wanted to meet.

Brian Battle, the school's compliance director, matched up the lists and assigned agents rooms. Players rotated each half hour in a high-stakes job fair.

"We're not going to stick our heads in the sand and pretend that agents aren't constantly contacting our players," Battle said. "We know most kids, if they have any NFL potential at all, have narrowed down the agent selection process now, as they should have. Our goal with agent day is to give agents an open avenue to play by the rules, introduce themselves to our juniors, and give another pitch to seniors they might already be talking to. If they do that, then maybe they'll be less likely to do something stupid."

Dye and Johnson, based in Atlanta, had just three Seminoles on their dance card, but they were three of the school's top prospects for the 2005 draft: defensive tackle Travis Johnson, along with Alex Barron and Willis, both offensive tackles.

It had been a rough day for the agents. The meeting with Johnson was not promising. A California native, Johnson told Dye and Bill Johnson he thought highly of Gary Wichard, who was based in Pacific Palisades (and, according to *Jerry Maguire* director Cameron Crowe, a main inspiration for the movie).

Barron, considered a lock for the first round, appeared on the verge of falling asleep. "Two years of work down the drain," Johnson said afterward. "He's clearly going in another direction."

Dye, Johnson, and Willis were hardly strangers. Johnson had met Willis during the player's sophomore year, and they sat down formally for the first time at the agent day at the end of the 2003 season, when Willis thought of leaving school early for the NFL.

It helped that Dye represented Montrae Holland and Brett Williams, two former FSU offensive linemen drafted in the fourth round of the 2003 draft by New Orleans and Kansas City respectively. It also helped that Kimberly Willis was unlike any player girlfriend or spouse the agents had encountered.

Kimberly Willis, who is five and a half years older and nearly a foot shorter than her husband, was completing work at Florida State on a doctorate in sport management. Before the wedding, she taught a sports law class that often included Seminole football players, who were forever complaining to Ray about his fiancee's imposed workload.

To keep Ray focused on football Kimberly assumed the task of vetting agents. She logged calls, asked pointed questions, created spreadsheets, investigated agents through the NFL Players Association, and built thick files. She reminded some agents a little of Marcee Tidwell, the outspoken player wife in *Jerry Maguire* who wasn't afraid to challenge Tom Cruise's character to do more for her husband:

> We majored in marketing, Jerry, and when you put him in a Waterbed Warehouse commercial, excuse me, you are making him common. He is pure gold and you're giving him "Waterbed Warehouse" when he deserves the big four: shoe, car, clothing line, soft drink. The four jewels of the celebrity endorsement dollar.

Kimberly took her agent research a step further by interviewing several at length for various doctoral projects and developed a quick rapport with Johnson, a former marketing executive for the NBA's Orlando Magic, who had joined Dye's firm in 1998.

Johnson had become so friendly with Ray and Kimberly that he was invited to their wedding in June of 2004. When the Willis party entered the room for agent day, it seemed like a reunion between friends. Besides Ray and Kimberly, there was Ray's aunt Vanessa, the sister of his late mother; and her husband Chris. Two of his mother's cousins rounded out the group.

Ray Willis walked in on crutches, having sprained an ankle in a loss to archrival Florida the night before. Kimberly helped him squeeze into a desk. The rest of the Willis party took their seats.

Dye cringed. "Are you okay? I was listening to the game driving in, and almost drove off the road when I heard what happened. To me, it was kind of a microcosm of the whole season, very frustrating."

Everyone in the room nodded. Willis had endured a series of ankle and shoulder injuries at Florida State. The Seminoles, accustomed to ten-win seasons and New Year's Day bowl games, finished a disappointing 8-3, losing at home to Florida for the first time since 1986.

"Yeah," Ray sighed. The mood of the room grew somber.

"So," Dye said, smiling. "You ready to take it to the next level, start getting paid for it? I know they've been paying you well here at Florida State, but not *that* well."

Everyone laughed.

Dye took a deep breath and began his presentation.

It's difficult to overestimate the impact of college football. To much of the nation, schools such as Auburn, Notre Dame, Clemson, and Miami are thought of first as football teams rather than institutions of higher learning.

Florida State University does little to discourage such thinking. Doak Campbell Stadium, which seats 82,300 chanting, tomahawk-chopping fans, is attached to a series of offices and classrooms, and the combined structure is the largest brick building in the southeast. From the outside the complex looks like a giant castle, even a small college—contrary to popular belief, it does not hold the entire FSU campus—or perhaps, more appropriately, the world's largest house of worship.

The edifice is not far from the Florida governor's mansion, and some would argue that neither Jeb Bush nor his predecessors have wielded as much influence in Tallahassee as Bobby Bowden, Florida State's head football coach since 1976.

During the 2004 season, Florida State unveiled a nine-foot bronze statue of Bowden, the winningest coach in NCAA Division 1-A history. The statue stands at the entrance of the four-story Moore Athletic Center, a recent $32 million addition that houses the football offices, meeting rooms, and locker facilities, along with upscale amenities such as a grand atrium, hall of fame, trophy room, and theater, that have become must-haves in the college football arms race.

To top off the shrine to FSU football, school officials unveiled a thirty-by-twenty-foot stained-glass window prior to the Florida game, the day before the agent gathering. The image depicts Bowden gazing at the playing surface, recently renamed Bobby Bowden Field, and is one of the five largest stained-glass windows in America.

"I only know one other guy on stained glass," joked Kevin Steele, FSU's linebackers coach. "I see him every Sunday morning."

For Brian Battle, working in St. Bobby's Cathedral is a mixed blessing, one that crystallized for the Florida State compliance director prior to the 2004 season when he interviewed for a similar position at the University of Virginia.

On the surface, the job of a compliance director is to make sure the school is adhering to the volumes of NCAA regulations governing what athletes, coaches, administrators, and boosters can and cannot do.

That's a hectic, full-time position for anyone, and, not surprisingly, the gig usually is filled by a single, thirty-something like Battle, with a masters degree in sports administration.

The role of compliance director at many schools also has come to include everything that the vast football staffs would rather not handle. A player needs disability insurance to protect against a career-ending injury? Go see the compliance director. An underclassman wants a rating from the NFL advisory committee to determine his potential draft position and whether he should go pro? Go see the compliance director. Need someone to deal with agents? Get the compliance director on it.

Since arriving at FSU in 1996, Battle had fulfilled all of those roles, along with giving up his Tuesday nights in the fall to teach a class called "A Career in Professional Sports." Now held in the theater in the new Moore Complex, it's popular with athletes, who learn about such things as NCAA guidelines, sports agents, and the media.

For the princely adjunct professor stipend of two thousand dollars a semester, Battle helps ensure that the school avoids a repeat of the free shoes episode, for which the program received a year of probation. To illustrate his lessons, Battle focuses on actual college misbehavior. He'll show episodes of ESPN's *Outside the Lines* and distribute copies of landmark investigations in *Sports Illustrated*, including the report that detailed the free shoes incident.

"This is not a Jim Harrick Jr. course," Battle says, in reference to the former University of Georgia assistant basketball coach whose "Principles and Strategies of Basketball" class reportedly included such exam questions as *How many points is a three-point field goal worth*? "I've flunked some prominent athletes."

Battle spends an entire class on the rules of agent recruiting. That's probably more time than most students need, though with nearly the entire football team taking the class at some point, he knows it's not time wasted.

Battle explains how it's permissible for players and their parents to talk to agents, so long as nothing of value is accepted, not even a soda. He also explains the rules of engagement. Under Florida law, an agent may not make the initial contact with a player or parent. If a player or parent contacts him, all is fine. But if the agent calls first, he's breaking Florida law. The rule applies to every contact.

It's a rule, of course, that's flagrantly violated. Battle understands this, sees agents hovering around after games outside the players' exit, and realizes that he's powerless to enforce it. Almost every year, Seminoles players—along with those from the University of Miami and the University of Florida—sign with prominent agents not licensed in Florida. Still, Battle stresses to players that the agents who play by the rules probably are the most ethical.

Battle requires agents to register with him. All contact with players, whether via mail or by phone, is supposed to go through him, another regulation that's impossible to enforce. He and his boss, associate athletics director Bob Minnix, schedule agent day each fall, inviting dozens of agents to meet one-on-one with players. FSU was among the first to schedule such an event, and the nine-year-old program has been adopted by many schools around the country.

The irony of agent day is that it's held in late November. By then most players have been talking with agents for months and probably have narrowed the search to three or four representatives. Battle acknowledges this and believes agent day is more valuable for players who will be searching for agents the following fall. Unlike schools such as Miami, which hold a similar late-season event and restricts it to seniors, Battle lets juniors attend.

As for the draftees-to-be, "I tell guys if they haven't narrowed their search to three agents by November, then they must not be serious about going pro," Battle says. "If you want to be ready to train for the combine in January, you have to have these things in order."

A month before agent day, Battle sends invites to agents registered with FSU. He asks them for a list of players they'd like to interview and matches that up with agent lists he receives from the players.

"The whole process is kind of funny," says Ken Harris, a Tampa-based agent. "You know you'd better list everyone, in case there's some guy you thought you had no chance with who really wants to meet you. But usually you show up just to cover your butt. If you're feeling pretty good that you're going to land a certain guy, you know you'd better show up, since everyone else is going to be there."

Because Battle has been assigned or assumed so many ancillary roles, he gets to know Florida State football players well. By dealing with agents, submitting requests to the NFL advisory committee on behalf of underclassmen, and helping players apply for disability insurance—which is granted in part by a player's pro potential—he would have a good feel for where Seminole players stand in NFL eyes, even if he did not talk frequently to team officials.

People like Tim Ruskell, the Atlanta Falcons assistant general manager who got to know Battle during his time with the Tampa Bay Buccaneers, turn to Battle for character insight on players.

So, when Battle traveled to Charlottesville, Virginia, prior to the 2004 football season, he felt qualified to become the next director of compliance for the University of Virginia. Though head coach Al Groh was starting to produce more NFL talent, the school never would attract the beehive of agents that Florida State saw on an annual basis.

After interviewing with Groh, Battle realized the gig would be easier on other fronts. Groh, ever the micromanager, made it apparent that he and not the compliance director would organize such matters as agent day. Though Virginia players could petition the NFL advisory committee for an underclassman draft rating, Groh preferred to rely on his own vast network of contacts in the league. As for teaching "A Career in Professional Sports," Battle need not worry about *that* appearing in the course catalog at Thomas Jefferson's university.

Battle could not have felt more qualified; but he lost the job to an applicant from Vanderbilt, the prestigious academic school in Nashville, Tennessee, known for a sterling compliance record and for a football team that perennially finished at the bottom of the Southeastern Conference. Agents and NFL scouts spent relatively little time in Nashville.

"We're always going to struggle with that big football school image," Battle says. "I'm not saying it's undeserved, of course it is. But we've implemented a lot of things on the compliance front that a lot of schools might do well to emulate."

So Battle resumed his hectic schedule at Florida State. Though the Seminoles struggled during the 2004 season, at least by their lofty standards, they again fielded a roster of talent that made pro scouts and agents salivate.

Battle rose early on Sunday, November 21, 2004, the morning following Florida State's loss to Florida, to oversee agent day. Fifteen agents were to meet one-on-one with seventeen players. Battle produced a schedule based on which agents players wanted to meet with and vice versa, staggering thirty-minute meetings over a dozen rooms between noon and 5:00 P.M.

Alex Barron, the prized offensive tackle, surprised the agents by asking to speak with eight of them. Harris, the Tampa-based agent with twelve NFL clients, figured he scored a meeting by virtue of being invited by Battle to deliver an informational session to players' parents a month earlier.

Unlike most players, who brought an entourage of family members,

Barron met with agents alone. Like his meeting with Dye and Johnson, Barron said little during his chat with Harris and seemed on the verge of falling asleep. "A guy like Alex should have narrowed the field by this point," Harris said afterward. "My guess is he already has, but for whatever reason just wants to cover all of his bases."

Defensive tackle Travis Johnson was the next most coveted prospect, having enjoyed a breakout season in his first as a starter. Johnson's stock was soaring, despite character issues that included being arrested in April of 2003 and charged with felony sexual assault. A jury acquitted him after it was revealed that he had previous consensual relations with the woman.

Johnson's case illustrated how quickly a player's draft status can change. His pre-season scouting grades of 1.85 by BLESTO and 4.4 by National Football Scouting were those of a fringe prospect. Hundreds of players received higher grades. Now he was projected to go in the first round.

Johnson wasn't the biggest Florida State character risk for the 2005 draft, though he was the only one still enrolled. Adrian McPherson had started at quarterback for much of the 2002 season as a true sophomore before being arrested in late November of that year on charges of stealing a blank check and receiving nearly three thousand five hundred dollars after it was cashed. He was kicked off the team and three months later was charged with gambling on pro and college games. The six-three McPherson pleaded no contest to misdemeanor theft and gambling charges and spent the 2004 season playing for the Indiana Firebirds of the Arena Football League, where he was named the league's rookie of the year.

After Barron and Johnson, cornerback Bryant McFadden and wide receiver Craphonso Thorpe were the next most promising, at least at this stage, along with Ray Willis.

Though Pat Dye Jr. and Bill Johnson were the front-runners to represent her husband, Kimberly Willis was keeping their options open. Dye and Johnson were the first of four agencies on their schedule. Rich Moran, a former Green Bay Packers offensive lineman, would come next, followed by Roosevelt Barnes, who along with his partner Eugene Parker represented a long line of Seminoles, including Deion Sanders, Corey Simon, Peter Boulware, and Greg Jones. Phil Williams, a former Florida State wide receiver whose clients included ex-Seminole quarterback Brad Johnson, got the last meeting.

Battle and three colleagues played traffic cops, directing players to rooms and keeping warring agents away from one another. The most unpopular man on hand was Darrell Wills, who Battle allowed to meet with players, despite being decertified by the NFL Players Association seven months earlier.

Wills, who had reinvented himself as a player "manager," partnered with Matthew Couloute, who was a certified player agent, and brought him along with Thom Park, a former college football coach turned sports consultant and financial advisor. Wills scored three meetings, with McFadden, wide receiver Chauncey Stovall, and tight end Paul Irons.

Wills, wearing a gray suit and bow tie, kicked off his schedule by speaking to Stovall and his family. He revisited some familiar themes from a talk he gave to Battle's class in September.

"Most of the things you've heard about the agent business are bad," Wills told the Stovall contingent. "I'm not going to tell you it's any different. Most of these guys are crooks. You have twenty-one- and twenty-two-year-old kids. How do they know the difference? I'm about education. You always hear that saying, that what you don't know won't hurt you. That's completely false. What you don't know can and will hurt you. If you don't handle your business, the business will handle you.

"Fifty percent of players have no money after five years. What about the other half? They've lost a lot of it. I started a corporation to stop that. Seventy percent of NFL players are African American and 50 percent have no money after five years. So it stands to figure that a significant percentage of African-American players have no money after five years. It's a sad story. If you're going to take those violent hits for five years and have no money to show for it, you're an idiot."

Battle reluctantly granted Wills an audience with players. After all, he had twice invited the former FSU track captain to speak, to the class in September and to a gathering of players and parents in early October. From what Battle figured, the decertified Wills was playing within the rules as long as he had a certified agent with him.

Wills was just one of Battle's concerns. Early in the day, a young agent crashed the session, figuring he could just grab some players.

"This isn't a job fair," Battle told the man, escorting him out.

"How am I supposed to break into this business?" the agent asked.

"You're asking the wrong guy."

Battle shook his head as he stood in the atrium and watched the elevator and the would-be agent descend. Light reflected off the stained-glass Bowden window.

"Look, we're Florida State," Battle said. "You don't want players going with people who haven't been in the business that long. We have top-caliber guys and they should have top level representation. You don't want them going with people who haven't been in the business long. In our defense, we always try to bring some new people into the fold. Each year we invite a few up-and-comers. The fact is that there were no players that wanted to speak to the guy.

"I always tell players that the better your representation, the more likely you're going to get into a NFL camp if you're a fringe player. Of course, none of these guys think they're fringe players. They're all going to be NFL stars. But if you're in an NFL camp and get cut, at least that opens the door for NFL Europe, the Arena league, Canada. Dreams will be shattered in the next few months. Hopefully, the athletes have made the right choice to get someone to help them make it. You see some of these guys back around school a year or two later, not knowing what they're going to do. It's sad."

Back in Room 2302, Pat Dye Jr. addressed Kimberly and Ray Willis and his family. At this point, the player and his wife knew everything they needed to know about Dye and Bill Johnson, but they wanted to see what Aunt Vanessa thought.

"Let me give you an overview of who we are and what we're about. I'm Pat Dye, and I know you know a little about us. Bill and I grew up together in Greenville, North Carolina. I grew up in a football family. My father coached at Alabama under Bear Bryant and then was a head coach at East Carolina and finished at Auburn his last twelve years. So I've been around football literally all my life. I went to law school and decided I wanted to meld this legal training with my football heritage and be a sports attorney. My father wasn't too pleased with that, as you could imagine.

"That was seventeen years ago, and I've had the good fortune of negotiating hundreds of NFL contracts for several hundred-million dollars in total value. Bill and I have done a half billion dollars in the last five years alone. I've represented fifteen first-round draft picks in the last decade, twelve second-rounders. I've negotiated for players picked as high as the third pick in the draft, so nothing is going to come up that we can't handle, as far as a contract-negotiation standpoint. We have done landmark rookie and veteran contracts.

"As a coach's son, I have what I think are three distinct advantages. I know the game, can talk intelligently to Ray about it, articulate his strengths, address his weaknesses with teams intelligently, and with credibility, talk to the general managers, scouts, and coaches at any level. That gives us added credibility when we lead clients through the draft and negotiate contracts. I've been around major Division 1 programs all my life and I've seen the price someone like Ray has had to pay to get to this point. It gives me an even stronger sense of obligation to see him capitalize on this. Thirdly, and perhaps my most important advantage, is that because of being a coach's son and having this football heritage, imagine the network of contacts and relationships that I have. There are people that have known me since I was a little kid roaming the sidelines with my father.

"Al Davis came up to me at the Senior Bowl a couple years ago and said, 'Did you know I scouted your father at this game in 1960?' Those relationships help when we sit down at the bargaining table; we're seen as football people first and agents second, and that adds to our credibility. They don't care for agents; they think they're out there getting over on players, being a bad influence. But we have great relationships with people around the league. We're not looking to be golf buddies with them; they know we'll come strong to the table, be well prepared, and we'll show you that in our contract presentation. We're going to max out every opportunity for you.

"I started this firm eleven years ago. We have seven people, including myself, and we have fifty years of combined experience representing professional athletes. We have two attorneys on board. Bill is vice president and is independently qualified to represent Ray himself. You're getting two for one, and we work very closely together. We have a full-time marketing guy we hired away from IMG, which is the world's largest sports marketing company. All he does is bang that phone twenty-four/seven trying to get our guys free stuff. Free cell phones, free suits, free cars, Nike shoe contracts, paid personal appearances, trading card deals—all of those things. I'm not going to sit here and lie to you. The opportunities are going to be a little more limited for Ray because he's not scoring touchdowns. He's not throwing TD passes, and those kind of things, but there will be opportunities for him out there and we'll see to it that he'll maximize those, keeping in mind that he doesn't want to do too much, because we don't want to distract him from making his main income through football.

"We currently represent thirty-seven players on active NFL rosters. We've had eight different guys in the Pro Bowl in the last three years. That speaks to two things: the selectivity that we use when we recruit and also the caliber of our clients. With thirty-seven clients, that makes us the tenth or eleventh biggest firm in the country. We're not a small firm, but not too big. We're right where we want to be. We have enough leverage with our client base around the league that GMs treat us with respect. Yet we're not spread too thin with sixty or eighty clients.

"That's important, because we're in the personal service biz. We're accessible to our clients twenty-four/seven and the only way we can do that—because I have twenty-four hours in my day just like you do and Bill does—is we're very selective. A third of our base is first-round draft picks, and Ray is one of only two offensive tackles in the country that we're recruiting. The only other one is his teammate [Alex Barron], so we're not going to be out there hawking five or six different offensive tackles in this year's draft. When you get to that point, you're pushing too many guys. Two or maybe three, fine, but any more than that, you're stretching your credibility.

"Like I said, we're all about personal service. We have two young ladies in our office that handle the day-to-day services of our clients. Rental cars, limousines, dinner reservations. We're planning [Falcons linebacker] Keith Brooking's wedding right now. Our girls are out there looking for caterers, florists, photographers, churches, places to have the reception. We do it all from soup-to-nuts, and we'd do it for [Falcons guard] Steve Herndon, who you've never heard of and who never got drafted. We're a full-service operation, and if there's something we can't handle, we'll find someone who can. Bill and I have sat in with a dozen or more of our clients when they chose their engagement rings, making sure they didn't get taken advantage of by the diamond people. There are a lot of crooks in that business, too."

Kimberly Willis and the other women in the room nodded.

"We help with buying cars, buying homes—they see Ray coming and they'll try to cave his head in. Here comes the professional athlete with all this money in his pocket. They'll add all the bells and whistles, but then Bill comes in and works the deal and Ray walks out smiling. The car dealer isn't that happy about it, but that's what we're here for.

"We have a full range of predraft services. That involves going to scouts and getting a competitive, definitive assessment of his strengths, weaknesses, and providing it to Ray and his personal trainer, and doing everything we can to polish him up before he has a chance to go to an all-star game or go to the combine, or working out for scouts here for his pro day. We will map out a calendar of everything he's going to be doing, everything we'll be doing on his behalf leading up to the draft. That will also include us being there at different events: all-star games, pro day, and combine, not only for moral support, but to solicit feedback and continue lobbying and promoting him as the total package to scouts and GMs."

Most players leave school after New Year's to train for the NFL combine, the February event where they're stripped and tested in front of NFL personnel. The combine training period is geared to improve speed and strength quickly, and add or subtract weight if needed.

Agents must pick up the tab, which can be up to twenty-five thousand dollars, and over the last decade combine training has become a major perk NFL hopefuls expect.

"Part of the predraft process is identifying a good training solution for him," Dye says. "I'm sure we'll talk more about that later, but the thing I want to say about training is that we're not married to any one trainer. We'll send him wherever he wants to go. If he wants to go to Tom Shaw or Mackie Shilstone in New Orleans, Chip Smith or Velocity, they've trained our guys before. There's Cris Carter in Boca, [Mark] Verstegen in Phoenix. We get calls from all these people because they want to work with our clients. If Ray wants to visit these facilities, test drive the car if you will, we'll facilitate that. Once he plugs into that training solution, we pay for all the training fees, lodging, meals; he won't be coming out-of-pocket for anything associated with training. As much money as we invest in this process, we want to make sure he's with somebody that's outstanding and has a great track record. We don't want to waste our money."

Dye continued. "Our fees for all of these services is 3 percent of the contract. We don't charge for any expenses associated with training. We're going to go to these various events, fly around to see you play, take you to dinner—that's on us. That way, there are no hidden charges at the end of the year. You'll hear from guys who will say, 'Man, my agent threw me a slamming draft party.' Then at the end of the year he gets a bill for the chicken wings, beer, all that stuff. Not with us."

By now Dye was focused on Willis's relatives.

"We're all too conscious of the fact that he's not going to be doing this when he's my age. He'll be long out of the game. I'm forty-two. I can be doing this for the next twenty years or longer if I want to. Ray's got a limited window of opportunity to make it big, and we confess to being greedy on behalf of our clients. You know that movie *The Grinch Who Stole Christmas*, where the Grinch reaches down to get that last crumb away from Cindy Lou Hoo? We try to do that, recognizing that we're going to have to do business with that team again some day. There's the low end of reasonable and the high end of reasonable, and we like to be in the high end, plus a little bit. We're never going to burn bridges or take a scorched-earth approach to negotiations, but we are going to be a little aggressive, because at the end of the day he's judged by how many sacks he's given up. We're judged by how much money we get for a third-round pick, based on what the guys got above and below him, and we're very competitive like that. We're not out there buying and paying clients, and doing some of the things that our competition does to get clients. The only way you're going to get them is by your own clients bragging on you and showing good, solid results every time you negotiate a contract."

Dye leaned in toward Willis's relatives. "We're only going to have one or two offensive tackles in this year's draft. We might have one, we might get skunked, you never know. But he's very, very important to us."

Of all the rivalries in sports, few are as unlikely as the Atlanta Falcons and Tampa Bay Buccaneers. There's no track record of hard-fought games—neither team has a lengthy competitive history period—and there's no bad blood between players.

But when the Falcons arrived at Tampa's Raymond James Stadium on the morning of Sunday, December 5, 2004, they lit the fire of a growing rivalry fueled by two men who would not be wearing helmets that afternoon.

SOUTHERN FEUD, read the front of the *Tampa Tribune* sports section. MCKAY–GRUDEN SPLIT HAS TURNED DIVISION RIVALS INTO NFL'S HATFIELDS AND MCCOYS.

The headline topped a half-page cartoon featuring Falcons general manager Rich McKay and Bucs head coach Jon Gruden dressed as hillbillies and scowling at each other from the front porch of an old shack, divided down the middle.

Tribune sports columnist Martin Fennelly, channeling the prevailing pro-McKay, anti-Gruden sentiment of Buccaneer fans, wrote a tongue-in-cheek column projecting the futures of the two men. While Gruden struggled through a series of progressively lower-profile coaching jobs, McKay ascended to NFL commissioner, Florida governor, and U.S. president before becoming Pope Rich I.

Not even two years had passed since McKay, as Buccaneers GM, and Gruden stood on a podium in San Diego and celebrated a Super Bowl championship together after the Buccaneers routed the Oakland Raiders in Super Bowl XXXVII.

It didn't take long for the winning glow to fade. Gruden and McKay began feuding over personnel decisions, with Gruden favoring veteran free agents and McKay wanting to stay the course by building through the draft.

With the Bucs struggling late in the 2003 season, McKay resigned his longtime post on December 11. Four days later, he accepted a new job as president and general manager of the Falcons, whose next game was back in Tampa against the Buccaneers.

Television cameras zoomed in on McKay's suite frequently during the contest, usually catching him smiling. The Falcons won, 30–28, putting an end to the Buccaneers faint playoff chances.

That might have been the end of the rivalry, if not for the Falcons surprising 9-2 start and the Buccaneers 4-7 record in 2004. Gruden was diplomatic whenever McKay's departure was raised, as it frequently was leading up to the latest Falcons game, saying it would forever be a "sensitive issue." Still, Gruden bristled under the line of questioning, especially when an Atlanta reporter showed up at One Buc Place earlier in the year. To Gruden, it implied that McKay was responsible for the success of the Buccaneers and that the team might still be winning if he were still in Tampa. After all, the sports radio theorists argued, McKay quickly turned the hapless Falcons around.

Actually, the Falcons turnaround was more due to the return of quarterback Michael Vick, who missed much of 2003 with a broken leg. McKay, like Gruden, dodged the rivalry issue.

Others were happy to stoke the fire. When the Falcons defeated the Buccaneers in Atlanta three weeks earlier, head coach Jim Mora presented game balls to McKay, assistant general manager Tim Ruskell, and Reggie Roberts, the public relations director—all former Bucs employees.

Gruden made it a point not to let reporters bait him on the McKay issue, even when Gruden had a strong argument, like when someone asked him why the Bucs had the oldest roster in the NFC.

"I'm not criticizing anybody," Gruden told reporters early in the season. "But in the last ten or twelve drafts how many offensive players are [still] in the media guide? So you've got to fill the roster. If you look at the free agent list, the guys who make it to free agency are not twenty-six years old and they aren't cheap."

Bruce Allen, McKay's replacement as general manager, was careful not to say anything negative about his popular predecessor. But like Gruden he made it clear that the Bucs were hamstrung by an aging roster and the salary cap issues they inherited.

The Buccaneers traded two first-round picks in 2000 to acquire wide receiver Keyshawn Johnson from the New York Jets and dealt a pair of firsts and two second-round selections to Oakland as compensation for Gruden in 2002. Signing free agents such as quarterback Brad Johnson and defensive end Simeon Rice didn't help the cap situation.

Still, McKay didn't dispute Gruden's charge. In fact, it validated the argument he made when he became general manager of the Buccaneers a decade earlier. A team that's in constant flux, changing offensive and defensive coordinators frequently, will squander draft picks. A player that's drafted for one scheme likely will be a poor fit in another. The Buccaneers, from 1999–2001, had three different offensive coordinators and then brought in Gruden, an offensive-minded coach.

"When you have three coordinators in three years, then that's our fault," McKay said. "You let [Tampa Bay defensive coordinator] Monte Kiffin and his staff leave, bring in a new set of defensive coordinators, and I guarantee you that within three years you'll have nothing left. Nothing. Now do it every year for three years in a row. Good luck. Tell me what you have left.

"The thing I learned in Tampa that I say to owners all the time when they ask about how to have success in the league is that continuity matters. It's hard to adhere to sometimes, because you say, 'I could be better.' Yeah, you could be. But at what cost? You might get a little short-term gain, but you may have a long-term failure. We took a shot with Keyshawn with two ones. I don't regret the shot, because we felt like we had to force the issue. We were getting older and we had to hurry up and win, and then we continued to exchange schemes and accordingly had players falling out everywhere."

Russ Hochstein was part of the fallout. A fifth-round pick by Tampa Bay out of Nebraska in 2001, the guard spent his rookie season on the practice squad and then was cut early in Gruden's tenure. New England signed him, and the following season Hochstein started at left guard during the Patriots' win over Carolina in Super Bowl XXXVIII.

"He wasn't a pretty looking lineman," McKay says. "We threw him out immediately because we got a new staff in, and you know what? It was the right decision at the time. But that's what happens in that situation."

As for Tampa Bay's salary cap quandary, McKay viewed it as the cost of a Super Bowl championship. By acquiring veteran players such as Rice, Keyshawn Johnson, and Brad Johnson, the Bucs mortgaged part of the future.

"We never had a cap issue until we jumped into free agency, because we could feel our run coming to an end," McKay said. "You look back and say, 'Look at the cap problems.' It wasn't hard to see. Once we jumped into free agency it was going to happen, because those contracts are so much higher than the rookies. That's what you're going to get."

As for Kiffin, he remained as the Bucs defensive coordinator, though defensive pillars Warren Sapp and John Lynch had followed McKay out the door. Still, there was a strong nucleus, led by Rice, linebacker Derrick Brooks, and cornerback Ronde Barber.

The defense stifled the Falcons in Tampa, sacking Vick five times as the Bucs routed the visitors 27–0, keeping McKay and the Falcons from clinching a playoff berth.

Gruden had cut McKay's lead to 2-1.

The Renaissance Hotel in Orlando was the site of the 2004 Butkus Award, presented to the top linebacker in the nation. Like many Disney-area resorts, the Renaissance projects a faux tropical feel, with a ten-story atrium, palm trees, and a waterfall cascading into a goldfish pond. The Florida humidity gives it the feel of an upscale greenhouse.

Seven glass elevators, wrapped in red ribbon for the holidays, carry guests to and from their rooms. Early in the evening on Friday, December 10, 2004, an elevator descended to the lobby and out popped Al Groh, the University of Virginia's head football coach, clad in a black tuxedo and accompanied by Virginia linebacker Ahmad Brooks and his parents, Perry and Vergie Brooks.

Ahmad was a finalist for the Butkus Award, along with Derrick Johnson of Texas and Matt Grootegoed of Southern Cal. Groh and the Brooks family proceeded to a silent auction table laid out in front of the ballroom. There was plenty of Dick Butkus–signed memorabilia, certificates for various Orlando golf and lodging packages, items autographed by Arnold Palmer and Sandy Koufax, and a framed *Caddyshack* movie poster signed by Rodney Dangerfield, who had died two months earlier.

Groh surveyed the auction, focused as always on football. "I think the kid from Texas is going to win it," he said. "Then Ahmad will come back next year and win it."

Groh did not toss praise around lightly, but Brooks was an exception. The former NFL linebackers coach, who worked with Lawrence Taylor, already put Brooks in a special category. "I coached ten Pro Bowl linebackers," Groh said. "There's only one who had better skills."

Two weeks had passed since Virginia's regular season ended with a loss to Virginia Tech. Agents were circling around four of Groh's underclassmen: Brooks, linebacker Darryl Blackstock, tight end Heath Miller, and offensive tackle D'Brickashaw Ferguson.

Groh was asked how many of his underclassmen he thought would leave. "Why is it nobody asks a kid if he's staying? It's always, 'Are you going?' I think all of them will be back. Why wouldn't they? Look at the Mannings [quarterbacks Peyton and Eli]. They stayed four years. Why? Because they loved the college experience. The players will realize they're better off coming back."

That seemed like wishful thinking, especially with all four players getting a full-court press from agents. With so many departing seniors, including defensive end Chris Canty, guard Elton Brown, and running back Alvin Pearman, Groh could ill afford to lose underclassmen, especially after a disappointing 8-3 season. Ranked sixth in the nation in mid-October, with a 5-0 record, the Cavaliers were humiliated 36–3 at Florida State and lost two of their last three, falling to Miami and Virginia Tech.

Groh's job was secure, and his assistants were in the process of signing one of the nation's better recruiting classes. But if Groh hoped to keep the Cavaliers at the level where he wanted, contending for a national championship, he needed all of his underclassmen back.

Groh had reason to feel confident they'd all return, perhaps more reason than he had all year. Miller, who a day earlier had won the Mackey Award as the nation's best tight end, was suffering from a nagging abdominal injury. Though it had long been a foregone conclusion that the redshirt junior would leave, the condition could keep him from participating in the NFL combine and predraft workouts. Even for a talented, accomplished player, that could be enough to wait a year, though Groh knew it was a long shot.

Brooks, Groh knew, was coming back. Though he was eligible for the draft by virtue of spending a season in prep school, Brooks had played just two years of college ball. Money was not an issue, not with a father who had enjoyed a lengthy NFL career.

As for Ferguson, Groh was willing to bet the value of everything on the silent auction table he'd be back. Ferguson was the rare college athlete who had both NFL potential and aspirations of attending law school. An older brother had graduated from the University of Virginia. Ferguson was one of the more cerebral members of the Cavaliers, delivering quotes to the local media like, "I don't need anything deviating— or, excuse me—diverting my attention," as he told the *Roanoke Times and World News*.

The six-five Ferguson had finished his true freshman season two years earlier weighing just 260. But he put on thirty-five pounds and by the end of the 2004 season had become a favorite of NFL personnel people like the Redskins' Vinny Cerrato, who spoke frequently with ESPN draft guru Mel Kiper Jr. By November, Kiper was projecting Ferguson as a top-fifteen pick in the 2005 draft if he came out. *Pro Football Weekly* touted him as one of the best tackle prospects to come along in years.

Blackstock was the wild card. He was no scholar, unlike Ferguson. Unlike Miller, he still was a raw talent that could benefit from another year of college football.

There was another factor. Blackstock was the father of a son, Savion, born August 13, 2003. Blackstock shared custody with the mother, a fellow student, but they no longer were together. The linebacker estimated he had run up twenty thousand dollars in loans supporting the mother and child, but did so willingly. He wore his fatherhood proudly, with a tattoo of SAVION on his right wrist and STRONG DEDICATED DAD on his left forearm.

Groh had taken on Blackstock as a pet project from the moment the linebacker arrived in Charlottesville in 2002, following a year at prep school, where he earned a high school diploma. During the season, they would meet on Sundays at the football office to break down the previous day's game. They'd watch film, with Groh providing a candid assessment. Sometimes they'd line up head-to-head in Groh's office and walk through techniques.

Though Groh likened Brooks, who lost the Butkus Award to Johnson, to Lawrence Taylor, he assigned Taylor's number 56 to Blackstock, who had long since tired of the comparisons and asked to change numbers throughout the 2004 season.

Groh dismissed such talk, but finally relented before the Cavaliers appearance in the MPC Computers Bowl game against Fresno State on December 27 in Idaho, and had a number 1 jersey placed in Blackstock's locker.

The player remained noncommittal when asked by reporters if he would be going pro early. A week before Christmas, he said the bowl game would not be his last time wearing number 1, seemingly a telling indicator, since the NFL does not allow linebackers to don the number.

The statement was more in jest; Blackstock had not made a decision. But like the rest of the prospects for the 2005 NFL Draft, he knew that, if he did go pro, preparations for the draft would need to begin immediately.

Chapter Eight:

GOING PRO

F
red Gibson crouched down, pulled back his cue stick, and sunk the eight ball in a side pocket. It was early evening on December 30, 2004, and Gibson was shooting pool at Game Works, a video arcade and bar for adults in Tampa's popular Ybor City district.

Game Works was closed to the general public for a few hours while the football teams from the University of Georgia and University of Wisconsin had the run of the place as part of weeklong festivities for the Outback Bowl, which pitted the third-best teams from the Southeastern Conference and the Big Ten.

After devouring a dinner of pizza and barbecue—one of the few meals all week not catered by the Tampa-based Outback Steakhouse empire—most of the players fanned out to the state-of-the-art video games, all free for the evening.

Gibson and a few other teammates hung back at the pool tables near the buffet. Quarterback David Greene sat nearby playing a tabletop version of Ms. Pac Man, the type that was popular at Pizza Hut restaurants when the game came out in the early 1980s.

"I'm old school," said Greene, shattering the high score.

Gibson, known to teammates as "Freddy G.," racked up another game of eight ball. At six-four, he was a prototype NFL wide receiver, an attractive blend of size, speed, leaping ability, and good hands. On his good days, some scouts compared him to Minnesota Vikings star Randy Moss, minus the attitude and bad behavior. Unlike the perpetually scowling Moss, Gibson possessed a gregarious personality and a winning smile.

On his bad days, scouts compared him to, well, any number of athletic college stars who never cut it in the NFL. Gibson, some scouts believed, had a tendency to hear footsteps and lose concentration. Though he could leap and grab passes as well as any draft-eligible player—he also had played basketball at Georgia—he would drop easy balls caught against his body.

Gibson was an enigma in other areas. He could lock in on a game of eight ball or a pass through the air, but other times seemed unable to focus. Early in his college career a psychologist diagnosed him with attention deficit disorder, though Gibson never took medication for it. He struck everyone as a good kid, though he tended to be immature, or at least naïve. During a basketball game against Florida in 2002, he scored six points in a one-minute span, including four from the foul line. After the final free throw, he taunted Florida fans by clapping his arms in the school's "Gator chomp."

In May of 2003, he was suspended with eight teammates after they sold their 2002 SEC Championship rings. NCAA regulations prohibit athletes from reaping a financial benefit from their athletic fame. Gibson says he received four thousand dollars, but had to pay all of it back. The rings were recovered and he and his teammates were reinstated before the 2003 season.

Gibson was full of contradictions. Though he could come across as immature, he actually was one of the older members of the draft class of 2005, especially considering he never had a redshirt season. Born October 26, 1981, he grew up in a modest home next to the post office in Waycross, Georgia, the oldest of six children. Brenda Gibson gave birth to Fred when she was just thirteen and, according to Fred, never was around much. Dad was never in the picture either, and Fred was raised by his maternal grandmother, Delores Bethea, who had him repeat kindergarten.

"The first thing I want to do is buy her a big house with a lot of space for Christmas and Thanksgiving," Gibson says.

Still, it was not exactly a hardscrabble childhood. Early in high school, Gibson started competing in the privileged, quasiprofessional world of AAU basketball, playing on a Nike-sponsored team out of Atlanta that included Kwame Brown, the number-one pick in the 2001 NBA Draft. The team traveled the country and Gibson regularly went up against future pros, including Tyson Chandler, Eddy Curry, and Dajuan Wagner.

Gibson was the only member of his team not to accept a basketball scholarship, though he received offers from Auburn, Florida, and South Carolina. He verbally committed to Florida, but head coach Billy Donovan was reluctant to let him play football for the Gators. So Gibson headed to Georgia, where head coach Mark Richt had no problem with him playing both sports.

Gibson played just one full season of basketball at Georgia, averaging 4.9 points per game in a reserve role, before leaving the team early in his sophomore year to concentrate on football.

Throughout the 2004 season, Gibson was rated a strong prospect for the NFL Draft, as high as the first round by some analysts, though he was by no means a sure thing. At a lean but lanky 193 pounds, he was built more like a shooting guard than a wide receiver and still was a little raw on the football field. His biggest challenge in the months leading up to the NFL Draft would be to put on weight and shake the image of being a skinny basketball player.

Like most draft-eligible players, Gibson dealt with an endless barrage of phone calls and mailings from agents. Changing cell phone numbers helped. So did delegating much of the communication with agents to a close friend of the family.

The agents approached from all angles. Gibson says some agents—he won't say who—offered money and other incentives to get him to sign. A few sent attractive women his way.

"I don't care if agents were going to pay me a couple thousand dollars," Gibson said. "You can't buy me. If you were thinking of doing that, then I didn't trust you from the get-go. I didn't care if they had girls coming at me; they were wasting their time. I see pretty girls all the time."

At the end of 2003, Gibson's junior season, he briefly entertained the idea of going pro and met with Todd France, the young Atlanta-based agent. Pat Dye Jr. was in the running during Gibson's senior year, at least until Gibson found out that Dye and his partner, Bill Johnson, also were recruiting his fellow Georgia wide receiver Reggie Brown.

"That was a red flag right there," Gibson said. "I just stopped talking to them at that point. Do they think players don't talk to each other? How are they possibly going to sell the two of us?"

It's a common agent recruiting tactic to tell players that it's impossible for an agent to objectively represent two players for the draft at the same position, unless the difference in talent and pro potential is pronounced. The theory is that an agent, in marketing players to teams, will inevitably show favoritism. The problem with the argument is that teams are influenced little by a player's choice of representative, let alone the agent's efforts to talk up his client. Teams spend huge amounts of time and money scouting and will draft based on need and scheme. A team running a West Coast offense, for instance, will be more likely to go with a taller receiver than a shorter, faster one. Few players, even at the same position, are that similar.

France, as part of his presentation, shows a chart of prominent agents and how they represent multiple players at the same position.

"It's ridiculous to not go with someone because they have two players at the same position," France says. "I tell players not to do that, whether it be me or another guy. If you buy into that then, now you start thinking the agent affects your draft status. That's the biggest bullshit that's out there. We can affect them by the tools we give them to succeed—training before the combine, advice based on what we hear from contacts around the league—but I can't go convince Jerry Jones to pick one guy over another. He'd laugh at me."

Still, the *perception* of an agent having a conflict by representing two comparable players at the same position is enough to scare away most from even recruiting them.

"I can do it one of two ways," says SFX Sports agent Ben Dogra, who did not recruit Gibson. "I can recruit, say, the top five running backs and figure I'll get one and lose out on the other four, since the top five probably want bigger companies but don't want to go to the same agency. Or I can target the player I like best, spend more time with him, and not get caught up in the conflict game."

Two days before the Outback Bowl, Gibson had narrowed the agent field to two: Octagon and Joel Segal. Octagon, which represents athletes in many sports, has a football division based in Walnut Creek, California. Gibson had spent the most time with Demetro Stephens, a former Florida State linebacker based in Georgia, who worked for Octagon for two years recruiting athletes, becoming a certified agent just five months earlier. Stephens, as the junior agent of the firm, would defer to agent Doug Hendrickson to handle Gibson's contract negotiations.

Segal, based in Miami, is a one-man show best known for representing Atlanta Falcons quarterback Michael Vick. Gibson planned to make his decision shortly after the Outback Bowl, which kicked off the New

Year's Day marathon of bowls at 11:00 A.M. Two days later, he planned to be on a plane to Phoenix to begin training for the NFL combine.

Players cannot hire an agent—or commit to one orally—until after they've played their final college games. Some give less-than-subtle hints, though Gibson has played his cards close to the vest.

By revealing his choice of precombine training centers, the Phoenix-based Athletes' Performance, he tipped his hand, since Octagon is one of the seven agencies with a relationship with the training center. Segal, who previously sent clients there, no longer has such a deal.

"I think the two guys in the running probably have an idea," Gibson said between pool shots. "Bottom line is that an agent isn't going to get you drafted. *You* are going to get you drafted. An agent is there just to do your contract and make sure everything goes well. I don't believe all these agents calling me and telling me I'm going to go in this round. Agents are trying to sell you a dream and most kids get caught up into that."

Midway through the first half of the Outback Bowl, Greene rifled a pass to Gibson along the sidelines, hitting the wide receiver in the numbers. With Wisconsin defenders closing in, Gibson bobbled the ball. By the time he gained control, he had stumbled out of bounds.

In the press box of Tampa's Raymond James Stadium, two NFL scouts groaned.

"Fred, Fred, Fred," said one NFC scout.

The other scout, a twenty-year personnel veteran from an NFC team, shook his head as he picked at a complimentary "Bloomin' Onion."

"If he drops one ball early, he's done for the game,"

"I wouldn't even throw it to him," the first scout said. "He'll just break your heart."

The scouts scribbled their latest thoughts on Gibson. By now, they have spent five months watching film, practice, and live action of college players. Bowl games offer another glimpse of a player against top-quality competition.

For Fred Gibson, prototype wide receiver, world-class leaper, and all-around good guy, the scouting reports were not kind. *Pro Football Weekly*'s "Pro Prospects Preview," a widely read early-season scouting report, provided the consensus view:

Tall, lanky athletic playmaker with excellent size and natural athletic ability. . . . Has a thirty-eight-inch vertical jump. Lacks the polish of Randy Moss, but shows similar ability to stretch the field, sky for the ball, and make tough catches look easy. . . . Has been hampered by injuries and inconsistency throughout his career. Will show ability to adjust and make outstanding grabs but will also drop easy balls. . . . Not physical and does not like to be hit. Makes too many drops due to poor concentration and needs to take better care of the football. Will take some plays off. . . . Has first-round talent if he wants it badly enough, but has yet to show the toughness and consistency of a first-round receiver.

In the minds of many NFL scouts, Gibson was squandering his talent and needed to get his head in the game. He represented a typical dilemma for NFL executives, who spent much of their time trying to figure out if they were better off with a lesser athlete with mental toughness or a blue-chip talent who was inconsistent.

Greene represented the other side of the quandary. A calm competitor and leader who following Georgia's Outback victory would leave as the winningest quarterback in Division-1 history with forty-two victories, Greene lacked the bazooka arm and mobility of many NFL quarterbacks.

Pro Football Weekly:

Makes good decisions. Good poise. Very good touch but lacks the arm strength to drill it on a rope, and struggles with deep accuracy. . . . Very intelligent and knows how to manage a game. Top intangibles. . . . At the very least, he can be a solid backup at the next level, but demonstrates the accuracy, leadership skills and mental toughness to develop into a starter.

If only NFL teams could put Greene's head and a few extra pounds on Gibson's body, they'd have Jerry Rice. If they could install Gibson's natural athleticism in Greene's physique, they would end up with Steve Young.

Later in the first half at the Outback Bowl, Greene overthrew wide receiver Reggie Brown, another NFL draft hopeful. Again the two veteran scouts groaned. Their teams didn't especially need quarterback help, but every player gets graded.

"David Greene? No thank you," one said, jotting down notes.

"He's no Jason Campbell," said the other, a reference to the athletic quarterback of the Auburn Tigers whose stock had soared over the course of the season.

Greene completed nineteen of thirty-eight passes on the day for 264 yards and two touchdowns. Gibson finished with four catches for 42 yards, including a touchdown grab. The Bulldogs won, 24–21, and by any measuring stick the two NFL hopefuls had a strong showing.

Up in the press box the scout section was empty. They had departed before the end of the third quarter to beat the traffic and drive to Miami to scout Southern Cal and Oklahoma, slated to play for the national championship three nights later.

The numbers Greene and Gibson compiled meant little, and their performances only confirmed the extensive scouting reports. It was New Year's Day, the start of a whirlwind tour for Greene, Gibson, and the rest of the Class of 2005.

That group included Georgia defensive end David Pollack, who recorded three sacks and was named the game's MVP, and Wisconsin defensive tackle Anttaj Hawthorne, the leading target of agent Jack "Show Me" Scharf.

Greene, Gibson, and Hawthorne soon would compete in the Senior Bowl, train for the NFL combine, work out at the late-February event, and again at a pro day held back at their respective schools in March. No longer were they off limits to NFL scouts, who would use every opportunity to interview them and pick apart their brains.

Greene and Pollack—who, by virtue of his blue-chip draft status, would skip the Senior Bowl rather than risk injury—took victory laps around Raymond James Stadium, shaking hands and posing for pictures with Georgia fans. Their college careers were over, but NFL scouts had only begun their analysis.

Pat Dye Jr. walked through a tunnel in the bowels of Raymond James Stadium. The Outback Bowl had ended a half hour earlier, and now Dye carried a satchel that contained two standard player representation agreements.

Autograph hounds lurked around the Georgia team buses. Nobody was more anxious to get a couple of Bulldog signatures than Dye was. He staked out a position in a corridor, not far from the team bus, and spotted Rick and Kay Greene, David's parents. The couple approached and invited Dye to a reception back at a condo they had rented for the week. Dye smiled. After three years of recruiting the quarterback, he finally would get a signature.

Dye excused himself and retreated into the corridor. Reggie Brown, the Georgia wide receiver, approached in a pack of teammates. Fred Gibson was among the group, but Dye knew he had no shot with Gibson, who the following day would choose Octagon's Doug Hendrickson over Joel Segal.

Brown told Dye they needed to get together back in Atlanta. Dye nodded back. He knew, from years of experience, that it did not mean anything until he got a signature. But he felt good about Brown, who had been recruited mostly by Dye's colleague Bill Johnson, who was in Jacksonville getting ready to sign Florida State lineman Ray Willis after the Gator Bowl.

Dye's euphoria did not last long. Thomas Davis, the gifted Georgia safety, who many believed would bulk up and become a Ray Lewis–style linebacker in the pros, was walking toward the bus with his mother . . . and agent Todd France. Davis, a junior, had two weeks to decide whether to renounce his final year of eligibility, a decision Dye and everyone else believed was a foregone conclusion.

Dye had spoken several times with Davis, not often, but enough to think he was in the running, at least before learning New Year's Eve that Davis was leaning toward France. Now it was official.

Dye shrugged, exhaled, and went to find Kay and Rick Greene. He would drive back to the condo with them, picking his car up later. It would be a raucous celebration, with three dozen friends and relatives toasting the end of David Greene's college career and the beginning of his professional one. Dye enjoyed the moment, but could not help but wonder how many other prominent autographs France would obtain.

France had gone to bed long before the ball dropped in Times Square in order to make a 6:00 A.M. flight from Atlanta to Tampa New Year's Day. As Davis boarded the bus, France told Davis's mother she could drive behind him back to the downtown Hyatt, where the University of Georgia was staying.

By dinnertime, France had signed his first client with legitimate first-round potential. He hung around long enough to celebrate with Davis, but soon excused himself.

There were more first-rounders waiting.

Two days after the Outback Bowl, January, 3, 2005, Jack Scharf was sitting in an apartment in Phoenix. He had gotten an early start on getting his clients situated at Athletes' Performance, the training center that would prepare them for the NFL combine in February.

The group was mostly athletes whose teams either played in early bowl games or none at all. There was Jovan Haye, a defensive end from Vanderbilt, who had left school as a junior; Washington cornerback Derrick Johnson; and Jonathan Pollard, a linebacker from Oregon State. J.R. Russell, a wide receiver from Louisville, would be arriving in Phoenix shortly. Scharf's most intriguing client was Richie Incognito, an offensive lineman kicked off the Nebraska football team after a series of disciplinary problems on and off the field. Two other clients, Arizona State cornerback Chris McKenzie and defensive end Jimmy Verdon, had opted to stay nearby on campus to train. Ronald Bartell, a cornerback from Howard University, rounded out the Momentum Sports draft class of 2005, though Jeff Griffin, Scharf's colleague, represented him.

It was a solid recruiting class for Scharf, though it lacked a surefire, blue-chip prospect. With Russell and Haye on board, Scharf had landed two of the four players from his early September recruiting trip to the East Coast. He lost out on Justin Geisinger, the Vanderbilt guard, but was still in the hunt for Anttaj Hawthorne, the defensive tackle from Wisconsin.

Scharf had jumped through hoops to recruit Hawthorne since meeting with the player's uncle, Ed Hawthorne, and family attorney Ed Walsh in Connecticut in September. Scharf was not to contact Anttaj unless instructed. Scharf, dubbed "Show Me" by the Hawthorne camp, followed along, only contacting the player on November 15 with a happy birthday e-mail, as Uncle Ed advised.

That was two days after Scharf had agreed to one of the more bizarre requests of his career. Ed Hawthorne asked him to go see his nephew play. There was to be no contact with the player, however, not even a hello after the game. So Scharf traveled from San Antonio to East Lansing, Michigan, and endured forty-degree weather to sit in the Spartan Stadium stands and watch Wisconsin lose 49–14.

Scharf might have blown the trip off, if not the recruiting of the player, were it not for his relationship with Ed Hawthorne. The two talked three times a week, not just the usual recruiting stuff, but about football, other sports, and each other's lives. As an agent, Scharf knew better than to read too much into a budding business relationship; he was a salesman, after all, but he felt this was different.

Two weeks later, when Anttaj was home for a week over Thanksgiving, the Eds summoned Scharf to New Haven, Connecticut. Finally, Scharf got to meet Anttaj and felt confident, especially since Uncle Ed prepped him for the meeting, which would include Anttaj's high school coach. So Scharf memorized Anttaj's high school accolades—first-team Reebok/ESPN All-American, number-nine prospect in the nation by *Tom Lemming's Prep Football Report*—and learned everything he could about Hamden High.

Scharf spent two hours with Anttaj Hawthorne, his girlfriend, the Eds, and the high school coach over pizza and beer. By the time Scharf departed for San Antonio, he felt good about his chances, but knew Tom Condon, the IMG agent and New Haven native, also was in the picture.

Shortly before the Outback Bowl, Ed Hawthorne told Scharf he would gather with Walsh and Anttaj at Walsh's law office to make a decision a few days after the game.

It had been quite an education for Hawthorne and Walsh. When they met Scharf in September, they knew little about agents and the predraft process. But as they interviewed eleven agents in person between July and October, always in Walsh's office late in the afternoon, it quickly grew repetitious.

"I'm a lawyer, I can negotiate a contract," Walsh said. "But I didn't know about incentives, escalator clauses, the salary cap. You learn that from the agents. Since they don't know if they're the first or the last to talk to you during the process, they go through everything. They show you their success stories. They all pull out their lists and say, 'Look what I got for this guy. He was drafted sixteenth in the first round. This guy was fifteenth and this guy seventeenth. I got my guy number-fifteen money. I jumped the guy in front of me and here's how I did that and why I'm the best.'"

The Eds marveled at the cutthroat competition. "As a lawyer, I can go at it with another guy and at the end of the day still have a degree of professional respect and friendliness," Walsh said. "With these guys, there's no union holding them together, no association, no bar or medical association. They're just a whole bunch of guys out there, half lawyers, half not, worried about who is stealing their clients. They all hate each other, and you can see why."

The Eds heard from twenty-five agents. There were others, but they were eliminated for continually calling Anttaj directly. To narrow the field, the Eds contacted the NFL Players Association, which, though not the equivalent of a bar association, serves as a governing body. Through that research, they eliminated agent David Dunn, who had eluded a two-year suspension from the NFLPA by filing for bankruptcy after a jury awarded his former boss, Leigh Steinberg, $44.6 million in damages.

(Though a federal appeals court overturned the decision on March 30, 2005, Dunn still would face discipline from the NFLPA.)

"How could somebody consider that guy, with all that was hanging over him?" Ed Hawthorne wondered.

The Eds also heard from Neil Cornrich, a Cleveland agent who represented Barry Alvarez, Anttaj Hawthorne's head coach at Wisconsin. The Eds eliminated Cornrich because he was under investigation by the NFLPA for working as an expert witness for General Motors and against the estate of deceased NFL player Derrick Thomas, who died in an automobile accident in 2000. (In January of 2005, the union would suspend Cornrich for one year for violating the NFLPA's agent regulations against conflicts of interest by accessing proprietary information on the union's Web site about the market value of NFL veterans and passing it on to General Motors. In August of 2005, an arbitrator upheld the decision and Cornrich began serving his suspension.)

The Eds narrowed the field to three: Scharf, Condon/IMG, and Joe Linta, a Connecticut-based agent. All three made their final presentations Thanksgiving week. Doug Hendrickson, the Octagon agent, managed to circumvent the rules about not dealing with Anttaj directly and staged a meeting with the lineman in Wisconsin.

IMG pulled out all the stops for its final presentation. Condon came, along with fellow agents Ken "Fuzzy" Kremer and Chris Singletary. Kremer, like Condon, was a former Kansas City Chief, having played nose tackle and defensive end from 1979 to 1984. Singletary, the only African American in the contingent, had played football at Michigan and for the last few years had helped with IMG's recruiting and precombine preparations, before becoming a licensed agent three months earlier.

The Powerpoint presentation was impressive, breaking down IMG's client list and the amount of money IMG had negotiated for its clients in recent years. Kremer, the former defensive lineman, took the lead, talking to Anttaj about the position. Singletary, who had played Big Ten football as recently as 1998, outlined the predraft preparation process. Condon pulled out a three-ring binder full of recent IMG football contracts, including the one for top pick Eli Manning the year before. Aware that Anttaj would fall a semester short of graduating at Wisconsin, Condon mentioned that they could require the team that drafts him to permit him to do his off-season conditioning work at Madison. They had inserted a similar clause in the contract of Chris Hovan, a Boston College defensive tackle selected in the first round by the Minnesota Vikings in 2000.

Six weeks later, sitting in Walsh's office, Anttaj made a decision. It would be IMG and Condon.

"Jack Scharf is a great guy," he said later. "He's really dedicated to his work, but Tom Condon has been around for a long time. He has a lot of connections in the NFL, played fifteen years [actually twelve] himself. I had to go with the experience."

Ed Hawthorne called Scharf's cell phone. Sitting in his apartment in Phoenix, Scharf knew it wasn't a good sign when he saw Hawthorne's number on caller ID. Had he been the chosen one, it would have been a conference call on speaker phone from Walsh's office.

"This is a tough call for me to make," Hawthorne said. "I couldn't make the decision for him. I didn't want him to come back to me later if it didn't work out and say, 'You told me to go with this guy.' It was his call. He's a man now, and it's time for him to stand on his own two feet."

Scharf didn't have to ask for an explanation. He didn't need to hear a listing of Condon's advantages again. Instead, they talked football and promised to share dinner and cigars at the Senior Bowl in Mobile, Alabama, at the end of the month.

"It's disappointing," Scharf said later while watching his clients train at Athletes' Performance. "I had the kid. I really thought I had him. But I can't compete with the client list of IMG. The bottom line was that Anttaj Hawthorne wanted to be a client of Peyton and Eli Manning's agent, of Marvin Harrison's agent, and you can't fight that. Plus, Tom Condon is from New Haven. So not only is it Jack Scharf up against the IMG giant, but also Tom Condon, local boy made good. At the end of the day he won, and second place means nothing. Can I accept that? Yeah, I guess I have to. I know I did everything I could and I know I made an impression. They saw the passion, the work ethic, and a guy who is going to be in this business the next twenty years."

That evening, Auburn defeated Virginia Tech, 16–13 in the Sugar Bowl in New Orleans. The Tigers capped a perfect 13-0 season and laid claim to the national championship.

For agents Todd France and Ben Dogra, there were bigger things at stake. They were hot on the trail of three of Auburn's top stars: running backs Ronnie Brown and Carnell Williams, and cornerback Carlos Rogers.

Brown and Williams somehow had done the impossible. They managed to put their egos aside and share the Auburn backfield without diminishing their stock in the eyes of NFL scouts. In fact, their willingness to set aside personal goals for the good of the team was one reason scouts referred to them as high character guys. Along with Cedric Benson of Texas, they were considered the best running back prospects for the draft.

France and Dogra were latecomers to the Brown/Williams sweepstakes. Though both backs considered going pro the previous year, neither agent recruited them. France began contacting Brown in the summer of 2004. Unlike Pat Dye Jr., who went after both players, France figured he needed to make a choice.

"I didn't know if they'd want to go with the same guy, or if they cared," France said. "But I figured they had been bunched together so long, I had to go with one or the other."

Dogra was even later to the party, not contacting Williams until October, and meeting just once with Williams and his family. That's unusual, but Dogra had gotten word that Williams, unlike many players, had not narrowed the field.

Dogra had no Auburn clients and attended no regular season games. He recruited no other Auburn players, not even Rogers, Williams's roommate. Dogra has a well deserved reputation among agents as a sniper, a tireless recruiter able to pick off top talent across the country at will.

He does not fit the agent profile, and not just because he is the only NFL player rep of Indian descent. With a squatty physique and thick black hair, Dogra is gregarious and polished without being slick. "Polite and cerebral," is how *Street & Smith's SportsBusiness Journal* described him in its annual ranking of forty sports powerbrokers under the age of forty. (Drew Rosenhaus was the only other football agent included.)

Dogra turned down an invitation to the magazine's "Forty Under 40" banquet at the Waldorf Astoria in New York before being told the date. He knew he would be working. Dogra, it seems, has not stopped working since his family moved to the United States from New Delhi when he was five. His father owned two restaurants outside Washington, D.C., and his mother cooked in them. At age ten he began working in the restaurants for no pay. He logged ten-hour days during summers in high school, and his parents expected him to take over the restaurants.

Instead, he graduated from George Mason University in Fairfax, Virginia, and enrolled in law school at St. Louis University because it was near Sports Management Group, a football agency run by Jim Steiner. After twice applying for an unpaid internship at SMG, he finally was accepted in his third and final year.

Dogra demonstrated his parents' work ethic, was hired full-time, and by 1997 was Steiner's equity partner. In 2000, they sold the company to SFX Sports, which was on a buying spree of boutique agencies that included David Falk's basketball practice and Arn Tellem's baseball/basketball business.

Steiner and Dogra continued to operate essentially independently, though with the marketing muscle and global power of SFX Sports, part of the Clear Channel Communications empire. Steiner let Dogra handle most of the recruiting and Dogra did not let up on his workload. He figures the closest thing to a vacation he's taken since law school was when his wife and two young daughters accompanied him to the Pro Bowl in Hawaii in 2002.

So when Dogra made his pitch to Carnell Williams and his family, he trumpeted not only his work habits, but also the marketing power of his company, no small concern to a player nicknamed "Cadillac." Dogra also mentioned his many successful running back clients, including Shaun Alexander, Warrick Dunn, and Deuce McAllister.

"Our company can bring a lot more to the table than a lot of other companies, and that gives us an advantage," Dogra says. "We can be a little more selective."

Dogra, like France, arrived in New Orleans fairly confident he was going to sign a client. Parents generally don't suggest agents attend otherwise.

The day after the Sugar Bowl, Dogra met with Williams and his family in New Orleans. The agent produced a standard player representation agreement, and Cadillac became the newest member of SFX Sports.

France, meanwhile, wasted no time. After the game ended around 10:00 P.M., central time, he hustled back to the New Orleans Hilton Riverside and waited for the players. Unlike the autograph hounds casing the hotel, France was in search of more valuable signatures. He signed Rogers first and then zipped down the hall to sign Brown.

As much as schools try to police agents during the season, all bets are off once the bowl game is completed. Many seniors do not even return to school with their teammates. Thomas Davis, the Georgia junior who signed with France following the Outback Bowl, drove back to Georgia with friends.

Brian Battle, the Florida State compliance director, makes it a point to sit sentry on the floor of the Seminoles' hotel during the week of the bowl game, just to make sure agents don't try to sign paperwork before the game.

When Florida State defeated Virginia Tech in the Sugar Bowl on January 4, 2000, clinching a national championship, the team hotel was a mob scene, with players, fans, and family members celebrating everywhere. Battle was returning to his room and found kicker Sebastian Janikowski standing in a stairwell with his soon-to-be agent, trying to sign some paperwork. Apparently there were too many people celebrating in Janikowski's room.

Battle rolled his eyes and pointed toward *his* room. At least they would have a level writing surface there.

Janikowski was a junior with a year of eligibility remaining. Before he signed the standard player representation agreement, Battle reminded him that there was no turning back once he signed. Janikowski nodded and signed. As an underclassman, he was required to notify Florida State within seventy-two hours of his intention to go pro. With Battle present for the signing, it was the quickest notification of all time.

Then, according to Battle, the agent pulled out a wad of hundred-dollar bills and laid out four thousand dollars for Janikowski on Battle's bed. Whether it was a loan or a signing bonus did not matter. Either way, it was legal through the NCAA, the NFL Players Association, Florida State University, and the state of Florida, now that Janikowski was a professional.

Battle shook his head and excused Janikowski and his agent. A player could accept cash, cars, and anything else from an agent, so long as it came *after* the signing, even thirty seconds later. Promising something beforehand was illegal, but the next time an athlete turns in an agent for making an illegal inducement, Battle knew, would be the first.

Back in New Orleans five years later, Todd France sat down for dinner at 11:30 P.M. with the families of Ronnie Brown and Carlos Rogers for a celebratory dinner in a private room of the hotel restaurant.

France picked up the check, which he now could do legally, and, he knew, he'd be expected to do so for as long as he represented the client. With Brown, Rogers, and Thomas Davis, he finally had not one but three legitimate, first-round draft prospects. France said he lost out on Roddy White, the wide receiver from Alabama-Birmingham, when he declined to accept a 2 percent commission if White landed in the first round.

Barring injuries to Brown, Davis, and Rogers, rival agents no longer would be able to rip France for not having represented a first-rounder.

"You work so freakin' hard, but it's so anticlimactic," France says. "You should take a step back and get excited, pat yourself on the back. But I guess not being satisfied, that makes you good. It's an asset and a liability, a liability because you should step back and smell the roses sometimes. I don't. It should surprise me or make me totally excited, it just didn't. Afterward, I went to bed. When it was done, it wasn't like I was a bachelor and there were two other guys and a girl and she made the decision and I had no clue. I kind of knew."

Rogers came to his decision shortly after Christmas, choosing France over Jeff Sperbeck, an agent for Octagon. Rogers said other agents brought up France's lack of experience representing first-round picks.

"Every agent has something bad to say about the others," Rogers says. "Todd France has no first-round picks. That didn't matter to me. Look at Priest Holmes and Takeo Spikes. They're Pro Bowl guys. A lot of guys are first-round picks, but they're not standout guys in the league. I didn't want to go with a big company. I wanted to go with the one I could get personal attention [from]. Todd was that guy."

Under NCAA rules, France and his competitors could not offer or promise players anything of value before they signed, with one notable exception. They could promise to send them to a training center to prepare for the NFL scouting combine in February. The agent could pick up the tab for the trainer and nutritionist, along with all lodging, meals, transportation, and related costs. Depending on the training center and lodging, it could run as much as twenty-five thousand dollars a player for three months.

It was a valuable inducement, though hardly an unusual one. These days, no agent recruits a player without a training plan in place. Players know they have to make a decision on an agent immediately in order to begin preparing for the late-February combine, where they'd be tested, poked, prodded, and interviewed by all thirty-two NFL teams.

Not surprisingly, the business of precombine training had mushroomed over the last decade. For Brown, Rogers, and Cadillac Williams, their college days were over, though they'd be reunited within a few days to prepare for the biggest test of their lives, the NFL combine.

Chapter Nine:

WORKOUT WARRIORS

Each February, NFL scouts and executives gather in Indianapolis to take an in-depth look at the top three hundred or so prospects for the draft. The National Invitation Camp, known as "the combine," consists of four days of intense workouts, interviews, and drills.

How the players perform at the combine can mean the difference in several slots, or even rounds, in the April draft, which can mean a difference of hundreds of thousands, even millions of dollars in signing bonus money.

The NFL combine seems more like a track meet than a football-related event and, on one level, seems irrelevant to the game. But it provides a different perspective for NFL scouts and executives, who by the time the event is held in late February in Indianapolis have broken down long hours of tape, interviewed countless sources for background checks, and watched plenty of practice and live games.

The combine gives NFL officials a chance to get inside a player's head. Prospects travel to Indianapolis in four-day segments staggered over a week, depending on their position, and they are subjected to intense drills and interviews in which team officials try to assess their physical skills, mental acumen, and psychological makeup.

At the combine, the players undergo physicals, endure a Cybex test to measure their knee flexibility, take a fifty-question I.Q. test known as the Wonderlic, and go through a rapid-fire series of fifteen-minute interviews with teams.

They also complete seven drills, with players from certain positions excused from certain tests. Quarterbacks and wide receivers, for instance, do not have to bench-press, since their position is not one of raw power. Kickers and punters are excused from almost everything and spend their time at the combine demonstrating kicking ability.

Players have the option of doing all, none, or some of the drills. Some players, coming off injuries, do little more than interview with teams and take the Wonderlic, though there are plenty of able-bodied draft hopefuls who also sit out the combine. Some agents advise clients to skip all or portions of the event, and instead let their performances at individual school pro days in March serve as their showcase. Whether they perform at pro day and/or the combine, players go through the following:

- Forty-Yard Dash: Starting from a three-point stance, the player sprints forty yards and is clocked at increments of ten, twenty, and forty yards. Forty yards is the distance a player runs on punt coverage, Hall of Fame coach Paul Brown believed, or on long passes. The drill tests pure speed, along with power and explosion. The ten-yard split is especially important for linemen, who usually run no further on any one play.
- Bench Press: A player lies on a bench and presses 225 pounds off his chest as many times as possible. Though the drill tests nothing more specific than overall strength, scouts believe a poor performance on the bench shows a lack of dedication to the weight room and to conditioning.
- Vertical Jump: The combine uses a device called a "Vertec" to measure vertical leap. It's a pole with plastic flags that the athlete swipes with his hand at the top of the jump. The flags are spaced a half inch apart and rotate when hit. Before jumping, the player stands flat-footed and raises his arms straight up. The Vertec is lowered to the tips of his fingers. With the exception of wide receivers and defensive backs, for which there's a premium on leaping ability, the rest of the players are showing that they can generate explosion and power from their lower bodies.
- Broad Jump: In this standard drill from grade school gym class, the player leaps forward from a standing position on a line. Distance is measured from the line to where the back of his heels

land. The broad jump tests leg explosion and the player's ability to generate power by uncoiling his body. It's especially important for players working at or near the line of scrimmage: linemen, running backs, and linebackers.

- Three-Cone Drill: Three cones are placed on the field in the shape of an L, five yards apart from one another. Call them A, B, and C. The player begins in a three-point stance next to Cone A, runs to Cone B, bends down and touches the ground near the cone with his right hand. Then he runs back to Cone A, bends down and touches the ground with his right hand. He then runs back to Cone B and around the outside of it, weaves inside Cone C, then cuts around the outside of the two cones before sprinting back to Cone A. The drill tests change of direction and body control, especially valuable for running backs and the defenders chasing them.
- Short Shuttle (twenty yards): A player straddles a yard line on the field and places one hand down in a three-point stance. He can start by going to his right or left, though most players go to the right. He runs five yards to his right and touches the line with his right hand. He then runs ten yards to his left, touches the line, then runs back to the starting point. The short shuttle is a measure of change-of-direction ability and lateral control.
- Long Shuttle (sixty yards): A variation on the short shuttle, similar to basketball practice "suicide drills." Here the player runs five yards and back, then ten yards and back, then fifteen yards and back. He must bend down and touch the line at each interval for a total of six touches. This is less a test of lateral control as it is of overall conditioning and endurance.

As recently as the early 1990s, most players relied on their college strength coaches or a local weight-room guru to prepare them for the combine. The players worked out after class, continuing to progress toward their degrees, and pretty much enjoying the lives of pampered college athletes. That changed in the mid-1990s, when a few unsung players trained specifically for the seven events and dazzled scouts in Indianapolis.

The investment, paid for by agents, made sense. Not only could a player improve his draft position, thus earning more money, but by being drafted higher, he gave himself a better shot at a long-term NFL career. The more money a team invests, the more likely it is to be patient with a player. The lower a player is drafted, the more disposable he becomes.

By 2000 an entire combine preparation industry had sprung up. Agents, forever looking for an edge in recruiting, began sending athletes to these training centers. Much like high school students who spend months on expensive SAT prep courses, the players undergo grueling training regimens to give themselves an edge in the draft.

Most NFL draft hopefuls drop out of school after the fall semester to embark on a crash course on combine preparation. Some already have graduated, some never will. Others postpone their college educations for their NFL off-seasons. Some remain on campus working with their strength coaches, while others try to complete their coursework long distance.

Whatever route the player chooses, the most important class is Combine Preparation 101. The class is ungraded, the performance measured solely in numbers posted at Indianapolis and in dollars earned through the NFL Draft.

Mike Boyle figured it would be easy to beat the NFL combine. Working as a strength coach for Boston University in the mid-1980s, he became the football version of Stanley Kaplan, the popular service employed by high school kids looking to ace the SAT.

The way Boyle saw it, the combine was an open-book test, the questions provided well in advance. What if a player spent the weeks leading up to the mid-February event in Indianapolis training specifically to ace the test? Had nobody thought of this before?

"I was the first one to look at the test and realize you could cheat your ass off," Boyle said. "Then again, is it cheating if you're following the rules? I didn't think so, especially with the amount of gray area there is with these tests."

Boyle thought the vertical jump was the easiest drill to beat and it had little to do with training to jump higher. At the combine, a player's reach is measured from the ground to the tip of his fingers. The Vertec is lowered to that height to establish a benchmark. Plastic flags are attached higher up the pole, spaced a half inch apart, and rotate when hit. The player jumps straight up and hits as many plastic flags as he can.

During the initial reach, most players shrug their shoulders and reach as high as possible. Boyle taught his clients to do the opposite, depressing the shoulder blades, keeping the lat muscles of the upper back tight,

Top Left: Atlanta Falcons president Rich McKay. *(Courtesy of Jimmy Cribb, Atlanta Falcons)*

Top Right: Chris Canty, former University of Virginia defensive end. *(Courtesy of Eric Kelley,* The Cavalier Daily*)*

Bottom Left: University of Virginia head coach Al Groh.

Bottom Right: Brian Battle, Florida State compliance director during the 2004–2005 NFL draft season. *(Courtesy of Florida State University)*

Above: Jack Scharf, Momentum Sports football agent. *(Courtesy of Momentum Sports)*

Right: Tim Ruskell, Seahawks president and former Falcons asst. general manager (left) chats with Al Groh pregame.

Bottom: Chris Canty tore three of four ligaments in his left knee on September 25, 2004 against Syracuse. *(Courtesy of Danny Neckel,* The Cavalier Daily)

Top Right: Kimberly and Ray Willis, former Florida State offensive tackle.

Above: Fred Gibson, former University of Georgia wide receiver.

Right: Logan Mankins, former Fresno State offensive lineman, (right) and others line up for the weigh-in at the Senior Bowl.

Above: Roddy White, Cedric Houston, Cadillac Williams, and Fred Gibson stretch before Senior Bowl practice at Fairhope Municipal Stadium.

Right: Heath Miller, former University of Virginia tight end.

Below: University of Wisconsin defensive tackle Anttaj Hawthorne (middle) was guided through the agent selection process by family attorney Ed Walsh (left) and his uncle Ed Hawthorne.

Above: Olympic champion Michael Johnson instructs three future first-round picks, from left, David Pollack, Chris Spencer, and Alex Smith at the IMG Academies in Bradenton, Florida.

Left: Darryl Blackstock, former University of Virginia linebacker.

Below: Falcons president Rich McKay (left) and team owner Arthur M. Blank. *(Courtesy of Jimmy Cribb, Atlanta Falcons)*

Above: Tim Ruskell (with helmet) is introduced as president of the Seattle Seahawks along with, from left, team owner Paul Allen, CEO Tod Leiweke, and board member Hoon Cho.
(Courtesy of the Seattle Seahawks)

Right: David Greene speaks with the media at the NFL combine.

Below: Scouts take note of heights and weights during Florida State's pro day.

Top: Offensive tackle Ray Willis completes the forty-yard dash during FSU's pro day.

Above: Falcons assistant coach Brett Maxie (left) works out defensive backs during FSU's pro day.

Right: Seahawks president Tim Ruskell times players in the forty-yard dash at Auburn University's pro day.

Above: (From left to right) Agent Bill Johnson, Georgia wide receiver Reggie Brown, quarterback David Greene, agent Pat Dye Jr., and quarterback guru Zeke Bratkowski.

Right: Falcons owner Arthur M. Blank welcomes top draft pick Roddy White. *(Courtesy of Jimmy Cribb, Atlanta Falcons)*

Below: Todd France (top center), along with FAME staffers Jennifer Thatcher and Brushaud Callis. Bottom row: clients Carlos Rogers, Ronnie Brown, and Thomas Davis. *(Courtesy of France Athlete Management Enterprises)*

and extending the elbows. The beauty of it was that the player created the illusion of straining to reach as high as possible, even though he was establishing a base about four inches below where he would have been by elevating his shoulders. As a result, his vertical leap already was ahead of the competition.

There was nothing illegal about Boyle's advice. The only instruction players received at the combine, at least back then, was to extend their elbows. By keeping the lat muscles tight, it shortened the distance they could reach.

Like the Kaplan people, Boyle coached his clients on how to beat the tests. He looked at the twenty-yard shuttle drill and marveled at how players lost time with poor technique, not because they necessarily lacked lateral quickness and change-of-direction capabilities, which the shuttle is designed to test.

During the shuttle, performed on a football field, players must run five yards to one side and touch the line, then ten back to the other side and touch the line, and then five back to the other side. Boyle taught players to complete the drill in twelve steps, covering each of the five-yard segments in three steps and the ten-yard portion in six. Many players took extra steps so they could touch the line with the appropriate hand. That cost them precious time.

Even the bench press could be manipulated, Boyle felt. At the combine, players must bench 225 pounds as many times as possible. They're told not to bounce the weight off their chest. They also must "lock out" their arms at the end of each repetition.

In traditional strength training, coaches tell athletes to keep the bar in control. Often players are instructed to employ a slower routine (and lighter weights) to build strength and muscle. Boyle told his combine clients to toss that out the window and bench as fast as possible. Let the bar drop down quickly, as soon as the elbows begin to lock. That way, it was possible to create the illusion of the arms being fully extended.

Boyle had no reservations about his clients beating the bench press, especially since he saw the test as outdated and more a measure of endurance than strength, which was what it was supposed to test.

"A more telling measure would be if they had guys bench 275 or their body weight," Boyle said. "There are much better routes to find out how strong a guy is. If he's benching 225 for thirty or forty reps, that just means he has good endurance. But the NFL would rather do the same things they've been doing forever."

Even the forty-yard dash, the drill most associated with the NFL combine, could be tweaked in favor of the athlete, Boyle felt. At the combine, players were forced to place their feet six inches behind the starting line. At pro days, held later on the college campuses, the rule was loosely enforced and players could bring their front foot up to the line. In a three-point stance, the front foot and hand were on the line, the shoulders leaning ahead. (These days, the difference is one reason agents have clients skip the forty at the combine and run at school weeks later, though some combine coaches believe the foot placement makes little difference.)

"Some guys end up running forty-one yards," Boyle said. "The problem a lot of guys have is they try to learn from track coaches. But track coaches have no idea how to run the forty, because sprinters start with blocks. The shortest race they run is fifty-five meters, and it's run out of blocks. You want to have all of the weight forward, because you don't have a block to push off of."

Boyle found the easiest way to shave time off of a forty was during the first ten yards. A 4.5 time usually could be broken down to 1.5 seconds over the first ten yards, 1.2 for the next segment and .9 for each of the last two. Boyle trained his clients so they could run each ten-yard segment, especially the first, in just seven steps.

"You go back to the physics of running," Boyle said. "The average guy takes ten or eleven steps in the first ten yards, and that's a guy who is not putting a lot of force into the ground. Running is a function of how much force you put in the ground and how much horizontal vector that creates. When people do that correctly, they move further in fewer steps. So it's actually less movement in the same amount of time. But the illusion is that you don't see force production, how hard he's pushing against the ground, or how hard he's being propelled. You just see turnover. Some guys run like the Roadrunner; their wheels are spinning but they're not going anywhere, because they're not putting force into the ground. They look fast, but they don't run fast."

In 1986, Boyle began training Boston University athletes for the combine, a group that included wide receiver Bill Brooks and center Gary Walker. Brooks invited his young agent, Brad Blank, to stop by and check out his precombine program.

Blank packed a bag lunch and arrived at Boyle's "training center," a dark, windowless weight room of no more than three hundred square feet, nestled in the bowels of the BU athletic complex. Weights were locked in a cage. Nobody was around, so Blank ate his lunch, unimpressed with this early precombine facility.

An hour later Blank was a believer. He watched mesmerized as Boyle put Brooks and Walker through drills that, at the time, looked downright bizarre. Here was Brooks, trying to run with a harness around his waist and Boyle holding on to rubber tubing behind him to provide resistance. Boyle had the players jump up and down on platforms and boxes. When Blank asked for an explanation, Boyle pulled out a magazine called *Bigger, Faster, Stronger* and turned to an article on "plyometrics," a new regimen of jumps to make an athlete more explosive and powerful.

Boston University, which would disband its football program a decade later, was not exactly a finishing school for NFL prospects. With games against the likes of Holy Cross and New Hampshire, the team attracted few scouts. Boyle figured he could help BU's off-the-radar players make an impression at the combine and earn a spot in the twelve-round NFL Draft.

Brooks excelled at the combine, held that year at the Superdome in New Orleans, and caught the attention of the Indianapolis Colts, who selected him in the fourth round. (As a wide receiver, he caught sixty-five passes as a rookie and played eleven years in the league.) Walker, heeding Boyle's vertical-jump guidelines at the combine, leaped forty inches, an eye-popping result for a 270-pounder. The Colts took him in the fifth round.

"He got drafted solely off that jump," Blank said. "When that happened, Mike and I knew we were on to something."

Walker never played a down in the NFL, but teams kept biting on Boyle's workout wonders. In 1989, Mike Graybill arrived at the combine, having never played a down of college football. In other years, the Terriers basketball player might not have received an invite, but more than eight hundred players ended up at Indianapolis that year, the third year since the combine moved to the spacious Hoosier Dome and convention center.

Using Boyle's techniques and his own raw athleticism at the combine, Graybill sufficiently impressed the Cleveland Browns to take a flyer in the seventh round.

Graybill never advanced beyond the Browns practice squad. Stan Jones, a Hall of Fame lineman with the Chicago Bears, who as a prep star in the late 1940s was among the first football players to undergo a formal weight-training program, was the Browns strength and conditioning coach in 1989. He cornered Boyle at a convention and gave him grief for selling teams a bill of goods.

Boyle laughed. "It's not my job to watch film and figure out if they can play."

The 1989 draft also included the first of Blank's many clients from the University of Virginia to train with Boyle. Linebacker Jeff Lageman's stock rose after the 1988 season, with a strong performance at the East–West Shrine Game and the combine. Still, he was hardly a surefire first-round pick.

Until 1988, the NFL Draft was held on Tuesdays and Wednesdays at a series of hotels, most recently New York's Marriott Marquis. Now ESPN was in its second year of televising the weekend affair from a five thousand–seat theater at Madison Square Garden. The audience was dominated by rowdy Jets fans clad in full team regalia. When the Jets selected Lageman with the fourteenth overall pick, the crowd howled in protest.

Mel Kiper Jr., more combative in his early years working as ESPN's draft analyst, ripped the selection on air. "It's obvious to me the Jets don't know what the draft's all about," he said. (Lageman would go on to enjoy a solid decade-long career in New York and Jacksonville.)

Boyle remained under the radar, even after 1991, when he trained Eric Swann, who, coming out of high school two years earlier, was ruled academically ineligible to play at North Carolina State. He ended up playing for the Bay State Titans, a minor league football team in Lynn, Massachusetts. Dick Bell, the Titans coach who was serving as Swann's agent, brought the six-four, 300-pound lineman to Boyle.

The trainer put Swann through the usual routines and the lineman ran a 4.99 in private workouts for NFL scouts. Swann was so far off the radar screen that he wasn't invited to Indianapolis.

The Arizona Cardinals selected Swann with the sixth overall selection, four ahead of Herman Moore, the University of Virginia wide receiver and fellow Boyle trainee.

Even with Swann's unlikely background, his workout performance went largely unnoticed, and it might not have made a difference to Boyle's business if it had been noticed. Few reporters went to Indianapolis to cover the combine, and those that did were shut out of the Hoosier Dome, forced to loiter in the player hotel for scraps of information. The Internet was years away from widespread use. Few "draftniks" existed beyond Kiper and Joel Buchsbaum, the eclectic, well-connected Brooklyn hermit who wrote for *Pro Football Weekly*. Even ESPN had yet to expand its coverage into a full-blown, all-weekend affair.

So Boyle, working mostly with Blank's clients, continued to toil in obscurity. That changed in 1995. With interest and media coverage of the NFL Draft season mushrooming, an obscure Boston College lineman jump-started the combine training industry and caused NFL officials to rethink how they evaluated talent.

Mike Mamula was hardly a can't-miss prospect heading into the 1995 NFL Draft. As a redshirt junior for Boston College in 1994, he racked up thirteen sacks from the defensive end position and was named to the Big East's all-conference team.

Mamula, however, was a "tweener," a linebacker-sized player at defensive end. Though he possessed raw NFL potential, he lacked the fire, drive, and nonstop "motor" scouts like to see from players in charge of attacking the quarterback.

"The motivational level just wasn't there," Boyle recalled. "But once he was put in a situation where the combine mattered and he could make some money, he started concentrating and made this quantum leap."

Boyle had never encountered a player like Mamula, a talented but raw player with an upside. His precombine players typically had fallen into two categories. There were unheralded Boston University players such as Brooks and Graybill, who parlayed strong combine performances into better-than-expected draft days. Then there were Blank clients with solid skills and athleticism such as Herman Moore and fellow Virginia Cavalier Chris Slade (second round, New England, 1993), who, as expected, went on to long careers in the NFL.

Boyle compared his work with the Moore-Slade group to polishing what were already fairly flawless diamonds. With Mamula, he had a hunk of rock to chisel.

Mamula had turned down his fifth year of eligibility, entering the draft as a redshirt junior. Unlike seniors, who are put through combine testing by NFL scouts in the spring before their final years of eligibility, Mamula had not produced any data. As far as combine testing, he was a clean slate.

Armed with Boyle's strategies, the twenty-one-year-old Mamula went to Indianapolis, and on February 10, 1995, dazzled more than three hundred NFL scouts and executives at the newly renamed RCA Dome, posting numbers never before seen at the combine by a man his size. Following Boyle's advice, he kept his lats and shoulder blades pulled down when he stepped up for the vertical jump, then leaped thirty-eight inches, a feat normally reserved for elite wide receivers and NBA players.

Six years after 270-pound center Gary Walker leaped forty inches, few players had caught on to Boyle's bait-and-switch reach technique. Only six of the other 230 players jumped higher than Mamula did.

Mamula bench-pressed 225 pounds twenty-six times, the same number as Tony Boselli, the six-seven, 323-pounder from Southern Cal, considered the best offensive tackle in the draft. Mamula broad-jumped ten feet, five inches—an inch further than Michael Westbrook, one of the best wide receivers in the draft. He completed the twenty-yard shuttle in 4.03 seconds, faster than every wide receiver, and even scored an impressive thirty-three on the Wonderlic, a stunning performance for someone who carried a C average at Boston College.

By the time Mamula stepped up to run the forty, he had become the focal point of the workout. Scouts sat poised, stopwatches in hand. Before a crowd that included Bill Parcells, then head coach of the New England Patriots, and longtime Miami Dolphins head coach Don Shula, Mamula took off.

He didn't appear especially fast, but covered the first ten yards in just seven steps and 1.55 seconds, better than some of the running backs. Many scouts couldn't believe their stopwatches. According to the official electronic timer, Mamula ran a 4.62, unheard of for a man his size.

When the combine ended, Mamula had soared up the draft boards. Never before had someone put up such eye-popping numbers, especially not a six-five, 252-pound lineman. By the time *Sports Illustrated* ran a two thousand, eight hundred-word Mamula feature by senior writer Peter King the week before the draft, Mamula's combine performance had become a legend.

"He's a rare athlete, the kind who comes along once every five or ten years," King quoted Ray Rhodes, then the first-year head coach of the Philadelphia Eagles. "I judge players by production, and he could be the most productive player in the draft this year."

A "real genetic freak," said Jerry Angelo, Tampa Bay's director of personnel.

Dwight Adams, the Buffalo Bills director of personnel, still was blown away by the combine showing. "If he'd done anything more, they'd have had to put a cape on his shoulders."

"As the combine showed," King wrote, "Mamula may be one of the most gifted pass rushers to enter pro football in the past decade."

Rhodes certainly thought so. On April 29, 1995, he made the first of several bad investments in Boyle's workout warriors, selecting Mamula with the seventh overall selection, five picks ahead of Warren Sapp, who fell to Tampa Bay at number twelve, after reports of drug use while at Miami, and well before future stars such as Michigan defensive back Ty Law (number twenty-three, New England) and Florida State linebacker Derrick Brooks (number twenty-eight, Tampa Bay). The Eagles even traded a pair of second-round picks to Tampa Bay in return for swapping draft slots and a third-round selection.

With their existing third-round pick, the Eagles drafted another Boyle combine star, Greg Jefferson, a defensive end out of the University of Central Florida.

Blank landed Mamula a four-year contract worth $7 million, a package worth at least $4 million more than Mamula would have received had he gone late in the first round.

That's where Blank believed he would have gone without Boyle's help. If nothing else, Blank knew Tom Coughlin was a Mamula fan and had the number eighteen pick. Coughlin, formerly Mamula's BC coach and now head coach and general manager of the Jacksonville Jaguars, drafted future five-time Pro Bowl offensive tackle Tony Boselli out of USC at number two and spent the number-eighteen pick on Tennessee running back James Stewart, who would go on to have a solid career with the Jaguars and Lions.

Others pegged Mamula before the combine as, at best, a third-round pick. When Mamula applied to the NFL's notoriously conservative advisory committee before making his decision to turn pro, he received a rating of "he will not be drafted higher than the fourth round."

Either way, Boyle, Blank's precombine training secret weapon, was exposed. Soon every player would want the equivalent of the Mamula program. Two years earlier, IMG had established the "International Performance Institute" for veteran clients in all sports, at its training complex in Bradenton, Florida. Mark Verstegen, the young IPI director, had urged IMG's head football agent, Tom Condon, to send his NFL Draft hopefuls to IPI. Condon, a former Boston College player who lost Mamula to Blank and Boyle, finally agreed for 1996.

By 1999, most top draft hopefuls were dropping out of school after their last football games and training full-time with Boyle, Verstegen, Chip Smith, Tom Shaw, and other "performance coaches" around the country. Smith and Shaw, operating out of Atlanta and New Orleans respectively, were best known as speed gurus, but soon put together versatile staffs to handle every part of combine training. Mackie Shilstone, a former 140-pound Tulane wide receiver known for his work with boxers and baseball players, launched a precombine program out of New Orleans.

Agent Pat Dye Jr., who spent nothing on precombine training in 1998, realized times had changed when Georgia offensive tackle Matt Stinchcomb asked him to foot the bill for Smith's services prior to the 1999 draft. Soon Dye and his competitors were spending fifteen thousand dollars or more per player for precombine training and expenses.

Boyle's precombine work and publicity fueled his growing Mike Boyle Strength & Conditioning business. He continued to work with the Boston University hockey program and served as the strength and conditioning coach for the NHL's Boston Bruins.

As for Mamula, he never lived up to the promise he showed in Indianapolis. A chronic underachiever on the field his first three seasons, he missed all of 1998 after tearing the ACL in his left knee during a preseason game. Remarkably, the Eagles responded by handing him a four-year, $11.5 million contract before the 1999 season. Even Blank and Mamula were stunned, figuring the player would need to try out for teams as a free agent.

Mamula saw only a fraction of that money. Andy Reid, who replaced the fired Rhodes before the 1999 season, was not nearly as enamored with the defensive end, and cut him after the 2000 season. Mamula soon retired. Sapp, named the NFL's defensive player of the year with Tampa Bay in 1999, often would cite Mamula whenever asked about the 1995 draft and the money Sapp lost falling to number twelve.

Under Reid, the Eagles would become a model for shrewd personnel decisions and building through the draft. Though Mamula still is cited throughout the league as a cautionary tale of irrational combine exuberance, Boyle does not consider it his finest work, or even Philadelphia's biggest blunder under Rhodes.

In 1997, the Eagles spent the twenty-fifth overall pick on Jon Harris, a six-eight defensive end from the University of Virginia. Rhodes compared Harris to former Cowboys star Ed "Too Tall" Jones and expected similar results.

Blank had signed Harris's teammates, linebackers James Farrior and Jamie Sharper, considering Harris a throw-in to his Virginia recruiting efforts. Like Mamula, Harris embraced Boyle's teachings and performed well at the combine, though not nearly as well as Mamula did.

Harris was projected as a fourth-round pick in most mock drafts, the fifth-best player out of his own school, behind Farrior, Sharper, and brothers Tiki and Ronde Barber. The New York Jets selected Farrior seventh overall, but Harris went ahead of everyone else, signing a five-year, $5 million deal.

Like Mamula, Harris never lived up to his combine performance. After two forgettable seasons in Philadelphia, he was dealt to Green Bay, where he was reunited with Rhodes. The Packers cut him a year later, and by 2002 Harris was out of the NFL.

In recent years, Boyle has scaled back his combine prep program, especially since Blank's pipeline of University of Virginia recruits has dried up. After Mamula, Boyle agreed to train Blank's clients exclusively, though after 1997 Blank allowed Boyle to accept other players.

"The one mistake I made was going exclusive with Brad," Boyle said. "Guys like Mark [Verstegen] and Tom [Shaw] saw what was out there and really capitalized on it."

In 2004, Boyle relocated to California to run the Carson branch of Athletes' Performance for Verstegen, but returned to Boston not long after the combine. Working with a full combine class for the first time in years, Boyle found the only thing that had changed was that now everyone knew how to beat the system. He wonders why the NFL refuses to tweak its roster of combine tests.

"NFL coaches have a Pygmalion complex," Boyle said. "They think they can take a great athlete and make him a great football player. In reality, it's easier to take a good football player and make him a great one. Jon Harris could run and jump and had a great body, but the bottom line was that he had limited football talent. It's funny. Every year you hear coaches say the combine doesn't matter and that it's more about talent and character. And teams like the Patriots actually believe that. But every year someone falls in love with a guy who blew up at the combine. As long as that keeps happening, combine preparation will be a booming business."

Nobody knew that more than Verstegen and his Athletes' Performance staff, who were training the equivalent of a college all-star team for the 2005 draft.

Chapter Ten:

FIGHTING FOR
ALVIN PEARMAN

red Gibson parked his rented white Chrysler 300 in front of the Athletes' Performance training facility. It was Thursday, January 6, 2005, and Gibson was officially a professional. Shortly after the Outback Bowl he had signed with Doug Hendrickson, an agent with Octagon, and after a few days back in Georgia to gather his belongings, he boarded a plane to Phoenix.

Now, as he entered API—the pros used the full acronym for "Athletes' Performance Institute," even though the company had dropped the "Institute" from its name—he knew he was in a different world. The University of Georgia enjoyed one of college football's finest training facilities, and Gibson had viewed the DVD of Athletes' Performance that Hendrickson's colleague, Demetro Stephens, had provided. Still, the wide receiver was struck by the thirty-three thousand-square-foot facility, with its cavernous workout room, cafe, massage rooms, athlete lounge, and swimming pool.

Boxes of clothing and shoes were stacked up next to the front desk, having arrived via UPS or overnight delivery. The names were scrolled on the sides in black marker, and as Gibson surveyed the mail it looked like a college all-star-game roster. There were a lot of packages for Carnell "Cadillac" Williams, the Auburn running back.

Ronnie Brown, Williams's backfield mate, and teammate Carlos

Rogers, a cornerback, also were expected soon, having signed with agent Todd France after Auburn's Sugar Bowl win over Virginia Tech three nights earlier.

Two of the stars of the Oklahoma football team, wide receiver Mark Clayton and offensive tackle Jamaal Brown, were expected shortly, having just signed with Ben Dogra. (Southern Cal had routed the Sooners 55–19 in the Orange Bowl two nights before, to claim a share of the national title.) Dogra, who also had signed Williams, was in the hunt for Brodney Pool, a junior safety at Oklahoma expected to turn pro.

There was mail for Erasmus James, the defensive end from Wisconsin who, like Gibson, had played in the Outback Bowl. Marcus Johnson, an offensive lineman from Ole Miss, already was in the house, as was Andrew Walter, who was training in his backyard after quarterbacking Arizona State.

There were rumors flying about which other players might arrive at Athletes' Performance, all contingent on which agents they selected.

"You take the guys that are going to be training here, put us all on one team, and we'll win a Super Bowl in three years," Gibson said.

Gibson walked out to the pool and glanced at nearby Sun Devil Stadium, nestled between mountain buttes. Overhead was the steady cackling of traffic from Sky Harbor Airport. Near the pool there was a fifty-yard Astro Turf practice field and the Arizona State University softball stadium. The perimeter of the area was lined with pink oleanders and towering fan palms.

Octagon was paying ten thousand dollars to API to train Gibson for the combine in late February and for his pro day at Georgia in late March. The fee did not include housing for the three-month period—a pricey proposition in Phoenix during the winter—the Chrysler 300 rental, and meals not provided by the training center. Throw in nearly four months of spending money for the budding professional athlete and the bill easily could approach twenty-five thousand dollars.

Given that NFL agents worked on a commission of 3 percent—some worked for less—a player had to generate almost a million dollars in signing bonus and first-year salary to cover the costs of predraft training alone. Anyone drafted below the second round usually does not cover.

"With a lot of guys, you're working toward a long-term relationship," said agent Jack Scharf, who had six players training at Athletes' Performance for the 2005 draft. "If I do everything I can for my client and honor all promises, then they'll honor me for the second contract by allowing me to negotiate. By then I'll have no overhead."

Scharf used Nate Burleson as an example. Relatively unheralded coming out of the University of Nevada-Reno in 2003, Burleson trained at Athletes' Performance and was drafted by the Minnesota Vikings in the third round. He received a three-year contract with a signing bonus of $529,000, generating a 3 percent commission of $15,870 for Scharf. Burleson's salaries in 2003 ($225,000), 2004 ($305,000), and 2005 ($380,000) accounted for another $27,300 in commissions.

Deducting precombine expenses and the money Scharf spent recruiting, he figured he might make fifteen thousand dollars over the first three years of Burleson's contract. The wide receiver had emerged as a solid number two receiver, playing alongside Randy Moss, and was setting himself up for a huge payday after his third year in the league.

Yet that was no guarantee for Scharf, who like the rest of his thirteen hundred colleagues had to deal with the widespread practice of client stealing. After all, it was more cost-effective to grab a three-year veteran on the verge of free agency than pay the freight for the first three years. There also was the potential for career-ending injury; the average NFL career lasted just three and a half seasons.

Athletes' Performance was the most expensive of the combine training centers, and each year its draft class became more distinguished. In 2002, API trained one player that was drafted in the first round (offensive lineman Levi Jones, Cincinnati), three in 2003, and five in 2004, including top-ten picks Roy Williams of the Detroit Lions and DeAngelo Hall of the Atlanta Falcons.

Players quickly discovered how little precombine training resembled the work they did in the weight room back at school. There were some similarities; they were training to bench-press at the combine, after all. But they were just as likely to harness a sled weighted with plates across a field, balance on a giant rubber Physioball, or undergo a series of moving stretches that seemed more like yoga routines.

Unlike college strength coaches, trainers at Athletes' Performance were not just trying to bulk players up, though they could do that, too, for players that needed it. Instead, they concentrated on the player's hips, shoulders, and midsection, tapping into the power of the "core" region to generate ferocious power and explosion. An emphasis was placed on flexibility and lateral movement. Scouts were forever looking at hips to see how well a player, especially an offensive lineman or cornerback, could move.

Mark Verstegen, the founder and president of API, could not believe how his training center had become a negotiating tool in the cutthroat world of draft recruiting. It's not that he did not believe his product was the best. By limiting his combine training class to thirty players and offering a complete array of services—physical training, meals, nutritional supplementation, massage, physical therapy—all under one roof, he believed his ten thousand dollar-per-player cost was fair, especially given his staff's reputation for improving strength, speed, and overall performance at the combine.

What surprised him was how prominent a role the combine training industry played when athletes made their decision on agents. After all, the work of his twenty-person staff over the course of two or three months was a minor part of what could be a career-long relationship with an agent.

The thirty-five-year-old Verstegen, who wears his hair in a flattop and looks like a younger, more muscular version of the actor Ed Harris, briefly played football at Washington State until an arm injury ended his career. Not long after he opened Athletes' Performance in mid-2001, he sent out feelers to agents about combine training for 2002. Having run precombine programs as the director of IMG's International Performance Institute in Bradenton, Florida, for the 1996–1999 drafts, he had a strong resume.

In 1998, San Diego State's Kyle Turley was considered, at most, the fifth-best offensive tackle prior to the combine. Working with Verstegen, he gained fourteen pounds, lowered his time in the forty-yard dash, and dazzled scouts in Indianapolis. The New Orleans Saints picked him with the seventh overall pick. The following year, Notre Dame offensive tackle Luke Petitgout was projected as a mid-to-late-second-round pick. He packed on twenty pounds before the combine, impressed the scouts with his strength and speed, and was taken by the Giants with the nineteenth selection in the first round.

Between the success of the combine program and other clients such as baseball's Nomar Garciaparra, whom the trainer had met in 1993 while working at Georgia Tech, Verstegen began to feel the entrepreneurial bug. Not long after the 1999 draft, Verstegen, then thirty, and his wife, Amy, moved to Arizona armed with little more than a sponsorship agreement from Adidas and a dream of building an independent training center for elite athletes.

Verstegen, who as recently as 1994 was earning $22,400 a year at Georgia Tech, financed the facility to retain 100 percent ownership. The Adidas agreement helped. So did other sponsors and loans. While the building went up, Verstegen worked with a small group of athletes out of an old ASU building scheduled for demolition.

There was an old-school, Rocky Balboa charm to the temporary housing. Garciaparra, the no-nonsense shortstop in the midst of back-to-back American League batting titles, embraced the place, as did fellow Boston Red Sox teammate Lou Merloni.

Verstegen, with just his wife and two other coaches, attracted a modest combine class for 2000. The San Francisco 49ers selected Giovanni Carmazzi, a quarterback from Hofstra, in the third round. Tyrone Carter, a defensive back from the University of Minnesota, went to the hometown Vikings in the fourth.

The new building was not quite finished in time for the 2001 draft, though Verstegen trained Leonard Davis, a massive offensive tackle from the University of Texas, who was drafted by the Arizona Cardinals second overall after the Atlanta Falcons selected Michael Vick.

Amy Verstegen, serving as the original director of sales and marketing while wearing nine other hats, contacted agents in the fall of 2001 to "presell" slots for the inaugural Athletes' Performance draft class of 2002. In return for their commitment, the agents could use API's new facility as a recruiting tool.

It wasn't quite an exclusive arrangement for either party. API did not want ten clients from one agent, nor did agents want to foot the bill for high-end training for players with limited draft potential. API also wanted to leave a few slots open, in case an agent representing a top-ten pick came calling.

By the fall of 2004 API could be more selective. Most of the original agencies were still on board, though occasionally there was a replacement. Todd France and Octagon earned slots for the 2005 draft after Joel Segal and Eugene Parker opted to take their business elsewhere. Agents Pat Dye Jr., Drew Rosenhaus, and others called later asking for availability, but there was no more room.

"We can't continue to leave slots open," said Percy Knox, a former All-American track athlete at the University of Arizona who joined API in 2002 as director of athlete management. "We don't want agents to be using API as an incentive unless they're already in the fold. It's only fair to the guys that have been with us all this time."

Dye lost out on three Auburn clients—Williams, Brown, and Rogers—that opted to go with agents with slots available at API.

"I don't want to use that as an excuse, but I don't have any doubt that it made a difference," Dye said. "I know it did with Carnell. I was told his father said point-blank, 'You can't go with Pat. He can't get you into API.' I think it definitely made a difference with Ronnie [Brown] and Carlos

[Rogers], to the extent that they were locked in to going to Arizona, and knowing that I couldn't get them in there because the slots were filled."

Williams, who signed with Ben Dogra of SFX Sports, said that wasn't the case. "I wanted to come to API, and it influenced my decision a little bit, sure. I had heard different players talk about it and I wanted to be away from home, where nobody could bother me and I could focus on football and getting better. But that's not why I didn't choose Pat Dye. I just thought Ben could do a better job for me."

Dogra, who like France enjoyed a banner recruiting season for the 2005 draft, said the facility does not make that much difference in recruiting. In 2004, he represented first-round picks Lee Evans, a wide receiver from Wisconsin, and Vernon Carey, a guard from Miami. Neither trained at API, nor did clients such as 2005 draft prospect Jonathan Clinkscale, a guard from Wisconsin, or Bryant McKinnie, a first-round offensive tackle out of Miami in 2002.

Players from Miami and Wisconsin fall into their own categories, since those players almost always stay at school to train. Anttaj Hawthorne, the Badgers defensive tackle Jack Scharf lost to Tom Condon and IMG, was training in Madison and would not have come to API anyway. Erasmus James, Hawthorne's Wisconsin teammate who was at API, was the exception.

"This is just one piece of the puzzle," Dogra said. "I don't get players because of this facility. I would if I was the only one using it. I'm competing with a lot of these other agents that have slots here, so it neutralizes the training advantage."

"It might make a difference for some," said France, who also had clients training with Chip Smith's Competitive Edge and Velocity Sports, both in Atlanta. "But I'd like to think a kid isn't making decisions based on a six- or eight-week training program."

Dogra has a point. Sometimes even having slots at API was no guarantee for an agent. In January of 2004, cornerback DeAngelo Hall enrolled at the training center as a client of Ethan Lock. Hall fired Lock a few weeks later and signed with Joel Segal, who represented Vick, who, like Hall, played at Virginia Tech. At that point Lock asked API to kick Hall out.

Knox, as director of athlete management, let Hall stay, but made it clear to Segal that it could not happen again. Knox also crafted a new policy.

"I tell kids, 'You're here because your agent brought you here,'" Knox says. "If you go with someone outside the group, you can't train with

API. If it's within the group, it's okay only if the agents can work something out—or at least agree to disagree. If the original agent doesn't want the kid here, then the kid can't be here. Because, who am I here to protect—the athlete or the agent? That's a no-brainer. I get new kids every year. I'll work with the agents forever."

Hall was drafted eighth overall by the Atlanta Falcons. Defensive end Will Smith, a Segal client from Ohio State that trained at API, went to New Orleans at number eighteen. Segal's slots at API were grabbed by France for 2005.

Now, a week into combine training season, the Athletes' Performance staff had little time to spend wondering what impact they had on a player's selection of representation. It was all they could do to keep up with which players were coming. Though the thirty slots in the 2005 combine class had been sold for months, they still were being filled. Some players still had not selected agents—or, in the case of underclassmen, even decided if they were going pro.

At one point it looked like Braylon Edwards, the talented wide receiver from Michigan, was coming to API. But he signed with an agent (Lamont Smith), not affiliated with the training center. Dogra thought he had Miami cornerback Antrel Rolle, who, unlike most Hurricanes, would have come to API had he not chosen agent David Dunn. (Rolle, ironically, would fire Dunn and hire Dogra in mid-February, too late to start training at API.) At least two agents with slots at API had talked to D'Brickashaw Ferguson, the talented junior tackle from the University of Virginia who opted to remain in school.

Whoever ended up at API would be affiliated with one of seven agencies: SFX Sports (Dogra); Octagon (Hendrickson and partners Mike Sullivan, Ken Landphere, and Jeff Sperbeck); Momentum Sports (Scharf, Jeff Griffin); FAME (France); Professional Sports Marketing (Rich Moran); Lock, Metz & Malinovic (Lock); and Priority Sports (Ken Zukerman, Rick Smith, Mark Bartelstein).

By the morning of Friday, January 7, the API roster was still in flux. Lock, whose agency is based in Tempe, felt so confident in his chances of signing Miami's Frank Gore that API prepared a training binder emblazoned with the running back's name. The junior was expected to go pro and, for all the API staff knew, would be walking in at any time.

Back in South Florida, Gore placed a call to agent David Levine around three o'clock. "I want to get this done," Gore said. "Declare for the draft, sign with you. We can do it for the six o'clock news."

Levine's hard work had paid off. Though he represented only a handful of NFL veterans, he was no newcomer to the business, having been an agent since 1989. His clients had included former Hurricanes and NFL players Alonzo Highsmith, Winston Moss, and Darryl Williams. All three called Gore on Levine's behalf.

Levine contacted South Florida media outlets, setting up a press conference at the Coconut Grove home of Gore's mother, who had endured a history of kidney ailments and underwent dialysis three times a week. Gore himself had torn anterior cruciate ligaments (ACLs) in both knees during his college career, missing most of the 2002 and 2003 seasons. It was time to take advantage of his health and earning power.

By the time the media arrived at the Gore residence, a modest five hundred-square-foot bungalow the running back shared with his mother and two siblings, Lock had turned his attention to another running back from the Atlantic Coast Conference, one that was barely on the radar screen when the 2004 season started. But now Lock and Dunn were in a fierce battle to land Virginia running back Alvin Pearman.

Pearman wanted to train at Athletes' Performance.

Two days earlier, Ethan Lock had brought Pearman to API and Pearman came away impressed. It helped that he roomed for a night with Chris Canty, his former University of Virginia teammate who had signed with Lock and now was training at API.

David Dunn also wanted to represent Pearman, and unlike Lock did not have slots available to offer at the training center. Dunn also was in the hunt for Heath Miller, Pearman's former roommate at Virginia, who was considered the best tight end prospect in the nation. Miller, a redshirt junior, had yet to declare for the draft, and was having some second thoughts of turning pro after undergoing surgery for athletic pubalgia, a tear of the abdominal wall. Though not serious, it likely would keep him from working out at the combine in Indianapolis and during the school's pro day on March 23.

Miller had won the Mackey Award in December as the nation's top tight end, but wondered if he'd fall in the draft by not working out in the coming months. A training center with strong rehabilitation facilities was a must.

Late in the afternoon on Friday, January 7, one of Dunn's staff members called Athletes' Performance. He was told the facility could not make an exception and offer Dunn training slots in Arizona. But there was an alternative. API had a second facility on the campus of the Home

Depot Center, a 125-acre complex in Carson, California, near Los Angeles, that featured Olympic-caliber training facilities and playing fields for many sports, including soccer, track and field, and basketball.

The complex was owned by the Anschutz Entertainment Group, and API planned to build a training center there equivalent to its Arizona headquarters. Since 2003, API had operated out of a temporary facility that featured state-of-the-art equipment, a full team of performance specialists, and access to the entire Home Depot Center. But there was no way agents could convince potential clients that it was equivalent to the Arizona complex. Dunn had hired a trainer to work with his clients in California. Unable to get into the API facility in Arizona, he stuck with his existing program.

Pearman personified how a player's draft stock could soar in just a few months. As recently as mid-October, the thought of the five-nine Pearman attracting the type of agents that would pay twenty-five thousand to send him to Arizona and Athletes' Performance for combine preparation would have seemed preposterous. He began the year as the backup to Wali Lundy at running back, and though he was a solid college performer, contributing on special teams and in a reserve role, he projected as an undrafted free agent, lacking the speed, strength, and size needed at the next level.

That changed after Lundy and the rest of the Cavaliers were held to just twenty yards in an embarrassing loss at Florida State at midseason. Head coach Al Groh benched Lundy, and over the next four games Pearman rushed for 582 yards, continuing his stellar work at punt returner and even emerging as the Cavaliers' second-leading receiver.

Soon scouts were jumping on the Pearman bandwagon, comparing him to Brian Mitchell, the versatile back who played in the NFL for fifteen years, mostly for Washington, and ranked as the all-time career leader in total yardage. Groh began touting Pearman for ACC Player of the Year. Pearman didn't do anything exceptionally well, but he was the type of versatile performer NFL coaches loved to have in their running back rotation. A true scholar-athlete, Pearman majored in sports medicine and had graduated in just seven semesters.

By the end of November, *Sports Illustrated* was calling Pearman the most underrated player in the ACC. Scouts also began calling more frequently. Pearman, Miller, and their roommates did not have an apartment phone, relying on cell phones, and Pearman marveled at how Miller's rang incessantly. Now his was ringing nearly as often. Miller would spot an agent on his caller ID, ignore him, and moments later Pearman's phone would ring. Sometimes, after Pearman refused to pick up, the agent would call Miller again.

"We'd be watching TV and it was as if we had a land line, waiting for the other guy to get up and deal with it," Pearman said. "We just learned to ignore it."

Dunn had recruited both heavily, meeting with them together in Charlottesville late in the season. It helped that both remained close with Dunn's client Matt Schaub, the former Virginia quarterback drafted by the Atlanta Falcons in the third round in 2004.

Agents wondered how Dunn could recruit at all, given that he still was waiting for the result of his appeal of a jury award to Leigh Steinberg of $44.6 million in damages against him. (In fact, a federal appeals court overturned the decision on March 30, 2005, though Dunn still faced discipline from the NFLPA.)

With that hanging over Dunn, at least in January, not having slots at Athletes' Performance seemed like a minor issue. Pearman signed with Dunn and his agency, Athletes First.

"A lot of agents were using [the judgment] against him, and it was definitely an issue," Pearman said. "It was an issue that had to be discussed on a personal level, and it wound up that it wasn't going to affect my relationship with him, and vice versa, in the near future."

Miller, a soft-spoken young man from tiny Swords Creek, Virginia, disliked the agent selection process. He wasn't too fond of anything that drew attention and was happy to let his parents handle the process. They had narrowed the field to Dunn and IMG's Tom Condon and Ken "Fuzzy" Kremer.

Miller met with the IMG agents a few days after the Cavaliers' season ended with a 37–34 loss to Fresno State in the MPC Computers Bowl. Miller, like many of his teammates, figured they'd look back years later and wonder how a team with so much future NFL talent could finish the season 8-4. The tight end signed with IMG over Dunn, figuring Condon had the most high-profile contract experience, to say nothing of a training center that Verstegen himself had created before moving to Arizona.

"I felt like I couldn't go wrong with either choice," Miller said. "The entire process just wasn't very fun for me."

For Ethan Lock, losing Pearman and Gore stung, but he and his partners still had a solid draft class that included Erasmus James, Michigan lineman David Baas, Nebraska linebacker Barrett Ruud, and Charlie

Frye, a quarterback from Akron. Lock also had a Virginia Cavalier in Chris Canty, who, like Pearman, was emerging as one of the more unlikely stories of the 2005 NFL Draft.

Canty stood neck-deep in a small pool of fifty-five-degree water. It was late afternoon on Friday, January 7, and Canty, wearing swim trunks, was alternating between the "cold plunge" and an adjacent hot tub alongside the Athletes' Performance swimming pool. Most of his fellow members of the API precombine class had departed for the day, or at least were playing video games and Ping-Pong inside in the lounge. Canty had been at API just five days, but already he had established a pattern of being the first to arrive and the last to leave.

The idea behind the contrasts in pool temperature was to force the blood to move fast, from the organs to the skin and back again. That's a good thing, even for people who do not exercise. When done after a workout, the contrasts stimulate muscle recovery without much effort—though, as Canty had learned, sitting in a pool of ice water for up to two minutes takes some effort.

The cold plunge, in particular, decreases the natural inflammation in the muscles created by working out. Lifting weights creates tiny tears in the muscle fibers, which the body repairs in between workouts, leaving the athlete bigger and stronger. The contrasts jump-start the process.

Trainers at Athletes' Performance sometimes struggled with getting clients to put their full effort into the cold plunge. Some stood waist deep or jumped out before the interval was over. Nobody had to encourage Canty, who, despite one of the more grueling and painful precombine regimens, had embraced every element of the program.

Nearly four months had passed since Canty shredded three of the four ligaments in his left knee in the University of Virginia's game against Syracuse. While the rest of API's draft hopefuls dove right into training for the forty-yard dash, bench press, vertical jump, and the other tests they would face at the combine in Indianapolis in six weeks, Canty was on his own program.

Under the direction of Darcy Norman, an API physical therapist, Canty spent a lot of time doing plyometrics, a series of jumps and squats. Canty had undergone months of rehabilitation, first in Birmingham, Alabama, and then at home in Charlotte, North Carolina, but he still was in the early stages of preparing for the NFL combine. Much of the work at API took place in the swimming pool, where the water offered resistance but not a heavy impact on the knee.

"When you've had surgery, tissue atrophies," Norman said. "You spend your life developing tissue tolerance to activities, and after an injury you have to relearn a lifetime of tolerance, so that you're as good as you were. Guys have a tendency to come back too early and try and be a hero. If they don't have things taken care of, they're going to reinjure themselves, or another part of the body, trying to overcompensate.

"So much of rehab is psychological. You're going to react based on your experiences. If you've never had injuries, you're going to be sensitive to any pain or discomfort. Chris has had a laundry list of stuff, so he's able to push through the pain and move on. That's what makes him special. He's here every day doing whatever we tell him to do."

Canty already could train with the rest of the group on the bench press. The plan was for him to run in three weeks. It was too ambitious to think that he could run at the NFL combine, but the University of Virginia's pro day on March 23 was a possibility.

It also was imperative that Canty ace the Cybex test at the combine. In Indianapolis, every athlete is strapped into a chair and told to extend and pull back the leg. During the test, the machine is set at various speeds and it tests the player's ability to produce force in both directions. For players with healthy knees, the test is a routine procedure. But for those like Canty with knee issues, the Cybex is given considerable weight.

Canty already was well ahead of Willis McGahee, who tore three of the four ligaments in his left knee two years earlier in the Fiesta Bowl at Sun Devil Stadium, which Canty could see while seated in the cold plunge. McGahee, then a running back for the University of Miami, declared early for the NFL draft anyway, and still was selected in the first round by the Buffalo Bills. He was unable to play in his rookie season, 2003, but rushed for 1,128 yards in 2004.

"You've got to work very hard to make it back," Canty said. "The toughest part is not being able to do the things I was capable of doing. I've been blessed that so far the knee hasn't hiccupped even a little bit. It's not painful now."

When Canty considered applying for the NFL Draft in 2004, the league's advisory committee projected him as a "not higher than second-round" pick, which Canty interpreted as strong second-round potential.

"I'd like to get back to that, if not improve," Canty said. "And I think that's possible, once teams see how my body looks, the athleticism, and how hard I've worked to get back. All I can say is look at the tape. The tape doesn't lie. I'm a good player. I have confidence in my ability. If I'm not a first-round or second-round guy, as long as I get an opportunity to get into the league and prove myself, I know I'll be there for a long time."

Darryl Blackstock kept people guessing until the end about whether or not he'd go pro. On January 13, just days before the deadline to declare for the NFL Draft, the linebacker opted to leave the University of Virginia after his junior season.

Unlike Canty, Pearman, or Miller, Blackstock did not wear the student athlete title well, struggling at Virginia. His son, Savion, now was seventeen months old and he had to pay off the twenty thousand dollars in debt he accrued supporting the child and his mother by the end of the 2004 football season.

Not long after the Cavaliers season ended, Blackstock applied to the NFL's advisory committee for a rating on where he might go in the draft. Virginia head coach Al Groh didn't discourage underclassmen from doing this, but he didn't exactly encourage it either. He preferred to have players rely on him and his vast network of NFL sources. Given Groh's well-traveled NFL past, it was hard to argue with him.

Heath Miller did not bother with the NFL committee. Groh told him he was ready to be successful at the NFL level and that he would be one of the top tight ends taken, either in the first or second round. "That was good enough for me," Miller said.

Blackstock, however, wondered if Groh could provide an objective opinion on his status. After all, nobody believed that Miller, who was polished as a player and on track to graduate in May, should return for a fifth season. Blackstock, for all his skill as a pass rusher, still was a raw talent who could benefit from a fourth season in college.

Like many players, Blackstock interpreted his rating from the NFL advisory committee of "will not be drafted higher than the second round" to mean "strong second-round possibility." After all, the next-highest rating was "he will be drafted in round one." But the next-lowest rating was "he will not be drafted higher than the fourth round."

What Blackstock and others interpreted as strong second-round status really was a wide range, from early in the second round to late in the third round. During the 2004 draft, that was a difference in signing bonus of $400,000 and $2.3 million.

Blackstock called Groh and told him about his second-round rating.

"That's not what I'm hearing," said Groh, whose sources told him mid- to late-third round.

Until the letter, Blackstock still was on the bubble. He wanted to go pro, but didn't want to leave if it meant getting drafted low. He gave little credence to the predraft Internet hype about how he was the perfect outside linebacker for the NFL's increasingly popular 3–4 defenses, relentless in pursuit of quarterbacks, and equally capable of covering receivers out of the backfield. He thought little about the knee injuries to Canty and Anthony Poindexter, the Virginia running backs coach who, like Canty, gave up a chance to go pro after his junior year.

Given the NFL advisory committee's history of conservative ratings—nobody wants a player to be overly optimistic—Blackstock expected a third-round projection, which is what it was. But by misinterpreting the NFL's rating as strong second-round status, the decision was easy for a player with one foot already out the door.

"Any athlete that is good will tell you, 'You love football, man. That's what you want to do while you can do it,'" Blackstock said. "Can't nobody sit there and lie and tell you that school is first, football is next. That's a lie. That's just a big lie. Any athlete that really loves football—basketball, baseball, golf, hockey—you think about it all day long. You think about it all day. When you walk, you try and walk so you can plant at the corner. I'll be walking by people in the mall and they're thinking I'm crazy. It's something that comes with it. I love football. I'm not a school guy, anyone can tell you that. I have a problem doing things I don't like to do. It's not like a lot of stuff. It's not like I can only do this and hate everything else. Out of ten things, I won't like two. It's a matter of doing things you don't want to do."

Groh issued a statement that, while diplomatic, clearly lacked the hearty endorsement that he had given Miller days earlier.

"Darryl played a significant role in a lot of games that we have won," Groh said. "He is a talented player and we wish great success for him with this next challenge."

On Miller: "There is a significant difference between a player's being ready to be drafted and that of a player being ready to play well in the NFL," Groh said. "Heath clearly fits into both categories. We fully support his decision to start his NFL career."

Blackstock had spoken frequently with Chris Slade, the former Virginia defensive end whose school-record forty career sacks Blackstock had a chance of breaking by returning. Slade, who had played for the New England Patriots while Groh was linebackers coach under Parcells, stressed the benefits of an extra year of seasoning without lobbying for a return. "Ultimately, it's your decision," he said.

Slade made a strong pitch for his former agent, Brad Blank, who was actively recruiting Blackstock and trying to reestablish the Cavalier client pipeline he enjoyed for most of the 1990s. Blackstock considered Blank seriously before signing with SFX Sports agent Ben Dogra.

For Groh, who liked to think he had a big influence on his players' predraft decision making, Blackstock's agent selection meant not one of Virginia's five major draft hopefuls selected a representative from the group Groh invited to Charlottesville the previous summer.

That group included Blank and Anthony Agnone, who represented Atlanta Falcons defensive end and Virginia alumnus Patrick Kerney. There was Ralph Cindrich, whose forty clients included former Virginia linebacker James Farrior. There was Jimmy Sexton, agent for numerous NFL players and coaches, including Bill Parcells. There was Joe Linta, a Connecticut-based representative; and Alan Herman, who represented veteran wide receiver Ricky Proehl, who had played for Groh at Wake Forest.

In addition to Miller (IMG), Canty (Ethan Lock), Alvin Pearman (David Dunn), and Blackstock (SFX), guard Elton Brown chose Joel Segal. (Agnone signed defensive tackle Andrew Hoffman, considered a possible late-round selection.)

Groh said that in return for the access of agent day he asks agents "not to harass the players during the season, without asking them to put themselves at a competitive disadvantage."

"We play by Al's rules, not bothering players when Al doesn't want them bothered," Blank said. "I don't know. It seems if you play by the rules, you get shut out."

Not long after signing with Dogra, Blackstock flew to Phoenix, where he became one of the last members of the Athletes' Performance combine-training class of 2005 to arrive. He would have an opportunity to catch up quickly, since, as a junior, he was ineligible to play in post-season all-star games.

So, while Blackstock hung back at Athletes' Performance the last week of January with fellow juniors such as Brodney Pool and Richie Incognito, fifteen players left to showcase their talents for NFL scouts at the most prestigious of the postseason bowl games.

The Senior Bowl combined the medical exams and interviews of the combine with a week of practice and a game. It was a sort of Twilight Zone experience between college and pro football, and the first important signpost to the NFL Draft.

Chapter Eleven:

THE ALL-STAR
MEAT MARKET

F red Gibson stepped off an escalator into the second-floor lobby of the Riverview Plaza Hotel in Mobile, Alabama, and suddenly felt like a rock star. Everywhere he turned someone wanted a piece of him. There were kids and adults looking for his signature on footballs, NFL scouts looking for a quick interview, and television crews hoping for a few sound bytes.

Having played four years of college football at the University of Georgia, Gibson was used to the attention. But this was something else entirely.

It was Sunday, January 23, 2005, the opening day of Senior Bowl week, the undercard to the NFL combine that would take place a month later in Indianapolis. One hundred and three of the top seniors were on hand for a week of interviews, practices, and glad-handing in the hope of improving their stock for the NFL Draft.

The Senior Bowl itself, played the following Saturday, would be anticlimactic, with most NFL executives long since departed, having watched a week's worth of practice. They would watch tape of the game later. The real action would take place on the practice fields and in the Riverview lobby.

Gibson negotiated his way through the crowd. Many teams had staked out tables, as if set up for a career fair, which in a sense it was.

The New Orleans Saints were alongside a local radio outlet, 93-BLX, "The Big Station." A potted palm separated the Saints from the Seattle Seahawks. The Washington Redskins and Chicago Bears carved out territory across the room.

Long white banners were posted on the walls, with the words FOOD WORLD in bold red type, the words separated by a globe, in reference to the local supermarket that served as the game's title sponsor.

Scouts, decked out in official team logo clothing, corralled passing players to fill out questionnaires. In the center of the room, Senior Bowl staff members handed out green credentials that were the same for everyone: agents, NFL officials, media, family members, hangers-on. Jerry Jones, the owner of the Dallas Cowboys, wore the same credential as David Levine, a South Florida agent who had no clients in the game but, like so many other agents, came to Mobile looking to tout his clients to NFL brass. (Levine's top client, University of Miami running back Frank Gore, had given up his final year of eligibility two weeks earlier. As a junior, Gore was ineligible for the Senior Bowl.)

All told, the Senior Bowl issued more than 1,200 credentials, including more than 700 to NFL officials (an average of more than 20 per franchise), 300 to agents, family members, and job seekers, and more than 200 to media members.

Though it was an impressive gathering of NFL talent and administration, there were few sportswriters on hand, as evidenced by the boxes of Krispy Kreme donuts in the middle of the lobby that had gone virtually untouched. NFL team beat writers had little interest in the event, since none of the players were yet affiliated with a pro franchise.

Not only that, but many writers were in Philadelphia for the NFC championship between the Eagles and Falcons, or in Pittsburgh for the AFC title game between the Steelers and New England Patriots.

Gibson walked by the Krispy Kremes. Players knew better than to grab an original glazed in full view of potential NFL employers, though Gibson might have been given some leeway. At six-four and 193 pounds, he needed at least seven more pounds on his lanky frame to compete in the NFL. As if to take the focus off of his frame, he wore a baggy gray Georgia sweatshirt, baggy white-and-blue shorts, and black Nike sneakers. A yellow badge worn around his neck—FRED GIBSON, UNIVERSITY OF GEORGIA—completed the ensemble.

Ever gregarious, Gibson worked the lobby like a politician. He hugged fellow players and his agents. He embraced other agents—most players got to know at least four or five well during the recruiting process—even reporters. Gibson spotted Georgia quarterback David Greene and greeted him with a sweeping handshake and embrace, as if he had not seen him in months, instead of hours. The lobby lights sparkled off Gibson's diamond stud earrings as he signed official thirty-five-dollar Senior Bowl footballs, among the many souvenir items available in the lobby.

"It's like Mardi Gras in here," said Gibson, unaware that the event had just kicked off in Mobile, site of the original Mardi Gras celebration. "I'm not sure how I'm going to get out."

Doug Hendrickson, one of Gibson's two Octagon representatives, watched him and smiled. "Fred is so outgoing. He loves people. When teams get to know him, they'll love the guy on a personal level. He just has to show teams he's consistent on the field. He's got great hands and doesn't have many flaws. If you look at receivers in the NFL, he can overcome any shortcomings through practice and repetition. And a year or two from now, he could weigh 220 pounds."

As Gibson signed for fans, professional autograph hounds jockeyed for position. Along one wall, Jim Dodson of Palm Beach Autographs worked out of a duffel bag. He spotted Kay-Jay Harris and cornered the running back from West Virginia University.

Harris, who had played three years of minor league baseball for the Texas Rangers, was no stranger to the autograph transaction. "I see these going for twenty-five bucks on eBay," he said.

"I'll give you seventy-five for twenty-five," Dodson said.

Harris shrugged and dropped to one knee beside a console table, a Luis Vuitton bag slung over a shoulder. Dodson handed him a black Sharpie pen and the first photo. Players, agents, NFL scouts, and reporters filed by, unfazed by the transaction. Scouts from the San Francisco 49ers and Carolina Panthers waited patiently for a Harris interview.

As Harris finished each signature, he handed the photo to Dodson, without looking up. Dodson shook each photo to dry the signature. It was an action shot of Harris running in his Mountaineers uniform. Harris completed his work in less than two minutes.

"Won't these photos be worthless once he's drafted?" Dodson was asked.

"That's the irony," Dodson said, opening his wallet and handing Harris the money. "You can't get to these guys when they're in school, but diehard West Virginia fans want the stuff of them in school. So you have to move fast to capitalize on the market."

At the moment, the market for Fred Gibson was white hot. The Miami Dolphins had taken over some key lobby real estate beyond the ballrooms, behind a piano. Two scouts escorted Gibson out of the main lobby fray, past the Alabama Ballroom.

Gibson poked his head in the door. Inside, more than a hundred scouts were watching the NFC championship on a movie theater–sized screen. The Eagles led the Falcons 20–10 at the start of the fourth quarter. As a Georgia native, Gibson felt a connection to the hometown team. His Georgia Bulldogs had practiced several times at the Falcons indoor facility during bad weather in Athens.

"It doesn't look too good." he said.

Inside the Alabama Ballroom, nine members of the Atlanta Falcons scouting department occupied a center table. They wore stylish black-and-red Falcons gear, their faces showing no emotion as their employer's unlikely storybook season ended one game shy of the Super Bowl.

Their boss, Falcons president and general manager Rich McKay, was scheduled to arrive the next day to oversee the scouting process. So was Tim Ruskell, the assistant general manager. Both would arrive disappointed, though no doubt consoled by having reached the NFC title game in their first full seasons since leaving the Tampa Bay Buccaneers.

Across the Alabama Ballroom, Buccaneers head coach Jon Gruden sat at a table with Monte Kiffin, his defensive coordinator. Gruden and Kiffin, like the players, were among the few people wearing yellow passes instead of green.

Gruden and his staff were on hand to coach the Senior Bowl's South team, a unit dominated by players from the Southeastern Conference and Atlantic Coast Conference. The Oakland Raiders, led by head coach Norv Turner, would coach the North squad.

For many years, Senior Bowl coaching duties were offered to the two teams with the best records that did not make the playoffs. It was a plum assignment, the opportunity to spend a week working with potential draft picks. Not surprisingly, teams that coached the Senior Bowl often selected players from the game, picks that often turned out well.

The Raiders and Buccaneers coached the game in 1999, and the Bucs produced a stellar draft that included defensive tackle Anthony McFarland in the first round, quarterback Shaun King in the second, kicker Martin Gramatica in the third, and safety Dexter Jackson, the future

Most Valuable Player of Super Bowl XXXVII, in the fourth. The Raiders picked up one of the draft's biggest steals, defensive lineman Rod Coleman, in the fifth round.

"Coaching the event gives you one more behind-the-scenes look," McKay said. "When you go into the colleges in the fall, you can see the kid practice, and talk to coaches. But even that, to a certain extent, can be staged, depending on the approach of the coach to protecting the players. Here, you can't hide and there's no question there's a benefit to coaching the game."

In recent years, the NFL has offered Senior Bowl coaching duties to the teams with the worst records. For the 2005 game, the invitation went first to the Miami Dolphins and San Francisco 49ers. Both teams declined, what with their staffs in flux with recent coaching changes. The NFL went down the line until Tampa Bay and Oakland accepted, thus pitting teams that had met in the Super Bowl two years earlier but finished 5-11 in 2004.

With 3:21 left in the fourth quarter, the Eagles scored again to push the lead to 27–10. The Falcons table did not flinch. Nor did Gruden, a former Eagles assistant who no doubt took some pleasure in seeing McKay fall short of a Super Bowl return.

With 1:47 remaining, the Eagles began celebrating. Head coach Andy Reid was doused with Gatorade. Two Falcons scouts stood up. Matt Berry, one of the younger members of the staff, shook his head as he walked out the room. "I didn't need to see that."

By the time the Atlanta Falcons season had officially ended, the scouting staff was back in the lobby preparing for 2005. Scouting director Phil Emery grabbed Ole Miss offensive lineman Marcus Johnson in the lobby and they sat down at a table abandoned by the Bears. Berry and Bob Harrison, the Falcons mid-Atlantic region scout, nabbed Virginia Tech cornerback Eric Green and escorted him to a semiprivate enclave of leather chairs off of the main lobby. Alex Page, who was not a scout but worked as a "college scouting assistant," pinned down Georgia quarterback David Greene for an interview.

"What other sports did you play in high school?" Page asked.

"Baseball."

"What position?"

Four hours later, the New England Patriots had defeated the Pittsburgh Steelers to advance to meet the Eagles in Super Bowl XXXIX. The lobby crowd had thinned and there were more empty tables. The Falcons had the largest presence in the room; all nine scouts continued to grab players for interviews. Perhaps it was because they missed time watching the NFC title game—or found added motivation because of the result.

"Not necessarily," said Taylor Morton, a younger Falcons scout who works the Southeast. "We'd love to be going to the Super Bowl, but our job is to get ready for the draft."

Morton stood in the middle of the lobby scanning for players, as if playing safety. He held a deck of business-sized cards with the Falcons logo and spaces to fill in an interview date and time. Like the rest of his colleagues, he was filling the dance cards of McKay and Ruskell.

"We'll do some interviewing here in the lobby, but later in the week we'll sit them down with Rich and Tim and go more in-depth," Morton said.

Fred Gibson reemerged in the main lobby and was nabbed by Boyd Dowler, who at sixty-seven was the elder statesman of the Falcons scouting staff and, technically, the tallest wide receiver at the Senior Bowl. At six-five, the former star of the 1960s Green Bay Packers had more than an inch on Gibson.

Dowler caught 448 passes for the Packers, was named to the NFL's All-Decade team, and served as an assistant coach for five NFL teams in the '70s and early '80s. Were this a hotel in Wisconsin, Dowler would have been the one signing autographs. Instead, he was stalking twenty-two-year-olds alongside scouts young enough to be his grandsons.

Not surprisingly, McKay and Ruskell put a lot of stock in Dowler's interview reports. All-star games like the Senior Bowl are the first chance for scouts to talk to players. Though they've been around the athletes for months, watching practices, standing on the sidelines before games, and watching games from press boxes, they never talk to players. By now they've spoken to coaches, tutors, compliance directors, and anyone else they think might hold a valuable opinion on the character and work ethic of a player. Now they get their first shot at hearing from the players firsthand.

"There are some con guys out there," Dowler said. "When the answers come out of their mouths before you're finished with the question, you know they've been prepped by their agent. They know what you're going to ask and they've got a canned answer, and you can tell. They try to tell us what they think we want to hear, not necessarily what they believe. They'll answer the question to make themselves look good to the scouts. Sometimes you notice, sometimes you don't. You won't know for sure what they're like until you've spent a few years around them. The goal is to have a pretty good idea between now and April."

Dowler wasn't entirely sold on Gibson. "He's a good kid and has the talent, but is he consistent enough to thrive in the NFL? I'm not sure."

After just three hours at the Senior Bowl, including an hour-long interrogation by the Miami Dolphins, Gibson was a veteran of the NFL scouting interview. Already the questions were becoming repetitive, in that sense not unlike the pattern of media queries he had endured for years.

"They want to know what you love most about football. Obviously, to win—that's a pretty simple answer. They ask about background. 'Have you been arrested? Do you have a valid driver's license—or has it been suspended?' They try to know everything about you because they're investing millions of dollars in you. They ask you, 'Who is the best cornerback you've ever faced? What are all the positions you played in college?' They ask, if I was a defensive back on the other team, what would worry me about Fred Gibson? What are his weak points?"

Dowler gave Gibson a Falcons card and a time to meet with McKay the following evening. "I feel like they've grabbed me ten times already, which is great," Gibson said. "I hope they're interested. They've asked me about my speed and ability to catch balls in a crowd. They asked for one weakness I could get better on. I said, 'I get all the hard catches, but some of the easy ones I miss. I try to run before I catch the ball, and I need to work on that.'"

David Greene emerged from another interview and signed a few autographs; the hounds never leave the lobby. He too had faced the Falcons scouts, though it was unlikely Atlanta would take the hometown quarterback. The team had superstar Michael Vick at quarterback, along with promising backup Matt Schaub.

"You never know," Greene said. "You have to assume everyone has sincere interest. What Georgia kid wouldn't want to play for the Falcons? The key is to be prepared for anything. Guys have different tactics. Some are informal, some are as formal as it gets, like an interrogation. You have to be prepared for both situations. It's almost like a good-cop/bad-cop routine. One guy loosens you up and the other one drills you. They want to see how you're going to react. It's really like an interrogation. 'Tell me about this. You ever been arrested? What do you hate most about football?'"

Greene had a clean track record, but Gibson had one major blemish.

In May of 2003 he was one of nine Georgia players accused of violating NCAA rules for selling their championship rings. The NCAA did not penalize the players, because of the lack of precedent and the unclear nature of the rules involved. Still, it's something NFL teams want to investigate, just to make sure Gibson is not a character liability.

"I'm up front about it," Gibson says. "You have to be. The teams know and they want to see if you're going to bring it up. They wait until the end of the interview and then ask, 'Anything else we should know?' So I explain everything. I gave it to one of my teammates. He said this dude wanted to buy it for four thousand dollars. I thought he was kidding, but I gave it to him and got four thousand dollars in cash. Someone's ring ended up on eBay and then it all came out. I had to pay the school back. You learn from your mistakes. Nobody is perfect. If that's the worst thing I've ever done, I don't think that should count too much against me."

At 10:30 on Monday morning, January 24, 2005, the Alabama Ballroom was packed. More than six hundred scouts had taken their seats, waiting for the meat market to begin.

A small dais was constructed in the front of the room, with an electronic scale. Tape was posted on the back wall, marked in increments from five-six to seven feet.

Outside the ballroom, the members of the South Team stripped down to identical black shorts and white socks. As the doors opened, a hush fell over the crowd and the players entered the room alphabetically, lining up stage right along the wall.

Senior Bowl officials had given out sheets with each player's name listed, along with their arm and hand measurements. There were spaces for scouts to fill in height, weight, and "body type," referring to whether the player was muscular or soft, lanky or fat.

The players were announced one by one. Each player entered from the right of the stage, stood on the scale, and then had his height measured. After his vitals were announced, he walked through the center of the room, giving scouts a closer look. All that was missing was a catwalk.

Over the years, players tried to stack the odds in their favor. There were stories of rocks hidden in pockets, multiple layers of socks. At least one player had wet his pants on the stage, having chugged too much water beforehand.

Fred Gibson, looking thinner than ever without a shirt, was announced at 6.035 (translation: six-three and five-eighths inches) and 194 pounds. David Greene, appearing even paler than usual amid the mostly African-American roster, was announced at 6.027, 223 pounds.

A few players flexed their biceps before leaving the stage, mimicking a boxing weigh-in. The scouts did not react; they had seen every attempt to lighten the mood through the years. When the players reached the back of the room, scouts approached to set up more interviews.

"It's like a meat market, which I guess is the point," Gibson said as he got dressed outside in the lobby. "I was proud of the way I looked. I didn't weigh what I wanted to, but nobody else did either. You're half naked up there, but that's how it is. Everyone's got to do it."

Greene nodded. "You've got the spotlight on the stage and you're in there with nothing but your shorts on. If you've got any flaws, you will be exposed."

The North squad came in next. Darren Sproles, a talented if undersized running back from Kansas State, showed no emotion as he endured the most embarrassing moment of the weigh-in. Since he fell just shy of five-six he had to wait as officials readjusted the height chart. If there was anyone in the room unaware of Sproles's lack of size, they had a few awkward seconds to consider it.

The verdict: five-five and six-eighths inches.

"It wasn't that bad," Sproles said afterward. "I've dealt with it all my life. When you're a running back, it really shouldn't matter. You have to run low to the ground anyway. I consider it more of an advantage to be so short. Look at Warrick Dunn in Atlanta and LaDainian Tomlinson with the Chargers. They're little guys."

Mike Nugent, a five-nine kicker from Ohio State, looked the most out of place amid the giants. He tried to appear confident as he took the stage. He tipped the scales at 179.

"Couldn't they have just given me the extra pound?" Nugent asked. "Like it's going to matter for a kicker. I might have just experienced the only time a guy would ever feel so inadequate about measuring five-nine and 179 pounds. I'm basically the size of the average American male. I guess they needed somebody like me up there to remind people of how huge everyone else is."

The road to the NFL goes through some unlikely places. On Monday afternoon many of the NFL's top executives and coaches drove fifteen miles east of Mobile to the town of Fairhope, and Fairhope Municipal Stadium, a field normally used for high school football games.

As school kids scampered through an adjacent playground and townspeople gathered around the fences, Jon Gruden's South squad got ready for practice. A five-lane asphalt track separated the fans from the field, which was ringed three deep by NFL executives, scouts, and media.

Among the luminaries were Dallas Cowboys owner Jerry Jones and head coach Bill Parcells, Indianapolis Colts head coach Tony Dungy, and Dick Vermeil, head coach of the Kansas City Chiefs. Agents walked circles around the field, talking on cell phone headsets.

The onlookers knew to keep a close eye on the action. Though the players were practicing in shorts, in theory going at three-quarters speed, they also were trying to impress NFL scouts. A year earlier, Falcons assistant general manager Tim Ruskell suffered a broken leg when he failed to get out of the way of players running out of bounds.

On this, the first day of Senior Bowl practice, the agent community was abuzz about young Todd France, the Atlanta agent who landed Auburn stars Ronnie Brown and Carlos Rogers, along with Georgia safety Thomas Davis—all projected as first-round picks.

Only Rogers was playing in the Senior Bowl. Davis, a junior who gave up his final year of eligibility, was ineligible. Brown, like a lot of projected top-ten picks, opted not to play in the game, figuring it could not help his draft status—and possibly hurt with a bad showing or injury. Interestingly, fellow Auburn running back Carnell "Cadillac" Williams, who competed with Brown for carries, had opted to play on the advice of his SFX Sports agent Ben Dogra, wary that the Buccaneers and Raiders, with early first-round picks, both were in need of running backs. Gruden, the coach of the South team, would get a chance to test drive a Cadillac.

The scouts carried roster sheets, though none were necessary. The players wore their college helmets, and, besides, the scouts had been watching them for six months already. The Senior Bowl was the last and most prestigious of the six postseason bowl games, and the talent pool was deep, though not as deep as it could have been.

Many of the top stars like Brown turned down invitations upon the advice of their agents, preferring to spend the week training for the NFL combine. Why risk injury or tainting a sterling college career with a bad week of practice for an exhibition game?

Blue-chip prospects could afford such a position, which explained the absences of Texas running back Cedric Benson and Michigan wide receiver Braylon Edwards. Miami cornerback Antrel Rolle did not accept his Senior Bowl invite. Nor did defensive ends David Pollack (Georgia) and Erasmus James (Wisconsin), or Alex Barron, the promising offensive tackle from Florida State.

The Senior Bowl was more attractive for players who had soared up the draft boards during the season and wanted to build upon that momentum. The South roster was full of such players, like Auburn quarterback Jason Campbell and Demarcus Ware, the defensive end from Troy State.

The week leading up to the game gave players a chance to address shortcomings in practice. Greene, the Georgia quarterback, needed to show athleticism. Matt Jones, who played quarterback at Arkansas, wanted to demonstrate that he could play wide receiver or tight end in the NFL. For Oklahoma's Mark Clayton, the idea was to show that a five-ten wide receiver was worth a first-round pick.

As the South practice ended, scouts, agents, and reporters swarmed the field. Fans and VIPs who had scored the familiar green passes also converged, pens and autograph material in hand. In a repeat of the previous night's lobby scene, scouts conducted flyby interviews and arranged times for more thorough investigations.

Todd Brunner, a scout for the San Francisco 49ers, managed to get an audience with Florida State cornerback Bryant McFadden between autograph seekers.

"Would you say you consider yourself a leader?" Brunner asked.

"Definitely," McFadden said, signing an autograph.

"Who was the vocal leader of the secondary? You? Jerome Carter?"

Jerome Carter played safety for the Seminoles. Unlike McFadden, who was projected as a first- or second-round pick, Carter was considered a lesser prospect. He played two weeks earlier in the Gridiron Classic, an Orlando game featuring players likely to get drafted in the later rounds, if at all.

"Mostly J. C., but both of us to some degree," McFadden said.

"How do you learn: classroom, film, on the field?"

"A combination of everything."

"What's your vertical [leap]?"

"Thirty-nine, forty [inches]." The players will be tested in the vertical jump at the NFL combine in Indianapolis.

"Think you can do that in Indianapolis?"

"Oh yeah."

All around the field, agents huddled with their clients. They were not there for any particular purpose, other than to offer congratulations on a fine practice, show support, and, perhaps most important, keep other agents from approaching their hard-earned, recently signed clients.

As Todd France chatted with Carlos Rogers, Pat Dye Jr. and his partner Bill Johnson spoke with two of their clients: Greene, the Georgia quarterback, and Ware, the defensive end from Troy State. Dye and Johnson already had touched base with Georgia wide receiver Reggie Brown and offensive tackle Ray Willis, whom they had successfully reconnected with during Florida State agent day in November.

Ware was Dye's prized signing, a product of the existing client network. Mike Pelton, who coached the defensive ends at Troy State, had played at Auburn for Pat Dye Sr. in the early 1990s. Dye Jr. represented Pelton during his brief NFL career.

Dye had heard the buzz about France and had taken note of the snickering about how the kid beat the veteran at Auburn and Georgia.

"He kicked our ass on three guys we wanted bad: Rogers, Davis, and Brown. I don't get it. He's never had a first-round player since he's been in the business, and to sign three top-twenty picks—wow, what a year! My hat's off to him. I told him congratulations. He works hard. I'll give him that. He's a hell of a lot smoother a talker than I am. This is my eighteenth draft and Senior Bowl, and I've had fifteen or twenty first-round picks and he's had none. If I'm one of those players, I don't know. I would have thought one of them signs with us. But I give the guy credit. He worked hard and I'm sure he'll do a good job for them. We'd been talking to those guys for two years. Between the two schools [Georgia and Auburn], we've got upwards of twenty-five clients from those two schools. Out of thirty-six guys we have on active rosters. That's two-thirds of our client base. But, hey, he's working hard. He's single. He doesn't have to worry about being on the road all the time, family. I was his age not that long ago."

Not that Dye had a bad recruiting season. Besides Greene, Brown, Ware, and Willis, he also signed Ben Wilkerson, a center from LSU. Still, in a year in which Auburn and Georgia were arguably the two most attractive colleges for agent recruiting, the agent that had dominated those schools for more than a decade couldn't help but feel defeated.

"We signed a good class. Ben Wilkerson is a top-rated center. Demarcus Ware, who many people have never heard of, is going to be a first-round pick. Reggie Brown is a climber in the draft, will go in the first two rounds, and David Greene is a freakin' icon in the state of Georgia. So it is a good class.

"But when you've got Thomas Davis, Ronnie Brown, Carnell Williams, and Carlos Rogers, all of whom we recruited very actively for two years, and don't get any of those guys, that is *very* disappointing and it's one of those things that just makes you shake your head on the rationale. I'm sure they have different reasons for not choosing us and I'm going to do everything I can in the next three months to learn why."

It was hardly time for Dye to panic. He had a solid draft class, to be sure, to say nothing of one of the deepest client rosters in the game. But as he told Greene his room number at the Riverview Hotel, he shook his head at the irony. No longer did he have a stranglehold on Auburn and Georgia, which presented a crisis of sorts for ProFiles Sports Management.

Dye was staying in room 911.

France's recruiting efforts also had yielded Kerry Rhodes, a safety from Louisville, Wake Forest cornerback Eric King, and Josh Davis, a wide receiver from Marshall. France did so well that he actually lost a client, Oklahoma State cornerback Darrent Williams, because Williams believed France could not give him the attention he needed while dealing with three consensus first-round picks. Williams fired France and hired Momentum Sports agents Jeff Griffin and Jack Scharf.

Williams was training at Athletes' Performance, setting up a potential replay of the previous year, when DeAngelo Hall fired Ethan Lock and hired Joel Segal after arriving in Arizona. Under the new rules, France could ask Williams to leave the facility, but he let him stay. Momentum, of course, would foot the bill.

France, having seen Carlos Rogers back to the team bus that would take the South squad back to the Riverview Hotel, made no apologies for his success.

"If I had just started in the business and had no clients and had never done any contracts and got a first-rounder, then even I would ask, 'How the heck did this guy do it? That's phenomenal. How did he do it?' I'm not going to sit here and pat myself on the back and say nobody without a first-rounder has ever gone out and gotten three first-rounders. It's hard work. They made their decision. I won; I almost won before, but being second doesn't count. The reality is I have a great list of clients, some big names, some medium, some smaller names. Some more well known. The reality is I've done good deals and have some big deals. I don't have to apologize for anything."

On Wednesday night during Senior Bowl week, Jack "Show Me" Scharf sat down at a table near the lobby bar at the Riverview Hotel with some unlikely companions: Ed Hawthorne, Ed Walsh, and Chris Singletary, an agent from IMG.

Nearly three weeks had passed since Ed Hawthorne called Scharf with the news that his nephew, Anttaj, would be signing with IMG agent Tom Condon. That decision cost Scharf a possible six-figure commission and his first surefire blue-chip client. Still, the men talked as if they were all old friends.

They sat near the foot of the escalator and watched as a parade of Mobile socialites and their husbands proceeded to the Alabama ballroom for the latest VIP reception. Actually, anyone with a green pass could attend, which included just about everyone. The buffet of fried foods was the same each evening, even if the sponsor and theme changed. Tonight's motif was "Seafood Jubilee," sponsored by a wireless phone company. A cloud of smoke hung over the lobby; Alabama had yet to ban indoor smoking.

"You're watching something that never happens," Scharf says. "An agent that lost out on a prominent client is sitting with the family. It never happens."

The group visited for more than an hour. Scharf picked up a bar tab in excess of one hundred dollars before the party broke up.

Of course, it's not uncommon for runner-up agents to keep in touch with would-be clients. Football players switch representatives frequently. Could Scharf have been jockeying for rebounding position?

"There might be a little bit of truth to that," he said later. "The bottom line is that it's rare in any profession when you have an opportunity to meet people you respect as much as I got to know Ed Hawthorne. It's very rare. I don't keep a relationship for the sake of it becoming fruitful in the business sense, bringing me some monetary reward. Though, if it happens, it happens."

Norv Turner's North team defeated Jon Gruden's South squad, 23–13, to win the Senior Bowl. Even in defeat, it was a good afternoon for David Greene, who completed eleven of sixteen passes for 102 yards and a touchdown. Fred Gibson caught two passes for 43 yards, but also fumbled a kickoff return.

Back in Tempe, Arizona, Chris Canty watched the Senior Bowl at his apartment after a brief workout at the Athletes' Performance training center. The place seemed empty, what with half of the NFL hopefuls in Mobile for the week.

That was fine with Canty, who for the last month had worked tirelessly to rehabilitate the knee he injured in September. So, while players like Gibson, fellow Virginia player Darryl Blackstock, and Auburn running backs Ronnie Brown and Carnell "Cadillac" Williams worked on their vertical leaps and forty-yard dash performances, Canty endured a grueling regimen of physical therapy.

The hard work was beginning to pay off. Training at Athletes' Performance began at 8:00 A.M. each morning. Canty always was the first player there, no later than 7:30. Though the combine was a month away, he felt confident that he would be ready to perform many of the drills in Indianapolis. Draft Web sites already were touting Canty's remarkable comeback.

Canty was, by his own admission, something of a loner. That had become more apparent during the season after his injury, when he no longer felt like a member of the Virginia Cavaliers. It was not that he was not friendly and approachable; his mother, Shirley, was a pastor in Charlotte, and Chris inherited her outgoing demeanor, but Chris preferred solitude, even living alone during his final year at school. After undergoing surgery in Birmingham in September, he returned home to Charlotte. Having graduated the previous May, there was little incentive to stay at the University of Virginia, not even the school's legendary reputation for partying.

It was Saturday night in Phoenix, the one night where Canty and the rest of the NFL hopefuls did not have to go to bed early to be ready for early-morning training. So he decided to accompany a few of his new friends to a pulsing, two-story nightclub called Axis/Radius, in Scottsdale. One of Canty's agents, Vance Malinovic, held a modest, indirect ownership stake in the club, having invested in a partnership that purchased several Scottsdale properties.

It's usually not a good idea for prominent athletes, especially larger ones, to enter a contained area where liquor is served. Canty arrived with Erasmus James, Jovan Haye, and Richie Incognito, all of whom stand at least six-two and weigh more than 270 pounds.

The club was packed when the group arrived around 11:30 P.M. and the players got separated. Canty and Incognito, a six-two, three hundred-pound lineman with a history of anger management issues, ended up in a VIP section upstairs. While navigating the area around

1:00 A.M., they brushed up against a patron sitting at the bar. The man jumped up and began yelling and waving a small flashlight in their faces.

Words were exchanged and accounts of what happened next vary, according to the Scottsdale police report. Canty said he and Incognito headed downstairs toward the exit after a profanity-laced exchange with the flashlight-wielding patron. Incognito said that the situation upstairs escalated into pushing and shoving, and bouncers escorted everyone downstairs.

Either way, Canty and Incognito were standing near the exit when Canty was struck in the face with a beer bottle. Canty says he never saw it coming; Incognito told a Scottsdale detective the assailant was the guy from upstairs. (Canty did not decide to press charges until days later. Incognito could not pick the alleged assailant out of a photo lineup and no arrest ever was made.)

In the darkness and cacophony of Axis/Radius, Canty fell to the floor. He reached up to his left eye and came back with a handful of blood. Someone helped him take off his shirt to apply pressure.

Though vision in his left eye was blurry, Canty assumed it was from blood trickling from his forehead or eyelid. It wasn't until an EMT took a look at the eye on the ambulance ride to the hospital that Canty grew concerned.

"Buddy, your eye has been cut," the EMT said.

From there, things seemed to proceed on fast-forward. Doctors were telling Canty he had a detached retina and they would need to operate momentarily. Two of Canty's agents, Malinovic and Ethan Lock, hustled to the hospital.

It was nearly 2:00 A.M. Mountain Time. Feeling disoriented and suffering from blurred vision, Canty managed two coherent thoughts. First, he did not want to call his father and mother, the Rev. Shirley Canty, and wake them up at 4:00 A.M. Eastern Standard Time.

Mom and dad eventually would understand, Canty knew, but as nurses prepared him for surgery, Canty wondered if he had not endured four months of agonizing knee rehabilitation, only to throw his NFL career away in a Scottsdale bar.

Chapter Twelve:

THE NEED FOR
SPEED

C hip Smith is a devout Christian and a proud American. But when he's asked how he developed his training regimens to prepare for the NFL combine, he's quick to credit the former Soviet Union.

In 1987, Smith was part of a contingent of American trainers who visited the Soviet Sports Institute in Moscow to study the Russians' training methods. The facilities were every bit as drab and depressing as Smith expected, but their philosophies were cutting edge.

Unlike trainers in the United States, who at the time focused their efforts on making athletes big and strong, the Russians concentrated on sport-specific movement, athleticism, and especially speed.

"Their runners were among the fastest in the world," Smith says. "I figured if the Russians could make white guys this fast, they were really on to something."

At the heart of the Russian philosophy, Smith learned, was the notion of "overspeed" training. Children, from a young age, realize they can run downhill at extraordinary speeds. The brain triggers a neuromuscular response that keeps the body from falling.

The Russians discovered that it was possible to replicate that response, through training, by tricking the fast-twitch muscle fibers that fire first when movement begins.

"When you watched [sprinter] Carl Lewis, it looked like he'd accelerate in the middle of the race, leaving everyone behind," Smith says. "But what actually was happening was that he was maintaining that fast-twitch response and everyone else was decelerating."

In Moscow, Smith watched Russian athletes step into a harness attached to a motorized contraption that looked like the grill of a car. The machine would begin to reel in the athlete, who would need to continue that fast-twitch response to maintain his pace. As a result, he ran 10 to 15 percent faster than he normally could.

Back home, Smith simulated the device by using surgical tubing. Soon his athletes were working with harnesses and bungee cords. The muscles work harder while stretching the bungee, and when the cord contracts it produces overspeed, training the athlete to run faster.

"When you take the contraption off, the muscle fibers still think they have resistance," Smith says. "They fire just as fast."

By combining overspeed and resistance training, Smith found athletes could increase both the length and frequency of strides. Contrary to popular belief that speed was something an athlete was born with, Smith discovered it could be taught.

The training had obvious applications for football. After all, it didn't matter how strong a player was or how well he tackled if he couldn't catch the opposing player. The NFL, with its annual combine, became Smith's training ground.

Smith began preparing athletes for the NFL combine in the early 1990s, and when the market exploded at the end of the decade he was in position to capitalize. With a training center located just north of Atlanta in Duluth, he's conveniently located for players from Southern schools, to say nothing of the many agents operating out of Atlanta.

It's hard to overestimate the importance of speed. Ask any NFL rookie to explain the difference between the college and pro game and he'll inevitably talk about how everyone in the NFL is so much faster. It's why NFL scouts spend so much time on evaluating a player's raw speed and quickness.

Smith, fifty, touts his company as the largest preparer of NFL talent, estimating that he's trained more than six hundred players for the NFL combine. Agents who send clients other places use the larger numbers against him, arguing that it's impossible for any staff to provide hands-on guidance to a group of sixty or more kids each year.

The results would seem to indicate otherwise. In 2003, Smith trained the fourth, fifth, and sixth picks in the draft: Kentucky defensive tackle

Dewayne Robertson, Kansas State defensive back Terence Newman, and Johnathan Sullivan, a defensive tackle from the University of Georgia.

Then there was Brian Urlacher. After the 1999 season, agent Steve Kauffman sent the University of New Mexico player to Smith. Urlacher was hardly an unknown, but he was somewhat off the radar screen playing for the Lobos. Plus, he was undersized by NFL linebacker standards, weighing just 235.

Urlacher got a head start on his combine training, since the Lobos did not play in a bowl game after finishing the 1999 season 4-7. Two months of Competitive Edge training later, he weighed a chiseled 258. At the combine, he benched 225 pounds twenty-seven times and ran the forty in under 4.6. With fourteen of the future first-round picks sitting out the event, the fiery Urlacher stole the show. The Chicago Bears selected him with the ninth overall choice.

Smith tells potential clients that he can shave two-tenths of a second off their forty-yard-dash time, increase their bench press by four to five repetitions, improve their vertical leap four to six inches, and help them run faster shuttles.

"From the time I got back from Russia, I realized I could take a guy straight out of Division I football and have phenomenal results," Smith said. "In defense of college strength coaches, they don't have five or six hours a day to spend with players. But when you can get a kid off campus and put him in this focused environment, you can accomplish a lot in two months. Look, I'm not going to take credit for Brian Urlacher. He was a workout warrior who would have played in the NFL whether he met me or not. But I like to think of what I do as taking a diamond in the rough and polishing it and tilting it toward the sun so it sparkles."

Smith's 2005 draft class included Mike Williams, the former Southern Cal wide receiver who tried to enter the 2004 draft after his sophomore season. Williams announced his intention to go pro after a federal judge ruled in favor of Ohio State running back Maurice Clarett, who had challenged the NFL rule requiring that a player be three years removed from high school to enter the draft.

Williams trained with Smith before the 2004 draft, only to have Clarett's ruling overturned on appeal. The NFL managed to keep Williams and Clarett out of the draft and the NCAA refused to let Williams return to the college football ranks.

So Williams spent part of the fall semester training with Smith. Once the college football season was over, Smith's training center again filled up. There was Adam Terry, the offensive lineman from Syracuse, Clemson linebacker Leroy Hill, Kentucky defensive end Vincent Burns, Oklahoma quarterback Jason White, and Karl Paymah, a cornerback from Washington State.

Pat Dye Jr. and Todd France, the Atlanta agents who went head-to-head on Auburn and Georgia recruits, also had talent at Competitive Edge. France sent Auburn's Ronnie Brown and Carlos Rogers to Athletes' Performance in Arizona and Thomas Davis, the Georgia safety who turned pro early, to Velocity Sports, another Atlanta training center. Smith got Louisville safety Kerry Rhodes and Eric King, a cornerback from Wake Forest.

"Different players like different things, so I give them a choice," France says.

Dye believed in Smith and had sent players to him ever since Georgia offensive tackle Matt Stinchcomb asked for him to foot the bill for Smith's services prior to the 1999 draft. Dye sent many of his clients to Smith, including Georgia quarterback David Greene and Ray Willis, the offensive tackle from Florida State. Dye's top client, Troy State defensive end Demarcus Ware, was training at a Velocity center in Alabama.

At Competitive Edge, players train six hours a day, five days a week. Each day consists of two hours of weightlifting, two hours of speed and agility work, and two hours of position-specific training. The players are forever donning harnesses and bungees and weighted vests, whatever it takes to become stronger, faster, and more explosive for the combine.

Smith has versions of the Wonderlic, the fifty-question cognitive ability exam given at the combine, and has the players practice. To prepare players for interviews with NFL scouts, he brings in Ken Herock, a longtime personnel man for the Tampa Bay Buccaneers, Oakland Raiders, Atlanta Falcons, and Green Bay Packers. Herock puts the players through mock interviews and provides pointers.

Herock is not viewed by current NFL executives as the turncoat one might expect. Team officials realize agents hire interview coaches and figure they might as well use someone experienced in the process.

Herock worked in Tampa during John McKay's coaching tenure and later did a lengthy stint as general manager of the Falcons. No one is more familiar with Herock's work than Rich McKay, the Falcons current general manager, who still values the interview process, even if players are coached.

"It's very scripted, because you have the Kenny Herocks of the world out there giving seminars," McKay says. "But I still get a lot out of interviews. A lot of times 30 to 40 percent of what a kid says isn't true, and we know it's not true because we've done our research on the kid. How truthfully he answers is a pretty good indicator of his character."

There were no questions about Greene's character. A high school star growing up in the Atlanta suburbs, he won a record forty-two games in four years as the starting quarterback at Georgia. With a perpetual smile, self-deprecating sense of humor, and enormous in-state popularity, he could run for governor.

According to scouting reports, the All-American boy lacked quickness and foot speed, which trumped character in the minds of NFL officials. Dye asked Smith to work on those areas, even hiring a special quarterback coach to help. Zeke Bratkowski, a former Georgia player, NFL quarterback, and assistant coach, had developed a reputation as a pre-draft specialist for quarterbacks such as Michael Vick, Patrick Ramsey, and Philip Rivers.

Smith had his own quarterback guru, Roger Theder, a former San Diego Chargers assistant and University of California head coach. Between the three of them, they thought Greene's foot-speed issue was overblown. Still, Smith put Greene in harnesses and cords, even for some quarterback drills.

"We don't add so much resistance that he can't do a three-step drop," Smith said. "The idea is to work on muscle memory. You take off the resistance and the muscle fibers think it's still there. They fire just as fast."

Willis presented a different challenge. He still was recovering from the high left ankle sprain sustained during Florida State's final regular season game against Florida in November. Smith's staff went to work helping Willis rediscover his "proprioception," the system of sensors in the joints that helps the body maintain balance. After an ankle is immobilized or not used after an injury, the proprioceptive system needs to be reactivated.

Dye and his colleague, Bill Johnson, had told Smith about Willis, how he was married and possessed a maturity and work ethic unlike that of most football players. Not long after arriving in Atlanta, Willis asked Smith if he would work with him on Sundays and Smith agreed, showing up after church services.

"Ray's not blessed as a natural athlete," Smith says. "But he has a drive and a motivation that you see only in the great ones. His performance in the NFL won't be affected by a lack of effort, that's for sure."

Though Smith had one of the larger combine classes, with clients representing more than a dozen agents, he was working with just one consensus first-rounder in Williams, who, because of his failed early entry into the NFL draft, had undergone more precombine training than any player in history.

Down in Bradenton, Florida, a much smaller group of athletes prepared for the combine. There were just five of them, all clients of the International Management Group, and four had realistic first-round aspirations.

Michael Johnson opened the trunk of a rented Ford Taurus and pulled out a rope ladder. The man considered the fastest human in the world for much of the 1990s walked across a well-manicured grass soccer field, crouched, and laid out the ladder.

Temperatures already were approaching eighty degrees shortly before 10:00 A.M. on Thursday, February 3, 2005. Johnson was the first to arrive at the International Management Group's soccer fields, part of 190 acres of prime Bradenton, Florida, real estate. The IMG Academies are a sprawling complex of condominiums, private schools, and athletic facilities that attract kids with parents willing to pay up to one hundred thousand dollars a year for high-end, sport-specific training and accommodations.

In 1978, tennis coach Nick Bollettieri created a tennis academy on what was then a twenty-two-acre tomato farm. He welcomed students from around the world and trained young prodigies such as Andre Agassi, Jim Courier, and Monica Seles. In 1987 he sold the facility to IMG, the Cleveland-based sports colossus that represents hundreds of athletes, entertainers, and sports properties.

Over the next decade, IMG expanded upon Bollettieri's residential sports concept and transformed it into a major recruiting and development tool for young athletes in tennis, golf, soccer, baseball, and basketball.

IMG did not develop football players; high schools and colleges did an adequate job of that. Instead, it used the training center, specifically the coaches at the International Performance Institute (IPI), to help lure promising NFL hopefuls to IMG. Between IPI and the reputation of lead agent Tom Condon for representing top NFL players, IMG was able to land promising draft classes most every year.

Johnson checked his watch as two sport utility vehicles rolled up alongside the field. Out popped his pupils for the morning, IMG's 2005 NFL Draft class, clad in shorts, sneakers, and gray IMG Academies T-shirts that read "World's Toughest Playground."

It had been another good haul for Condon and his partner, Ken "Fuzzy" Kremer. The rookie-to-be class included Alex Smith, the quarterback from Utah projected as a possible number-one overall pick; David Pollack, the three-time All-American defensive end from Georgia; Heath Miller, the Mackey Award–winning tight end from the University of Virginia; Chris Spencer, a talented center from Ole Miss; and Rob Petitti, a 350-pound lineman from Pittsburgh. The other member of IMG's recruiting class, Wisconsin defensive tackle Anttaj Hawthorne, had opted to stay in Madison to prepare for the combine.

The players fanned out across the field. Brook Hamilton, a trainer at the International Performance Institute, guided the group through a series of stretches and movement drills.

Scouts referred to Pollack as a "high-motor" player, meaning his intensity level never wavered on the field—or off, according to his Georgia teammates. Pollack maintained a running commentary through the warm-up routine, with nobody off limits.

Petitti, sidelined with a foot injury, opened a can of Skoal and folded a pinch under his lip. "There's Rob Petitti and his precombine workout," Pollack said.

Pollack turned his attention to the Ford Taurus. How could a rental agency assign such an everyday vehicle to the world's fastest man? "Nice ride, MJ."

Johnson nodded. "I'm taking that car to Pimp-my-Ride."

At thirty-six, Johnson had assembled a full slate of postcareer endeavors, including television commentary, helping coach at alma mater Baylor, and launching a sports consultancy company. For the past few years, his former agency had brought him to Florida to train the football players how to best run the forty.

It was an odd pairing, a world-class sprinter with athletes that averaged more than 250 pounds, sort of like enlisting Warren Buffett to teach financial planning to college kids. IMG flexed all of its resources when it came to recruiting and preparing athletes for the NFL Draft.

Johnson, who won Olympic gold medals and world championships in the two hundred and four hundred meters, never ran forty yards for time. But he believed the mechanics and philosophies of running still applied. Johnson wasn't about to stay in Florida for the entire precombine season, but he flew in several times for three-day stints. Today was the first time the group would run the forty for time.

Besides his rope ladder, Johnson had laid out a forty-yard course. Johnson gathered the group in a huddle and recapped his main points from a previous session. The start was essential, especially because the players would not have the normal sprinter's luxury of blocks.

"You want to have maximum force coming out to propel you forward," Johnson said. "Once you start moving, the clock starts, so everything has to be moving as fast as possible. This is not a buildup. Your initial move sets up the rest of the run, so it's got to start off with aggression, force, and speed all together at the same time."

The players lined up to run, first a pair of twenty-yard dashes. Petitti sat out, along with Miller, who was nursing an abdominal injury sustained late in the season. Here, running on grass did not simulate the RCA Dome track they would use for the NFL combine in Indianapolis in three weeks, but that wasn't the point. Johnson was more concerned with their techniques.

Pollack, already in a lather from the heat, ran first. He assumed a three-point stance, with his right hand on the ground and left in the air. Unlike his football position, where he stared ahead at his opponent, he kept his head down. Pollack waited a few moments then lurched forward, barreling through the distance and walking back to Johnson for feedback.

The sprinter pumped his arms. "You've got to keep your hands by your hip, as if you're pulling a gun out of a holster each time."

Pollack nodded and walked away. Smith, the Utah quarterback, prepared to run.

"You have to use different types of analogies," Johnson said. "David tends to run with his chest out and his arms back, and they never come forward. You can't get very much power that way. You want it to come from further back every time. It's easier for him to remember if I say it's like drawing the gun out of a holster instead of saying, 'Make sure your arm always comes up in front of your body and passes by your hip.'

"To do what I need David to do, he has to keep his head down, and that's very difficult for a guy used to starting the opposite way. Linemen are used to having their hands at a certain position, and I need them to keep their hands down. It's only temporary. Whatever they do after I'm finished with them, it doesn't matter. But for that one day, those scouts want to see them run the forty as fast as they can."

Pollack watched Smith. "A lot of this technique is beyond what I've ever learned," he said. "I might have run forty yards on the football field ten times in my entire career. But it's a test to show how fast you are. You hear the word 'potential' used a lot right now. 'This guy has a lot of potential, a lot of upside.' Most of the evaluation should come from film, and most of it does; but this is something else they're going to look at. If I'm even with somebody else, this is going to push me over the top. So how can I not listen to the fastest human being to ever walk the planet?"

After Smith and Spencer ran, the trio waited a few minutes and ran twenty yards again. Johnson showed no emotion as he looked at his stopwatch.

"You can't measure progress by the watch, not after just fifteen days down here," Johnson said. "We've spent quite a bit of time on the start and the drive. Now we proceed into the full run, and the question is, how are guys going to make the transition? I'm looking at what he's doing right and what we have to work on. Which parts of this will he get and which ones will he not get, based on the time we have here? Which battles should I choose to fight?"

Pollack ran the forty first, pumping his arms and looking more like a gunslinger than previously. Johnson glanced at the stopwatch and then reset it.

"How'd I do?" Pollack asked.

"We're not worried about times."

"C'mon, how'd I do?"

"It's grass, man. Even if you ran a 4.3, I wouldn't tell you."

Two hours later, across the IMG campus, Steve Shenbaum prepared the IMG football class of 2005 for the interview portion of the combine. During their stay in Indianapolis, players would spend two evenings shuttling between hotel rooms to speak with NFL teams in fifteen-minute blocks. It was Shenbaum's job to make sure they put their best face forward.

Shenbaum was part of the growing number of consultants specializing in image-building and media coaching for professional athletes. The idea, borrowed from the corporate world, was to show pros how every interview contributed to their public image and to create strategies to get their messages across. A well-spoken, accessible athlete that avoided controversy but still projected personality and flair could generate millions in off-the-field endorsement money. He also could use the playing career as a springboard for lucrative retirement opportunities in business, broadcasting, coaching, or motivational speaking.

That was the big picture, anyway. For now, the players needed to impress NFL officials in Indianapolis in this high-stakes game of speed-dating. The key was to project confidence, respect, intelligence, passion, knowledge of football, and personality, without coming across as cocky, self-entitled, or coached.

Most agents hired media coaches to prepare players for the combine interview. Shenbaum was IMG's answer to the likes of former NFL executive Ken Herock, Chip Smith's guru. IMG, being an agency with its own training center, brought the interview process in-house. Shenbaum had relocated his Game On business from California to Bradenton and worked year-round with IMG's sports prodigies from a well-appointed office on campus. His top priority for the first six weeks of the year was combine preparation.

"Most of their college classmates are interviewing for real jobs," Shenbaum said. "This is a similar process, but there's much more money at stake."

Cynics, including those in the media and NFL officials, suggest people like Shenbaum don't build images so much as they sanitize them, creating vanilla personalities like IMG clients Tiger Woods and Derek Jeter that offer guarded comments and little insight into what makes them tick. In that sense, the industry is merely an advanced version of the famous bus scene in the baseball movie *Bull Durham*, where veteran catcher Crash Davis, played by Kevin Costner, lectured young pitcher "Nuke" LaLoosh (Tim Robbins) on how to handle the media.

"You're gonna have to learn your clichés," Davis said. "We gotta play it one day at a time . . . I'm just happy to be here and hope I can help the ballclub . . . I just want to give it my best shot and, the good Lord willing, things will work out."

The red-haired Shenbaum taught players how to act in Indianapolis, and he brought solid credentials to his work. He had a lengthy list of television and movie credits, with bit roles on *Married with Children* and *Will and Grace*, and a turn as "band camp director" in the second film of the *American Pie* trilogy. Still, Shenbaum bristles at the suggestion that there's anything disingenuous about interview coaching.

"Good actors are trying to be truthful, they're not trying to act. The basis of our program is for an athlete to be truthful. I don't want an athlete to try and be somebody he's not. If you don't go to church every Sunday, don't say you go to church every Sunday. If you're close to Mom, great. But if you don't talk to your parents then don't say you're close to your family. I'm not going to try and make Rob Petitti into a choir boy. That's not fair to him, and coaches and general managers are smart enough to know who is putting on an act."

Most bigtime football players think they're prepared for the combine interview, having undergone hundreds of sessions with the media in college. Unfortunately for Shenbaum and his competitors, they find that the constant media obligations have conditioned many players to spout the Crash Davis playbook on autopilot, rather than project the passion and personality NFL scouts and executives want to see, at least in Indianapolis. (Once they enter the NFL, the *Bull Durham* approach is heartily encouraged.)

Miller suffered from a version of the syndrome. A soft-spoken native of tiny Swords Creek, Virginia, with close-cropped hair, Miller came across as shy, expressionless, even disinterested. Teammates at the University of Virginia hung the nickname "Big Money" on him, mostly because of his reliable pass-catching skills, but also because he seemed like the last guy who would have such a flashy moniker.

So Shenbaum filmed an interview with Miller and had him watch it.

"Your issue is going to be that you don't come across as very dynamic," Shenbaum said. "But whose issue is that? Is it yours or the media's? I worked with Pete Sampras and he had this same problem. But do you think he's banging his head up against the wall with his $55 million in the bank and fourteen Grand Slam titles and a beautiful wife and child because he's called boring? Yeah, it hurt him for a while and it was frustrating, but whose issue is that? We ask athletes to be sportsmen and to be respectful and gentlemanly, and when they do exactly that, we call them boring. So don't worry about it."

Miller nodded. "I've always been the type of guy to deflect attention to the team. I don't really cherish the individual attention or the interviews." (It was no wonder Miller was one of Virginia coach Al Groh's all-time favorite players. Groh, like his longtime colleagues, Bill Parcells and Bill Belichick, prefers players that say little if anything that could be construed as colorful or insightful.)

"And that's a great attitude to have," Shenbaum said. "But look at yourself here. It's almost as if you're mourning a death. Let's work with what you've got. You've got a great smile; you're a good-looking guy. Talk about things that excite you. Use some facial reactions. The way you play speaks for yourself."

Shenbaum turned the video camera back toward Miller and began asking questions about his family. Miller relaxed, smiled, and spoke of family vacations to the beach. Shenbaum put the interview on screen.

"What's the difference?" Shenbaum asked.

"I'm smiling," Miller said.

"Of course you are. You're talking about something you enjoy. This is how it all starts. We're not going to make you into a silver-tongued Charlie, and that's okay. I don't need to tell you to smile more; you know that. Instead, think of things in your life that bring a smile to your face. Think of them as coins you can put in your pocket and take out when you need to smile."

Unlike other interview gurus working with combine players, Shenbaum did not have to spend time coaching his players on how to address questions about drug use, arrests, suspensions, and other red flags. Smith, Miller, Pollack, and Spencer were going to register high on any team's character evaluation; Petitti only had to address a hard-partying reputation.

Still, there was room for improvement, especially since Petitti was the only one of the group that had endured the nonstop interviews at the Senior Bowl. Smith, Miller, and Spencer, as juniors, were ineligible for the game. Pollack, who finished his college career with three sacks in the Outback Bowl and was considered among the top prospects in the draft, figured there was nothing to be gained by playing in Mobile.

Shenbaum worked with the players for four hours a week. There were one-on-one sessions and group workshops that included mock interviews, public speaking—even improvisation skits. There was plenty of discussion on typical combine questions—strengths and weaknesses, toughest opponent faced, biggest likes and dislikes about football—but Shenbaum drew upon his acting experiences to create a free-flowing classroom atmosphere. That way, players improved their communication skills instead of just memorizing what they thought scouts wanted to hear.

"We want them to be able to tell stories, not just provide canned answers," Shenbaum said.

Pollack represented a different challenge. He was always passionate and animated and shifted gears quickly in interviews, transforming from the smack-talking, alpha male of the locker room into a polite, "Yes sir," young man. Before his junior year, he declined a spot in Playboy's preseason All-American team photo, saying it conflicted with his religious beliefs. Prior to his senior season, he revealed to *ESPN the Magazine* that he planned to remain a virgin until marriage.

It was a shtick that struck some as a little too Mr. Goody Two-shoes. Pollack also had a tendency to credit God and his Christian faith frequently.

Pollack didn't worry if his public testimony rubbed some the wrong way. During Outback Bowl week in Tampa in January, he appeared at press conferences in a white T-shirt with a knocked off emblem of the NFL shield that read FML (For My Lord).

"I'm going to be outgoing about my faith," Pollack said. "That's the reason I'm here today. That's the reason I've been given this gift to play football. God has been so good to me in so many ways, and I love to share it. There's a difference between sharing it and telling people why you have that faith, and cramming it down someone's throat."

Shenbaum wasn't about to steer Pollack away from public testimony, though he did remind him of devout athletes who were skewered in the press for their transgressions. The former actor just hoped Pollack and the rest of the players found the happy medium in their combine interviews.

And the good Lord willing, things would work out.

On the morning of Saturday, February 19, 2005, one week before the NFL combine, Fred Gibson stepped on a scale. He weighed 196, just three pounds more than when he arrived at the Athletes' Performance training center more than six weeks earlier.

The trainers and nutritionists at Athletes' Performance prided themselves on helping athletes put on weight or take it off, depending on what they needed to perform in the NFL. Though the staff had less than two months between when an athlete arrived and when he needed to depart for the combine, the training and diet program produced dramatic results.

A year earlier, Shawn Andrews showed up weighing 401. By working out and eating properly, the right tackle from the University of Arkansas dropped 35 pounds in a little more than a month before the NFL combine. The Philadelphia Eagles selected him with the sixteenth overall pick.

Most players need to gain weight for the NFL, with its longer season and higher level of competition. Football players at Athletes' Performance consume six meals a day, including at least two protein-rich shakes. Among the facility's sponsors is EAS, the Colorado nutritional supplement manufacturer best known for producing the Myoplex shake powder popularized by the Body-for-Life fitness craze.

Carlos Rogers, the former Auburn cornerback, had gained 7 pounds since arriving at API, becoming such a believer in EAS that his agent Todd France signed a deal with the company to make Rogers an official spokesman. Running back Ronnie Brown, a fellow Auburn teammate and France client, received a similar deal.

Gibson was another story. He was lactose intolerant, which made it difficult to handle many of the shake mixes. He also tended to be a picky eater, even though the training center included an in-house chef and café that most of the players loved.

In college, players have access to special dining halls and world-class training facilities. Blessed with the hummingbird metabolisms of young adulthood, most eat whatever they please, never drawing a connection between what they consume and how it affects energy levels and performance.

"Very few athletic departments have hired sports nutritionists," says Amanda Carlson, the director of nutrition at Athletes' Performance. "College athletes spend all this time in the weight room, which is good, but some of those gains are never realized because of poor nutrition."

At Athletes' Performance, players learned the importance of regulating energy levels and creating an efficient, speedy metabolism by eating roughly every three hours. They're taught to consume a high-protein shake immediately after workouts to jump-start the muscle recovery and repair process. Carlson took some players on a field trip to the supermarket to examine food labels for future reference. At least in Phoenix, they could eat virtually every meal at the training center—as long as their agents picked up the meal option on top of the ten-thousand-dollar training fee.

Gibson, gregarious as always, didn't seem to grasp the magnitude of the training. He enjoyed the camaraderie of being around Brown, Rogers, and Carnell "Cadillac" Williams, and talking shop with Mark Clayton, the Oklahoma wide receiver who became something of a legend at the Senior Bowl when he did not drop a pass in practice all week.

API trainers tried in vain to convince Gibson that he needed to work harder; there were millions of dollars at stake. They wished he could be like Cadillac Williams, who despite consensus first-round status trained like a fringe prospect. "I might not even get drafted," Williams told the trainers, quite seriously.

Gibson shot pool in the player's lounge between workouts, once launching a cue ball through a window, which cost four hundred dollars to repair. The concept of this level of training was new to him. Having played both basketball and football throughout high school and early in his college career, Gibson never underwent a formal off-season football conditioning program.

"Scouts might look at him as not developed, but he does have upside, because there's so much room for improvement," said Darryl Eto, the

API coach who directed the speed and movement portion of the pre-combine training. "He's capable of a lot more physically. The thing that will be a challenge for Fred is seeing the value in strength training and work off the field. He'll go out and run routes and catch balls all day long. He goes beyond the call of duty there. But will that effort translate into working in the weight room or in the classroom in the NFL?"

By 1:00 P.M. on Saturday, the training center was virtually empty. Saturdays are considered "regeneration" days in the Athletes' Performance system, and players undergo just light workouts in the morning before being dismissed until Monday.

The lone football player still training was Chris Canty, just three weeks removed from suffering a detached left retina in the Axis/Radius nightclub in Scottsdale. Since the injury, he had worked out during off hours with physical therapist Darcy Norman, who had been overseeing his knee rehabilitation.

The left eye was bandaged, the area black and swollen. Canty looked like he had sustained a few blows from Mike Tyson. The ghastly appearance was the main reason Canty preferred to train alone, that and not wanting to keep recounting the episode.

He knew he would have to discuss it as many as thirty-two times, depending on how many teams wished to interview him at the combine in Indianapolis. Unlike the rest of the draft hopefuls at Athletes' Performance, Canty would not be flying to the combine.

To stabilize the retina, doctors inserted gas that would dissipate over the next eight weeks. Until then Canty could not fly. If he did, cabin pressure could cause the gas to expand and then things could get really ugly.

Canty did not plan to work out at the combine, but would be there to undergo interviews that now seemed more important than ever, especially with teams wondering if they had to worry about character issues on top of a rehabilitated knee and a detached retina.

Instead of flying, Canty planned to board a train from Tucson in just five days. An uncle would accompany him.

"I know I have to face up to this," Canty said, sitting in the lobby of Athletes' Performance after a brief workout. "I have to go in there and have the confidence to address these questions head-on. You always hear that for a football player the combine is the most important interview of your life. I don't know if I believed that before. I do now. And I've got a long train ride to think about it."

Chapter Thirteen:

INDIANAPOLIS

T here is no event in the NFL calendar that generates as much discussion, debate, and controversy as the weeklong National Invitation Camp, known more commonly as "the combine."

For seven days in late February, more than one thousand NFL coaches, scouts, executives, and even a few owners, descend upon downtown Indianapolis and fan out among the Westin, Hyatt, and Marriott hotels. A number of shrewd scouts, like their fellow Marriott point-collectors in the press room, book the hotel months in advance.

Indianapolis is a miserable place to be in late February, which is one of two reasons the city has served as an effective site for the event since 1987. Nobody cares that they're cooped up inside for a week; it's not like they'd be playing golf.

The other reason is that the RCA Dome, home of the NFL's Colts, provides a climate-controlled atmosphere for testing, and is attached to the Indianapolis Convention Center, an upscale shopping mall; and all three hotels connect by a labyrinth of indoor walkways. It's possible to go days without venturing outside, though many NFL officials find time to enjoy several popular restaurants.

The combine is an outgrowth of an earlier era when teams pooled information in the interests of saving money on travel and scouting departments. Just as combines such as BLESTO and National Football Scouting continue to provide subscriber teams with information that becomes the basis for their yearlong evaluations, the midwinter workout gives clubs another look at draft-eligible talent.

These days, teams spend enough manpower and resources on data collection to make the CIA envious. BLESTO and National serve a more modest role as an initial rating of draft-eligible talent. By the time teams gather in Indianapolis, they have spent thousands of man-hours on background checks, film evaluation, attending practices and games, and debating the merits of players.

The combine still serves a valuable purpose. Players undergo drug tests and thorough physicals. Drills such as the forty-yard dash, vertical and broad jumps, and shuttle runs, provide standardized "measurables" of speed, quickness, and strength, albeit not necessarily directly applicable to football. Given the preparation most players undergo in the seven weeks leading up to the combine, the tests arguably are as much a measure of the effectiveness of the trainers as of a player's athleticism.

"This is the president's physical fitness workout," said New York Jets head coach Herman Edwards, a former NFL cornerback. "When I was playing, I never worried about a guy that ran a 4.4 forty, if I watched the film and saw that he had 5.2 hands. Coach would say, 'What are you going to do if he runs by you?' I said, 'I won't worry about it too much, Coach, because he can't catch. I'll handle that guy all day.'"

Players do go through some football-related drills, though they're often overshadowed by the seven measured tests. In either case, teams know better than to fall in love with a workout warrior or dismiss someone who performs poorly.

The 2005 combine marked the tenth anniversary of Mike Mamula's legendary workout, and the former Philadelphia Eagle still served as a cautionary tale. On the other side were players like Ben Roethlisberger, who in 2004 looked less than impressive during quarterback drills in Indy. His passes lacked zip and he didn't appear to have the arm strength scouts coveted. Roethlisberger, from Miami of Ohio, lasted until the eleventh pick, behind Eli Manning and Philip Rivers, and proceeded to lead the Pittsburgh Steelers to a 15-1 record and the AFC title game.

If players needed another reminder of someone who overcame a poor combine, they only had to visit the set of the NFL Network, which was televising the 2005 event. Former Denver Broncos star running back Terrell Davis, a sixth-round pick out of Georgia in 1995, was serving as the cohost of the network's daily combine wrap-up show.

Then there was Tom Brady, a visible reminder that exhaustive scouting reports, and where a player is drafted, often mean little when it comes to predicting success. In 2000, the New England Patriots selected the Michigan quarterback in the sixth round, with the 199th overall pick.

The Patriots, winners of three Super Bowls in four years, were held up as the gold standard for building for the draft, though the Brady selection was mostly luck.

Rich McKay, the Falcons general manager, preached to his troops the importance of emulating the New England Patriots, along with perennial contenders the Philadelphia Eagles, by remaining committed to players. The Falcons arrived at the combine having narrowed their universe of draftable players to 225. Between the combine, the March pro day schedule, and three weeks of meetings in April, they would whittle the field to less than a hundred.

"The one thing the Patriots and Eagles do very well is stay committed to the players they draft," McKay said. "When they show up, players don't always look exactly the way they were projected to look. Maybe they're not quite as fast, or quite as quick, or pick up the scheme quite as fast, and I think, as an organization, those are two that have had a lot of success because they have stayed committed to it."

The combine is a blur for the players. With 332 invited to Indianapolis, they're staggered over the course of a seven-day period, with each group staying three nights. Offensive linemen and kickers, along with about half of the running backs, were the first to arrive on the evening of Wednesday, February 23. The players were given identical gray sweats, with either OL, RB, or PK on the left breast, along with a number. That number and the player's name also were on the back.

As usual, there were players who would not work out. Some, such as Virginia guard Elton Brown, Florida State tackle Ray Willis, and tackle Rob Petitti of Pittsburgh, were nursing lingering injuries. A few others, most notably Texas running back Cedric Benson and Michigan wide receiver Braylon Edwards, planned to just undergo physicals and submit to interviews.

Agent Drew Rosenhaus advised much of his contingent not to undergo full workouts, a group that included lineman Chris Myers from Miami, Oklahoma defensive end Dan Cody, and Vernand Morency, a running back from Oklahoma State. Roscoe Parrish, a wide receiver from Miami, planned to do everything.

Rosenhaus was among the agents who told their clients they'd be better off limiting their workouts to their pro timing days—better known as pro days back on their college campuses—where there would be less pressure and a more comfortable environment. Many players, especially those from Florida schools, were convinced—at least by their agents—that they were better off working out in the Sunshine State than indoors at the RCA Dome.

This kind of thinking drove team officials crazy. At the combine players had an audience of every decision-maker in the league. Every general manager and head coach showed up, along with dozens of scouts, assistant coaches, and executives from every front office. Many owners flew in to sit in on the interview portions or watch from the stands. Rarely did a college pro day attract more than one hundred scouts. They were an important part of the process, to be sure, but why not look at the pro day as a makeup exam for a poor combine performance? If they aced the combine, they could sit out some or all of the pro day.

"I don't see why anyone would come down here and not do all the drills," said Charlie Frye, the quarterback from Akron. "That's what we're here for, right?"

Agents made some compelling arguments to sit out. At the combine, players are put through a nonstop schedule of physicals, interviews, and tests. Sleep and eating habits get disrupted. It's hardly the formula for an ideal workout, especially if a player is suffering the effects of a lingering injury.

When each group of players arrived at the combine, one general manager addressed the group. Without mentioning agents by name, they implored the players not to listen to those telling them to sit out the combine.

Charley Casserly, general manager of the Houston Texans, drew the duty the first night. He didn't have to worry about punters and kickers skipping drills—they had a limited slate as it was—and he knew offensive linemen were less likely than running backs or wide receivers to be prima donnas. But he, along with his counterparts on other nights, made it a point to give the address every evening, regardless of position.

"This is like a job interview," Casserly said. "You have guys you grew up [with] and guys you went to college with and what are they doing? They're trying to find a job. So what are you trying to do? You're trying to find a job. You're auditioning for a job over the next couple of months. So let's start off there. Number one, be on time. Be honest with people.

When they ask you to do things, do them, okay? You're going to be pulled a million different ways during this combine and it's going to be tough on you, but think of it as a job interview.

"You're going to be told things like, 'Don't work out at the combine. It's not a good environment for you to work out in. It's not a good surface to run on.' I disagree and so do the general managers in the league on those points. Number one, you should work out. First of all, the surface? The surface is fast, men. It's an AstroTurf surface, indoors. Now, at the end of the day, when we're sitting in the draft room, we take your best performance in each individual category. We take your best time, your best jump, your tallest height if you will, your best weight. So the more times you do something, the more chances you have to do your best. If you don't work out here, some of us are never going to see you work out. But more importantly, head coaches aren't going to see you work out. Position coaches may not see you work out. So what you're doing, you're cutting your window down by not working out here. Number one, you're only giving yourself one workout and number two, you're limiting the number of people who are going to see you who are going to make the decisions on your career. That's what it comes down to, men. It's a dollars-and-cents thing. I can't be any more blunt than that about it.

"Don't pay attention to all these predictions about where you're going to be drafted. Men, we haven't finished our draft ratings. We have a rough draft board like everybody else in the NFL, but we don't have your physical. Some of you we don't have a time on. So, what we're saying is that none of this stuff you read in the paper is accurate. Because the people writing it don't make those draft decisions. So, conversely, don't get your hopes up or get deflated by draft predictions. Finishing up now, what are the points here that you want to come out of this with? Number one, it doesn't make any difference where you get drafted. Every one of you in this room has a chance to be Tom Brady. Don't worry about where you're drafted. This is a job interview process you're going through over the next couple of months. So be cooperative, be honest in the process. The next thing here we have is the combine. Work out and give yourself the best chance to get drafted, and make the money I talked about by giving yourself the best workouts. Why? Because we take the best workout. If you only work out once, maybe you're the guy who gets hurt in the warm-up, doesn't work out, and drops in the draft. It happened last year. It's going to happen this year, because somebody is going to make that mistake again. Don't you make that mistake."

When Casserly was through, the players were taken to Methodist Hospital for preliminary medical evaluations. Few players make it through college football careers without a significant injury, and it was the job of the doctors to address every concern, no matter how far removed from the injury the player was.

Chris Spencer, the lineman from Ole Miss who had been working out at IMG's training center in Florida, found doctors spending time on a wrist he had broken in the fourth grade.

"It happened so long ago, I didn't even remember," Spencer said. "I think I was playing football when it happened, but I'm not sure. I guess these background checks turn up everything."

The following morning, the players were awakened at 5:30 for urine tests. The league tests players for both recreational and performance-enhancing drugs. The league would send out letters to anyone that tested positive in April. (Two Wisconsin players, offensive guard Jonathan Clinkscale and defensive tackle Anttaj Hawthorne—the target of the Jack Scharf vs. IMG recruiting battle—tested positive for marijuana use.)

From there, it was off to the bowels of the RCA Dome for more extensive physical exams. Players with lingering medical issues could be sent back to Methodist Hospital for more X-rays or an MRI. After that, they were paraded in shorts and socks into an auditorium, a reenactment of the Senior Bowl weigh-in for those who were there. Unlike that event, where arm length and hand size numbers were provided beforehand, the measurement is taken at the combine.

The next two days go quickly. Players are brought to the press room in the Indiana Convention Center to answer questions from the media for fifteen minutes apiece. Maurice Clarett and Mike Williams drew the biggest audiences, with the media curious about how the two failed challengers to the NFL's underclassmen rule would fare at the combine.

The players spend their second and third evenings shuttling between hotel rooms on one floor of the Crown Plaza Hotel, interviewing with teams in fifteen-minute increments.

Then there's the bench press. NFL Network officials, televising the event extensively for the first time in 2005, quickly realized the bench press was riveting programming, especially with John Lott, the newly named strength and conditioning coach of the Cleveland Browns, running the show.

Before each group benched, Lott gathered them in a circle and implored them in his Texas twang to put on a show for the assembled scouts.

"Running backs, I'm going to hype you up today," he said. "You get off today on the bench press. After this, you don't have to lift a weight the rest of the spring, as far as the bench press. You concentrate on the skills and drills you have to do. Push yourself today. Talk to each other. Don't sit up there like some stinkin' mannequins. You've got one chance on this thing. Keep your elbows up and your head down and let's work. Every strength coach in the NFL is over there right now, every running backs coach, several coordinators, several head coaches and GMs—a lot of strong people over there right now. Fellas, it's first impression and it's a big impression. Get your stinkin' minds right and let's do this thing, all right?"

Finally, on the fourth day, the players take the field at the RCA Dome. Even with hundreds of NFL employees in the stands, the dome seems empty. It's quiet, except for when a player's name is announced or when he begins his forty-yard dash.

The forty is the first order of business. Each player runs twice. After that, he undergoes on-field, position-specific drills. Wide receivers catch balls, quarterbacks throw. Defenders run through simulated game situations. From there, it's back to the sidelines to complete the broad jump and vertical jump, followed by the three-cone and shuttle runs.

Then there's the Wonderlic, the twelve-minute, fifty-question test that measures cognitive ability and—depending on your vantage point—success or failure in the NFL.

More than 130 million people have taken a version of the Wonderlic Personnel Test (WPT). Developed in 1937 as a tool to measure the mental abilities of potential job candidates, it became part of the NFL scouting process in the mid-1970s. Tom Landry, the longtime head coach of the Dallas Cowboys, believed there was a correlation between cognitive ability and how a player processed data to performance on the field.

According to Wonderlic Consulting, the Libertyville, Illinois, publisher of the test, cognitive ability, or general intelligence, is the single greatest predictor of job success in any position. The Wonderlic provides employers with "quantifiable data about whether candidates can learn new skills, think effectively, and make important decisions under pressure."

NFL teams want players with such traits, though in the modern era of exhaustive scouting, where no stone is left unturned, few teams rely exclusively on the Wonderlic to gauge a player's ability to learn, let alone predict his future importance.

After all, the college football ranks are full of star players who, coming out of high school, struggled to post the requisite score on the Scholastic Aptitude Test (SAT) to be eligible to play. Many players who scored below the average NFL Wonderlic score of 19–20 went on to stellar NFL careers.

Dan Marino, for instance, posted a mere sixteen. Randall Cunningham scored just fifteen. Both showed exceptional abilities to quickly process information while performing the role of NFL quarterback, arguably the most stressful job in sports.

Brett Favre and Tim Couch both scored twenty-two. Favre, a second-round pick in the 1991 draft, is considered one of the smartest quarterbacks ever. The oft-injured Couch, the first selection in 1999, is viewed as one of the biggest busts of all time.

It's difficult to make sweeping generalizations about the Wonderlic, but one rule of thumb is that the closer a player is to the ball, the higher his score will be, or at least should be. Quarterbacks and offensive linemen will score higher than wide receivers. There does seem to be a correlation between academic intelligence and a high Wonderlic score. Pat McInally, a receiver/punter from Harvard, scored a perfect fifty in 1976. Players from prestigious academic schools often are among the high scorers.

Many of the questions are not especially difficult, but the challenge is to complete the exam in the allotted twelve minutes. In that sense, it mimics the NFL, where players must digest complex schemes, lengthy playbooks, and react quickly on the field.

Here are a few examples of Wonderlic questions, directly from the company's Web site:

1. When rope is selling for $.10 a foot, how many feet can you buy for sixty cents?

2. Assume the first two statements are true. Is the final one:
   1=True   2=False   3=Uncertain

   The boy plays baseball.
   All baseball players wear hats.
   The boy wears a hat.

3. Paper sells for 21 cents per pad. What will four pads cost?

4. How many of the five pairs of items listed below are exact
   duplicates?

Nieman, K. M.	Neiman, K. M.
Thomas, G. K.	Thomas, C. K.
Hoff, J. P.	Hoff, J. P.
Pino, L. R.	Pina, L. R.
Warner, T. S.	Wanner, T. S.

5. RESENT–RESERVE
   Do these words:

   1. have similar meanings?
   2. have contradictory meanings?
   3. mean neither the same nor opposite?

Answers:
   1. 6 feet
   2. True
   3. 84 cents
   4. 1
   5. 3

In addition to the Wonderlic, some NFL teams distribute their own questionnaires and psychological exams. The most notorious is the three hundred-plus question test given by the New York Giants, which includes the question, "If you were a cat or dog, which would you be?"

"I'm definitely more of a dog person," said David Greene, the Georgia quarterback.

Some questionnaires ask about a player's family history of heart disease or cancer. Others ask for the parents' height and weight; teams figure some players might still be growing.

"I thought it was kind of personal to ask how much your mom weighs," said Chris Myers, the offensive lineman from Miami. "I didn't want to disrespect my mom, so I left that question blank."

As for the Wonderlic, it's viewed by most teams the way they weigh the rest of the combine: a valuable exercise, but just part of a yearlong evaluation. In Atlanta, Rich McKay advises his scouting staff to include questions about how a player learns and processes information in every interview, and to seek out academic advisors and tutors as part of the background check.

"We don't consider the Wonderlic important at all," McKay said. "It's a marker to look at this issue in case it's there. But when you go back with guys with lower test scores and talk to coaches, you ask, 'How does he learn football? Is he a slow learner? What are the issues, if any?' We've never eliminated a guy because he was low or high. I don't know if it's even a tiebreaker. It's more of a red flag to make sure we've checked this guy out as much as we possibly can. More often than not, it's not a reference of how he learns."

"The Wonderlic is just another indicator," says Scott Pioli, general manager of the New England Patriots. "A guy isn't going to succeed or fail with us on the Wonderlic test. The range of socioeconomic backgrounds is so vast, and there are certain players from different parts of the country who, because of their backgrounds, may not test well. Maybe they have a learning disability or they just don't test well. The reason we have the interviews is because we want to spend time with players to find out if they get it or not. If you spend time with a person and ask the right questions, and you have a good feel for those kinds of things, you can figure out if a guy is smart enough for your system."

While most of the Atlanta Falcons contingent was settling in at the Indianapolis Marriott on Wednesday, February 23, 2005, Tim Ruskell was in Kirkland, Washington, being introduced as the new president of football operations of the Seattle Seahawks.

It had been a whirlwind few days for the Falcons' former assistant general manager. The Seahawks executive search committee called a week earlier. McKay, the Falcons general manager, gave the Seahawks not only permission to speak to Ruskell but also a hearty endorsement on his behalf.

Ruskell declined the overtures at first, telling the committee he did not want to talk until after the draft. If that meant he lost out on the job, fine. A year earlier, he left the Tampa Bay Buccaneers in mid-January to reunite with McKay in Atlanta. Changing teams so late in the draft preparation process was the toughest thing he ever did in his career.

Now the Seahawks were asking him to do it again, a month closer to the draft, and this time he wasn't going to be reunited with his closest friend in the game. He felt like he would be abandoning the Falcons at a crucial point in the draft preparation process. Not only that, Seattle's front office was in utter disarray.

More than a month had passed since the Seahawks had fired Bob Whitsitt, the team president. In that time, the general manager, vice president of football operations, and director of college scouting had departed. Head coach Mike Holmgren, who clashed with Whitsitt and once wore the dual title of head coach/general manager, remained, along with the scouts.

The Seahawks were persistent and called again. Ruskell was torn, and he turned to McKay for input. "I don't want you to be three months down the road feeling sorry that you didn't investigate it," McKay told him. "There's the money and security and the opportunity, but you've got to make that call."

Ruskell, forty-eight, soon realized it was time to leave. *Pro Football Weekly* recently had run a list of up-and-coming general manager candidates and tacked Ruskell's name at the end, noting that people throughout the league figured the accomplished talent evaluator would have such a position by now.

Steve Spurrier, during his brief tenure as Redskins head coach, had recommended the man he once knew as a Buccaneers ball boy to become GM. Ruskell had interviewed for several GM positions. Between the success of the McKay regime in Tampa and Atlanta, the phones were ringing more often.

Seattle was a good fit, with a team comparable to the Falcons roster McKay had taken over, not a rebuilding process but one in need of some minor repairs. Before the 2004 season, the Seahawks were a popular pick to reach the Super Bowl. But they finished a modest 9-7 and lost at home in the first round of the playoffs to the St. Louis Rams.

The move itself would not be a problem. As a kid, with a father in the military, Ruskell relocated every two years. He wanted his nine-year-old daughter and five-year-old son to be able to put down roots. The older they got, the tougher a move would be.

Negotiations proceeded quickly. Ruskell spoke several times on the telephone to Tod Leiweke, the team's CEO, and then met with Paul Allen, the billionaire cofounder of Microsoft who had taken a hands-off approach to running the Seahawks in his seven years as owner.

Speaking to reporters in Kirkland, Allen said, "It's safe to say that Tim has a strong and successful background in recognizing and securing talent, and communicating and motivating as a football executive."

Ruskell pledged to reunite the Seahawks front office.

"One of the keys is unifying," Ruskell said. "People working together where there are no walls, no agendas, and everybody's got a common focus on the goal, and that's winning. The answer is within. I know how it can go south when it's dysfunctional. What I'm hearing is we can do better."

For the first time in more than a decade, Ruskell would draft without McKay. They would not have their usual "popcorn night," where they would kick back and watch interview tapes of players from the combine. They would have to be guarded in their conversations, at least regarding the draft. On the flip side, Ruskell would have final say on draft picks.

In the past, when McKay and Ruskell would debate the merits of players before the draft, Ruskell sometimes would stop before wasting too much verbal energy. "I'm not going to say anything more," Ruskell would say. "I know one thing. You're never going to draft this guy."

Not that there were big disagreements. Having run their character-based draft evaluation for so long with an emphasis on background checks and interviews, they often came to the same conclusions on players. Now Ruskell would take that same system across the country.

He also would take an intimate knowledge of what the Falcons intended to do during the 2005 draft, although much of the final evaluation of players remained to be determined between the combine and during March, as players worked out one last time during campus pro days. Ruskell knew the Falcons' draft strategies to this point, knowledge that might be valuable, since the Seahawks drafted four picks before Atlanta. The information figured to be only so useful, since the teams had different needs and schemes.

If nothing else, Ruskell's anonymity was blown. Seattle sportswriters portrayed him as a hardworking mystery man operating in the shadows of the high-profile Rich McKay: son of John, team turnaround specialist, and future commissioner candidate. That soon would change for Ruskell, with much of the success or failure of an NFL club resting on his shoulders.

"This is a dream and a culmination of years of hard work," Ruskell told reporters in Kirkland. "Who would have thought twenty years ago that a struggling scout working in Saskatchewan would twenty years later be named to help run an NFL team?"

By Saturday, February 26, 2005, the lower level of the Indiana Convention Center was packed. In the hallways, NFL officials passed young girls attending a cheerleading convention, as well as those on hand for a gathering of the Indiana Association of Home Educators, as they shuttled between the RCA Dome, the press room, and their hotels. For some reason, a large number of Amish folks also were on hand, though the autograph hound contingent was modest. The main exhibit hall, adjacent to the RCA Dome and across from the press room, was set up in a country fair theme for the homeschooling crowd. Men wore stickers that read MY WIFE HOMESCHOOLS AND SHE'S MY HERO.

In the midst of the chaos, NFL Radio has set up a broadcasting center. The station, launched on the Sirius satellite radio network late in 2003, already has developed a huge following among NFL personnel, especially scouts driving hundreds of miles on fall weekends. Unlike Super Bowl week, where dozens of all-sports stations compete for guests wandering along "radio row," NFL Radio producers have no problem grabbing dignitaries for a few minutes of on-air chat.

In another room, there's a fitness industry trade show related to the combine. There are gym equipment suppliers, nutritional supplement manufacturers, and even Athletes' Performance, the precombine training center. Representatives of EAS, the Colorado-based maker of meal-replacement powders and protein drinks, hand out free samples. Already EAS displays advertising featuring former Auburn running back Ronnie Brown and cornerback Carlos Rogers, the top draft prospects represented by agent Todd France.

The media is confined to a large rectangular ballroom, which was assembled by opening the doors of four conference rooms. Unlike the Senior Bowl, where press coverage was modest and access virtually unlimited, a large contingent of reporters is kept at bay. Though the entrance to the RCA Dome is only a few hundred feet away, blue curtains block the view. Security people stand alongside signs that read CREDENTIALS ONLY.

The NFL's public relations staff brings a steady stream of players, head coaches, and general managers to the room for press conference–style interviews. The players wear numbered jerseys underneath their gray sweats, assigned by positions. Offensive linemen and running backs wear red, tight ends navy. Defensive linemen, quarterbacks, and wide receivers wear white.

The players stand on podiums at either end of the room. With so many players and more than two hundred credentialed media, the questions tend to be basic. Having undergone mock interviews at their training centers, the players know what to say, most answering in detached monotones. Everyone is willing to play whatever position or role an NFL team requests. Nobody has a preference of which team drafts them. Everyone is confident in their ability, but realizes they have a lot to learn.

Fred Gibson, the Georgia wide receiver, rolled in not long after weighing in (again) at 196 pounds. After seven weeks at Athletes' Performance, he had yet to put on more than three pounds. He strode to the podium and fielded questions.

Q: Who's the best cornerback you faced?
A: I'd have to say Carlos Rogers from Auburn. He has the speed.
   He's very strong in the upper body, just has the total package.
   He's the only defensive back that gave me a challenge.

Q: Did you have a lot of offers to play college basketball?
A: Yes, a lot of SEC schools: Florida, Georgia, Tennessee. I didn't
   start playing football until the eleventh grade. You find so many
   tall shooting guards in the NBA. You don't see too many six-
   four wide receivers in the NFL.

Q: Could you have been a NBA player?
A: I think so, if I would have dedicated myself and worked hard. I
   haven't played in two years. I kind of miss it, but football is my
   future now.

Q: Who do you compare yourself to?
A: I'd have to say Randy Moss. He goes deep, gets the deep ball,
   and I do the same things.

The oddest sight, aside from Bill Parcells weaving between reporters, the Amish, and prepubescent cheerleaders, is Gil Brandt, the former Dallas Cowboys personnel guru, cast as an NFL public relations staffer. Brandt spends much of the combine shuttling players between the dome and the press room, introducing the players to the media, and telling war stories to the many reporters who approach him. It's a role that would seem beneath the pioneer of NFL scouting and one of the architects of the Cowboys' early success, but Brandt embraces it, writing insightful columns for NFL.com and serving as all-around goodwill ambassador for the combine.

Though the combine is an NFL event, it's actually run by National Football Scouting, which at times creates some strange tensions. "National" is made up of NFL franchises, but the NFL has little control over the affair. Even the new NFL television network, a wholly owned subsidiary of the NFL, had to lobby for the right to televise portions of the workout. The 2005 combine marked the first time any portion of the event was televised live, and NFL officials credited the network for the large percentage of players that worked out.

For reporters who have traveled to Indianapolis to be confined to the press room, the lack of access is frustrating. They're reduced to watching the combine unfold on the NFL Network (in the press room—if not in their hotel rooms during the first two days of the combine, when the network broadcasts only a nightly wrap-up show) and that didn't always produce accurate reporting.

On Saturday, the combine finally moved to the RCA Dome field. The group that arrived Wednesday night, having completed their interviews with teams and the media, their medical tests, Wonderlics, and bench presses, would compete first.

Ronnie Brown and Maurice Clarett were among the first running backs to run the forty-yard dash. Clarett, who had unsuccessfully sued to enter the NFL Draft after his freshman year at Ohio State, was in the unusual position of attending his second combine, having not played in more than two years.

Clarett had become something of a pariah in college and pro football circles, not only for his defiant stance against the league and its draft eligibility rule but also for claiming in an interview with *ESPN the Magazine* that he had been given cash and grades he did not earn while enrolled at Ohio State, allegations the university denied. It didn't help that a year earlier, before a court ruled against him, he had come to the combine with a chip on his shoulder. By any measuring stick, NFL teams viewed Clarett as a major character risk.

Brown was among the first to run, clocking in at an eye-popping 4.32, at least according to the NFL Network. Clarett, running moments later, managed only a 4.82.

Or did he? The media soon learned that they were not watching *reality* television. An NFL Network official took the podium to announce that its times were unofficial. Later, the NFL released the official top five times among the group, and Brown's 4.48 ranked second, behind J. J. Arrington of California. In the interest of not embarrassing Clarett, or other low performers, the league did not reveal the other times. (Clarett ran a 4.78.)

Todd France, Brown's agent, could not have been more thrilled. The decision to hold Brown out of the Senior Bowl in favor of another week of precombine training looked like a wise one. With Cedric Benson opting to postpone his workout until his University of Texas pro day, Brown had managed to separate himself from the rest of the running back pack. Even Carnell "Cadillac" Williams, his former Auburn backfield mate, was now clearly behind him.

"Ronnie took the extra week to train, and look what happened," France said. "He's blown up the combine. There's no question that he's the top back in this year's draft. If anyone had any doubts, he eliminated them today."

Chris Canty almost missed the combine.

While the rest of his fellow NFL hopefuls at the Athletes' Performance training center took flights from Phoenix to Indianapolis, Canty and his uncle, Kenya Lee, drove to Tucson and boarded a train. A long delay caused them to miss their scheduled connector, so they got off in San Antonio, spent the night, and then got on another train to St. Louis, where they rented a car and drove to Indianapolis, arriving twenty-four hours behind schedule.

Canty showed up too late for physicals, but was able to interview with teams and take the Wonderlic test, which was all he had planned to do anyway given the condition of his knee—which, though much improved, was still not 100 percent. Canty scored a thirty-four on the Wonderlic, tops among defensive ends, and part of a strong showing by the University of Virginia. Heath Miller's thirty-nine was highest among tight ends and third overall. Alvin Pearman tied for the best running back score with twenty-six. (Virginia guard Elton Brown and linebacker Darryl Blackstock, however, managed only a thirteen and sixteen, respectively.)

Canty interviewed with nineteen teams in the Crown Plaza hotel over Saturday and Sunday nights. Like the rest of the players, he collected a bag of team logo goodies. The Seahawks, his first interview, gave leather briefcases. The Redskins and Rams handed out T-shirts, the Denver Broncos ski caps. The Falcons gave out a combination of ball caps and shirts.

"I hate the giveaways," Falcons president Rich McKay said. "It's ridiculous. It's not like we're recruiting them. We get to draft them."

Interviews were held each evening between six and eleven at the Crown Plaza, originally part of the nation's first "Union Station." Some rooms are converted from Pullman train cars, and the décor pays tribute to early 1900s figures such as Charlie Chaplin and Amelia Earhart. The

Pullman Restaurant, a small eatery and bar, is the only part of the facility not cordoned off for the week. Agents spend much of their time hanging out at the bar, waiting for updates from their clients.

NFL teams are assigned rooms on the first floor, with their logos placed in the window to the hallway. Players receive a spreadsheet of their meeting schedule, usually scheduled over two nights, and shuttle between rooms in fifteen-minute increments. A warning horn blows when there's one minute remaining and again when it's time to switch rooms.

Canty, trying not to appear self-conscious about the eye, addressed the issue head-on, providing copies of the police report and stressing that he did file charges. He also distributed copies of an eye report from a retina specialist in Arizona and a DVD from Athletes' Performance that showed him running and jumping.

Teams were willing to overlook Canty's poor judgment in heading to a nightclub in the midst of combine training; his otherwise impeccable character trumped one bad decision. But the eye, on top of the ailing knee and a history of injuries, gave some cause for concern.

You're never healthy. What's going on?

"I really don't have an answer for that," Canty told teams. "I'm a tough player. I play through injuries. I've had a lot of adversity and I've overcome it. If I do get hurt, it's only temporary, and I'll overcome the injury and I'm going to play. After every injury, I've come back stronger and a better player, and that's not just me talking. You can look at the tape. I'll always be a hard worker; it's been instilled in me and that's what I'll continue to do."

Canty could tell Al Groh and his Virginia staff had put in a good word for him. Teams that employed former Groh colleagues—Miami, Cleveland, New England—seemed to know everything about Canty. Four other teams—Houston, Jacksonville, Washington, and the Jets—employed assistant coaches who served on Groh's staff during Canty's time at Virginia. The Dallas Cowboys and Groh mentor Bill Parcells did not interview him in Indianapolis, but the team planned to fly Canty to Dallas before the draft.

The well-traveled Groh's sphere of influence had widened since the end of the 2004 NFL season. Already, he had former colleagues serving as head coaches in Dallas, New England (Bill Belichick), and New York (the Giants Tom Coughlin). The league's three new head coaches—Miami's Nick Saban, Cleveland's Romeo Crennel, and San Francisco's Mike Nolan—also had worked with Groh.

Bill Musgrave, Groh's offensive coordinator in 2001–2002, recently had left Jacksonville to join Joe Gibbs's staff in Washington. The Houston Texans had hired Groh's defensive line coach, Mike London, who became the fourth Groh assistant to join the NFL in three years.

"If you ever didn't buy into the way Coach Groh harps on the NFL experience of his coaching staff," said Miller, who bumped into Canty for the first time in more than three months at the combine, "you definitely realize it when you're at the combine."

Canty and the rest of the players shuffled between hotel rooms for two evenings. Upon arriving, they were given a schedule of interviews and times. Before 2003, NFL teams grabbed players as they could, much like at the Senior Bowl. To bring some order to the process, teams were asked to submit a list of no more than sixty players.

With 332 players, that does not sound like much, but teams already had interviewed many players at the Senior Bowl and other all-star games. The Falcons, for instance, had spoken extensively with wide receivers Roddy White and Fred Gibson at the Senior Bowl, and reserved combine slots for players like Canty and Georgia defensive end David Pollack, neither of whom they had interviewed. They also interviewed Miller and almost every junior of interest, since none had played in all-star games.

Besides quarterback, the last thing the Falcons needed was a tight end; Alge Crumpler had emerged as one of the league's best in 2004. But the Falcons did not want to dismiss Miller, whom they regarded as an intelligent, high-character player, the best tight end in the draft, and a perfect fit for their West Coast offense, having played it at Virginia. Matt Schaub, the Falcons backup quarterback who came out of Virginia the previous year, had shown Miller his playbook before his first minicamp. They figured more than 70 percent of the plays were run at Virginia.

The Falcons believed there was little downside to spending fifteen minutes chatting with Miller, a player who could play for them down the road. Miller, well-coached for the combine interview by IMG's Steve Shenbaum, was up for playing anywhere.

The interview process was more relaxed than Canty expected. The Falcons contingent, which included Rich McKay, head coach Jim Mora, scouting director Phil Emery, and a rotating cast of scouts and coaches, was eating pizza when he walked into the room. The Falcons ate pizza most evenings, and McKay believed it lightened the mood of the room. They even offered players a slice, which presented a quandary. No interview coach had addressed that situation.

Am I rude if I decline? I don't want to talk with my mouth full. Do they want to see how healthy I eat?

Canty turned down the pizza. Like most teams, the Falcons spent the first five minutes asking about the knee and the eye before querying him about schemes and fits. Canty, like every player, was willing to play wherever. If that meant bulking up twenty pounds and moving to defensive tackle, he was ready to do it. Having played the 3-4 defense (three down lineman, four linebackers) under Groh, Canty felt confident he could make an easy transition to the NFL, where an increasing number of teams played the scheme. He also, of course, told teams he would welcome the chance to play in the 4-3.

The Falcons had scrapped the 3-4 defense in favor of the 4-3 before the 2004 season, which had helped another former Virginia defensive end, Patrick Kerney. Instead of facing double teams each play, Kerney was freed up and recorded thirteen of the Falcons' league-high forty-eight sacks.

For the Falcons, Canty was not what teams call a great "scheme fit." Still, he was a tall, strong defensive end, and such players could fit any scheme to some degree. McKay liked what he saw on film, mostly from the 2003 season, since Canty was injured so early in 2004. If nothing else, he passed the Falcons' character filters—no small accomplishment.

"He's a nice kid," McKay said. "What happened off the field (in Scottsdale) is not an issue for us. Nobody says it was his fault. But the issue with the eye and the knee, those are serious things to consider. It's a shame. Without those, he doesn't last beyond the end of the first round."

If there were a Mike Mamula Award for the most unlikely, eye-popping performance at the 2005 combine, it would have gone to Matt Jones, the former University of Arkansas quarterback who posted a 4.40 mark in the forty-yard dash.

That's a great time for any player, let alone a six-six, 242-pound player without a position. Lacking the traditional bazooka arm, he didn't figure to play quarterback in the NFL. Some teams saw him as a wide receiver, others a tight end. A few projected him as a quarterback/receiver in the mold of Kordell Stewart, who had played the dual role for the Pittsburgh Steelers.

Jones, who had shot up the draft boards, wasn't the only player to earn money at the combine. Georgia defensive end David Pollack made his first appearance in front of NFL scouts since the Outback Bowl on New Year's Day a memorable one. Using Michael Johnson's gunslinger, arm-pumping technique, he completed the forty in 4.75 seconds, among the lowest times for defensive ends. He posted the best mark in the twenty-yard shuttle (3.94 seconds) at his position and scored a solid thirty on the Wonderlic. To nobody's surprise, he came across as confident and engaging in the interview rooms, expressing an interest in playing either linebacker or defensive end in the NFL.

"I had a great combine," Pollack said. "Nothing here surprised me at all."

Fred Gibson, Pollack's Georgia teammate, did little to distinguish himself in Indianapolis. He reached 38½ inches in the vertical leap, among the higher marks among wide receivers. But Reggie Brown led the field with a 41½ inch leap, further distancing himself from his former Georgia teammate. Gibson ran just a 4.55 in the forty, a slower time than twenty-one other receivers. That was significant, since scouts weighed the forty most prominently for wide receivers, because breakaway speed was a crucial trait at the position.

Gibson scored a nineteen on the Wonderlic, about average among receivers. After the forty, his most disappointing number was 196. Despite seven weeks on the weight-gain diet at Athletes' Performance, Gibson added just three pounds.

"I can't help it that I'm lactose intolerant," Gibson said. "I'm not able to put away protein shakes like everyone else."

David Greene put up solid, if unspectacular, numbers at the combine. The most puzzling one was his Wonderlic score (nineteen). With agent Pat Dye Jr. touting Greene's leadership and intelligence, trying to downplay his lack of athleticism, Greene's score was noticeable, especially considering that scouts tend to weigh the Wonderlic more heavily with quarterbacks. Top prospects Alex Smith, Aaron Rodgers, and Charlie Frye scored thirty-five or higher.

"I just didn't take it seriously enough," said Greene, who won an eighteen-thousand-dollar, post-graduate scholarship as the NCAA's National Scholar Athlete. "I'm not going to say I didn't try. I did, but I didn't prepare for it the way I should have."

"There's nobody around here that's going to question David Greene's intelligence," Dye said.

Darryl Blackstock's Wonderlic score (sixteen) was second-lowest among outside linebackers, which perhaps was not surprising for a player who struggled academically at Virginia. Still, scouts enjoyed their first postseason look at the pass-rushing specialist. Blackstock ran a pedestrian forty (4.70) but recorded a thirty-nine-inch vertical leap and twenty-five repetitions on the bench. Blackstock came across as engaging in interviews, though several of Al Groh's former NFL cronies challenged him about reneging on a promise to Groh to return for a senior year.

Blackstock never made such a pledge but spoke highly of Groh, while emphasizing his desire to play at the next level and provide for his young son.

Florida State's Ray Willis tipped the scales in Indianapolis at 327 pounds, third-heaviest among offensive tackles. Still hampered by the ankle injury suffered in November, Willis opted not to work out, though he bench-pressed 225 pounds a respectable twenty-seven times and scored a twenty-four on the Wonderlic.

Having arrived with the first group of players on the first day of the combine, Willis was able to leave on Saturday, February 26. That gave him just two and a half weeks to further rehabilitate his ankle and prove to NFL scouts that he was recovered.

Willis planned to return to Atlanta and train with Chip Smith. For guys like Pollack and Ronnie Brown who dominated the combine, the individual March workouts back on campus were meaningless. They'd sit out the bulk of those, standing by their combine performances, and perhaps undergoing position drills.

For Willis, the date of March 15, 2005, was the most important one on his calendar. On that day in Tallahassee he'd have to run forty yards and undergo the rest of the tests. He did not have the option of sitting out his pro day.

Chapter Fourteen:

PRO DAYS

Brian Battle stood at the podium in the projection room in Florida State's Moore Athletic Center. The 180-seat theater was more than half full of NFL scouts and executives on the morning of March 15, 2005, for the Seminoles' pro day.

The side walls were decorated with images of FSU standouts such as Derrick Brooks, Warrick Dunn, Corey Simon, Deion Sanders, and Peter Warrick. Not that the NFL officials, comfortably seated in deep-cushioned garnet-red theater chairs, needed any reminder of the talent pipeline that had brought them to Tallahassee for a 9:00 A.M. meeting.

It was midway through the March pro day calendar, when schools staged mini-versions of the NFL combine to give scouts one last look at their prospects. By then, almost every player with any hope of being drafted had been weighed, measured, tested, and interviewed extensively at postseason all-star games and/or the combine, but team officials nonetheless scoured the country to get an additional glance at talent.

Many of the scouts on hand were regulars at Florida State, having visited several times during the season as part of their southeastern coverage area. Pro days also brought out general managers and head coaches trying to get another look for themselves. The morning's contingent included Pittsburgh Steelers head coach Bill Cowher, New Orleans Saints head coach Jim Haslett, and Floyd Reese, the general manager of the

Tennessee Titans, who was in the midst of a grueling tour of twenty-five pro days. With the sixth pick in the draft by virtue of a 5-11 record in 2004, and eleven selections overall, the 2005 draft was especially important to the Titans.

"Usually I'll go to eight or ten of these, but we have some extenuating circumstances," Reese said. "This year especially, you want to know what you're getting. You don't come to pro days to see anything real dramatic; it's more of a stabilizing act than anything. By now you expect to see something, and if you do, you leave satisfied that you had this guy pegged."

As with Agent Day in November, Battle planned to spend much of the day playing traffic cop. The school discouraged agents, friends, and family members from attending, but they showed up anyway. The weight room and projection room, where players would be weighed and measured, was the only part of the state facility they could effectively cordon off.

"I'm here to help you do your job," Battle told the group. "I have two police officers with me. If any agents or family members start hassling you, flag one of us down."

Jon Jost, the FSU strength and conditioning coach, took the podium next. Jost was the lone member of Bobby Bowden's coaching staff not on a Caribbean cruise. Jost outlined the day's protocol, which followed the NFL combine schedule and varied little from school to school. The players would enter the room for their height and weight and to have their hand size and arm lengths measured. They'd proceed outside for the forty-yard dash and then come back inside to the weight room for the vertical jump, broad jump, and bench press. From there, they'd go to another indoor room to run the three-cone and shuttle drills on artificial turf before heading back outside to the practice fields for position-related work.

Position work tended to be the most intriguing portion of the day. Many teams dispatched assistant coaches to pro days to work out players. Jost had no problem enlisting volunteers from the audience to work out the Seminoles highly regarded offensive and defensive linemen. A long silence followed when Jost asked for someone to work with the linebackers. FSU had nobody at that position that would hear his name called during draft weekend. Finally, someone accepted the duty.

Brett Maxie, the Atlanta Falcons defensive backs coach, raised his hand to work out the secondary. Maxie was part of a large Falcons contingent that included area scout Boyd Dowler, defensive line coach Bill Johnson, and offensive line coach Jeff Jagodzinski, recently shifted from tight ends coach when longtime NFL assistant Alex Gibbs moved to a consulting position with the team.

Following the combine, Falcons general manager Rich McKay and scouting director Phil Emery took their list of 225 players and assigned the coaching staff cross-checker scouting duties by position. The idea was for the coaching staff to provide input on whether the players were true scheme fits, along with an overall opinion.

Since the Falcons season ended in late January with the NFC championship game, Maxie had taken a crash course on top draft talent, like the rest of the coaching staff. He spent the weeks between the Senior Bowl and the combine watching film and reading scouting reports and now served as a cross-checker, writing reports on defensive backs of particular interest to Atlanta.

Secondary was a need for the Falcons, especially the safety position. But there were few blue-chip prospects at safety. The best of the bunch, Georgia's Thomas Davis, would be long gone by the time the Falcons drafted, and even he was projected by some teams as a linebacker.

The Falcons viewed defensive line, wide receiver, and linebacker as more pressing concerns, but McKay sent Maxie to a few pro days just in case. Two weeks earlier, Maxie came away from the University of Miami's pro day impressed with Antrel Rolle, even though the cornerback would not last until it was the Falcons' turn, picking twenty-seventh in the first round.

Later in the month, Maxie would head to the University of Iowa to take a look at Sean Considine, the Hawkeyes free safety. Maxie's primary assignment at FSU was to serve as a cross-checker for the Seminoles cornerback Bryant McFadden.

McFadden was a legitimate first-day selection, but Maxie would take a long look at the Seminoles' lesser secondary talents, having been in their position two decades earlier.

Maxie never expected to play in the NFL, let alone for thirteen years. During his senior year at tiny Texas Southern in the spring of 1985, he harbored no hopes of being selected in what was then a twelve-round draft. He planned to take his degree in biology and enroll in optometry school, but he made the New Orleans Saints roster as an undrafted free agent. He played nine seasons in the Big Easy before moving on to Atlanta, Carolina, and San Francisco.

Since retiring after the 1997 season, Maxie has retraced his playing career as a coach, working for the Panthers and 49ers before joining Jim Mora's staff in Atlanta.

"The one thing I've learned over the years is that a guy doesn't have to be the strongest, fastest, or tallest player, but he has to have some redeeming quality that catches your eye," said Maxie, who despite his earlier interest in optometry has shunned laser surgery and wears eyeglasses. "So you keep doing research and studying, talking to all your sources and gathering information. You can't overlook a guy just because he doesn't fit the physical mold."

Maxie planned to study Jerome Carter, the Seminoles strong safety. Despite a muscular physique honed by boxing in high school, Carter's strength did not translate on the football field and he tended to get overpowered by receivers. Still, he was regarded as one of the leaders on his team, always a plus in the Falcons' character evaluation.

"He has some redeeming qualities," Maxie said. "I like the way he approaches his craft, very businesslike. He's not the most athletic guy, but he has some size and some instincts. The things I'm going to look for today in the skill drills are how well he moves his body in space making plays on the ball. On film, I don't see the range."

Scouts from other teams figured that Bill Johnson, the Falcons defensive line coach, was on hand to get a look at Travis Johnson, the talented defensive tackle whose stock had soared during the 2004 season.

Though the Falcons needed help along the defensive line, they were unlikely to draft Travis Johnson, who between an acquittal on felony sexual assault charges in 2003 and a reputation for being a handful for coaches virtually disqualified himself from consideration under the Falcons character-based evaluation system. There was no denying his talent; most scouts believed he'd be long gone by the time Atlanta picked in the first round anyway.

Instead, Bill Johnson planned to pay close attention to Chauncey Davis, who unlike Travis Johnson had remained off the radar screen. Dowler, who scouted the state of Florida for the Falcons, believed Davis was a better prospect than Eric Moore, the more highly touted FSU defensive end, and perhaps a better long-term value than Johnson.

Dowler and Emery had met Davis in August while making an early visit to FSU. Though NFL officials rarely get a chance to talk to players during the season beyond a friendly hello, Dowler was able to have a brief conversation and was struck by the player's maturity and presence.

At that point, Davis was nothing more than a well-mannered college backup who had played just one season for the Seminoles, following two years at Jones Junior College in Mississippi. Once Davis got a chance to start in 2004, Dowler noticed a hardworking player who applied constant pressure on the quarterback, even if he did not rack up sacks. Dowler interviewed people throughout the school about Davis and tracked down his high school coach. Everyone, it seemed, had nothing but positive things to say.

"The more you watched, the more you liked the guy," Dowler said. "You're thinking, 'This guy could be a real solid pick on the second day. Not an instant star, but he'd be in the rotation.' He works his butt off, runs well, is a pretty good athlete. You see guys at the combine rated as some sort of future superstar and pretty soon you're thinking, 'I like this guy better.' He's probably playing just as good as the number-one draft choice tackle [Johnson]. But that guy is his own biggest fan. He's an attention-seeker, always putting on a show. He's not my idea of a real good teammate."

Davis was a prototypical McKay player: a late-blooming overachiever with plenty of upside. It also helped that McKay had a successful track record with FSU draft picks in Tampa, from first-rounders Derrick Brooks and Warrick Dunn to safety Dexter Jackson, a fourth-rounder in 1999 who would become Super Bowl MVP following the 2002 season.

The NFL officials in the room had been given nine-page packets of information produced by the strength and conditioning staff. There was a small grid for each player where scouts could write in height, weight, arm length, hand size, and performances in each of the drills.

Twenty-one draft-eligible Seminoles were scheduled to participate in the pro day, along with four special guests.

Linebacker Nate Hardage and quarterback Fabian Walker had transferred from FSU to Valdosta State (Georgia). Since the tiny school did not have a pro day, FSU welcomed them back. Former Seminole Stanford Samuels was signed as a free agent by the Indianapolis Colts before the 2004 season, but was cut in early September. Robert May, a linebacker, had played two seasons in the Arena Football League since leaving Florida State.

Samuels and May represented a sad fringe element of pro days— players desperately clinging to the NFL dream. Most schools require "additional players" to work out last in each session—or in their own group. Brian Battle, hoping to keep the event from deteriorating into an open tryout, limited pro day to those that had played for the Seminoles within the last two years.

Battle drew the line with Adrian McPherson, the quarterback who pleaded no contest to misdemeanor theft and gambling charges. McPherson and his agent, Leigh Steinberg, petitioned FSU to attend, and the decision was close enough that McPherson's name was listed in the scout packet.

McPherson's request did not seem that unreasonable compared to that of Maurice Clarett, who had the unmitigated gall to ask Ohio State if he could return for the Buckeyes pro day, even though he recently alleged that Buckeyes football players were paid by boosters, among other infractions, all of which the university denied. McPherson ended up staging his own workout for scouts at his Bradenton, Florida, high school.

"There were too many open wounds for us to have him back here," Battle said. "Apologies were supposedly given, but it just wasn't enough."

After Jost and Battle finished housekeeping duties, the players entered the projection room from the right in alphabetical order, dressed in shorts and either snug-fitting T-shirts—Under Armour being the brand of choice—or no shirt at all.

Offensive tackle Alex Barron, first alphabetically and in pro potential, led the line. As with the Senior Bowl and the combine, the audience remained silent. The players, most of which were now veterans of the drill, needed little prompting. Scouts announced height, weight, arm length, hand size, and the results of the "sit and reach," a test to measure hamstring flexibility.

Barron, wearing a sleeveless gray T-shirt, checked in at 6.073 (six-seven and three-eighths inches) and weighed 312 pounds. Travis Johnson walked in shirtless, heavily tattooed, and looking chubby. He measured 6.037 and 296 pounds. Ray Willis, wearing a snug red Under Armour shirt, stood 6.053 and 325 pounds.

The scouts dutifully wrote the numbers down out of habit. By now, they had seen most of the players poked and prodded. It's not like anyone was going to gain or lose significant weight from the combine three weeks earlier; certainly nobody was going to get taller. Still, the scouts wrote down data for everyone, even those with no hope of playing in the NFL.

"You never know who might be that one-in-a-thousand guy," said Reese, the Titans general manager. "Some of these guys don't go to an all-star game or combine. Some have been out a year. It's a long-shot, but you want to cover all bases. You're here anyway."

When the scouts were finished with Willis, the audience rose and headed outside. The forty-yard dash often is staged near the end of a pro day, but Jost moved the event up in the schedule with the threat of rain.

To get outside, the scouts walked through the Seminoles locker room, newly renovated at a cost of 2 million dollars. It sprawled out over eighteen thousand square feet and featured spacious locker stalls made of light-colored wood and a wide-open carpeted area with a Seminoles logo woven in the middle.

Scouts never ceased to be amazed at the college football arms race.

Few pro teams possessed such elegant facilities. "These guys are going to be in for a letdown when they get to our building," one scout quipped.

Outside, several hundred people had gathered at the track, a mix of family members, agents, students, and athletic department officials. Most of the scouts headed into the bleachers, sitting near the finish line of the forty-yard dash. A few sat or stood at the finish line, stopwatches poised.

At many pro days, the forty is anticlimactic. Those players that ran well at the combine sit out the pro day run since there's nothing to be gained. Players from the state of Florida historically have not run at the combine, believing it's advantageous to run in a warm familiar setting, away from the pressure of Indianapolis. The more promising the prospect, the more he and his agent can get away with such maneuvers.

Florida State's rubber track had a reputation for being fast, which helped explain the modest Seminole turnout for the forty at the combine. The school's top prospects—Barron, Johnson, McFadden, Willis, and wide receiver Craphonso Thorpe—sat out the forty, though Thorpe and Willis were nursing nagging injuries. Davis posted one of the better times among defensive ends (4.80) in Indianapolis and performed well in the other drills. Carter's time of 4.47 was among the best among strong safeties.

Unlike the combine, where players are clocked electronically, pro day times are open to interpretation. Each scout brings a stopwatch and after each run compares his time to those around him. At the end of the session, the scouts huddle to get a general consensus.

The process is more scientific than it sounds. Since most scouts have clocked thousands of players in the forty, their times are usually similar. It also helps that everyone follows the same routine.

The clock starts at the first sign of movement. Since players begin the sprint from a three-point stance, the hand moves first. Once the watch is triggered, the scout turns to the finish line, ignoring the player's progress. On rare occasions, schools will string a tape across the finish line, but usually it's up to the scout to decide when a player breaks the plane.

Dowler, at six-five, makes it a point to sit in the bleachers above the finish line. "Some guys sit on the ground, but I like to back off. I try to line up directly down the finish line. It helps if you can find a guy with a cap on and just line it up that way. When the player crosses the plane, you have to hit it fast. It takes good reflexes."

Having played or worked in the NFL for parts of six decades, Dowler knew better than to read too much into a player's time in the forty. Jerry Rice, after all, ran a pedestrian 4.6 at the combine in 1985.

"You have to be able to tell the difference between forty speed and play speed, and a lot of that has to do with other factors, physical mostly. You have guys that are stiff who can't change direction very well, who can't get in and out of a break very well. Either they're stiff or don't have balance, or they're not strong enough to carry the football uniform very well. So the timed forty is objective and play speed is subjective. You have to make a call. You might have a 4.6 guy who can do a lot of things well. He's a good athlete, has balance, body control, and he might play faster than a guy that runs a 4.5 or 4.55. While the time is good to look at, you need to be careful and watch him in person. Sometimes you can see a guy on tape and think he isn't fast. If he's smooth and is somewhat of a strider, smooth and not shaking his shoulders, not bobbing his head, thrashing arms and overexpending energy. You think that guy is hardly running. Then you get down on grass next to him and you think, 'He's a little faster than I thought.'"

For the purposes of the workout, Jost, the FSU strength coach, opted to treat every player equally. At Miami two weeks earlier, the Hurricanes top five prospects worked out separately, expediting the process for the scouts. They could leave at the end of the first session, and many did.

In Tallahassee, each of the twenty-five players would run a forty-yard dash before the first one ran a second time. Barron, running first, posted a 4.87 mark—at least according to the consensus from scouts who huddled up to compare notes later—an impressive mark for a man his size.

As the scouts checked their watches, Barron's momentum carried him into a cameraman who had gotten too close. The two tumbled to the ground. For a nervous moment, it appeared Barron had lost millions. Both were okay.

Travis Johnson, forever putting on a show, grunted through his 4.91 dash and screamed as he hit the finish line. "That's called running angry," Maxie said.

Thorpe ran a 4.38, which would have been one of the better times among wide receivers in Indianapolis. McFadden ran a 4.44, though Maxie clocked him closer to 4.3.

"You don't want to go by my watch, but he's fast," Maxie said, sighing. "He's kind of an enigma. When you watch him on film when the ball is in the air, you don't see that 4.3 speed, that second gear. That's the thing; track speed doesn't always translate on the field."

Willis, running last in the alphabetical order, posted a 5.18, a respectable time for a man his size. From the stands, Kimberly Willis cheered and smiled at agent Bill Johnson. Her husband finally was running well, adequately recovered from the ankle injury he sustained against Florida in November.

The Falcons scouts watched Willis, if for no other reason than because he had not worked out at the combine, but he already had been eliminated from consideration. With Alex Gibbs running the offensive line in 2004, the Falcons had adopted his philosophy of employing quick, athletic linemen who moved well laterally, who get off the line fast and run outside to block. That meant there was no need for the Falcons to spend high draft picks on powerful linemen like Barron.

Willis no longer was viewed as more than a third-round pick by most scouts, but he still didn't fit the Falcons mold. Though tightly built and a powerful blocker, he did not change direction quickly. His hips did not shift as fast as the Falcons would like. In scout-speak, he was not "a bender." Not that he had to worry; few linemen made the cut for Gibbs, the offensive line coach for the Denver Broncos during back-to-back Super Bowl title seasons in the late 1990s.

Once each Seminole completed two forty-yard dashes, the scouts huddled inside the track to compare times. Mickey Marvin, a bearded former Oakland Raiders lineman who now scouted for the team, loudly announced that reporters were not allowed to listen in on the session. A couple of sportswriters scurried away, shaking their heads at the unnecessary secrecy. The results would be leaked within hours and posted on various Web sites, which reported all predraft minutiae.

The crowd moved back inside to watch the players perform the three-cone and shuttle drills. From there it was off to the weight room—scouts and players only—for the bench press, vertical jump, and broad jump. Ninety minutes later everyone reconvened on the practice field for position drills. The weather, though overcast and windy, had remained dry.

Maxie took the defensive backs to one end of the field. The group included likely draftees McFadden and Carter, along with four other players, including Stanford Samuels, the free agent the Colts had released in September.

Maxie played the role of quarterback. There were no wide receivers; they were showcasing their skills with quarterback Chris Rix. Maxie simulated various quarterback motions—dropping back, scrambling, looking downfield—to see not only how the players reacted but how their bodies moved. Since cornerbacks must move both laterally and vertically in response to wide receivers, it's vital that they can shift their hips.

"I'm looking to see how good their feet are and how well they control their bodies in a short area," Maxie said. "I'm looking for explosion and transition. Then I look at their ball skills. I take them out on the edge and see how well they move their hips, in terms of zone and man-to-man, turning back across the body and just how they move their bodies in space."

The rest of the Falcons staff fanned out across the practice field. Dowler, like the other Falcons area scouts, was assigned a position to cross-check. Dowler, whose scouting area included Florida State, also was serving as cross-checker for wide receivers, having played the position for the Packers. Neither Thorpe nor Chauncey Stovall was big enough or talented enough for the Falcons, who needed a larger receiver, possibly with their first-round pick.

Jagodzinski, the offensive line coach, watched Barron and Willis, who worked together, alternating in the role of defensive lineman. Though neither Barron nor Willis fit the Gibbs philosophy, Jagodzinski still paid attention. If nothing else, he'd have a better feel for Barron if the Falcons pursued him as a free agent in the future.

Bill Johnson watched the defensive linemen. While much of the crowd focused on Travis Johnson and Eric Moore, he studied Davis. Like Dowler, he was impressed with the player's size and athleticism. Unlike Travis Johnson, who seemed intent on mauling the poor coaches conducting the drills, Davis took direction from the coaches.

Brian Baker, the defensive line coach for the Minnesota Vikings, was in charge of working Johnson through a thirty-second hand-deflection drill to test the player's reaction and balance. When the coach puts his hands on the player, the player must slap them away.

It's a routine drill, but Johnson takes it too seriously. He yells and grunts and even knocks Baker's cap off, which draws cheers from the fans and students watching.

It's not what teams want to see. "Whoever gets that guy will have his hands full," one scout says. "Is he going to take direction or just do his own thing?"

On the other side of the field, Maxie concluded his session with the defensive backs by having them go deep, as if defending a fly pattern. Afterward, he was ready to select McFadden with the Falcons second-round pick, though he knew the team had higher priorities.

"He moved a little better than I expected," Maxie said. "He showed a lot of short-area quickness, which is good. A lot of these guys aren't ready for the anaerobic stuff we throw at them, all of the starting and stopping and bursting. I wish I had thrown more deep balls than I did, but you'll kill them if you give them too many. It's kind of ironic. They've spent all this time training for the forty and the three-cone, and they're not as prepared as they could be for football."

The day after Florida State's pro day, Fred Gibson pondered his draft future over lunch. Rain pelted Gibson's white GMC Yukon parked outside the Taco Mac restaurant just off the University of Georgia campus in Athens. Gibson, along with fellow ex-Bulldog wide receiver Reggie Brown, was to have caught passes from David Greene, but the weather foiled those plans.

Gibson, as usual, was being a finicky eater. Though he skipped breakfast, he barely touched a burger and fries over a leisurely ninety-minute lunch. The staff at Athletes' Performance, the Arizona training center he left two days earlier, had given up putting weight on the skinny former basketball player.

It felt weird being back in Athens. Technically, Gibson and his fellow Bulldogs were still part of the Georgia football program, but, like most draft hopefuls around the country, had spent no time on campus the previous eleven weeks.

The time passed quickly. Gibson had flown to Phoenix shortly after the Outback Bowl and remained at Athletes' Performance, except for a week at the Senior Bowl in late January and four days at the NFL scouting combine in February. He left Arizona ten days before Georgia's pro day and planned to spend the bulk of the time preparing for the event with Greene, Brown, and Zeke Bratkowski, a former Georgia player, NFL quarterback, and assistant coach, who in recent years had served as a predraft quarterback instructor for players such as Michael Vick, Patrick Ramsey, and Philip Rivers.

Agent Pat Dye Jr. hired Bratkowski to work with Greene, who, though not in the same class as Vick, Ramsey, and Rivers (all former first-round picks), had the potential to hear his name called on the first day of the draft.

It was not all work for Gibson. After arriving back in Atlanta, he appeared at the Colonial Mall of America in Macon with Greene, Brown, and David Pollack for an autograph signing. More than fifteen hundred people showed up, many willing to pay thirty dollars for either Greene's or Pollack's signature. The two main draws earned almost twenty thousand dollars each for their efforts, duplicating a payoff from the previous day, when they signed at a mall in Douglasville with Georgia safety Thomas Davis and linebacker Odell Thurman.

Gibson and Brown, not nearly as in demand as Pollack and Greene, commanded just four dollars a signature in Macon, but that still came out to about thirteen hundred dollars per player. Gibson also attended the Southeastern Conference basketball tournament in Atlanta, though even there his mind was never far from the NFL. His date was Tiara Dungy, a student at Spelman College and the daughter of the Indianapolis Colts head coach. The two had met through a mutual friend.

"She said her dad was very strict," Gibson said. "I hope I didn't mess anything up with the Colts."

Now, five weeks before the NFL Draft, Gibson's stock was volatile. He had performed well during the Senior Bowl. Ever gregarious, he interviewed well both in Mobile and at the combine in Indianapolis, though his 4.55 time in the forty-yard dash was a concern. Overall, he could not shake the reputation as a work-in-progress, a skinny, inconsistent, ex-basketball player who could not put on weight.

Considered a potential second-round pick or even a late first-round choice before the 2004 season, the consensus now was that he would go late in the third round. It was not that Gibson had done anything wrong, but that comparable receivers such as Oklahoma's Mark Clayton and Mark Bradley, Vincent Jackson of Northern Colorado, South Carolina's Troy Williamson, Roddy White of Alabama-Birmingham, Indiana's Courtney Roby, and even Gibson's teammate Brown had done more to distinguish themselves. Those that lacked Gibson's height made up for it with strength, speed, size, and consistency. (Michigan's Braylon Edwards and Mike Williams, the former Southern Cal star, were considered more talented than the rest of the pack.)

"I don't know what more I can do to sell myself," Gibson said. "I went up against some of the top defensive backs at the Senior Bowl. I interviewed well, caught every pass at the combine. I ran a 4.55 at the combine, which was the only thing I was disappointed in. That's why I'm going to run here, so I can get that 4.4 I know I'm capable of."

Gibson was presented with some predraft magazines over lunch.

"I don't go searching this stuff out, because people are going to say what they want to say. Like [ESPN's] Mel Kiper. I had a scout say to me, 'Do you think we actually listen to Mel Kiper?' But go ahead. Tell me what they're saying."

"Tends to drop easy balls."

"I've dropped a few, sure. Sometimes I try to get up the field before catching the ball. I see a whole lot of wide receivers do that. Mark Clayton dropped a bunch of passes at the combine. He's a great player, but everyone drops passes. Randy Moss does, and he doesn't even block. C'mon man. Be real. That's why NFL coaches are going to be drafting me and guys writing magazines are not."

"Not very physical and does not like to be hit."

"What kind of crap is that? What receiver likes to be hit? I'm going to catch the football, and if they hit me, they hit me. I've been doing this for four years. Did you see any of this stuff they're talking about at the Senior Bowl? Stuff like dropping passes, coming off the ball slow, taking off plays? I played for Coach [Mark] Richt for one of the best teams in the country. If my coach saw me doing that kind of stuff, I don't think I'd be starting as long as I did. I might as well not show up."

Gibson picked at the French fries.

"Look, I don't think there's a player that's been interviewed more than I have, and I'm going to be talking to more teams in the next month. I've told everyone that I'm not going to bring any problems to their organization. If they draft me, they'll get a great person who loves playing wide receiver and will do anything to help their team win. I'll do anything— play special teams—it doesn't matter. Bottom line is that whoever drafts me is going to have one heck of a player."

The following day, Pat Dye Jr. was back at his desk in Atlanta. It was a busy time of year, between pro days and the beginning of free agency for veteran players. Dye had only a modest slate of pro days to attend. Bill Johnson had worked tirelessly recruiting for ProFiles Sports Management and, as Dye would be the first to admit, had as good a year.

Johnson had recruited Florida State's Ray Willis, Georgia wide receiver Reggie Brown, and Ben Wilkerson, a center from LSU. Dye landed David Greene and Demarcus Ware, the defensive end from Troy State who since the fall had soared from the level of midround pick to potentially a top-ten selection.

Dye and Johnson would attend Georgia's pro day together the following Tuesday. As for Monday, when Auburn's talented draft class would work out just a two-hour drive from the ProFiles office, Dye was free to take the day off.

It still bothered Dye that for the second consecutive year he had been shut out at Auburn, where he graduated and where his father coached for twelve years. This year really hurt. Running backs Ronnie Brown and Carnell "Cadillac" Williams, represented by Todd France and Ben Dogra respectively, were projected as top-ten picks. Cornerback Carlos Rogers, another France client, was climbing the charts, as was quarterback Jason Campbell, who had signed with Joel Segal, whose client list included Michael Vick, quarterback for the Atlanta Falcons.

Dye still was kicking himself for recruiting both Brown and Williams. Unlike most agents, he did not see a conflict of interest in representing two players at the same position for the draft. He knew he lost out on Campbell, since he also was recruiting Greene. Other agents represented multiple quarterbacks in one draft, but it was different with Campbell and Greene, having played in close proximity.

That was the thinking, anyway.

"It's no different than when a Realtor has two houses nearby," Dye said. "The buyer is going to buy what they want to buy. I'm not going to push one house over the other. I'm not going to play favorites; I'm trying to sell houses here. If I had Ronnie and Carnell, I'd have nothing but great things to say about both of them. They're entirely different running backs. One is bigger than the other; one is faster. One catches better, blocks better. This notion that you can't represent two guys at the same position is a fallacy created by agents."

Dye was hardly the first agent to struggle at a school he once dominated. For many years, Drew Rosenhaus was the heavy favorite to land the top players from his alma mater, the University of Miami. That had changed in recent years, with Rosenhaus representing just one of the five Hurricanes selected in the first round of the 2004 draft. Though Rosenhaus landed wide receiver Roscoe Parrish and offensive lineman Chris Myers for the 2005 draft, he lost out on the top two Hurricanes: cornerback Antrel Rolle and running back Frank Gore. Agent Jimmy Sexton, once the dominant agent at the University of Tennessee, had seen his fortunes shift there.

"What happens is that agents will call and say, 'I know you're going with Pat Dye' and they feel like they have to knock me out of the way to have a chance. That's not the case now, but for a long time it was," Dye said. "If you're a prospect and you hear from agents that Pat Dye is getting too big or he doesn't get his clients enough money and you hear that from enough sources, pretty soon that perception becomes reality. Who knows?

"Maybe I get too emotional when I'm in a presentation with an Auburn client. I've heard theories that players thought I talked too much about my father. They don't want to know about my father, they want to know what *I* can do for them. Fine, I've never gone around wearing that on my sleeve or anywhere else. I mention my father in the context of, I know I can't afford to screw up down there or do anything inappropriate. My father's name and legacy makes me more accountable for my actions."

With two young children, Dye knew he probably was not as aggressive on the recruiting trail as he was when he entered the business in his mid-twenties in the late '80s. Many of his competitors were his age or slightly younger, and still single. How could he strike a balance? It's a topic he discussed at the combine in Indianapolis over dinner with Dogra, the SFX Sports agent who landed Carnell Williams. Dogra is three years younger than Dye, but also has two young kids.

Dogra, who did not become a certified agent until 1995, wonders if Dye did not get spoiled in his early years of agent work, before everyone jumped into the business and players began demanding combine preparation and higher levels of concierge service.

"It's a time-consuming, high-service business," Dogra says. "When Pat got into the business, he was getting better clients for less work than he is today, and that's because the competition and the time intensity has driven it up. When you're married and have kids, as I do, something is going to have to give. Are you willing to pay the price? Pat has done it his way for so long, but everything changes. Ten years from now, when I'm forty-nine, I don't know that I'll want to spend all this time before the draft with eight players to make sure everything is right."

In any other year, Dye would have felt good about his recruiting efforts. The following day, he would drive three and a half hours to Troy, Alabama, to see Ware's pro day, which, in the absence of any touted teammates, would be essentially a private workout for NFL scouts. Ever since Ware, who stood six-three and a half, arrived at the Senior Bowl weighing 247 pounds, fifteen more than his listed weight, scouts saw him as the type of versatile end/linebacker who could fit any defensive scheme.

Now Ware weighed 251. Dye's other client, Greene, also seemed to be climbing the charts, to say nothing of landing endorsement deals, largely based on his Q rating in Georgia. Dye's marketing director, Michael Perrett, figured Greene would enjoy more than two hundred thousand dollars in extra income for 2005.

Greene had spent much of the previous two months working with Atlanta area trainer Chip Smith on his footwork and quickness. Like Ware, he seemed destined to overachieve on draft day.

"An agent that takes credit for a guy going higher in the draft is kidding himself," Dye said. "What we do is give our client great advice at every juncture—whether or not to play in the Senior Bowl or work out at the combine. We solicit feedback on their strengths and weaknesses from teams, and we excel on that because of the access of information from my father's career and from my career. We can tell Demarcus Ware that teams want to see him at 250 and not 239. With David Greene, team after team is telling me he needs to work on his speed, agility, and lateral quickness. So we feel like we're going to put them in the best possible position to get them drafted as highly as possible. But I'm not going to run the forty. I'm not going to bench-press or catch passes or convince a team that he's a better player than the one over here. They're going to make that determination on their own, but I hope that through everything we put into it with advice, physical and mental preparation, soliciting and passing along feedback, taking things off their mind in terms of scheduling—anything we can do to allow them to focus can translate into higher draft stock."

Based on his discussions with NFL officials, Dye believed Ware would go in the first half of the first round. Reggie Brown could sneak into the first as well. "He's certainly a two," Dye said. Ray Willis was moving into the second round, Dye felt, Greene the second or third. As for Wilkerson, who had been hampered by an injured knee, who knew? "He's all over, anywhere from third to sixth."

Dye shrugged. "That's a solid year. They're great kids. But having graduated from Auburn and my father having coached there, and the presence we've had there representing three or four times as many Auburn players as any other agent—with all that in mind, this year will always have an asterisk beside it."

Todd France pulled his black Mercedes CLK 430 convertible into a parking garage near the University of Georgia's Butts-Mehre Heritage Hall. It was March 22, 2005, which not only was pro day for the Bulldogs but also the twenty-second birthday of safety Thomas Davis, France's client.

To mark the occasion, France carried a giant chocolate chip cookie inside a box large enough to hold a pizza. Davis, as an elite athlete, would eat little if any of the cookie, but that wasn't the point. France, like his competitors, was all about personal attention.

France walked briskly through wind and light rain into Butts-Mehre, another multi-million-dollar shrine to the flourishing business of college football, complete with vast workout and meeting facilities, a Bulldogs museum, and decorated in an elegant style normally reserved for luxury hotels and high-end law firms.

The Bulldogs, coming off a 10-2 season, were winning the college football arms race, though the large contingent of scouts and prominent agents filing into the building served as a reminder of how hard-pressed they would be to reload for the 2005 season.

France, like the other agents, stood sentry by a bank of elevators near the meeting room that would serve as the briefing area for the scouts and Georgia officials. He nodded at rival Atlanta representatives Pat Dye Jr. and Bill Johnson, who did the same, and greeted NFL executives as they passed. France, unlike Dye, had spent the previous day at Auburn at the pro day of clients Ronnie Brown and Carlos Rogers.

Once the NFL officials were seated and doors to the meeting room were closed, France sidled up to Tom Condon, the IMG agent whose draft clients included David Pollack, the Georgia defensive end projected as a first-round pick.

Condon and France exchanged pleasantries. In France's young career, he rarely had gone head-to-head with IMG for a client; Condon landed Pollack ahead of Ethan Lock, whose Arizona firm of Lock, Metz & Malinovic represented Wisconsin defensive end Erasmus James and Virginia's Chris Canty, among others, for the 2005 draft.

France had only a five-person staff, unlike the hundreds employed by the worldwide conglomerate of IMG that represented athletes and sports properties throughout the industry, including a vast football client list headlined by Indianapolis Colts quarterback Peyton Manning, San Diego Chargers running back LaDainian Tomlinson, and Chad Pennington, the quarterback of the New York Jets.

But France had arguably as impressive a class for the 2005 draft. Condon and partner Ken "Fuzzy" Kremer represented Utah quarterback Alex Smith, projected as the number-one overall pick, along with Pollack and potential first-rounders Heath Miller, the Virginia tight end, and Chris Spencer, an offensive lineman from Ole Miss. France had three surefire top-twenty picks in Davis and his two Auburn clients.

Condon and France stepped back as the meeting broke up and scouts flooded into the lobby. Georgia officials, like their Florida State counterparts a week earlier, rearranged the schedule to account for the weather, moving the forty-yard dash first.

As the scouts and players headed outside, Tim Ruskell adjusted his Seattle Seahawks cap. It had been exactly a month since he left his job as assistant general manager of the Atlanta Falcons to become president of the Seahawks. The move included a huge increase in salary, though it didn't feel like such a promotion at the moment.

With the exception of Titans general manager Floyd Reese, who was continuing his iron-man schedule of pro day events, Ruskell was by far the highest-ranking official at Bulldogs pro day. Many team presidents, including his former boss Rich McKay, were in Hawaii for the NFL's annual meetings. Most general managers and head coaches also were there.

Though Ruskell was well up to speed on the 2005 draft with the Atlanta Falcons, he was looking at it from a new perspective, evaluating talent with different needs in mind. Not only that, he had inherited a skeleton Seahawks staff that since the beginning of the year had lost its vice president of football operations, general manager, and director of college scouting.

So, instead of going to Hawaii, Ruskell packed his stopwatch and new Seahawks logo sportswear and hit the road, with Auburn and Georgia two of his more prominent stops. Outside at the Bulldogs' track, he took a prominent position at the finish line of the forty-yard dash.

"I'm always going to approach this from a scout's perspective, because that's where I came from," Ruskell said. "If I didn't do that, then the Seahawks aren't getting the benefit of why they hired me."

The wind seemed to help the Georgia players. Fred Gibson ran between 4.42 and 4.48, depending on the stopwatch. Teammate Reggie Brown ran slightly faster. David Greene and Pollack opted not to run, standing with their times at the combine. Davis, the star attraction, ran between a 4.48 and a 4.55.

Doug Hendrickson, Gibson's agent, was convinced his client's stock was strong. "He's a late first, maybe the second round," he said. "He's shed the basketball image."

With the sky growing darker and the wind beginning to gust, the players proceeded to a practice field for position drills. Like most major football programs, Georgia had one field made of artificial turf. Instead of the knee-punishing Astroturf of the 1980s, it was a synthetic blend of sand and shredded rubber, topped by the equivalent of a giant green welcome mat.

Greene, wearing gray sweats from the combine, loosened up at midfield, flanked wide by Gibson and Brown. Zeke Bratkowski watched nearby, as did Mike Johnson, the quarterbacks coach for the Atlanta Falcons.

The last thing the Falcons needed was a quarterback. In December, the team signed Michael Vick to an eight-year contract extension worth $130 million through 2013. Matt Schaub, selected in the third round of the 2004 draft, had quickly grasped the West Coast offense, having played it at the University of Virginia, and the Falcons were confident he could fill in capably if Vick were injured.

Still, Greene intrigued the Falcons. He was a proven winner, having led the Bulldogs to forty-two wins, a record for Division 1-A quarter-backs. He was unflappable under pressure and a leader by any measuring stick. He also possessed the rare gift of being able to treat members of the media like old buddies without divulging secrets or saying anything remotely controversial.

Greene also had grown up in the Atlanta suburbs, which was no small matter for McKay, who believed having local products on the roster was grossly underrated. Even in the modern mercenary world of sports, with wealthy athletes often detached from their communities, McKay found fans were more likely to give a team and its players the benefit of the doubt if there was a local connection, no matter how tenuous.

In Tampa, McKay drafted heavily from the University of Florida and Florida State. Shaun King, a marginally talented quarterback selected in the second round out of Tulane in 1999, became a fan favorite despite his erratic play. King had grown up in St. Petersburg and, like Greene, lacked the traditional size and athleticism NFL teams demanded of quarterbacks.

That thinking was shifting, especially now that former sixth-round pick Tom Brady had led the New England Patriots to three Super Bowl titles in four years.

"Brady was on the lower end of physical ability," said Mike Johnson, who evaluated him in 2000 as quarterbacks coach in San Diego. "But he was high on the intangible side. Same thing with Greene. If you're a guy that lacks physical ability, you better have the smarts, intelligence, and decision-making ability. For a guy like Greene, it balances out."

As Greene fired passes to Gibson and Brown, Ruskell approached Pat Dye Jr. Unlike his former Falcons colleagues, Ruskell had a pressing need for a quarterback to play behind starter Matt Hasselbeck. He also liked Dye's client Demarcus Ware, though he knew the Seahawks would have no shot at Ware, picking twenty-third in the first round.

When Greene was finished, Ruskell asked him how he felt about playing for the Seahawks. The question is a typical conversation starter this time of year, whether in interviews at the combine or in more casual settings. Greene, who had never been to the West Coast, expressed enthusiasm for the Seahawks and related a story involving Hasselbeck.

It was a predictable response. With players coached for interviews, scouts rarely hear anything but excitement about playing for any team, no matter how cold the climate or how poorly the team has played in recent years. *Are you kidding? I'd absolutely love to play for the Lions!*

"You take it half-seriously," Ruskell says. "You run across players that clearly have a preference. Either they grew up as a fan of a team or want to stay close to home. But you can use it to gauge passion and how excited a guy might be to play for you. You can only fake it so much."

When Ruskell finished with Greene, a scout from the Green Bay Packers took the quarterback to the other end of the field for some more drills. Greene had learned not to read anything into which teams seemed to be giving him more attention.

"You've got so many different teams and different schemes, and they want to see how you fit, and I don't blame them," Greene said. "If you're going to invest all that money in someone, you want to check everything out. Guys get picked by teams that never spoke to them. They had no questions because they knew they were going to be great players. I don't even try and figure it out. It's like chasing your tail."

The star of the morning was birthday boy Davis, who was rapidly ascending in the draft. Davis performed both linebacker and defensive back drills. The vibe France got from teams was that half of them projected him as a safety in the NFL, the other half a linebacker.

The Falcons and Seahawks were among the teams that coveted Davis, but they knew he would be long gone by their twenty-third and twenty-seventh picks. He had the thickness of a linebacker and the speed of a defensive back, but though he had the physique of a bodybuilder, he lacked traditional weight room numbers.

After position drills, the crowd moved inside. Georgia, unlike most schools, allowed everyone into the weight room: agents, media, friends, family, students, and underclassmen. If Georgia officials were concerned about agents talking with underclassmen, they didn't show it. Representatives spoke freely with up-and-coming players alongside motivational signs such as THE DESIRE TO WIN IS WORTHLESS WITHOUT THE DESIRE TO PREPARE, DO YOU HAVE A BAD CASE OF THE WANTS?, and RULE NUMBER SEVEN: ASK GOD FOR HELP.

The weigh-in took place first. Fred Gibson again checked in at 196. Davis, who did not bench-press at the combine, managed only twelve repetitions, barely half that of players of comparable size (six feet, 230 pounds).

No matter. For players with the talent of Davis, weight room performance was irrelevant. Later, while Davis showered, France waited to take his client to lunch. He sat on a weight bench near the sign for rule number six—SEE YOURSELF MAKING A GREAT PLAY.

The rest of the agents, scouts, and players had departed. The draft was one month away, and for thirty-three-year-old Todd France it was all coming together.

Chapter Fifteen:

RED-DOT SPECIALS

The Atlanta Falcons draft room, like the rest of the Flowery Branch training complex, is first class. Those fortunate enough to be invited inside must go to the second floor, where they arrive at a marble landing with the inlay of the Falcons logo. To the left is a large, softly lit portrait of team owner Arthur Blank holding a football, flanked by action shots of linebacker Keith Brooking and running back T. J. Duckett. Across the landing is a portrait of general manager Rich McKay and head coach Jim Mora, surrounded by action images of running back Warrick Dunn and quarterback Michael Vick.

Straight ahead is the executive conference room. Down the hallway to the right is a room identified with a sign outside that reads simply DRAFT ROOM. The Falcons, like the rest of the league, as well as ESPN, have refrained from using the term "war room" since the United States invasion of Iraq in 2003.

Inside the draft room is an NFL fantasy leaguer's dream come true. The room is slightly rectangular and has perhaps one thousand two hundred square feet of floor space. Rows of tables face the front. The head table is reserved for Blank, McKay, Mora, and scouting director Phil Emery. Scouts and other personnel people occupy most of the other tables. Assistant coaches remain in their offices, available for insight if needed.

Two walls, the front and right, are covered from floor to ceiling with white magnetic board. The front wall contains two identical groupings of about five hundred magnetic strips. Each strip is roughly the size of a business card. It represents a player and includes his name, position, college, agent's name, height, weight, and Wonderlic score, along with his rating by the Falcons staff. That rating contains a number between 5.0 and 8.0 and a double-letter grade of AA to FF. The numerical portion is similar to that used by several teams and is a descendant of a system developed by Bucko Kilroy, one of the NFL's first full-time scouts in the 1950s.

The front board is arranged as a grid, with positions listed horizontally along the top and the numerical ratings vertically along the left side. Magnets are arranged accordingly. During the draft, scout Matt Berry will distribute the magnets onto two boards on the right wall, continuing a duty he once performed as an intern. One is a round-by-round board, the other a team-by-team. The final board ranks each team's top-three needs by position, which is a valuable reference when trying to determine if the teams drafting close by might take the Falcons desired player.

The rating system is identical to the one the Falcons use to update their existing roster, generally once every four games during the regular season. Unlike grades that are based on professional track records, the draft grades are computed using college performances and pro projections.

Most players fall into the 5.6-to-5.9 range and are rated as solid starters or "backbone" (5.9), backups or "contributor" (5.8), and fringe players or "depth" (5.6 to 5.7). Anyone rated 6.1 or higher is considered a star, a player who consistently makes plays that win games. Though the numbers ranged from 5 to 7, scouts referred to them as if the decimal places did not exist. A guy is a "sixty-two" or a "fifty-seven."

Within the 5.7-to-5.9 range, players also can receive a plus or minus, depending on the projected period of transition. A 5.8-plus, for instance, might be a player that's on the border of being a starting player, either already as a veteran or, in the case of a drafted player, down the road. The plus/minus system also is a reflection of how well a player fits the Falcons' offensive and defensive schemes. No plus or minus is given at 6.1 or higher, since players projected that high inherently fit schemes and should need little transition time.

It's a tough grading system. Falcons such as linebacker Keith Brooking and defensive end Patrick Kerney, whom during the 2004 season many fans would have called stars, warranted only 5.9 ratings at the beginning of the year, but were bumped up to 6.2s after Pro Bowl campaigns. Quarterback Michael Vick, considered by some the best player in the league, or at least the "playmaker" most capable of transforming a game, is a mere 7.0, though the Falcons brass believes he can ascend to the 8.0 level. Alge Crumpler, the team's All-Pro tight end, is a 6.7.

McKay and his staffs, first in Tampa Bay and then in Atlanta, have typically assigned a rating of 6.1 or higher to just fifteen to twenty players heading into the draft. Not surprisingly, the players receiving such ratings for 2005 projected as high picks, including Georgia safety Thomas Davis (6.4), Auburn running back Carnell Williams (6.3), Troy State defensive end Demarcus Ware (6.2), Miami cornerback Antrel Rolle (6.2), and Roddy White, a wide receiver from the University of Alabama-Birmingham (6.2).

The two-letter ratings, from A to F, represent "football character" and "personal character," respectively. A player receiving a grade below a C in either category has little chance of getting drafted by the Falcons.

"With football character, we're not looking for Mr. Goody Two-shoes or guys that always do the right thing," McKay said. "That's the second grade, personal character. The first grade is about a million different things. It's about toughness, desire, work ethic. How many off-season workouts did he attend? How did he handle and play through injury? Does he command respect from teammates and instill fear in opponents? What did his coach say about his ability to learn football? Not math or science, but football. All of that goes into football character."

Personal character is a measure of citizenship. If a player has a criminal record, a history of disciplinary problems, or poor performance in the classroom, the Falcons believe he's more likely to be a distraction in the locker room and will not make the most of his talent.

"The object is to make sure you know very well who it is you're bringing in, and you accept both from the coaches' standpoint and the organization's standpoint, whatever the weaknesses are," McKay said. "Are we okay with that, and, if we are, what's our plan to manage it? Once you know the whole person you're dealing with, you're okay. It's surprises that crush you. It's not that we've set the bar so high we've eliminated everybody. It's just we want to know everything there is to know. There are certain guys, because of what we know, we're not going to take them."

Though McKay does not identify such players, it's clear where certain players rank in the Falcons character-based system. Adam "Pac Man" Jones, a highly rated cornerback and Atlanta native who played at West Virginia, was involved in a 2002 bar fight that led to a malicious assault charge, a felony that was later reduced to a misdemeanor. (Jones received a suspended sentence, along with probation and community service.) Richie Incognito, the former Nebraska lineman, had a history of suspensions from his college team. In February of 2004, he was charged with three counts of assault following a fight at a party and was found guilty of one misdemeanor assault charge. Then there was Odell Thurman, the Georgia linebacker with a history of troubles, including a suspension from the team as a freshman for a series of incidents, including a bar fight. Later he was arrested for underage possession of alcohol and having an open container of alcohol in a vehicle. These charges were dropped, and he was given a fine for a traffic violation.

Jones, Incognito, and Thurman were among the dozens of talented players eliminated from consideration by the Falcons' character filter.

The Falcons' character ratings are even more stringent than the numerical rankings. Davis, rated a 6.4, earned a CB rating. Rolle, the 6.2, ranked BC. Chris Spencer, a 5.9-plus center from Mississippi that the Falcons thought of highly enough to bring to Flowery Branch for an interview, was rated CC. Ware, the Troy State defensive end whose stock had soared between an impressive performance at the Senior Bowl and by gaining twenty pounds, rated AA. Nobody, it seemed, could find anything negative to say about Ware, a studious athlete, weight room warrior, and all-around good guy.

Then there was Williams, the Auburn running back nicknamed "Cadillac," who received an "AA" rating from the Falcons. Gregarious, humble, a team leader, and a tireless worker, Williams was a younger, more talented version of Warrick Dunn, a model citizen who could both run and catch out of the backfield.

Of course, the Falcons already had Dunn on their roster. Between Dunn, Duckett, and Vick, a constant threat to take off, running back was a low priority for the Falcons. Still, Cadillac's magnet in the Falcons draft room was one of just eighty stamped with a red dot.

At the moment, the eighty red-dot magnets were scattered along the front draft boards, across positions, and from 5.7 and up vertically. Barring something unforeseen, like a highly rated player that took a precipitous drop, the Falcons' eight picks would come from among the eighty.

They were not the eighty most-talented players or the eighty rated highest by the Falcons. After all, the Falcons, like everyone else, had to make late-round selections. But the eighty players were those that best fit the team's needs and schemes, while earning high grades as prospects and in both football character and personal character.

Which players would land in the Falcons lap depended on a host of factors. It was not as simple as ranking the group one to eighty and crossing players off as other teams drafted. McKay had tried that in

Tampa, and it only created problems if he decided to pick a player when there were five or six remaining on the list ahead of him. The list opened up the room for debate and gave scouts fodder to argue for players from their scouting regions, even during the draft.

Instead of drafting vertically, McKay chose horizontally, based on the 8.0 scale. During the draft, as magnets were transferred, it was easy to see which players remained at the highest levels across all positions. If, for instance, the team needed both a defensive tackle and a linebacker, the highest-rated player at either position usually would get the nod. The Falcons generally would wait until the next selection to address the other need, unless, of course, a more highly rated player at another position of need remained on the board. Scouts quickly learned McKay's mantra, "We do not want to drop down a level to draft a player."

That helped explain how the Carnell Williams magnet ended up with a red dot. Most mock drafts projected Williams going to Tampa Bay with the fifth pick. Though nobody put much stock in mocks—examine enough of them, and it's possible to find most players going to any of a half dozen teams, more in the later rounds—the Williams projection looked solid. Tampa Bay head coach Jon Gruden, who coached the running back during the Senior Bowl, made no secret of his feelings. Williams was the player to jump-start the Bucs' moribund running game.

At the same time, the offensive-minded Gruden could never have enough wide receivers and quarterbacks. Mike Williams, the Tampa native and former Southern Cal receiver, had made an impression. The Bucs needed an upgrade at quarterback, and there was talk of a trade up to land Alex Smith, the Utah junior.

It had become fashionable in NFL circles to suggest that running backs were disposable commodities. The Denver Broncos seemed to create a new backfield star each season. Still, if Cadillac made it past the Buccaneers, it was highly unlikely that he would fall to the Falcons at number twenty-seven.

Since Williams was such an ideal scheme fit, and a perfect AA character, the Falcons placed a dot on him. Former teammate Ronnie Brown, another AA character who even received the team's highest rating, the Falcon Filter, also had a dot, though there was even less chance he'd be available at number twenty-seven. The red dots also included tight ends Heath Miller of Virginia and Alex Smith of Stanford, both solid fits for the team's West Coast offense. Both figured to be available when the Falcons picked, though it made no sense for the Falcons to select either, with Crumpler entrenched at the position.

The Falcons even hung a dot on David Greene, the Georgia quarterback. The last thing the team needed was a quarterback. Greene, a high-character local product, would be tempting at the end of the draft if he was available. McKay figured he'd go in the third or fourth round, but that's what he thought in 2000, when Georgia Tech quarterback Joe Hamilton slid to the seventh round and McKay drafted him for the Buccaneers.

Players like Williams, Brown, Miller, Smith, and Greene were more the exceptions. Of the eighty red dots, about seventy were truly in the mix to become the next Atlanta Falcons.

Williams compared favorably to other smaller NFL backs, such as Tiki Barber of the Giants and Washington's Clinton Portis. But they were both second-round picks, in part because of size concerns, and teams rarely spent a first-round choice on the position, unless they lacked a featured back.

Cadillac was a long shot for Atlanta. The only way he would wear a Falcons uniform was if twenty-six teams passed. McKay would not be trading up to grab a running back, sacrificing future draft position and picks.

He would, however, consider trading up to land two of the biggest red dots on the Falcons board: Ware or Davis. Having played, respectively, at Troy State University (in nearby Troy, Alabama) and the University of Georgia, the players had plenty of exposure to Falcons scouts. The Falcons viewed Ware as a defensive end, unlike much of the league that saw him as a linebacker. As for Davis, the Falcons did not care if he played safety or linebacker, though the latter position was less of an immediate need with the signing of free agent Ed Hartwell from the Baltimore Ravens a month earlier. Davis, the Falcons believed, was a future star at either position.

McKay had his limits, however. If he could trade up from number twenty-seven to, say, number twenty to grab Davis or Ware, he would do it. Any higher and teams would command a number one or number two in the 2006 draft, a price McKay refused to pay. He wasn't about to do what Buffalo did in the 2004 draft, sending its number-one pick in 2005 to Dallas, along with second- and fifth-round picks in 2004, for the chance to draft quarterback J. P. Losman in the first round in 2004.

Buffalo's former first-round pick now was, ironically, the twentieth selection. With the Cowboys drafting eleventh and twentieth, and head coach Bill Parcells remodeling his defense into a 3–4 scheme, there was a good chance the versatile Ware would go to Dallas. McKay could live with that; he had learned never to stake too much on the selection of any one player.

"It becomes very pricey," McKay said. "What everyone tries to do in a trade up is they're hoping you've fallen in love and they're hoping you're willing to put next year's one or two on it. Not for me."

It had come to this, just eighty players, seventy really. From a pool of thousands that Falcons scouts began evaluating in May, they had narrowed the field to 225 by the combine. Through cross-checking and meetings, they had culled the list to eighty players.

Once pro days ended, roughly four weeks before the draft, the scouting staff reconvened at Flowery Branch. They spent the first three weeks going through the 225 players, rereading every one of the now voluminous files. They repeated the process the final week before the draft with head coach Jim Mora, defensive coordinator Ed Donatell, and offensive coordinator Greg Knapp.

During the process, McKay paired up scouts and assistant coaches to do a ranking of players at each position. Tim Ruskell came up with the idea before he left for Seattle. The idea was to take another close look at the players while also building camaraderie between the coaching and scouting staffs.

The process of elimination was now complete. At times, McKay cautioned his staff from taking it further. With players so thoroughly scouted by now, everyone had a few warts.

"Let's not kill everybody on the board," he said. "There are some guys who can be Falcons."

How much of the eighty-player list was a reflection of character evaluation? In the early 1990s, McKay believed teams weighed character just 10 percent in their overall ratings. These days, he figured it was up to 40 percent—more than 50 with the Falcons.

However, the Falcons' double-letter character grade did not serve as a tie-breaker during the draft. If it came down to two comparable players with the same numerical grade, McKay would call in the appropriate position coach to see if one player was a better scheme fit.

"The letters are confusing because we emphasize character so much," McKay said. "We're not going to draft anybody *because* of character, but we may *not* take somebody because of character. We're not going to draft because of these letter grades. But it plays a key role in the process of elimination."

McKay preached to his staff to watch what they said in the weeks leading up to the draft, not just to other teams, but to the media. He wasn't as paranoid as Parcells and New England head coach Bill Belichick, who did not allow their assistant coaches to speak to the press. But McKay didn't want anyone to be able to glean information about who the Falcons planned to pick.

On the Monday before the draft, McKay sat with Falcons beat writers Matt Winkeljohn of the *Atlanta Journal-Constitution* and George Henry of the Associated Press. Few sports executives are better at the give-and-take of informal interviews with writers than McKay, who, like his late father, is insightful, self-deprecating, and quick with one-liners. He appreciates journalists who try to better understand the personnel decision-making process and the salary cap implications of each move. The financial structure of a football roster is more complex than those of the other three major sports, which was why, upon taking the Atlanta job, he held a seminar for Falcons media on the salary cap.

Sitting with Winkeljohn and Henry in the office belonging to public relations director Reggie Roberts, McKay held court for forty-five minutes without addressing any draft prospect by name.

"I'm not going to talk about specific players," McKay said. "I don't think it's appropriate for me to grade them and scout them right here. Because then if I draft a guy and I had said something bad about him, you'll kill me. If I said something good and we didn't, you'll kill me. I'm not big on grading specific players."

Winkeljohn was familiar with McKay's tactics. "What about Shaun Cody?"

"Cody?" McKay asked. "What school did he go to?"

McKay figured he had done a successful job keeping a lid on the Falcons' plans, because most of the mock drafts were not coming close to predicting what the team planned to do.

The team had brought in four players for interviews in the weeks before the draft—Oklahoma defensive end Dan Cody, Alabama-Birmingham wide receiver Roddy White, Clemson cornerback Justin Miller, and Ole Miss center Chris Spencer—and even they were not drawing much attention in mock drafts.

Brodney Pool, the safety from Oklahoma, was a popular pick. Many predicted a defensive lineman, such as Iowa's Matt Roth or Shaun Cody from Southern Cal. *USA Today*'s mock draft had the Falcons taking Davis at number twenty-seven, an ambitious pick McKay gladly would have accepted. Paul Zimmerman, the longtime football writer for *Sports Illustrated*, projected White, the UAB wide receiver.

The hometown *Atlanta Journal-Constitution* threw out six names:

Pool, Roth, Cody, Tennessee linebacker Kevin Burnett, tight end/wide receiver Matt Jones of Arkansas, and Bryant McFadden, the cornerback that Falcons defensive backs coach Brett Maxie worked out during Florida State's pro day five weeks earlier.

Without a glaring need at any position, McKay could play his cards close to the vest. With the exceptions of quarterback and tight end, the Falcons were open to upgrading at any position. Between the roster McKay inherited in December of 2003, the 2004 draft, and several free agent acquisitions, he was in position to use the 2005 draft essentially to choose a developmental squad. The draftees would play, as backups and on special teams, but nobody needed to start immediately. They could be eased into the system slowly.

It was easy to sell patience in Atlanta, especially after a surprising 11-5 season in 2004. Atlanta never will be described as a rabid sports town. Fans were mostly ambivalent, even when it came to the Braves, a dominant team for more than a decade. In New York, Philadelphia, or Chicago, fans would be calling for major free agent acquisitions to put the team over the hump after a season like the Falcons had in 2004.

There were smatterings of discontent. Terrence Moore, sports columnist for the *Atlanta Journal-Constitution*, wondered in the days leading up to the draft if McKay wasn't overestimating his talent pool.

"He apparently has nerves of steel," Moore wrote. "That's because he doesn't see what I see, and that is an overachieving team that went to the NFC championship game last season by overcoming a lot of things. I'm talking about things such as a secondary that rarely was gouged by a deep pass, but that relinquished so many yards through the air that you figured the Falcons would get a certifiably awesome defensive back from somewhere. They didn't.

"Elsewhere, you have the Falcons' receiving woes. In a tribute to the NFL's Stone Age that featured Bronko Nagurski, three yards and a cloud of dust, and the forward pass only as a last resort, starting wideouts Peerless Price [forty-five catches] and Dez White [thirty-five catches] were virtually invisible. You know you're offensively impaired when your tight end [Alge Crumpler] is your go-to receiver, and nothing has changed."

McKay knew the wide receiver position needed to be addressed. He much preferred drafting at the end of the first round. That meant the team had done well the season before and probably had no pressing needs. The worst place to be was at the end of the first round with a glaring hole, as McKay had been in 2001, with the Buccaneers in dire need of a left tackle.

Not only did McKay have to surrender his second-round pick for the right to move up from number twenty-one to Buffalo's number fourteen in the first round, the Bucs were forced to start that player, University of Florida junior Kenyatta Walker, immediately. Walker quickly alienated teammates and coaches with his underachieving play, poor work ethic, and by voicing his complaints to the media.

"If we didn't get a left tackle, we didn't have anybody to line up there," McKay said. "That is very, very nerve-racking. Because now you're going to watch every card come off, from number five through fifteen, before you can get into range to move up, and that is not fun. You always want to pick last. The next place you want to pick is second to last. And you move up from there."

Picking later in the round requires a different mind-set. From the Buccaneers' first draft in 1976 through 1997, McKay's third as general manager, the team often selected among the first ten picks, including number one five times. As the team improved in the late 1990s and began drafting later, McKay, Tim Ruskell, and Jerry Angelo realized they had to change their thinking. A player they previously considered an early second-round pick needed to be viewed as a late first-rounder, especially with the additions of four new franchises between 1995 and 2002.

So, as the Falcons examined their eighty red-dot players for the 2005 draft, they needed to get an idea of where they might go by round, keeping in mind their late draft position.

The Falcons had pegged Courtney Roby, a wide receiver from Indiana, as a third-round pick. But the more they spoke to teams around the league, the more it became apparent that somebody would take him early in the third round. If the Falcons wanted Roby, they'd have to grab him with their pick at the end of the second—if they did not take a wide receiver in the first.

McKay believed there was danger in picking late in the round, especially the first round, because you're more likely to take a player who chronically underachieves, even though he has tremendous talent. The further he falls, the more of a bargain he appears.

"It's very tempting, because his card will be sticking up on that board and it'll have a fast time, and he'll jump real high. He's going to look great when he comes in here. The only thing is, he's got to go out and play, and he didn't quite do that in college, otherwise he'd have been picked higher."

Though eighty players was a small universe of players in a draft of 255, the red dots were spread out evenly across most positions, with quarterback and tight end being the exceptions. At linebacker, the Falcons had six red dots, all of which projected to go in the second or third rounds.

That group included Jordan Beck of Cal Poly, Southern Cal's Lofa Tatupu, Nebraska's Barrett Ruud, Matt McCoy and Kirk Morrison of San Diego State, and Michael Boley of Southern Miss. Technically, the group also included Davis and Ware, though the Falcons viewed Davis as a safety and Ware as a defensive end. Both would be long gone by number twenty-seven.

Which of the remaining six would fall to the Falcons? In a sense, it didn't matter. Each player fit the Falcons 4-3 defensive scheme, was sufficiently talented to warrant drafting in the second or third round, and passed the team's stringent character evaluations.

Though the Falcons needed help at linebacker, at least from a depth standpoint, there was no guarantee they'd select one in the second round. It depended on which players remained at the higher levels, regardless of position.

Two days before the draft, McKay took a piece of notebook paper and scribbled down the players he thought the Falcons would likely select. It was not a true best-case scenario—no Thomas Davis or Demarcus Ware—but a best case, given the players likely to be available at the end of each round when the Falcons selected.

It was a routine McKay followed every year. For all of the draft's variables and surprises, he usually manages to guess most of his team's selections.

First round: Roddy White, wide receiver, Alabama-Birmingham
Second round: Jordan Beck, outside linebacker, Cal-Poly
Third round: Chauncey Davis, defensive end, Florida State
Fourth round: Marviel Underwood, safety, San Diego State
Fifth round: DeAndra Cobb, running back, Michigan State
Fifth-sixth round: Kevin Dudley, fullback, Michigan

For each pick, McKay kept a "hot list" of five or six names. The idea was to identify players that were good values at each spot and have several contingency plans depending on how other teams drafted. Not even the scouts saw the hot list, just McKay, Blank, Mora, and Emery, the scouting director.

The Falcons first-round hot list consisted of Ware, Davis, White, Georgia defensive end David Pollack, and Marcus Spears, the LSU defensive end. Pollack wasn't the greatest scheme fit; many teams viewed him as a linebacker. Plus, Falcons scouts had learned from other Bulldogs that Pollack wasn't the most popular guy in the locker room, though even then it was hard to poke holes at a guy who rated an AB in character. Pollack's drive and intensity reminded McKay a little of Warren Sapp. There was no way Pollack would accept anything less than success.

Spears, like Pollack, was not a great scheme fit. Plus, there were some lingering concerns about a knee injury suffered during precombine training.

If all five players were gone by the time the Falcons picked, McKay planned to entertain offers to trade down. The top names on the trade-down list were Mike Patterson, the defensive tackle from USC, Fresno State guard Logan Mankins, and Chris Spencer, the center from Ole Miss.

So much of the draft was a chess game of trying to discern which teams would pick players at what spot. Nobody wants to pick a player earlier than they have to, no matter how highly they think of him. Emery and the scouts spent a lot of time gathering intelligence on who teams wanted.

"You never want to overpay," McKay said. "Sometimes coaches will say, 'If we want them, why don't we just take them? It doesn't matter what round.' That's like going to the grocery store really hungry; you'll come out with way too many groceries. Don't do that. Take them where they're supposed to be taken. If somebody else takes them, move on. Take the next guy."

McKay did not go too deep with his projections. He placed Dudley in the fifth- or sixth-round range, in part because the Falcons had two fifth-round picks, having acquired one from Denver in September in exchange for defensive tackle Ellis Johnson.

Most mock drafts had the Falcons taking a defensive player with their first choice, and even McKay publicly acknowledged the team's draft would be heavy on defenders. He still kept his eyes on wide receiver, his Achilles' heel for nearly a decade. No matter how he acquired one— draft, trade, free agency, or inheritance—the player ended up creating headaches.

In Tampa, McKay spent his second number-one pick in 1997, behind Dunn, on Florida's Reidel Anthony. In 1998, without a first-round pick, he chose Gator wide receiver Jacquez Green in the second. Neither became a consistent deep threat.

Free agency proved equally dangerous. In one of McKay's first acts as general manger in Tampa, he signed Alvin Harper away from the Cowboys. Without Michael Irvin by his side, Harper struggled and lasted just two seasons.

Bert Emanuel had posted three consecutive years of nine hundred-plus yards receiving in Atlanta when McKay signed him prior to the 1998 season. Emanuel didn't reach nine hundred yards combined in his two years in Tampa. His Buccaneer career ended appropriately, with disappointment. With the team driving against the Rams late in the fourth quarter of the 1999 NFC championship, Emanuel's catch was ruled incomplete when instant replay showed that the tip of the ball touched the field.

With the Bucs so close to the Super Bowl, McKay surrendered a pair of first-round picks in the 2000 draft to the Jets in exchange for the talented but high-maintenance Keyshawn Johnson, who continued his self-indulgent act in Tampa. Johnson spent the week leading up to one of his first games bashing new Jets head coach Al Groh and former teammate Wayne Chrebet. Johnson called himself a star, Chrebet a flashlight.

Groh issued Jets-logo flashlights to his team and, in one of the highlights of his brief tenure as head coach, the Jets held Johnson to just one catch, a shovel pass for one yard. Chrebet, meanwhile, caught the winning touchdown to cap an unlikely Jets comeback. (Groh keeps one of those flashlights on display in his office at the University of Virginia.)

Johnson, who as a rookie in 1996 authored the book *Just Give Me the Damn Ball*, was forever complaining in Tampa about Tony Dungy's conservative play-calling. Even when Jon Gruden brought his offensive wizardry to the Buccaneers in 2002, Johnson's mood rarely improved, even with a Super Bowl victory. The following season, McKay spent his last weeks as general manager refereeing the Johnson–Gruden feud.

The Bucs did not have a pick until the third round in 2002, having sent their first two selections to the Raiders for Gruden. McKay drafted Michigan wide receiver Marquise Walker in the third round, trading him a year later to the Cardinals for Thomas Jones. Walker made no impact for either team.

At least McKay could point to Joe Jurevicius, who played a key role for Tampa Bay's Super Bowl squad after signing as a free agent before the 2002 season. But even that had an unhappy ending. In the second week of the 2003 season, Jurevicius collided with teammate Mike Alstott, tore a ligament in his knee, and along with Alstott missed most of the season.

In Atlanta, McKay inherited Peerless Price, who parlayed a ninety-four-catch, 1,252-yard 2002 season in Buffalo into a seven-year, $42 million contract. Price caught thirty fewer balls in 2003 and only forty-five in 2004. This, after the Falcons surrendered their first-round pick in the 2003 draft to get him.

In his first draft in Atlanta, McKay targeted the wide receiver position. With the number-eight pick, the Falcons were ready to take Texas wide receiver Roy Williams or Virginia Tech cornerback DeAngelo Hall. When the Lions drafted Williams, the Falcons selected Hall, who had a promising rookie season. But not as promising as Williams, who caught fifty-four passes for 817 yards and eight touchdowns.

Meanwhile, Tampa Bay finally discovered a deep threat. Michael Clayton, the LSU wide receiver the Buccaneers took with the fifteenth pick, outperformed every rookie not named Ben Roethlisberger, catching eighty balls for 1,193 yards and seven touchdowns.

The Falcons traded up to draft a wide receiver with their second first-round pick, grabbing Ohio State's Michael Jenkins—rated AA in character and a Falcon Filter—at number twenty-nine. For the right to do so, the Falcons gave up their second, third, and fourth selections, also receiving the Colts' third-round choice.

Jenkins caught just seven passes as a rookie, but played a prominent role on special teams. McKay thought it was premature for anyone to pass judgment on Jenkins, who, unlike Tampa Bay's Clayton or Williams in Detroit, was not called upon to start in 2004.

With Vick as quarterback, it was difficult to judge the Falcons' receiving corps. Did receivers underachieve because Vick, the best running quarterback in the league, did not look to them enough? Or did he lack the precision touch to get them the ball more? Or was he forced to run more because he did not have enough downfield threats?

Whatever the reason, it was clear by the end of the 2004 season that Price and Dez White, the number-two receiver, were not the long-term solutions.

The 2005 draft did not offer as many promising receivers as 2004, when seven were chosen in the first round. Michigan's Braylon Edwards clearly was the class of the 2005 bunch, though he would be long gone before the Falcons picked.

So would Mike Williams, the former Southern Cal receiver who had missed a season following his unsuccessful attempt to enter the draft early. The Falcons had plenty of inside scoop on Williams, who grew up in Tampa not far from where McKay used to live and where scout Boyd Dowler still resided. During McKay's tenure in Tampa, Williams visited

Buccaneers headquarters as a guest of Keyshawn Johnson, who was pushing him toward USC.

Even if Williams fell to the Falcons, he wasn't a good fit. He reminded Dowler of Kellen Winslow, the Hall of Fame tight end whose son, Kellen II, was drafted in the first round in 2004. Dowler looked at how Williams's frame had thickened over the last two years. He still had a lean, powerful physique, but it was morphing into that of an H-back or tight end. That was of little use to the Falcons, with All-Pro Crumpler in the house.

Dowler, the former Packers receiver for Vince Lombardi, scouted the southeast for the Falcons in the fall and served as a cross-checker on wide receivers in the spring. By March, the Falcons had five wide receivers pegged as first-rounders: Edwards, Williams, South Carolina's Troy Williamson, Oklahoma's Mark Clayton, and Roddy White of Alabama-Birmingham.

Williamson's stock had soared. A six-one speedster, he left South Carolina with a year of eligibility remaining. The Falcons knew he would be long gone by the time they picked. They loved the sure-handed, five-ten Clayton, but felt they needed someone bigger.

That left Sharod "Roddy" White, whom Dowler had seen a lot of during the 2004 season, visiting the UAB campus three times and watching the Blazers game at Florida State. With UAB playing in Conference USA, the nonconference game against the Seminoles was by far the toughest competition White faced all year.

Dowler did not place too much weight on level of competition, remembering how some scouts knocked Randy Moss in college because his school, Marshall University, did not play the most imposing schedule.

"You could see where Moss dominated the competition," Dowler said. "Roddy White was clearly getting beyond the secondary, and it's not like he was playing 1-AA football."

Dowler visited UAB three times, once more than he visited Alabama, which had no blue-chip prospects for the 2005 draft. Following McKay's guidelines of interviewing five sources, Dowler spoke to everyone at UAB—coaches, strength coach, trainers, and academic advisors. He delved into White's high school days—White was a two-time all-state wrestling champion—and even rounded up a couple of youth coaches.

White was hardly perfect. He wasn't much of a blocker and his work ethic wasn't the greatest. He rated just a CC on the Falcons scale for football and personal character. But that was outweighed, the Falcons believed, by a huge upside and fiery determination.

"Everybody I talked to, going back to playing baseball as a nine- or ten-year-old, talked about how competitive he is," Dowler said. "He doesn't like to lose and he definitely doesn't like to look bad."

Dowler and the rest of the scouts had followed McKay's orders to be thorough in their background checks. Taylor Morton reached a point with Spears, the defensive end from LSU, where he almost felt like a member of the family.

Morton began his investigation in June of 2004, making an early visit to Baton Rouge. He returned in September and November. LSU was one of a handful of teams that had two pro days, and Morton attended both. Along the way, he spoke to anyone he could find that could provide insight into the defensive end.

"I met his dad three times and he knows me by name," Morton says. "I can tell you his sister's name, what his fiancée does, where he went to high school, and who his high school coach is. You get so much data, you hit a wall where you say, 'I know this guy.' But that's the level Rich wants you to be familiar with these players."

By mid-April White had emerged as the Falcons' most likely first-round draft pick. Other receivers passed the team's character filters and fit the West Coast offense, most notably Indiana's Courtney Roby, but the Falcons did not believe he warranted more than a third-round pick. Roby would serve as a fallback position in case the Falcons missed out on White in the first—or someone more desirable at another position fell to them at number twenty-seven.

The Falcons were not pinning everything on White. As with the other rounds, McKay had options for the first-round pick.

"One philosophy I've stayed with is to treat the draft just like a trial," McKay said. "Go into it with the idea that everything is put to bed. There are no surprises. Just realize that there will be a surprise or two involving trades."

McKay had whiffed on wide receivers with either a first-round pick or his first overall selection in three of the previous eight drafts, four if Jenkins was counted. Even McKay's wife, Terrin, got on him about his track record picking receivers. Other positions offered safer options, but McKay felt confident he'd finally catch a break at receiver with White.

Chapter Sixteen:

DRAFT DAY

E SPN's coverage of the seventieth NFL Selection Meeting, better known as "the draft," began at noon on Saturday, April 23, 2005. The broadcast unfolded with a flurry of graphics, ominous tones, Chris Berman voiceovers, and hyperbole. The theme was "Wall Street," and ESPN had brought many of the projected first-rounders to the floor of the New York Stock Exchange earlier in the week to pose, scowl, and boast in front of the camera.

"If value is what you're after, you better pick me," said Alex Smith, the Utah quarterback.

"I've put in the work already," Cal quarterback Aaron Rodgers said. "You just have to call my name."

Soft-spoken tight end Heath Miller of tiny Swords Creek, Virginia, and the University of Virginia, seemed the most uncomfortable following ESPN's scripted Wall Street smack talk.

"I feel there are no risks in drafting me," he said.

Back at the Falcons training complex in Flowery Branch, things were quiet. Rich McKay, clad in dress slacks, white shirt, and red tie, watched the broadcast unfold from the draft room along with the scouting staff, clad in team logo polo shirts. Team owner Arthur Blank, nattily tailored as always in a dark suit and red tie, stood in the back of the room with friends and invited guests. Lunch was available in the back of the room.

Downstairs, the media room was quiet. With teams allotted fifteen minutes per pick, the first round proceeded at a painstaking pace. The Falcons did not figure to pick for at least five hours. Still, technicians were working in small chambers off the press room, hooking up live video feeds for ESPN and The NFL Network, prepared in the unlikely event of a trade.

Like most sporting events, the draft did not start as scheduled. ESPN's Chris Berman, Chris Mortenson, and Mel Kiper Jr. spent the first thirteen minutes setting the stage, which for the first time since 1995 was not at Madison Square Garden's Paramount Theater. With Cablevision, the owner of the facility, and the New York Jets arguing over a proposed West Side stadium for the Jets, the NFL moved the event to the Jacob K. Javits Convention Center.

The Falcons table was occupied by video director Mike Crews, logistics manager Spencer Treadwell, and sixteen-year-old Hunter McKay, continuing his father's Tampa tradition of relaying picks via telephone.

At 12:13 P.M., NFL commissioner Paul Tagliabue strode to the podium and announced that the San Francisco 49ers were on the clock. The 49ers, under new head coach Mike Nolan, spent nearly their entire fifteen minutes deliberating, which allowed ESPN's Suzy Kolber enough time to interview IMG agent Tom Condon, who represents Alex Smith. Condon told Kolber he had not heard from the Niners in a day and a half.

Finally, at 12:26, San Francisco selected Smith, who smiled as he walked to the podium to greet Tagliabue, don a 49ers cap, and mug for the cameras.

That put the Miami Dolphins on the clock and Ronnie Brown on camera, chatting with agent Todd France. It had been a busy couple of days for France, who, as the agent for three top draft prospects, had become a story himself. In the weeks leading up to the draft, France's office fielded more than a dozen requests from media outlets looking to tag along with him and Brown in New York.

France knew there was a fine line between providing access that's beneficial to the client and generating unnecessary publicity that makes the agent look self-promotional. Guys like Drew Rosenhaus and Leigh Steinberg were forever pushing the envelope on that front. France knew other agents would be gunning for him after a blockbuster 2005 draft, and the last thing he wanted to do was provide them with more ammunition. The story, France believed, was Brown, Rogers, and Davis, not their agent.

In the end, France listened to his four-person staff. Maybe the exposure could help them add to the considerable endorsements they already had landed for the trio. France let the hometown *Atlanta Journal-Constitution* accompany him and Brown, not because France was based in Atlanta but because Brown is a Georgia native. As for the sports-business writers looking to explore the agent angle, he opted for ESPN.com and reporter Darren Rovell.

Brown and France checked into the Westin Times Square on Wednesday night. They spent Thursday shopping along Fifth Avenue, enjoying a one-thousand-dollar, please-sign-with-us buying spree at Niketown, listening to a Reebok sales pitch, and stopping in at Saks Fifth Avenue.

On the morning of the draft, France told Brown not to look disappointed if the Dolphins did not select him at number two. After all, cameras would be rolling. He and Brown arrived at the Javits Center at 11:00 A.M. and sat in a backstage green room, along with the agents and family members of the other five invited players.

After Smith was selected, France clasped his hands, as if in prayer. The second pick in the 2004 draft, Robert Gallery, received a package that included $18.5 million, guaranteed.

France, wearing a blue suit, stayed calm. He reminded Brown that the Dolphins could opt for Braylon Edwards, the wide receiver from Michigan. Instead, with just a minute remaining on the clock, the Dolphins selected Brown.

Brown stood, hugged his mother, and then France, who wiped away a few tears. The agent spent the next three picks following Brown around to his various media obligations. Dolphins beat writers asked France if he thought the rumored return of running back Ricky Williams from a one-year hiatus would affect his client's negotiating leverage. France deflected the queries, keeping one eye on the draft.

The Cleveland Browns selected Edwards with the third pick. Cedric Benson, the Texas running back, went to the Chicago Bears at number four. The Tampa Bay Buccaneers, to nobody's surprise, selected Cadillac Williams fifth.

France's decision to recruit Brown, who backed up Williams at the beginning of the 2004 season, paid off. Back in Flowery Branch, scout Matt Berry moved the Williams magnets to the right wall. For all the talk of McKay and Buccaneers head coach Jon Gruden differing on draft philosophy, the Bucs took a player at the top of the Falcons' chart.

In New York, with Brown now a Dolphin, France turned his attention to client Carlos Rogers, the Auburn cornerback. France believed Rogers could go in the top ten, but after five offensive picks, he needed some other corners to come off the board. Floyd Reese, the Tennessee Titans general manager who attended two dozen pro days, obliged by drafting Adam "Pac Man" Jones from West Virginia.

The Minnesota Vikings, using a pick acquired from the Oakland Raiders for Randy Moss, selected a potential replacement: Troy Williamson of the University of South Carolina, a favorite of Falcons scout Boyd Dowler. The Arizona Cardinals then took another cornerback, Miami's Antrel Rolle.

With reporters still interviewing Brown backstage, France left his client to watch Tagliabue announce the ninth pick. At 2:13 P.M., Tagliabue announced the Redskins took Rogers. France, standing next to Rovell, the ESPN.com reporter, pumped his fist and screamed, "Yes! Yes! Yes!"

France called Rogers, "I'm so, so, so, so happy for you . . . How fired up are you baby? . . . Just like we talked about!"

The next pick produced the day's first surprise, albeit a mild one. Mike Williams, the Southern Cal wide receiver who sat out the 2004 season after his ill-fated attempt to go pro after his sophomore year, went to the Detroit Lions, who for the third consecutive year took a receiver with a top-ten pick.

The night before, Williams ate dinner with Tampa Bay general manager Bruce Allen and now was hosting a draft party in his native Tampa at a restaurant around the corner from Raymond James Stadium.

"I really feel like it came down to me and Cadillac Williams, and they had a better feel for Cadillac Williams," Mike Williams told reporters.

With Mike Williams off the board, France and SFX agent Ben Dogra, who represented Cadillac Williams and Rolle, were the only agents with a pair of top-ten picks. It was nothing new for Dogra, whose client list included Lions wide receiver Roy Williams, the seventh pick in 2004. For France, it was more significant. No longer would rival agents be able to say he never had represented a first-round pick.

At that point he had two, with a third—Thomas Davis—waiting in the wings.

Back at Flowery Branch, McKay took a break from the draft room. He walked down the hall, over the marble Falcons inlay, past the Arthur Blank portrait, and into his office, where he kept an eye on a flat-screen television on his desk tuned to ESPN.

So far, the draft had unfolded as expected. The Falcons were fans of many of the first ten picks, especially Brown, Cadillac Williams, and Rolle, though they knew they had no real shot at any of them, especially after Williams went to Tampa Bay. Six weeks earlier, they believed they had a legitimate shot at Rolle.

"You've got to be prepared for anything," McKay said. "Who's to say someone doesn't call us and say we love one of your players and we're going to give you a one, and that one is the twelfth pick in the draft? Because of that, you can't treat players any differently. But when it comes to the end and you get within a week of the draft, things change. We're not spending any time in the last two weeks on Antrel Rolle. But before, when we looked at it, we did. Because you just don't know. The last thing you want to be is unprepared."

McKay remembered 1998, when Randy Moss began to fall toward the Buccaneers, who held the number-twenty-three pick before trading it to Oakland for a pair of second-round choices. Many teams had character concerns about Moss. Unlike 1995, when the Bucs investigated Warren Sapp, they had not done as thorough a job with Moss, believing he'd never fall so far.

"Had he come to us, we would have had an issue," McKay said. "The issue was that we hadn't done as much work as we would have liked. You should always be prepared, because you never know."

At the moment, the Falcons had not lost any of the players on their short list for number twenty-seven. Roddy White, McKay's projection, was still there. So, too, were Thomas Davis, David Pollack, Marcus Spears, and Demarcus Ware, though McKay knew what was coming next.

Tagliabue stepped to the podium and announced that Dallas had selected Ware. McKay shook his head. Ware didn't come close to falling to twenty, striking distance for a trade. "They got Ware, huh?" McKay said. "Good pick."

The selection of Ware salvaged the draft for Pat Dye, Jr., who watched as three Auburn clients, including two represented by France, went in the top ten. Ware's selection capped a meteoric rise for a player who, coming out of high school, was a 165-pound wide receiver with few scholarship offers. Now he was a dominant 251-pound player who could play linebacker or defensive end.

In Seattle, Tim Ruskell crossed Ware off his board. Ruskell viewed Ware as a defensive end and he needed one desperately. It was another example of how difficult it was to land a premium player at that position.

"The good ends go early," Ruskell said. "Just look at Ware. He had just one great year of production, at Troy State of all places, and we're not even sure what he'll be in the NFL. And yet we all wanted him."

The San Diego Chargers selected Shawne Merriman, a defensive end from the University of Maryland, at number twelve. Merriman was not a scheme fit for the Falcons; Maryland and the Chargers played in a 3–4 alignment. He also did not pass the Falcons' character filters.

At 2:53 P.M., the New Orleans Saints traded up with Houston at number thirteen and selected Jammal Brown, an offensive tackle from Oklahoma and the third Dogra client of the day. The Falcons, following the Alex Gibbs philosophy of not spending high picks on offensive linemen, had no interest in larger lineman like Brown or Florida State's Alex Barron.

France knew if he wanted to accompany Ronnie Brown to Miami, he could only stay at the Javits Center for one or two more picks. A car was waiting to take them to LaGuardia Airport. At 3:05 P.M., France stared at a television mounted on the wall in the green room. The Carolina Panthers took Davis at number fourteen.

France reached his client in Shellman, Georgia—one of France's staff members was attending the draft party—and congratulated "T. D." on his selection. "How happy are you?" he asked Davis. "Are we on it, or what?"

After a brief conversation with Davis, France leaned back against the wall. His eyes moistened. Given the information the agent had before the draft, Brown, Rogers, and Davis each had gone as high as he believed possible.

"We got [number] two," France tells Rovell, the ESPN.com reporter. "We got nine. We got fourteen. I'm fired up. But I'm absolutely drained."

The Davis pick ended any thought of the Falcons' best-case scenario taking place. It also caused the first nervous moments in the Falcons' draft room. Twelve selections remained before number twenty-seven. The key, the scouts knew, was for two quarterbacks to come off the board. Aaron Rodgers, the Cal quarterback, was the last of the six players remaining in the green room at the Javits Center. The NFL had invited Rodgers to New York for draft day, along with Smith, Ronnie Brown, Edwards, Benson, and Rolle. There were reports that the Redskins, who four days earlier traded their number-one pick in 2006, and two other choices, to Denver for the number-twenty-five selection, were interested in Jason Campbell, the Auburn quarterback.

Then there was the Ruskell wild card. The Seattle Seahawks president, having traded down with the Raiders from number twenty-three to number twenty-six, and also receiving Oakland's fourth-round selection, was just two months removed from Falcons' employment and one selection in front of his former team.

The picks began to fall in Atlanta's favor. The Chiefs selected Texas linebacker Derrick Johnson at number fifteen—too pricey for the Falcons' linebacker needs, and not a good scheme fit. Houston grabbed Florida State defensive tackle Travis Johnson, who did not pass the Falcons' character filter.

The draft already was more than three and a half hours old, with just sixteen picks on the board. Nobody was more impatient than McKay, who, as cochairman of the NFL's competition committee, had lobbied hard to cut down on the time spent on each selection

"I've tried three different times to move the first round to twelve minutes and the second round to eight, or doing something. But we haven't gotten there yet. I would even consider trying to say that the first sixteen picks be fifteen minutes and then the next fifteen be ten. I just don't think pick twenty-four requires fifteen minutes. It's very annoying. I have no idea how [ESPN] fills in that much stuff.

"If you want agony, just try doing it the year when your first- and second-round picks are traded away. Our first pick that year [2002] was at 9:00, maybe 9:30. We'd sit in [Ruskell's] office and we'd say, 'You know what? Let's go sit in my office.' We'd go over and hang out there. Then we'd go back in the draft room. We just couldn't do anything, nothing. And you can't leave. Somebody could call and say, 'We're going to trade you Bronco Nagurski.' So you've got to stay and there's nothing going on. You call other people. Hey, how's it going? You having fun? We're not doing anything. It is very, very, very tough."

After Johnson, there was a run on defensive ends and an offensive tackle. Pollack, the Georgia end who grew up in the Atlanta suburbs, went to the Bengals. At number eighteen, the Vikings selected Wisconsin defensive end Erasmus James, a player the Falcons did not view as a good scheme fit. The Rams then took Barron, the Florida State offensive tackle.

Dallas, still looking to revamp its defense, selected Spears, the defensive end from LSU, leaving McKay with just one player on his hot list: Roddy White, the wide receiver from Alabama-Birmingham, with seven picks to go.

At number twenty-one, the Jaguars provided the day's first surprise, taking Matt Jones of Arkansas. Jones, who played quarterback for the Razorbacks, but thrilled NFL scouts at the Senior Bowl and combine at wide receiver, soared up draft boards in March. The Falcons were intrigued with Jones, but like many teams saw him as a tight end. No need there.

The Baltimore Ravens drafted sure-handed wide receiver Mark Clayton from Oklahoma at number twenty-two, giving Dogra, the SFX agent, his fourth first-rounder of the day. The Falcons loved Clayton's character and performance, but felt they needed someone taller than five-ten in their West Coast offense. At number twenty-three, the Raiders selected

Nebraska cornerback Fabian Washington, who didn't pass the Falcons' character filters.

When it came to defensive backs, there were few among the Falcons eighty red dots. Besides Davis and Rolle, there were cornerbacks Bryant McFadden (Florida State), Dominique Foxworth (Maryland), and Justin Miller (Clemson). The Falcons thought enough of Miller to have brought him to Flowery Branch for a predraft interview. Miller had pleaded guilty to a drunken driving charge in July of 2002, and the Falcons were willing to give him the benefit of the doubt. However, Miller didn't help his character rating with a disorderly conduct arrest a week before the draft.

The Falcons were even choosier when it came to safeties. Besides Davis and Marviel Underwood, McKay's projected fourth-round pick, the only other red-dotter was Sean Considine of Iowa.

After spending nearly five hours in the green room, Rodgers finally got to come to the podium, the newest member of the Green Bay Packers. Washington, as expected, made it two quarterbacks in a row, drafting Auburn's Campbell.

Then the only thing standing in the way of the Falcons was Ruskell. It was tough to read Ruskell, who knew much of the Falcons' draft plan, having been employed at Flowery Branch until February 21. But though he sat in on the defensive team meetings, he left before the offensive side of the ball was discussed. McKay could not recall ever talking to his friend about Roddy White.

Like McKay, Ruskell had hoped to trade up, preferably to take a defensive end like Ware, to upgrade a defense that ranked twenty-sixth in the league in 2004.

When that didn't happen, Ruskell did not have any ends on the board that warranted the number-twenty-six pick. The Seahawks, like the Falcons, were not about to drop down a level to draft a player. Instead, the first draft pick of the Tim Ruskell Era in Seattle was Chris Spencer, the center from Ole Miss.

Ruskell, dressed in a suit and tie at the team's headquarters in Kirkland, Washington, anticipated the fallout. "It wasn't a flashy pick," Ruskell told reporters, "so I figured I'd be flashy."

McKay and the Falcons had no interest in using the number-twenty-seven pick on Spencer, whom they rated a 5.9-plus, CC player; Ruskell rated him higher in Seattle. The Falcons liked Spencer enough to have brought him in to Flowery Branch for an interview, and he was on the team's short list, in the event they could not get anyone rated sufficiently high at number twenty-seven and traded down.

Instead, they proved *Sports Illustrated*'s Paul Zimmerman correct and grabbed Roddy White, a 6.2 CC player and an excellent value at number twenty-seven. White was the last player on McKay's hot list. Had White been gone and had he been unable to trade down, he would have taken Southern Cal defensive tackle Mike Patterson, or Logan Mankins, a guard from Fresno State. Those players were the last two picks of the first round, going to Philadelphia and New England, respectively.

McKay was surprised how little his phone had rung throughout the first round; there was little trade action from teams looking to trade up or down. Before he could savor the White selection, he took a call he feared would come soon. His brother, J. K., was on the line from Tampa with the news that their mother, Nancy "Corky" McKay, had died after a four-year bout with cancer.

As the widow of John McKay, the former Southern Cal and Buccaneers head coach, Corky McKay understood the importance of draft day. Three days before the draft, Rich McKay traveled to Tampa and stayed for twenty-four hours before she ordered him back to Atlanta to be with his team. "We talked a long time," McKay said later. "I would have liked to have been there, obviously."

With the first round finally over after six hours, teams were given just ten minutes per pick. The Eagles, selecting third in the round, took Georgia wide receiver Reggie Brown, giving Pat Dye Jr. his second client in the first thirty-five. Brown, once considered the second-best Bulldogs receiver, had gone before Fred Gibson.

The Buccaneers, picking next, selected Barrett Ruud, the linebacker from Nebraska, and another one of the Falcons' eighty red dots. The Bucs, McKay wryly noted, were thinking along the same lines as the Falcons, at least with their first two selections.

Now McKay was hunting for a linebacker. He looked at his hot list. His projected second-round pick, Cal-Poly linebacker Jordan Beck, still was on the board. So, too, were defensive ends Dan Cody of Oklahoma and Southern Cal's Shaun Cody. Miller, the Clemson cornerback, was still there, along with Iowa defensive tackle Jonathan Babineaux.

Other teams obliged, with a run on cornerbacks and wide receivers, though McKay's hot list suffered a blow when Shaun Cody went to Detroit. Ruskell, also needing linebacker help, traded up nine picks with Carolina to select Southern Cal's Lofa Tatupu, projected by many as a third- or fourth-round pick.

McKay and Ruskell had watched USC's blowout of Oklahoma in the Orange Bowl in Miami, and McKay came away infatuated with Tatupu.

It seemed like he touched ten passes. When Tatupu, a junior, decided to go pro, they watched tape on him together.

After Ruskell's conservative first-round selection of a center, the drafting of Tatupu in the second was stunning.

"For Tim to take Tatupu is not fair. I found him," McKay quipped. "Tim will catch criticism for where he took him, thinking maybe he could have gotten him later, but he's going to be a good player."

With the Seahawks out of the way, the board began to fall in favor of the Falcons. The Dolphins took Matt Roth, the Iowa defensive end, and the Jets stunned their Javits Center faithful by making Ohio State's Mike Nugent the highest-drafted kicker since Florida State's Sebastian Janikowski in 2000.

ESPN producers cued the tape of Kiper's comments in 1989. "It's obvious to me the Jets don't know what the draft's all about," the younger Kiper says. The older Mel is kinder to the Jets and Nugent.

The Bengals, drafting next, took junior Georgia linebacker Odell Thurman, whose history of disciplinary problems took him out of consideration by the Falcons.

McKay looked at the board. There were ten picks remaining, and most of his second-round hot list remained on the front wall. That changed when Baltimore, selecting six picks before the Falcons, drafted Dan Cody. McKay looked at the team-needs board toward the back of the room and saw a nice problem developing. Babineaux and Beck both stood to be available for Atlanta.

Sure enough, the next five picks consisted of a running back and two wide receivers—no interest there—along with a cornerback (Darrent Williams of Oklahoma State went to the Broncos) that did not pass the Falcons' character filter. (Williams's resume included a positive test for marijuana as a freshman and not endearing himself to the coaches with his bad attitude.)

Momentum Sports agents Jeff Griffin and Jack Scharf had two picks with Williams and Howard cornerback Ronald Bartell, selected by the Rams three picks before Dan Cody. Scharf technically still was looking for his first drafted client; Griffin was the lead agent-of-record for Bartell and Williams.

The Jets, picking before the Falcons with their second choice of the round, took Clemson's Miller.

That left McKay with Beck and Babineaux. Both were rated 5.9 on the Falcons' board. Beck fit the McKay profile, a dynamic leader and classic overachiever who made the most of his talent. He earned a perfect AA character rating, along with the rare Falcon Filter designation. Babineaux had a solid CB character rating. Picking Beck looked like the logical move.

McKay preached to his staff that character was not to be used as a tie-breaker on draft day, but as a way to whittle down the universe of players beforehand. Perhaps Beck, his projected second-round pick, could last until the third round. If not, he had other red-dot linebackers for later in the draft, albeit ones for later round hot lists.

The Falcons did not expect Babineaux, unlike Beck, to last until the end of the second round. In that sense, Babineaux was the better value. Besides, the Falcons always were looking for athletic defensive tackles that fit their one-gap system. Babineaux, at 286 pounds, meshed perfectly. McKay, having missed out on USC's Mike Patterson when the Eagles took him at the end of the first round, snapped up Babineaux.

The rest of the second round took out some popular players in the Falcons' draft room. Wide receiver Vincent Jackson, the Northern Colorado favorite of scout Boyd Dowler, went to San Diego, though with the selection of White in the first round it didn't matter. The Steelers grabbed McFadden, the cornerback that Brett Maxie, the defensive backs coach, worked out at Florida State's pro day. The consensus in the room, however, was that McFadden warranted no more than a third-round pick. The Eagles, again thinking like the Falcons, chose San Diego State linebacker Matt McCoy, who was on McKay's third-round hot list.

With the draft now nine hours old, the 49ers led off the third round by selecting Miami running back Frank Gore. Three picks later, the Tennessee Titans went with Courtney Roby, the Indiana wide receiver the Falcons correctly predicted they'd have to take with their late second-round pick (had they not chosen White and still wanted a receiver.)

Tampa Bay, picking seventh in the round, chose "the other" Alex Smith, the tight end from Stanford. That inspired Buccaneers head coach Jon Gruden to quip that the rumors of the Bucs interest in Alex Smith had been correct after all. Back in Flowery Branch, scout Matt Berry moved the Smith magnet over to the right wall board, where it became the third straight red-dot player for the Bucs. Though Smith had a red-dot, he was never hot-listed since the Falcons did not want to spend such a high pick on a position where they did not need help.

The same was true for David Greene. With Matt Schaub entrenched behind Michael Vick, there was almost no scenario—barring Greene falling to the seventh round—that would have caused the Falcons to pick the former Georgia quarterback.

That wasn't out of the question for Greene, whose lack of quickness and arm strength scared off many teams. Unlike many players, Greene did not have a draft party, preferring to watch the event at home with immediate family, and politely turned down requests from Atlanta media to view the draft with him.

He need not have worried. Ruskell, who needed a backup quarterback in Seattle, selected Greene with his third-round pick, the eighty-fifth overall. Greene, speaking to Seahawks writers via a conference call, addressed his lack of arm strength yet again.

"There are a lot of guys in the NFL that have had great careers and didn't have the strongest arms, because they were able to throw on time and they were accurate. I'd rather have accuracy over arm strength any day of the week."

For Pat Dye Jr., Greene joined clients Demarcus Ware and Reggie Brown as draft overachievers, at least by their projections on New Year's Day. In Flowery Branch, Greene's magnet gave the Seahawks, like the Buccaneers, three of the Falcons' red-dot players, along with Spencer and Tatupu.

Five picks later, the Falcons still had a choice of red-dot linebackers. The Raiders took red-dotter and third-round hot list member Kirk Morrison at number seventy-eight, but Beck remained on the hot list. So did Chauncey Davis, the Florida State defensive end and McKay's projected third-round selection.

This time, McKay chose Beck, a two-year team captain at Cal Poly, with a nonstop motor on the field and tireless work habits in the weight room. Projected as a fourth- or fifth-rounder in some mock drafts, Beck found himself looking at a signing bonus of around four hundred and thirty thousand dollars, double what he might have received as a fourth-round pick and more than triple what a fifth-rounder would get.

Then there was Maurice Clarett, who went to Denver with the one hundred and first selection, the last of the third round. The pick jolted the ESPN crew, showing fatigue from eleven hours of coverage. Many teams figured Clarett would go in the sixth or seventh round, if he was selected at all. Instead, he was drafted by a team with a deep stable of running backs.

"His slate is clean and we're giving him an opportunity," Broncos head coach Mike Shanahan said.

As ESPN signed off on the first day of draft coverage, other players wondered where their opportunities had gone.

Chapter Seventeen:

DAY TWO

Suzy Kolber took over for Chris Berman as lead host of ESPN's draft coverage on Sunday. ESPN's panel of Chris Mortenson, Mike Golic, and Mel Kiper Jr. continued to analyze the shocking selection of Maurice Clarett the night before. Denver head coach Mike Shanahan appeared via teleconference to defend the pick.

Kiper presented his list of the top twelve remaining draft prospects. Anttaj Hawthorne, the Wisconsin defensive tackle who had tested positive for marijuana use at the combine, was number three. Ray Willis, the Florida State offensive tackle, was number six and Chris Canty was number eight. Fred Gibson, the Georgia wide receiver, was not on Kiper's list.

Willis was back in Tallahassee watching the draft alone with his wife Kimberly. They weren't especially surprised when he didn't hear his name called the first day. Agents Bill Johnson and Pat Dye Jr. had tempered their expectations. With Ray's ankle injury and history of ailments, it was hard to make a prediction.

At the Seattle Seahawks draft headquarters in Kirkland, Washington, Tim Ruskell was glad to see Willis still available. Ruskell, still only two months on the job as Seahawks president, had one of the more confusing draft rooms. One board was set up using the Atlanta Falcons' mold, another with the Seahawks' existing system.

Freed from the constraints of the Alex Gibbs offensive line philosophy, Ruskell used the fourth pick in the fourth round on Willis, a player deemed too tight and not athletic enough to play for the Falcons.

"I like him a lot as a person," said Ruskell, who used the pick he acquired from Oakland for trading down in the first round to draft Willis. "He's got toughness, character—and he's relentless when it comes to effort. For me, that's what being an offensive lineman is all about. Guys like Ray aren't always pretty, but they're tough and they usually pan out better than others. He's a quiet guy, but he's smart and there's a passion that comes out on the field."

Six picks later, the Arizona Cardinals selected Virginia guard Elton Brown, considered a first-round lock for much of the fall. But Brown left the Senior Bowl and combine early with a knee injury and then pulled a hamstring while working out during his pro day in Charlottesville. No player fell further since the end of the season without failing a drug test.

It had been a disappointing draft all around for the Virginia Cavaliers. Heath Miller became the school's first player to go in the first round since 2000, but he fell to Pittsburgh and the thirtieth pick because some teams had concerns about the tight end's abdominal injury. Linebacker Darryl Blackstock, who left school early in part because he misinterpreted his "not higher than the second round" rating from the NFL advisory committee, did not go until the end of the third round to the Arizona Cardinals.

Alvin Pearman, the fast-rising running back who was the target of the fierce recruiting battle between agents Ethan Lock and David Dunn in January, also was still seeking employment, though that was not unexpected.

Kiper suggested Brown needed to be more aggressive, while praising the Virginia program. "That's a talent-laden team at Virginia," Kiper said. "Al Groh has done a great job of recruiting."

Green Bay, with the fourteenth pick in the fourth round, selected Marviel Underwood, the San Diego State safety that Falcons general manager Rich McKay had projected as his fourth-round pick prior to the draft. A pair of Florida State players went next (wide receiver Craphonso Thorpe to the Chiefs, and safety Jerome Carter to the Rams), giving the Seminoles six picks on the day.

The Jacksonville Jaguars, with former Virginia assistant coach Andy Heck working in a similar role, selected Pearman, the versatile Cavalier running back, with the twenty-sixth pick in the fourth round. The Falcons, drafting next, chose Florida State defensive end Chauncey Davis, McKay's projected third-round pick.

The Falcons considered Davis at the end of the third round but did not want to pass up linebacker Jordan Beck. The Davis pick continued McKay's long tradition of drafting Seminoles, and he likened Davis to Greg Spires, a late-blooming former FSU end who was drafted in the third round by New England in 1998 and played a key role on Tampa Bay's Super Bowl team in 2002.

"We feel like Davis is on the upswing," McKay said. "He's a great kid, definitely has some pass rushing skills. He's just going to get bigger and stronger. He's not close to where he's going to be strength wise. He's a high-motor guy. You watch tape and he goes a hundred miles per hour on every play."

Back in Waycross, Georgia, Fred Gibson remained at his grandmother's house in his old bedroom, watching the draft with a cousin. The community center would not be hosting a day-two draft party; nobody had planned for it.

The Arizona Cardinals called early in the day, telling Gibson they might be selecting him, but they chose Elton Brown instead. Now he watched more wide receivers come off the board. With the thirteenth pick in the round, the Houston Texans chose Jerome Mathis, who played Division 1-AA ball at Hampton (Virginia) University, but ran a combine-best 4.28 in the forty. Kansas City chose FSU's Thorpe with the thirteenth selection and New Orleans selected California's Chase Lyman at seventeen, making him the sixteenth wide receiver drafted.

Two picks after the Falcons selected Davis, San Diego drafted Darren Sproles, the tiny running back from Kansas State. That put the Pittsburgh Steelers on the clock and it was then that Gibson's cell phone rang. He would be joining a team that finished 15-1 the previous season with rookie quarterback Ben Roethlisberger at the helm. The Steelers needed a tall receiver, having lost the six-five Plaxico Burress to free agency and the New York Giants.

"I can't wait to get to Pittsburgh and start catching the football," Gibson said. "I want to go out and prove everybody wrong."

The Steelers chose Gibson in the midst of Suzy Kolber's teleconference interview with David Pollack. Kiper didn't miss a beat.

The Steelers "lose one tall receiver in Plaxico Burress and get another one in Fred Gibson, who goes about six-four. What he needs to do is fill out that frame and become a little more consistent."

In Charlotte, Chris Canty waited patiently as the Philadelphia Eagles were on the clock. Or were they? His cell phone rang and he learned that he was the newest member of the Dallas Cowboys, who had traded up to get him.

Bill Parcells continued the overhaul of his defensive line, having already selected Demarcus Ware and Marcus Spears in the first round. ESPN showed a shot of a triumphant Dallas draft room, noting that Parcells had not officially committed to switching to the 3-4 defense that Canty had played under Parcells's protégé Groh at Virgina. Still, with Ware, Spears, and Canty on the roster, the 3-4 looked inevitable.

Canty was glad to be off the board and headed to a team where he was a perfect scheme fit. Still, he remained in shock. He thought he would be chosen in the second round, certainly no later than the third.

"I'm happy to be drafted," Canty said, "but this wasn't the excitement that I hoped for."

Still, the Canty household was downright jubilant compared to the scene at Ed Hawthorne's home in Connecticut, where his nephew, Anttaj, was watching his once-lofty draft status plummet.

When the Tennessee Titans drafted Tulane wide receiver Roydell Williams with the last pick in the fourth round, Anttaj Hawthorne's name moved to the top of Mel Kiper Jr.'s list of best available players.

That's where it remained throughout the fifth round. When the Philadelphia Eagles selected Brigham Young guard Scott Young, with the third-to-last pick in the round, Hawthorne was the only player left from Kiper's ten highest-rated players from the start of the day.

Hawthorne was among four players, including Wisconsin teammate Jonathan Clinkscale, to test positive for marijuana at the NFL combine in Indianapolis. Before the season, Kiper rated Hawthorne the best defensive tackle prospect for the draft and the eleventh-best overall.

From a character standpoint, Hawthorne rated high. Down-to-earth, levelheaded, and immensely popular with his teammates, "this kid could run for president," proclaimed one Internet scouting service. Still, scouts were concerned about Hawthorne's dropoff in production from the 2003 season. He could be a disruptive force, but at times seemed to take plays off. The positive drug test raised a red flag.

"One of the biggest knocks on Hawthorne is that he plays lazy, takes snaps off, and does not give great effort on every down, despite his natural physical talent," wrote *Pro Football Weekly*'s Nolan Nawrocki on April 12 when the test results became public. "The test results could give scouts a reason to explain his effort."

It didn't help that most teams identified Hawthorne strictly as a two-gap defender, which limited his stock. In a one-gap scheme, the lineman attacks a hole and either goes after the running back—if he comes that way—or proceeds to the quarterback. A one-gap lineman tends to weigh at most 290 pounds, and is quick and athletic.

In a two-gap scheme, the lineman must read the play, anticipate which gap a running back will choose, and fill the hole. A two-gap lineman tends to be heavier, like Hawthorne, who's 325 pounds.

No team plays either scheme exclusively, though almost everyone tends to lean on one or the other. A team playing a 3-4 defense, with three down linemen and four linebackers, tends to use a two-gap system more often. A 4-3 team like the Atlanta Falcons, with four down linemen, tended to use the one-gap more.

Hawthorne was highly regarded as a two-gap defender, at least before the drug test.

"When he went to the combine, you had the impression that he was going to go somewhere in the second round, because for a lot of schemes like ours, he doesn't fit," Rich McKay said. "Now, the two-gap scheme he fits and fits it well. So he's got twenty teams to choose from probably and there are twelve of us who he probably doesn't fit real well. And obviously the test positive did not help him."

According to Ed Hawthorne, IMG agent Chris Singletary remained in close contact with Anttaj throughout the spring, checking in by phone once or twice a week. Though Anttaj opted to train for the combine mostly at Wisconsin, instead of joining fellow IMG clients such as Alex Smith, David Pollack, and Heath Miller full-time in Bradenton, Florida, Singletary stayed in touch.

Ed Hawthorne says his nephew used marijuana following the Outback Bowl at a party in Tampa and knew about the positive drug test for three weeks before it came out.

"He didn't tell anybody," Hawthorne said. "Not me, his attorney, or his agent, until it came out in the paper three weeks later. He was so worried about what I was going to say that he went into a shell. He knew that he'd let me down, and he let everyone else down because of all the work we put into this thing, and he goes and does something stupid like that—even though he's been lectured one hundred times that 'you're high-profile now. Whatever you do is going to end up in the newspapers. It's going to be in there.' He just figured he had enough time to clean up before the combine. I guess he didn't."

Ed Hawthorne said IMG did not call during draft weekend. (Condon, head of IMG's football division, said he called Anttaj the day after the draft.)

Jack Scharf, who had remained in touch with the Hawthornes, did call. "I'm so sorry," he told Ed. "I can't believe what's happening. I don't know what to say."

Finally the wait ended. The Oakland Raiders, no strangers to drafting and acquiring players with baggage, selected Hawthorne with the first pick of the sixth round. Head coach Norv Turner and his staff, who coached Anttaj during the Senior Bowl, remained fans of the defensive tackle.

Ed Hawthorne did the math. Players selected early in the sixth round in 2004 received signing bonuses of around eighty-five thousand dollars. It was a far cry from the seven-figure bonus Anttaj figured to receive for much of the fall, when everyone from Kiper to IMG to Scharf viewed him as a first-rounder.

"If you learn from your mistake, you'll be a better person," Hawthorne told his nephew. "If you don't, then you're an idiot."

Late in the afternoon, Roddy White arrived at Falcons headquarters with his mother and younger brother for a news conference. As far as sports media events, nothing is more mundane than the player introduction. There's the inevitable praise lavished by team officials, the jersey presentation photo-op, and a brief question-and-answer period.

For Arthur M. Blank, former image-conscious chairman of The Home Depot and now the image-conscious owner of the Atlanta Falcons, no media event is ever mundane. Much planning and preparation went into the White introduction.

Reggie Roberts, the team's public relations director, sent a file of bio information to Kim Shreckengost, the executive vice president of operations for the AMB (Arthur M. Blank) Group, LLC. Shreckengost previously worked as Blank's vice president of investor relations at Home Depot and knew the importance of projecting a rosy, upbeat outlook to the media at all times, no matter how trivial the information presented.

By the time Blank approached the podium in the Falcons' media room, dressed impeccably as always in a black blazer, gray slacks, white shirt, and red team-logo tie, he had a detailed speech that he delivered as if it were off the cuff. The theme of the speech was family, and how White now was a treasured member of the Falcons tight-knit community.

Oddly enough, the wide receiver was not the first Roddy White in the organization. The Falcons employed a Roddy White as director of event marketing and client services.

Falcons beat writers Matt Winkeljohn of the *Atlanta Journal-Constitution* and George Henry of the Associated Press sat at their cubicles, views obstructed by a phalanx of television cameramen and reporters appearing at Flowery Branch for the first time in six days. Earlier in the day the beat writers were asked to leave the press room briefly while Blank sat for an updated portrait.

White's "background is really very interesting," Blank said. "Today, the young man to my right is 207 pounds. When he entered his first days of high school at James High School in South Carolina, he was 112 pounds. He joined the wrestling team, which is a tradition—a part of the DNA in their family (they have five members who were all state wrestling champs in South Carolina)—and he became a two-time state wrestling champion himself, the first time at 152 pounds and the second time at 182 pounds. So Roddy has grown up a good bit physically, and obviously matured a great deal in high school as well, and on through college.

"In high school he was an all-time state selection as a football player, broke all the school's receiving records, and was listed among the top receivers on a national basis. He's seven courses away from getting his [college] degree in sociology. His mother has made it very clear to me that Roddy will complete his college degree; and Roddy, we're here to make sure that we can help you in any way to do that, and we're as excited about you being that close to your college degree as you are today.

"So I want to welcome Roddy to our Falcon family. He's an exceptional young man on the field, off the field. We're thrilled that he's here, we're thrilled about the contributions he's going to make to us. I promise you, Roddy, that you'll get tremendous support from the coaching staff here. I promise you'll get tremendous support from this organization in every aspect.

"When you're part of our family, you're part of our family, and we're going to care for you on the days that your mom is not here, which I know she'll be here to watch you every Sunday or Monday night, or whenever we're playing. I promise you, the rest of the staff here will be supporting you and really treating you as family as well. So thank you for being here. We're excited about you being a Falcon. Come on up here and say hi to your new family."

White thanked God, Blank, Rich McKay, the coaching staff, and his family, before taking a few questions from the media. Head coach Jim Mora said the addition of Roddy would help open up the Falcons' languishing passing game.

"Right now you'd say we're a team that runs the football and throws to the tight end," Mora said. "We'd like to be a team that can beat you any number of ways, and that's why you want to keep adding quality players like Roddy to your program, and give a great player like Mike [Vick] more weapons, more places to deliver the ball, and more threats up the field."

With two selections in the fifth round, the Falcons had some flexibility. The draft had unfolded nicely, McKay believed. Glancing at his predraft predictions, he had landed his first-round pick (Roddy White) as expected, and grabbed Jordan Beck and Chauncey Davis, each a round later than projected, which meant he was getting good value for his draft position. Picking up Jonathan Babineaux in the second round was an added bonus.

Having selected wide receiver, defensive tackle, linebacker, and defensive end, McKay had addressed the Falcons' primary needs. A safety would have been nice, but after the like-minded Eagles took Sean Considine with the first pick in the fourth round and the Packers nabbed Marviel Underwood, nobody else jumped out at the Falcons.

McKay looked across the Falcons' draft board. Michael Boley, a linebacker from Southern Miss, was looming high with a 6.0 rating. The 6.0 was a wild card, sort of the sergeant-major of the Falcons' rating system. A 6.0 was not necessarily better than a 5.9 player, but had a much higher upside.

The Falcons called the 6.0 the "elevator grade," since the player had a high ceiling and a low floor. There were only a few 6.0 grades per draft, and they fell into three categories. The first was the "special specialist," the rare special teams player that commanded a premium draft pick. For the 2005 draft, there was only one such player, Ohio State kicker Mike Nugent.

The second category was a player that scouts were having a hard time putting a grade on, because he played at a lower level of competition, had recently switched positions, or would be expected to learn a new position in the NFL. Troy State's Demarcus Ware fit the bill in the fall, before he gained twenty pounds and solidified himself as a NFL-caliber defensive end with a strong predraft season. Already in possession of an AA character rating from the Falcons, he had been bumped up to a 6.2 long before the draft.

The final category consisted of players with bigtime potential who thus far had not made the most of their talents. McKay's character-based draft system frowned on underachievers. By thoroughly researching a player's football and personal character, the Falcons hoped to eliminate any potential problems down the road.

Boley received a CC in character, the same grade as White and Davis. He was a raw talent with a lanky frame and a reputation for not working hard in the weight room. On the field, he got by more with athleticism than proper technique. At least he had a long resume of community service endeavors, always a plus with the Blank-owned Falcons.

McKay still wanted an offensive tackle. Going into the draft, he didn't plan to take one, but figured if he did it would be in the fourth or fifth round. Using the stringent Alex Gibbs parameters, the Falcons had few red-dot linemen, and only three remained on the board. Tackles Anthony Alabi (Texas Christian) and Frank Omiyale (Tennessee Tech) were on the fifth-round hot list, along with Robert Hunt, a center from North Dakota State. DeAndra Cobb, the Michigan State running back and McKay's projected fifth-round pick, remained available.

With two fifth-round choices, just three picks apart, McKay could afford to play chess.

Boley and the 6.0 rating, in some respects, contradicted the core of McKay's draft philosophy, but then there was the cardinal rule of never dropping down a level to draft a player. Boley was, by far, the highest-rated player left on the Falcons' board. McKay could afford to spend a fifth-round pick on a 6.0 and let him develop on special teams and in a backup role for at least a year.

Whenever McKay considered a 6.0 player, the name Santana Dotson came to mind. In 1992, McKay was participating in his first draft with the Buccaneers as vice president of football operations. Head coach Sam Wyche had final say on personnel decisions, and that year the Bucs had two selections in the fifth round. As the rounds went on, the Bucs drafted 5.8 players, even though Dotson, a 6.0 defensive tackle from Baylor, remained on the board.

Finally, with their second pick in the fifth round, the Bucs drafted

Dotson, who recorded ten sacks as a rookie and went on to a productive, decade-long career with the Bucs and Packers. Michael Boley, like Dotson, was a player viewed as a potential underachiever.

"One of the things that hurts Michael is people want more out of him," McKay said. "He's such a good athlete and moves so well, you look at every play and say, 'Boy, he could have done this or he could have done that.' But every tape you watch, you see nothing but production."

McKay pulled the trigger on Boley. The Jets, picking next, chose Andre Maddox, a safety from North Carolina State. The Dolphins then chose an offensive tackle, Alabi, leaving the Falcons with Omiyale of Tennessee Tech, a Division-II school.

The run on offensive linemen continued with the next pick, as San Diego drafted Wesley Britt, a tackle from Alabama. The Colts then took Hunt.

McKay marveled at the intelligence-gathering operation of scouting director Phil Emery and his staff. Through their own evaluations and by talking to other teams before the draft, they identified three linemen that fit the Falcons' scheme and were fifth-round-caliber players. The rest of the league agreed, drafting the players in a span of four picks late in the fifth round. It was the draft equivalent of missing the Powerball Lottery by one number.

The art of the draft, McKay believed, was not just identifying talent but spending time with other teams to determine leaguewide value. The danger was that scouts would come to second-guess their own grades, which wasn't such a bad thing if it caused them to make one last check of the files. More often than not, the process provided the type of intelligence that gave McKay the confidence to wait an extra round on a Beck or Davis.

"You want to buy wholesale," McKay says. "You'll pay retail, but you never want to pay the marked-up price. Problems occur if you get your rounds all wrong and you start overpaying. Just because you like a guy doesn't mean you should take him in the second when you can get him in the fourth."

The Falcons believed they got good value in Omiyale, who showed an uncanny ability to explode off the line of scrimmage for a man his size (six-four and 310 pounds), a good fit for the Gibbs system, even if he was huge. The Falcons had depth on the offensive line, and McKay planned to give Omiyale the equivalent of a redshirt season in 2005, letting him learn the Falcons' system in practice.

Omiyale was something of an unknown, in that he seldom had played against top-level competition. But he showed tremendous upside, along with a mean streak, and posted a solid CB on the Falcons' character rating. Omiyale also possessed thirty-six-inch arms, believed to be among the longest in the NFL. "I don't know where you get that shirt," McKay said.

In the sixth round, the Falcons picked up McKay's projected fifth-rounder, Michigan State running back DeAndra Cobb. With Warrick Dunn and T. J. Duckett entrenched in the backfield, the Falcons had no interest in spending a higher selection on a running back.

Cobb, at five-nine, 196 pounds, was in many respects a younger version of Dunn. He was a skilled kickoff returner and figured to get a chance at that role, and as a third-down back as a rookie. Married, with a daughter, he also earned the second-highest character rating (BB) of any Falcons draft pick. With a rating of 5.8-plus, McKay believed he got a deceptively fast runner and a tremendous value in the sixth round with Cobb.

"He ran a 4.5 at the combine, but I defy you to look at any tape you want and tell me he runs a 4.5," McKay said. "He certainly looks like he runs a lot faster than that, because his play speed is really impressive."

Anttaj Hawthorne was not the only person disappointed in the sixth round. Florida State's Eric Moore, once rated among the better defensive ends, lasted until the twelfth pick and the New York Giants.

Two players that agent Jack Scharf and Momentum Sports spent ten thousand dollars apiece just to train at Athletes' Performance, not including housing and other expenses, lasted until the sixth. Jovan Haye, the defensive end who left Vanderbilt with a year of eligibility remaining, went to Carolina with the fifteenth pick. Cornerback Derrick Johnson of Washington—the other Derrick Johnson in the draft—went to San Francisco with the thirty-first selection. Neither player figured to generate enough in commissions in 2005 to cover their combine training. Nor would Louisville wide receiver J. R. Russell, drafted in the seventh round by Tampa Bay, or Oregon linebacker Jonathan Pollard, who went undrafted.

Hawthorne was not the lowest-drafted IMG client. Rob Petitti, the mammoth offensive tackle from Pittsburgh who was sidelined throughout the spring by turf toe, lasted until the Dallas Cowboys took him with the thirty-fifth pick, one of eight compensatory selections tacked onto the end of the round.

Though it had been a disappointing weekend for University of Virginia players at the front end of the draft, Al Groh's network of NFL contacts paid off for lesser prospects. Defensive tackle Andrew Hoffman, who was not even invited to the combine, went to the Cleveland Browns and new head coach Romeo Crennel, a fellow Parcells assistant with Groh with the Giants, Patriots, and Jets. Crennel planned to install a 3-4 defense similar to the one Hoffman played at Virginia.

Tight end Patrick Estes, another noninvite to the combine, who had played in the shadow of Heath Miller, went in the seventh round to San Francisco. There he would play for new head coach Mike Nolan, who in 2000 had served as defensive coordinator for the New York Jets during Groh's one season as head coach.

The Falcons concluded their draft by selecting Darrell Shropshire, a six-two, 301-pound defensive tackle from South Carolina. Shropshire received a 5.8-minus grade from the Falcons, which meant he wasn't the greatest scheme fit. Like White, Davis, and Boley, he received a CC character grade. Shropshire didn't figure to play much, not with promising second-yearman Chad Lavalais, a fifth-round selection in 2004, moving into an expanded role. Then there was Babineaux, the second-round pick.

"We just felt like we needed one bigger-bodied nose tackle to make sure we're stout enough inside," McKay said. "We believe we are inside with Lavalais and Babineaux, but neither is as big-bodied as this guy. He can eat up space inside."

Shortly after 7:00 P.M., once the draft was over, McKay met with the small Falcons press corps one more time in his office. Down the hall, the scouting staff worked the phones. It was time to pick free agents off the scrap heap of undrafted players, a process that would take no more than an hour.

Nobody wanted to stay on the phone long, especially with disappointed agents who would have to explain to their clients why they went undrafted.

Some agents prepared for the moment before the draft ended. Agents Bill Johnson and Pat Dye Jr. maintained close phone contact with Ben Wilkerson, the LSU center whose injured knee kept him from undergoing full workouts all spring.

By the time the seventh round got underway, the agents told him he'd be better off not drafted. At least then they could be selective and try and find the team that most needed a center. Wilkerson signed with Cincinnati shortly after the draft.

After the media departed, McKay examined his draft picks.

Roddy White, WR, Alabama-Birmingham—6.2, CC
Jonathan Babineaux, DT, Iowa—5.9, CB

Jordan Beck, LB, Cal-Poly—5.9, AA
Chauncey Davis, DE, Florida State—5.8-plus, CC
Michael Boley, LB, Southern Miss—6.0, CC
Frank Omiyale, OT, Tennessee Tech—5.7-plus, CB
DeAndra Cobb, RB, Michigan State—5.8-plus, BB
Darrell Shropshire, DT, South Carolina—5.8-minus, CC

For a team that placed such a premium on character, there were a lot of C grades on the board. McKay was okay with that—a C was an average grade, after all—so long as the area scout had investigated the player thoroughly. Getting a C in personal character was worse than in football character.

"If you give a guy a C in personal character, you go back and look at him from A to Z to make sure we know all the issues," McKay said. "If there's no alert, then you turn to the area scout and say, 'You're ready on this guy?' And if [the scout] is ready to go, then you're ready to go, If he's interviewed his three, preferably five or more sources, you're fine."

McKay's draft showed how little value the Falcons place on the Wonderlic. Only three players scored higher than the league average of 19: Boley (30), Beck (27), and Omiyale (20). McKay was fine with that, too, since among the variables that went into the football character grade was how well a player learned football.

Looking around the Falcons' draft room, most teams had at least one selection with a D or F grade in football character or personal character. It wasn't difficult to find the teams that shared the Falcons' philosophy. The magnets representing Tim Ruskell's first three picks in Seattle—Chris Spencer, Lofa Tatupu, and David Greene—had red dots. Ruskell's fourth pick, Florida State offensive tackle Ray Willis, did not have a dot, because he didn't fit the Alex Gibbs scheme, though Willis did receive a lofty BB character grade from the Falcons.

The first three magnets on the Tampa Bay board also had red dots, representing Carnell Williams, Barrett Ruud, and Alex Smith. For all the talk of how much McKay and Buccaneers head coach Jon Gruden differed philosophically, McKay could find little wrong with his former employer's draft, at least at the front end.

The Chicago Bears, led by general manager Jerry Angelo, McKay's longtime friend and colleague, did not have a red dot on their board, led by Texas running back Cedric Benson.

McKay shook his head in mock disappointment. "Jerry has abandoned us."

As McKay glanced at his own board, he liked what he saw. The Falcons had addressed their depth issue at defensive line and linebacker. They had a legitimate home run threat at wide receiver in White and an exciting addition to their already potent running game in Cobb. They drafted strong character players, receiving good value in each round.

Best of all, none of the players, with the possible exception of White, would be counted on to make significant contributions in 2005. They could play backup roles and on special teams, learning the system and advancing gradually into more prominent duties in 2006 and beyond. When that time came, McKay would be able to jettison aging, higher-priced veterans, thus managing the salary cap and keeping his team young and yet experienced.

Already he could look at his 2004 draft class, which collectively accounted for just ten total starts in 2004—and see the players stepping into more prominent roles in 2005. DeAngelo Hall, the first-round pick, would start at cornerback. Fourth-rounder Demorrio Williams, a linebacker, and fifth-round defensive tackle Chad Lavalais, projected as starters. So, too, did Michael Jenkins, the wide receiver selected late in the first round after Hall.

Even third-rounder Matt Schaub, who didn't figure to play much behind Michael Vick, had mastered the West Coast offense to the point where coaches were comfortable with him in the event of an injury to Vick.

That's why it didn't matter to McKay what 2005 draft "grades" the Falcons received from football writers and Internet pundits the following morning.

"How can you grade a draft? I hope the people in the top ten got better players than we got. They better. They had every advantage and in every round—and they should. Last year, when we had a number-eight pick, we should have had a very good draft grade, unless we screwed it up.

"Look, if you give me a C every time, I'm thrilled. If you give me an A, it means we didn't have a very good team and you're able to look at our draft and say that these two guys are going to have an immediate impact. That's great, but it also means we're not very good right now."

After reaching the NFC title game three months earlier, the Falcons appeared very good, but McKay knew how quickly that could change. The NFL maintained parity by giving the better teams low draft picks and tougher schedules. The Falcons had never produced back-to-back winning seasons, not even after appearing in the Super Bowl following the 1998 season.

Mastering the draft is the only way a team can stay on top. That's why there would be little time to rest for the Falcons scouting staff. By 8:00 P.M. they were heading out the door, through the press room. They had rounded up a dozen free agents, including Kevin Dudley, the Michigan fullback McKay had projected as a fifth- or sixth-round pick for the Falcons.

In just a few weeks the scouts would meet in Florida with the rest of the teams that subscribed to the National Football Scouting service; McKay planned to drop out of BLESTO and rejoin the combine he belonged to in Tampa.

In Florida, the scouts would discuss rising seniors and give them grades. Those ratings would become the starting point for the 2006 NFL Draft.

No matter how deep the scouts dug, some players would fail to live up to expectations. McKay's office includes a large framed action photo of Ricky Bell, the former USC running back the Buccaneers drafted ahead of Tony Dorsett in 1977 with the first overall pick. John McKay coached Bell at Southern Cal, and the running back was one of Rich McKay's all-time favorites. He hung a photo of Bell in his dorm room at Princeton and has displayed one at every office since.

Bell no doubt would have scored an AA character rating, had the younger McKay's system existed in 1977. McKay believes it's unfair to second-guess the selection. Nobody knew Bell would suffer from a rare heart condition that would take his life at age twenty-nine. Besides, Dorsett never had to run behind the lousy offensive line the Buccaneers fielded during Bell's rookie year.

The photo serves as a tribute to Bell and the Buccaneers, the room's only indication that the man that occupies the office is connected to the Tampa Bay franchise. It also serves as an unintended reminder that even the most gifted, high-character player does not always pan out, for whatever reason.

"The draft is not an exact science," McKay says. "But in my naïve thinking, there are two things we need to focus on: character and scheme fit. To give the player the best chance to succeed, he needs to fit what you do and what you're going to ask him to do. If you can get that person and get the character side of who you want to be a Falcon, then from a work ethic and durability standpoint, you give yourself the best chance of success. It's not a perfect system, but it gives you that best chance."

Chapter Eighteen:

AFTERMATH

The 2005 NFL Draft produced the highest draft ratings ever for ESPN. The show was the most viewed cable program during the month of April among men eighteen to thirty-four, eighteen to forty-nine, and twenty-five to fifty-four. Overall, a whopping 34.4 million people tuned in to at least part of the eighteen-plus hours of coverage.

The network's selection of a Wall Street theme for its 2005 coverage was an appropriate one. In the year between the 2004 draft and the time the San Francisco 49ers selected Alex Smith with the first pick in the 2005 draft, the stock of many players went up and down dramatically.

Anttaj Hawthorne, once regarded as the best defensive tackle prospect for 2005, fell to the sixth round, largely for testing positive for marijuana at the NFL combine in February. Chris Canty, rated a "not higher than the second round" talent by the NFL's advisory committee in the spring of 2004, and as a potential first-rounder by some prognosticators before the 2004 season, plunged to the end of the fourth round after suffering torn knee ligaments in September and a detached retina in January.

Ray Willis, though never as highly rated as Canty or Hawthorne, dropped at least a round, to the fourth, because of a nagging ankle injury that figured to be completely healed by the time he played in a regular season game for the Seattle Seahawks. Ben Wilkerson, once the draft's highest-rated center, never overcame a torn left knee patella tendon suffered late in LSU's season. Undrafted, he was signed by the Bengals as a free agent and cut when he failed a physical.

Fred Gibson did nothing from a strictly football standpoint to hurt his draft stock, though he ran a slow forty-yard dash at the combine and failed to put weight on his skinny frame. Like a stagnant company that fails to provide Wall Street analysts with consistently better earnings reports, he fell behind more than a dozen wide receivers that suddenly looked more promising.

At least Gibson was drafted. C. J. Brooks, an offensive guard from the University of Maryland, was rated highly by BLESTO during the preseason, and once was ranked by ESPN's Mel Kiper Jr. as the top guard prospect for the draft. Brooks did not impress scouts in 2004, however, and went undrafted.

James Butler, the Georgia Tech safety, was rated among the nation's top draft prospects by BLESTO, National Football Scouting, Kiper, and numerous draft gurus for much of the fall of 2004. Butler did not get hurt, fail a drug test, or participate in a nightclub scuffle, but he failed to deliver on the promise that he showed in his junior season.

For every David Pollack or Carnell "Cadillac" Williams that maintained a blue-chip rating throughout the twelve-month draft cycle, there was a Gibson or Butler that failed to provide NFL investors with enough promise to warrant a "buy" rating. For every Hawthorne or Canty that lost millions on draft day, there was a Matt Jones or Travis Johnson that parlayed a strong senior year or postseason run into a spot in the first round.

Given such volatility, it's no wonder NFL personnel people are mindful of the first rule of investing, the disclaimer that's included at the end of investment ads:

Past performance is not indicative of future return, and investors can and do lose money.

"It's not what you say about them in the fall, it's what you say about them on draft day," says Tim Ruskell, the president of the Seattle Seahawks. "James Butler had a high draft rating by the combines and the media, but at no time in Atlanta or Seattle were we that excited about him. We put him on the board based on the numbers from our combine, but that wasn't our opinion. But what happens is that initial opinion stays out there, and TV announcers keep talking it up when, in fact, what was really happening was that once people started looking at him, they weren't that high on him. I think that happens more times than any dramatic interview or bad combine workout."

At least NFL teams have until draft day to make an investment decision. Agents must commit much earlier. In September of 2004, Jack Scharf of Momentum Sports spent six thousand dollars and a grueling week of travel recruiting four players: Vanderbilt defensive end Jovan Haye and left tackle Justin Geisinger, Louisville wide receiver J. R. Russell, and Hawthorne, the defensive tackle from Wisconsin.

Russell was drafted in the seventh round, the rest of the group in the sixth. Scharf landed two of the four, Haye and Russell, and spent approximately forty thousand dollars on their expenses and training at Athletes' Performance prior to the NFL combine. Scharf's total commission for their signing bonuses and 2005 salaries will be less than twenty thousand dollars. Scharf and Jeff Griffin, his Momentum Sports colleague, can write off the losses against their two second-round clients, Ronald Bartell (Rams) and Darrent Williams (Broncos).

Haye and Russell, drafted by Carolina and Tampa Bay, respectively, still could recoup Momentum's investment, though few sixth- and seventh-round picks enjoy significant NFL careers.

Many players go into the draft with an overly optimistic view of where they're going to be drafted. After all, confidence and a belief in their skills have gotten them to that point, and most agents base part of their sales pitch on an ability to best position their clients to NFL officials. It's difficult for an agent to give his client anything other than the rosiest scenario, not with competitors lurking in the background promising more.

The irony, of course, is that no NFL team takes into account a player's agent, let alone his predraft marketing campaign. Players tend to ignore obvious red flags leading up to the draft—better all-star game and combine performances by players at the same position, their failure to address concerns about weight, strength, etc.—and they believe their college reputations will carry draft day.

No wonder that there's rampant postdraft agent-shuffling among disappointed players who thought they were going higher.

"There's so much hype in getting a college player now, that it's almost impossible to live up to expectations," says veteran NFL agent Brad Blank, who did not represent anyone for the 2005 draft. "It's gotten to the point where most guys don't stay with their first agent for the duration of their careers. I prefer to just wait and get guys the second time around."

Gibson stopped short of firing his agent, Octagon's Doug Hendrickson, but made it clear to him he wasn't pleased.

"He told me I could go either late first round or early second," Gibson said. "He really didn't give me a good explanation of why things happen the way they happen. I was kind of upset about that. You know how agents are. They tell you one thing, they tell you the world, I tell you that."

Hendrickson said he told Gibson that several teams were considering him for picks toward the end of the first round or early in the second, but that he could go as late as the third.

"I never envisioned him lasting to the end of round four, but I always tell clients that the draft is a crazy process," Hendrickson said. "I never tell clients they're going in the first round, unless I know for sure. Fred's situation was all over the board, and by no means did I tell him anything other than there was a *possibility* he could go in round one. All you can do is give your client a range, because there are only ten or fifteen guys you can ever be certain are going in the first round. For everyone else, it's a crapshoot."

The phrase "crapshoot" isn't thrown around during recruiting season, when agents go to great lengths to show how they can best position players for the draft and improve their stocks in the minds of NFL officials. But there's a difference, Hendrickson says, in preparing a player for the draft and promising to magically improve his status.

"Teams spend millions on scouting," Hendrickson said. "All we can do is prepare the players for the Senior Bowl, combine, Wonderlic, interviews—everything. They take it from there. No agent can get a guy drafted higher. That's just unheard of."

Even at the top there are no guarantees. Hendrickson and his Octagon partners represented Aaron Rodgers, the Cal quarterback who was invited to New York for the draft because of leaguewide assumptions that he'd go among the first ten selections. He lasted until Green Bay chose him at number twenty-four.

Hendrickson is right; the draft *is* a crapshoot. For every supposedly sure thing like Ryan Leaf who bombs, there's a sixth-round success like Tom Brady. The Pro Football Hall of Fame is full of players drafted in the third round or later, such as Johnny Unitas, Joe Montana, Steve Largent, Mike Webster, and Dan Fouts.

On Sunday, August 7, 2005, as the members of the draft class of 2005 underwent their first NFL preseason training camps, the Hall of Fame inducted Dan Marino and Steve Young.

Marino was the sixth quarterback chosen in the first round of the 1983 draft, behind standouts John Elway and Jim Kelly, but also after such forgettable names as Todd Blackledge, Tony Eason, and Ken O'Brien. The entire NFL, or at least the teams with first-round picks, also overlooked Texas A&I's Darrell Green, the future Hall of Fame cornerback chosen after Marino by the Washington Redskins with the last pick of the first round.

As for Young, he spent time in the USFL, played briefly for the Tampa Bay Buccaneers, and served four seasons as Montana's backup before achieving stardom after his thirtieth birthday.

A list of Hall of Famers that overcame being drafted low provides little encouragement for today's low-drafted players, who know there's no guarantee of a second contract in a league where the average career lasts less than four seasons. Not only that, the size of the first contract is proportional to the amount of leeway they will be given in ensuing seasons. The greater the investment, the less likely the team will be to cut ties.

Gibson figured there was no point to a protracted contract negotiation and was among the first picks to sign. The Steelers paid him a $296,000 signing bonus, along with salaries of $230,000 in 2005, $310,000 in 2006, and $385,000 in 2007. Unlike many draft picks that are forced to sign five-year deals, Gibson inked a three-year pact that makes him eligible for free agency earlier.

"It's not where you get drafted, it's where you end up," Hendrickson told Gibson. "If you are the player you know you can be, you can make up that money in three years instead of five."

Frank Gore, the Miami running back, didn't wait for the draft to fire his agent, unloading David Levine in favor of David Dunn. Levine, who won a spirited recruiting battle over Ethan Lock to land Gore, and hired a trainer to help the running back lose thirty-two pounds prior to the draft, received his termination letter by fax. Gore, who had overcome major surgeries on both knees, went to the 49ers with the first pick of the third round, and signed a three-year contract with a signing bonus of $599,500.

"Nothing's ever a surprise in this business," Levine said. "No matter how hard you're working, and the result, players are always wondering if there's another guy who could have done better. And there's always someone there to convince them there is. Plus, there's no penalty for switching agents."

There is some recourse for the agent who wants to recoup his predraft expenses. He can appeal to the NFL Players Association and an arbitrator, though typically the player asks his new agent to pick up the cost as a condition of switching. Levine also receives his commission on the marketing deals he negotiated for Gore, mainly from trading card companies.

"As bizarre as it sounds," Levine said, shortly before training camp, "I'm still Frank's marketing agent."

Canty, drafted near the end of the fourth round by Dallas, fired Lock via FedEx and hired IMG's Tom Condon.

Canty said he was disappointed at how Lock and his colleagues handled his medical issues, and wondered if they could have better communicated his progress to NFL teams.

"I was not satisfied," said Canty. "It was best that we move on."

Lock said that he felt "very comfortable and confident" about how he disseminated information on Canty's medical condition, drafting a six-page, single-spaced document that he sent to all thirty-two NFL teams that detailed his client's progress. Lock said several NFL teams commended him for being so thorough.

Lock said his firm spent between twenty and twenty-five thousand dollars on Canty in the months leading up to the draft, including providing him with a two-bedroom apartment in Phoenix during precombine training so his parents would have a place to stay. Lock said he spent three separate weeks leading up to the draft dealing exclusively with Canty at the expense of his other clients, which included Erasmus James, who was drafted in the first round.

"I've been in this business twenty years and did more for that kid than for anyone else in my entire career," Lock said. "I can't tell you how disappointed I am."

Condon negotiated a five-year deal for Canty, with a signing bonus of three hundred and ten thousand dollars. Canty was hoping for a three-year deal, which would have given him the right to become a free agent earlier, and that's essentially what Condon delivered, negotiating the last two seasons as "voidable years." That allows Canty to become a free agent after the 2007 season, if he reaches certain incentives based on minimal playing time.

IMG and Condon should be glad that Canty, before switching agents, didn't seek out Ed Hawthorne's opinion on IMG's predraft communication skills. A month after the draft, his nephew, Anttaj, fired Condon. Ed Hawthorne said he and his nephew were disappointed with IMG's advice to not talk to the media following the news that Anttaj tested positive for marijuana at the combine.

Ed Hawthorne pointed to Luis Castillo, the Northwestern defensive tackle that tested positive for steroids at the NFL combine. Castillo sent a letter to all thirty-two NFL teams saying that he was frustrated that an elbow injury wasn't healing properly, and used steroids to perform better at the combine. Castillo put up strong numbers at the combine and was selected by San Diego late in the first round.

Anttaj "got some bad advice, and we believe that's why he dropped in the press," Ed Hawthorne said. "He didn't say anything to anybody, and that's not what the NFL wanted to see. So he got taken off a lot of people's draft boards because he didn't respond to it. If we did respond, he might have dropped a round or two, but not to the sixth."

Ed Hawthorne said IMG agents never called Anttaj on draft day or afterward. "They never called to say 'Keep your head up. Don't worry.' The writing was on the wall. They were basically saying, 'You don't meet our criteria anymore.'"

Condon, head of IMG's football division, said he called Anttaj Hawthorne within a day of the draft and had every intention of continuing to represent him. Condon said the player wondered if, as a sixth-round pick, he would get the attention he needed from an agency that had four first-round picks. Condon assured him he would.

"'Taj is going to be a starter in this league by his second year," Condon said. "Why wouldn't we want to keep representing him?"

About six weeks after the draft, Anttaj Hawthorne hired Jack Scharf, the runner-up in the recruiting process. Scharf, after all, had plenty of experience guiding players with baggage. Scharf represented Richie Incognito, who was suspended several times and finally kicked off the team at Nebraska for disciplinary problems. The Rams selected Incognito in the third round.

Scharf's Momentum Sports colleague, Jeff Griffin, represented Darrent Williams, the Oregon State cornerback who was drafted in the second round by the Denver Broncos and carried a similar reputation as a problem child.

Before the draft, Griffin and Scharf worked to paint positive pictures of their clients, sending teams packets of information that included recommendations from coaches and professors. Scharf said a similar approach should have been taken with Hawthorne, who signed a five-year deal with a signing bonus of $157,500, a fraction of what he figured to earn before the failed drug test. The deal is loaded with incentives based on playing time and Pro Bowl appearances, though he's bound to the Raiders for five seasons.

"You have to do some damage control," Scharf said. "If Anttaj Hawthorne had come clean and addressed the issues with teams, he might have been able to overcome a lot of it, like Luis Castillo did. Would he have been a first-round pick? No, not based on what teams perceived as a lack of speed and strength his senior year. But he was too much of a talent to last beyond the first day."

Condon said IMG sent a letter to all thirty-two teams saying that Anttaj would give back his signing bonus if he failed another drug test. "We thought we did the appropriate thing," Condon said. "I couldn't give you a reason for why he chose to go in another direction."

For Scharf, the 2005 draft was a bit of a disappointment. It's not that he didn't think the world of his players, even those that were drafted late or not at all. His efforts yielded eight clients, but only one (Incognito) went on the first day.

Scharf was inching closer to his first huge payday, now that the Minnesota Vikings had traded wide receiver Randy Moss to the Raiders. That made Scharf's client Nate Burleson the number-one receiver in Minnesota heading into the 2005 season, the third and final year of his rookie deal.

Still, for all of his tireless recruiting efforts, Scharf had failed to land a blue-chip talent for the 2005 draft, though Griffin signed a pair of second-rounders in Williams and Bartell.

With the late signing of Hawthorne, Scharf landed three of the four targets of his September 2004 recruiting trip, but none of them went higher than the sixth round.

"I batted .750 on that trip, and a lot of agents would take that percentage," Scharf says. "But the thing is, you're dealing with so many unknowns, especially in September. All you can do is do your research and hit the road hard."

Scharf already was racking up frequent flyer miles for the 2006 NFL Draft before NFL training camps broke for the season, albeit with a different approach than for 2005. He planned to recruit only ten or twelve players, with more of an emphasis on consensus blue-chippers.

His targets included his alma mater (UCLA) and Marcedes Lewis, ranked as the second-best tight end, according to BLESTO. There was Arizona State wide receiver Derek Hagan, LSU offensive tackle Andrew

Whitworth, North Carolina State defensive end Manny Lawson, and Boston College's Will Blackmon, a cornerback who planned to play wide receiver as a senior.

As usual, Scharf would recruit promising juniors. His 2006 draft-eligible targets included N.C. State's Mario Williams, Jason Hill, a wide receiver at Washington State, and Joe Newton, an Oregon State tight end.

Scharf already scoured most of the country, but for 2006 planned to expand his efforts into Florida, perhaps the most hotly contested agent-recruiting ground in the nation. He aimed high, targeting Florida State's Ernie Sims. Though only a junior, Sims had developed a reputation as a ferocious hitter and a likely early entry into the 2006 draft.

It was only the second week of August, and Scharf still was negotiating a deal for Incognito with the Rams, but the forty-five hundred dollar Armani suit was out. There were red-eye flights to catch, presentations to make, Jaguar XJ8s to rent, parents and gatekeepers to woo.

"The only players I'm attempting to establish contact with are first- or second-round picks," Scharf said. "I'm not going to go after guys that are projected second-to-fourth-round and hope that they improve with a great combine. It's too much. Instead of signing eight guys, I'd much rather sign three studs."

Many of Scharf's rivals would be flocking to Charlottesville, Virginia, where Al Groh again had a promising crop of draft-eligible talent. Line-backer Ahmad Brooks, a redshirt junior, and senior offensive tackle D'Brickashaw Ferguson were projected first-round picks, at least before the 2005 season. Scouts and agents also had their eyes on running back Wali Lundy and kicker Connor Hughes.

A school-record seven Cavaliers were drafted in 2005, second only to Oklahoma and Florida State. In four seasons back at his alma mater, Groh had yet to take the Virginia program beyond the perennial eight- or nine-win showing of his predecessor, George Welsh.

Still, the emergence of more NFL draft talent confirmed the beliefs of school officials that Groh was raising the level of the program, even if it had yet to translate into additional victories. With coaching salaries soaring across the country, Virginia rewarded the sixty-one-year-old Groh, on August 19, with a six-year contract extension worth $10.2 million. The annual salary ($1.7 million) more than doubled Groh's previous income of $765,000. No wonder Welsh, seventy-one, who was enshrined in the College Football Hall of Fame a week earlier, was expressing interest in getting back into coaching after five years of retirement.

Groh's contract was negotiated by Neil Cornrich, who on August 10 began serving a one-year suspension by the NFL Players Association. Arbitrator Roger Kaplan upheld the NFLPA's decision to discipline Cornrich for violating the union's conflict of interest policy by working as an expert witness for General Motors in a lawsuit brought against the automaker by the estate of Derrick Thomas, the late Kansas City Chiefs linebacker.

The NFLPA suspension had no bearing on Cornrich's coaching representation. Groh hired Cornrich upon the recommendation of Bill Belichick not long after Groh's previous agent, Craig Kelly, died of pancreatic cancer in 2003.

Cornrich "is smart, hard-working, and has integrity," Groh said. "So if that's what a player is looking for, he might want to consider him."

With Cornrich suspended, the draft class of 2006 would have to look elsewhere for representation. So apparently would any of Cornrich's clients in need of free agent negotiation. Nate Clements, the Pro Bowl cornerback for the Buffalo Bills who could become a free agent after the 2005 season, left Cornrich and hired Todd France, who was a little late getting out of the gate for 2006 draft recruiting. His negotiations with the Miami Dolphins for Ronnie Brown, the number-two pick in the draft, took up much of the summer, before they agreed on August 15 to a five-year contract worth $34 million, including about $20 million guaranteed. It was the richest deal for a nonquarterback in draft history.

During recruiting season for the 2005 draft, rival agents noted that France never had represented a first-round pick. As negotiations for Brown dragged on, there were rumblings that France was waiting for number-three pick Braylon Edwards to sign with Cleveland, because France wanted a benchmark for negotiations. Edwards did indeed sign five days before Brown.

France laughed off the criticism. All he had to do was look at the money given to the number-two pick in 2004 (Robert Gallery, $18.5 million guaranteed), account for the annual increase across the board, and strike a deal. In that sense, baseball agent Scott Boras is right about the NFL Draft. It's not brain surgery.

"Negotiations are negotiations," France said. "If anything, I thought [first round] negotiations were easier because the market is set. It wasn't that confusing. It's a recruiting thing. 'He hasn't done a first-round pick.'

That notion is so overrated it's unbelievable. For me, it's harder to establish a market for a free agent tackle and not know who else the team is talking to and how far you can push it. Are they talking to other free agent tackles, too? What are they willing to pay? It's wide open. Here you're boxed in and have some parameters. I like free agency better, because your negotiation skills are called upon more. You have far less leverage in the draft. What are you going to do? Tell the team you're going back in the draft?"

Throughout the FAME office there were monuments to a blockbuster year. In the conference room were blown-up images of Brown, Rogers, and Davis, each holding their new jerseys at introductory press conferences. A large blowup of a two-page Reebok advertisement featuring Brown that appeared in national sports magazines waited to be hung, alongside a life-sized cardboard standup of Priest Holmes.

In the marketing room hung the EAS ads featuring Brown and Rogers, alongside posters of Takeo Spikes representing Taco Bell and Kendrell Bell for Subway. There was a rack of DVDs, each featuring one of France's clients, that were given to potential marketing clients.

It was Friday, August 19, 2005, a week shy of France's second anniversary of resigning from Career Sports Management. Lonnie Cooper's lawsuit against France continued to churn through Fulton County Superior Court. In early August, the judge handling the case denied motions by both parties for summary judgment. That left the case either to be settled or to go to trial.

In the meantime, the commissions paid by former CSM-turned-FAME clients for deals struck during France's employment remained in escrow. Not that France worried much about that, given his recent earnings.

In the last six months, France had negotiated $140 million in contracts, between the three draft choices and new deals for veterans Bell, Jonas Jennings, and Jason Craft, a defensive back with New Orleans. Almost $65 million of that was guaranteed, giving France a commission of almost $2 million. Two days earlier, he visited the Bills training camp to begin negotiations on a contract extension for his newest client, Clements.

Again, the existing client network paid off for France, who has a history of representing Buffalo players. France already was hinting that Clements, who could become a free agent following the 2005 season, wanted to be the highest-paid cornerback in the league.

Then there was the 2006 draft. Once again, Auburn and Georgia were loaded. Marcus McNeil, an Auburn tackle, was considered one of the top-ten prospects, at least before the season. Georgia featured guard Max Jean-Gilles, safety Greg Blue, and cornerbacks DeMario Minter and Tim Jennings.

Unlike Jack Scharf, France was keeping his targets close to the vest, though with the additions of Brown, Rogers, and Davis, his existing client network at Auburn and Georgia had grown stronger. France was starting with a list of twenty-five to thirty targets and would whittle it down as the season progressed, inevitably adding a few others. Rival agents already had him pegged as the frontrunner for Leonard Pope, a junior tight end at Georgia. France already was behind on 2006, though at least rivals no longer could say he never had negotiated a first-round contract.

"I know how hard I work," France said. "I sacrifice my personal life to do this job, and my philosophy is that I will never be outworked. I don't care who it is. I'm up so early and in bed very late. Starting your own company and putting your head down for two years and sacrificing your personal life and to have it all pan out. . . ."

He let the thought linger. Standing in the lobby of his office next to the *Jerry Maguire* goldfish bowl, France flipped through a photo album. There was a kaleidoscope of images from the last year, mostly of France with clients at various events.

It had all gone so quickly. With the Brown signing four days earlier, he finally could close the book on 2005. France placed the album next to the goldfish and headed out the door in pursuit of talent for the 2006 NFL Draft.

Much had changed for France and other figures from the 2004–2005 NFL draft season. Ruskell had gone from a behind-the-scenes role with the Atlanta Falcons to president of the Seattle Seahawks. Shortly before the 2005 college football season began, Brian Battle resigned from his job as compliance director for Florida State to take a similar position at Georgetown University.

It seemed like a lateral move—Georgetown does not field a Division-1 football team and is more than a decade removed from its "Hoya Paranoia" dominance in basketball—but Battle received the title of "associate athletic director." Unlike in Tallahassee, where he reported to Bob Minnix, Battle will run the Georgetown compliance department.

As the 2005 NFL season began, the Dallas Cowboys appeared to have found a bargain in Chris Canty, who had overcome his knee and eye injuries to take a prominent role in the team's new 3-4 defense, along with first-round picks Demarcus Ware and Marcus Spears.

Anttaj Hawthorne wasn't so fortunate. The Raiders cut their sixth-round pick a week before the season opener, citing depth at the position. Considered by some to be the best defensive tackle among college players a year earlier, he cleared waivers and was re-signed to the Raiders practice team, an eight-man taxi squad that serves as the last chance for NFL hopefuls.

Practice squad players can be moved onto the active roster and are free to sign with other teams. They can only remain on the squad one season, do not travel with the team to away games, and don't dress for home games. They earn roughly $4,700 a week, a fraction of the $230,000 rookie minimum for players on fifty-three-man rosters.

Fred Gibson also found himself relegated to a practice squad at the beginning of his rookie season. Gibson struggled to learn the Steelers' playbook and ran poor routes. At times he seemed to run away from the football. One of the highest-drafted players cut, he signed on with the Miami Dolphins as a practice squad player.

Still, Gibson remained upbeat. As was the case throughout the pre-draft season and the draft itself, Gibson continued to believe he ranked with the rest of the receivers in his class, though he now seemed to recognize the work ahead of him.

"It's going to come, just like in college," Gibson said. "I had to learn the offense my freshman year, and it's the same thing here. It's a different level; everyone's good here. It all starts in practice. Practice pays off. The thing you've got to do is separate yourself from everybody else."

AFTERWORD

THE 2006 NFL DRAFT
Saturday, April 29, 2006

E ven New York Jets fans could find nothing wrong with D'Brickashaw Ferguson. They cheered as the left tackle from the University of Virginia strode to a podium at Radio City Music Hall, shook hands with NFL commissioner Paul Tagliabue, and donned a green cap representing his new employer.

Ferguson had just become the fourth player selected in the 2006 NFL draft, the highest-drafted Virginia player since the Pittsburgh Steelers chose future Hall of Famer Bill Dudley first overall in 1942. Ferguson beamed as he posed for photographers with Tagliabue, who was announcing the first-round selections for the final time, having recently retired effective the coming summer.

All week long, there had been talk that the Jets would trade up from No. 4 and select one of the three high-profile skill position players that made the 2006 draft one of the most hyped in years. Instead, the Jets kept the pick. The Houston Texans surprisingly took Mario Williams, the defensive end from North Carolina State, at No. 1 and the New Orleans Saints grabbed Reggie Bush, the flashy tailback from Southern California. The Tennessee Titans, choosing third, opted for Texas quarterback Vince Young.

That left three players backstage at Radio City: Ferguson, tight end Vernon Davis of Maryland, and quarterback Matt Leinart, Bush's teammate who a year earlier stunned the NFL world by staying for his senior season at USC. With leading man looks and perpetual three-day stubble, Leinart hobnobbed with celebrities in Los Angeles and shortly after the draft would be linked to ubiquitous socialite Paris Hilton. He had spent the previous days lobbying to play for the Jets through New York media outlets, who touted him as the second coming of "Broadway" Joe Namath.

Instead, the Jets under new head coach Eric Mangini called for Ferguson, who four years earlier wasn't even considered Virginia's highest-rated signing from the state of New York.

Jets fans, packing Radio City Music Hall as they had previous Manhattan draft venues, continued to cheer Ferguson, even as he stepped away from Tagliabue and posed for a group photo with his parents, brother, friends, and a gaggle of former coaches that included Al Groh, the Virginia head coach who had endured a tumultuous, one-season tenure at the helm of the Jets in 2000.

Either Groh went unnoticed or the notoriously fickle Jets fans, who had booed the team's most recent ex-coach, Herm Edwards, when he appeared on Radio City's ESPN feed moments earlier, no longer cared. Everyone, it seemed, had only good feelings about the massive tackle teammates referred to as "Brick."

"D'Brickashaw" was inspired by Father Ralph de Bricassart, a fictional character of the 1983 television miniseries *The Thorn Birds* played by Richard Chamberlain. During the previous four months, Ferguson patiently explained his unusual name and the other aspects of his life that made him the most well-rounded, intriguing player in the 2006 NFL draft.

He majored in religious studies at Virginia and could hold a conversation on most any topic in an unmistakable voice that sounded both deep and squeaky at the same time. He had graduated in December, completing his studies in just three and a half years. Though an imposing presence at 6'6" and more than 300 pounds, Ferguson seemed part college professor, part statesman. He played the saxophone and held a black belt in karate. In Charlottesville, he cut his teammates hair and served as a youth minister at his church.

While other draft hopefuls wore league-issued gray sweats to team interviews at the NFL scouting combine in Indianapolis in February, Ferguson donned a suit and tie. "I figured it's a job interview and I should dress appropriately," he said.

Even Ferguson's choice of representation was unconventional. He eschewed big-name agencies in favor of Donald Yee, one of few Asian-American agents, who, although registered with the NFL Players Association since 1988, represented few players. His clients included just one superstar: Tom Brady, the Patriots quarterback. It helped that Yee's credentials included a diploma from the University of Virginia's law school.

Ferguson's unconventional choices and hobbies, along with his made-for-TV voice and extensive vocabulary, made him a media favorite.

"With offensive linemen, there's a stereotype that we're not very smart," Ferguson said during Senior Bowl week in Mobile, Alabama, where he shocked and impressed NFL personnel by attending while comparably rated players stayed away. "We're pigeonholed as guys who just think football, football, football. I've always liked to spread myself out, just to see how I deal with different tasks and issues. Being well-rounded helps you deal with different situations on the field, things that change in an instant."

Ferguson's extracurricular activities only cemented his character ratings, which were among the highest on draft boards around the NFL. But in the three months between the Senior Bowl and the draft, the NFL-obsessed media, led by ESPN and a growing NFL Network, so overanalyzed his personality quirks that some wondered if the sax-playing lineman was committed enough to football.

"It's not like I'm Kenny G," Ferguson said in the days before the draft.

Ferguson was skilled in the art of dealing with the media. Though a New York native, with ties to Groh—Ferguson grew up in nearby Freeport, just ten minutes from the Jets' practice facility—he expressed no preferences for playing for the Jets over anyone else. Nor did he take the bait in New York when reporters tried to dredge up Groh's Jets tenure, expressing nothing but praise for his college coach.

After all, it was Groh who had helped develop him from an above-average prospect coming out of high school into what some NFL scouts now were describing as the best lineman prospect to come out of college in years. It was Groh who urged him to return for his senior season at Virginia.

Groh, of course, needed Ferguson back after Heath Miller and Darryl Blackstock left school a year early for the NFL, joining seniors Chris Canty, Elton Brown, and Alvin Pearman for the 2005 NFL draft. The Cavaliers underachieved for the second consecutive year in 2005, salvaging a 7–5 season after a win over Minnesota in the Music City Bowl.

No player represented Virginia's downturn more than linebacker Ahmad Brooks, whom Groh had compared to Lawrence Taylor during the

2004 season. Considered a potential first-round pick for the 2005 draft, Brooks underwent knee surgery that summer, ballooned to 290 pounds, and played poorly in '05 when he wasn't sidelined with lingering ailments. A month before the draft, Groh booted Brooks off the team for undisclosed reasons, along with two other defensive standouts.

The Cincinnati Bengals would select Brooks in the supplemental draft in July of 2006. Team owner Mike Brown, aware of the fallout from the recent arrests of several young Bengals players, anticipated the reaction to the Brooks selection and issued a statement.

"We want our fans to know that we share their concerns regarding the recent off-field conduct of several Bengals players. We expect our players to be good citizens, as most are, and we hold them accountable for their conduct under team and league rules."

Kai Parham, another star Virginia linebacker with a year of eligibility remaining, declared early for the NFL draft. Four of Groh's assistants left for more prestigious gigs. The group included new Kansas State head coach Ron Prince, who as Ferguson's position coach at Virginia joined Groh on stage at Radio City.

Groh, who had signed a new contract the previous August that paid him $1.7 million annually, now was declaring the 2006 season a "rebuilding year."

That, however, was still four months away. Ferguson, along with his family and friends, made his way through the Radio City Music Hall lobby. They moved slowly, with ushers clearing a path through NFL jersey–clad fans that had swarmed the facility, giving the proceedings the feel of a boxing match.

The lobby was an NFL bazaar. There were kiosks hawking draft merchandise. Sirius Radio, which as the NFL's satellite radio provider was broadcasting live inside the theater, had a booth in the lobby and staffers were signing up new subscribers. A Hummer H3—official vehicle of the NFL draft—was parked on the red carpet.

Inside the theater, ESPN and The NFL Network were perched on adjacent platforms above the orchestra section, where team officials sat, waiting for the calls from the respective draft rooms. NFL Network host Rich Eisen went head-to-head with ESPN, his former employer, though Chris Berman and the ESPN army wielded a huge manpower advantage.

Though the theater was packed, fans quickly discovered it was perhaps the worst place in America to watch the event. Unlike at home or at a sports bar, where they could view endless highlight footage from each pick's college career on television and listen to an endless stream of commentary, their only vantage point at the draft was an empty stage and a clock that counted down the time to each pick. The ESPN and NFL Network crews could not be heard, nor were the feeds broadcast in the room.

The real show was in the lobby. The Ferguson party turned a corner and headed down a red-carpeted staircase to the media center where Reggie Bush was finishing his news conference. Though the Houston Texans had announced the selection and signing of Mario Williams the night before, Bush appeared flabbergasted that his NFL career would begin not in Texas but in New Orleans, which still was recovering from the sweeping destruction of Hurricane Katrina eight months earlier.

Ferguson, in contrast, was all smiles as he stepped onto the dais. The predraft poker face was gone; playing for the hometown Jets clearly was his preference. He'd suit up for the thirty-five-year-old Mangini, a former Groh colleague with the Jets and the latest member of the Bill Parcells–Bill Belichick family tree to get an NFL head coaching gig.

Ferguson answered four questions about playing for the Jets and how many tickets he would need for family and friends before someone asked yet again about his name.

"This is probably the most-asked question in America," he said, sighing. "Hopefully this will the last time I have to answer this. D'Brickashaw comes from the movie *The Thorn Birds*. It was a miniseries in 1983. . . ."

As Ferguson addressed the media on one side of the room, other reporters cornered Ben Dogra.

Dogra, the tireless SFX Sports agent who represented four first-round picks in the 2005 NFL draft, was off to another strong start. He represented the No. 1 selection, Mario Williams, and had what he believed were three more first-round possibilities. Dogra also represented Saints running back Deuce McAllister, who now faced a challenge for his starting job from newly drafted Reggie Bush.

Reporters queried Dogra on a number of fronts, but the conversation kept returning to Williams. While agents doggedly pursued Bush, Matt Leinart, and Vince Young throughout the 2005 college season, Dogra quietly had lobbied Williams, the North Carolina State defensive end. Dogra was hardly alone in his pursuit, but as far back as the summer of 2005 believed Williams might be the biggest dark horse of the 2006 draft.

At 6'7", with a lean chiseled physique, Williams looked and moved like he weighed 240 pounds. Actually, he tipped the scales at 290, perfect for an NFL defensive end. Throughout the league, teams were looking for the equivalent of Julius Peppers, the Carolina Panthers unstoppable pass rusher. By the end of the 2005 season, Williams's stock had soared and he bypassed his senior year, signing with Dogra.

Dogra, as usual, sent his best prospects to the Athletes' Performance Institute (API) in Tempe, Arizona, for pre-combine training. The group included Michael Huff, a speedy defensive back from Texas, and Davin Joseph, an offensive lineman from Oklahoma. Cornerback Kelly Jennings, like most University of Miami players, opted to stay in Coral Gables to train for the combine, and that was fine with Dogra.

Williams's draft stock rose further at the combine when he ran the forty-yard dash in 4.66 seconds, leaped forty inches in the vertical jump, ten feet in the broad jump, and bench-pressed 225 pounds thirty-five times. The numbers were by far the best by a player of his size. Williams and Vernon Davis, the Maryland tight end with a bodybuilder's physique who also trained at Athletes' Performance, put on the biggest shows in Indianapolis.

Agents rarely offer public praises of another's work, but Dogra's competitors conceded his efforts with Williams were masterful. Dogra knew the Texans, with the No. 1 pick, were interested in Williams. But even after meeting with team general manager Charley Casserly in Houston less than two weeks before the draft, he thought the Texans were just posturing and really had their eyes on Bush to jumpstart a franchise that finished 2–14 in 2005.

The Texans concluded that running backs were more disposable than defensive ends and that Williams had no downside. From meetings with the player and Dogra, they got the feeling that Williams, unlike Bush, would jump at a chance to sign the six-year, $54 million deal Houston was offering. There would be no holdout.

On April 27, two days before the draft, Williams appeared at a luncheon at the Lighthouse Restaurant on Pier 60, located at Chelsea Piers along the Hudson River on the West Side of Manhattan. He was joined by Bush, Davis, Leinart, Young, and D'Brickashaw Ferguson. Before food was served, each player was assigned a table for one last predraft press conference.

Williams drew the smallest contingent of media. Asked about his chances of being the first pick, Williams said, "It's not likely, but it's a possibility. It would be kind of shocking, especially for a defensive end."

While Williams was eating, Dogra was in his Manhattan hotel room talking to Casserly on the phone. By the end of the afternoon, Williams was shocked. Casserly and Dogra were hard at work on the contract.

Remarkably, it wasn't the largest deal Dogra was working on, though the bigger one was on the backburner until the end of the draft. Earlier in the month, agent Tom Condon left IMG after the sports conglomerate announced it no longer would be representing team sport athletes. Condon and his partner, Ken "Fuzzy" Kremer, reaped a reported $30 million from the sale of their eighty-client football business to the Creative Artists Agency, the Hollywood talent firm that represents the likes of Tom Cruise, Brad Pitt, and Julia Roberts.

That prompted Leinart, who already had enlisted CAA to represent him for marketing purposes, to hire Condon and fire veteran agent Leigh Steinberg. Meanwhile, Dogra and his business partner, Jim Steiner, also were in position to sell their company.

Live Nation, the parent company of SFX Sports and part of the Clear Channel Communications conglomerate, also planned to divest itself of team sport athlete representation. CAA approached Steiner and Dogra about selling. In late July, three months after the draft, Dogra and Steiner agreed for a reported $30 million, joining Condon and Kremer and forming a football superagency.

For the 2007 draft, CAA would have the two most prominent NFL agents in Condon and Dogra. The agents, meanwhile, could leverage CAA to offer perks to potential clients that would include endorsement and marketing deals, to say nothing of access to Hollywood premiers, award shows, and parties. Such incentives had little to do with football, but in the cutthroat world of draft recruiting, they were increasingly significant, especially for players like Leinart who thought of themselves as Hollywood material.

The plan was for Steiner and Dogra to remain in St. Louis, with Condon and Kremer relocating from Kansas City. The agents would work closely with CAA headquarters in Los Angeles.

With IMG out of the football business, there would be no more pre-combine training at the IMG Academies in Bradenton, Florida. Condon, who a decade earlier had to be coerced by young trainer Mark Verstegen to let him prepare clients for the combine in Bradenton, again would be sending his top draft hopefuls to Verstegen, who now operated Athletes' Performance training centers in Tempe, Arizona; Carson, California; and Las Vegas.

The business of pre-combine preparation had grown increasingly competitive for the 2006 draft, with more trainers setting up shop. At the high end, the field had narrowed to three: Athletes' Performance, Chip Smith's Competitive Edge near Atlanta; and the Tom Shaw Performance Enhancement Program.

Shaw, the former Florida State speed guru, had trained players for the combine for a decade, most recently from New Orleans. When Hurricane Katrina ripped through the gulf region, his training center in nearby Kenner was needed to house relief supplies and delivery trucks.

Shaw relocated to Disney's Wide World of Sports Complex near Orlando and reopened for business at the same facilities used in recent years by the Tampa Bay Buccaneers for preseason training camp. His clients included Reggie Bush, D'Brickashaw Ferguson, Vanderbilt quarterback Jay Cutler, and Santonio Holmes, the wide receiver from Ohio State.

The players worked out on a state-of-the-art track, where Shaw unloaded a truckload of training contraptions, including a full-length mirror he attached to a tractor so players could see their running form live. In the weight room, they trained alongside the Atlanta Braves, in town for spring training.

Cutler, chosen eleventh overall by Denver, and Holmes (No. 25, Pittsburgh) joined Bush and Ferguson in the first round. Athletes' Performance boasted eight first-round picks for the second year in a row. Besides Dogra's three clients and Vernon Davis, there was Laurence Maroney, the Minnesota running back taken twenty-first by New England. Maroney, like Davis, was a client of Ethan Lock. Tye Hill, a cornerback from Clemson represented by Octagon's Doug Hendrickson, went to the Rams at No. 15. UCLA tight end Marcedes Lewis, who trained at the Athletes' Performance facility in Carson and was represented by Sean Howard and Bus Cook, went to Jacksonville at No. 28.

Todd France represented the other first-rounder from API: Florida State linebacker Ernie Sims, who left Tallahassee with a year of eligibility remaining and was selected by the Detroit Lions with the ninth overall pick.

After breaking into the upper echelons of the agent business in 2005 with three first-round picks (Ronnie Brown, Carlos Rogers, and Thomas Davis), France was named to SportsBusiness Journal's "40-under-40" ranking of sports powerbrokers under the age of forty. Early in 2006, he reached a confidential settlement with his former employer, Lonnie Cooper and Career Sports Management.

France signed nine players for the 2006 draft, though only Sims and Leonard Pope, a tight end from Georgia who went to Arizona in the third round, were selected on the first day. That was mildly disappointing, though not much of a surprise to France. More importantly, in a year in which no players from Auburn, Georgia, or Georgia Tech were selected in the first round, France managed to maintain and build his existing client network at all three schools by signing two players from each team.

The schools would have promising seniors and juniors for the 2007 draft. Georgia Tech projected to have the lightest stable of the three, but France's two Yellow Jackets signings for '06 were every bit as important as his Auburn Tigers and Georgia Bulldogs. Damarius Bilbo was a fringe prospect that went undrafted, signed by the Dallas Cowboys as a free agent, cut before the season and re-signed by Dallas to the practice squad. But Bilbo played wide receiver at Georgia Tech and was close to Calvin Johnson, who would be a true junior and draft eligible in the fall of 2006. As the '06 season began, Johnson was considered by many the best wide receiver in college football.

France's client Dawan Landry, a Georgia Tech safety drafted in the fifth round by the Baltimore Ravens, no doubt would be of value on the Johnson recruiting front. But he was more important as the older brother of LaRon Landry, a safety at LSU who opted to return to the Tigers after a third straight all-SEC season because there were an unusual number of high-end safeties available in '06. Barring an injury, the younger Landry figured to go in the top half of the 2007 draft.

By signing Sims of Florida State, France managed to expand his southeastern territory into arguably the most fertile ground for draft talent. The Seminoles, who finished 2005 with the worst record (8–5) in Bobby Bowden's tenure since 1981, still produced four of the first nineteen picks of '06 draft. The team's two top draft prospects for 2007—senior Buster Davis and junior Lawrence Timmons, both linebackers—had played alongside Sims.

France, having never recruited FSU players until 2006, never dealt with Brian Battle, the school's compliance director who left for Georgetown before the '05 season. Battle's position reopened before the '06 season began and FSU athletic director Dave Hart brought Battle back, with a reconfigured job description and the associate athletic director title he did not have before.

This time, Battle would not be dealing as much with agents. Instead, he would have broader, more-encompassing duties that no doubt would prepare him for his eventual goal: athletic director at a major university.

"I won't miss having to run Agent Day or Pro Day," Battle said.

France, meanwhile, was making inroads into Florida State. Since starting his own agency in 2003, France had become the dominant agent at Auburn, Georgia, and Georgia Tech. He had claimed the jurisdiction formerly dominated by fellow Atlanta-based agent Pat Dye Jr. as his own.

Dye and his Pro-Files Sports colleague, Bill Johnson, had endured another tough year on the recruiting trail. Johnson was the lead agent for their most prominent draftee, Alabama linebacker Roman Harper, chosen in the second round by New Orleans. Dye's top client was Clemson quarterback Charlie Whitehurst, drafted by San Diego in the third round.

"We picked up a lot of silver medals," Johnson said, referring to runner-up status in player recruiting. "That doesn't mean much in this business."

Dye and Johnson still fared better than Jack Scharf, the flashy Momentum Sports agent who in August of 2005 decided to pursue only players projected as first- or second-round picks. Scharf's targets included Sims, Mario Williams, Marcedes Lewis, and Manny Lawson, who, like Williams, played defensive end for North Carolina State.

All four players went in the first round—Lawson to San Francisco with the nineteenth pick—but Scharf's efforts produced no clients. By March, he no longer was listed on the Momentum Sports Web site and was fired by his top veteran client, wide receiver Nate Burleson, a highly regarded free agent who within weeks signed a seven-year, $49 million deal with Seattle negotiated by Ken Sarnoff.

That left Scharf with a modest stable of clients. One of his more prominent, third-year linebacker Marquis Cooper, was a surprise cut by the Tampa Bay Buccaneers shortly before the '06 season began.

Even with fewer clients, Scharf continued to lobby hard for players eligible for the 2007 draft and remained busy. Reached twice for comment at the start of the 2006 season, he said he was too busy to talk, and did not call back.

As was the case in 2005, the Atlanta Falcons participation in the 2006 NFL draft began later in the day. This time, it was not because they were picking lower following a stellar season—the Falcons finished 8–8 in 2005, extending a streak of never producing back-to-back winning seasons—but because a month earlier general manager Rich McKay dealt the team's first-round selection, the fifteenth choice overall, to Denver in exchange for a package of draft picks. The best of the lot, the Broncos first-round pick (twenty-ninth overall), McKay sent to the New York Jets in return for veteran defensive end John Abraham.

The Falcons announced the trade on March 22nd, the same day McKay was scheduled to participate in a conference call with the media. As cochairman of the competition committee, it was McKay's job to address the agenda for the NFL's annual meetings, to be held in Orlando the following week.

The reporters who dialed in to the conference call had modest interest in the meetings or the Abraham trade. The more intriguing issue was the possibility of McKay succeeding Paul Tagliabue as commissioner. Two days earlier, Tagliabue had announced his retirement, effective July. After years of being mentioned as a candidate, McKay's talking points were well practiced.

"I appreciate the fact that anyone would mention my name," he said. "It's a long process and for me to say anything, I'm not sure that's appropriate. Anybody that ever gets mentioned in a top list of five hundred (candidates) isn't going to get real caught up on it. In this league, there's plenty to do on a daily basis other than worry about what may or may not be."

The media installed McKay as one of the frontrunners, along with Roger Goodell, the NFL's chief operating officer, who had worked closely with Tagliabue. Addressing the media in Orlando following a meeting of the competition committee, McKay looked downright commissioner-like, fielding questions with his usual mix of confidence, humor, and sarcasm.

Though McKay was later interviewed by a league-appointed executive search committee, the media's lofty perception of his candidacy might have been more a product of McKay's accessibility and popularity among the press corps. His background, intelligence, and public relations savvy were unquestioned, but he was not among the eleven finalists.

Just as NFL owners selected Tagliabue, a relatively unknown veteran of the league office to succeed Pete Rozelle in 1989, they gave the nod to Goodell, Tagliabue's right-hand man for five years. "Roger was going to get it no matter what," Steelers' owner Dan Rooney, cochair of the search committee, told reporters in August upon Goodell's selection during meetings in Chicago.

Tagliabue was a difficult act to follow, much as Rozelle was in 1989. Under Tagliabue's watch, the NFL had grown into North America's most popular pro sports league. While Major League Baseball, the NBA, and the NHL endured work stoppages, Tagliabue presided over an unprecedented era of labor peace. One eye-popping television contract followed another. Average franchise values soared from $160 million per team in 1995 to $898 million prior to the 2006 season, according to *Forbes* magazine.

The NFL draft, like the league itself, continued to grow each year.

More than 36 million fans tuned in to coverage on ESPN and ESPN2 in 2006, establishing a record for a fifth consecutive year. The NFL draft was providing year-round content for the growing NFL Network. Already holding exclusive rights to the NFL combine, the network's additions since the 2005 draft included the Senior Bowl, several college bowl games, and year-round ratings and commentary on draft prospects—to say nothing of regular season NFL games beginning late in 2006.

Goodell somehow would have to grow the NFL brand further. That was fine with McKay.

"I am flattered to have been even mentioned as a potential candidate," McKay said in a statement when the five finalists for commissioner was announced. "My focus and energy, along with Arthur Blank and Jim Mora, has been and will continue to be on building a championship team here in Atlanta."

That continued to be a tough task. After reaching the NFC title game following the 2004 season, the Falcons took a step back in '05, still wrestling with the quandary of how best to harness the explosive talents of quarterback Michael Vick. The Falcons continued to struggle with the passing game. Backup Matt Schaub, the traditional pocket passer, continued to look impressive whenever given an opportunity, which was mostly in the preseason. McKay turned down trade offers for Schaub, the former Virginia star who in 2006 would begin his third season holding a clipboard on the sidelines.

After two drafts, the Falcons' roster had a definitive McKay stamp on it. DeAngelo Hall, the team's first pick in the 2004 draft, already had emerged as one of the league's top cornerbacks. The Falcons liked Hall so much they dipped again into the Virginia Tech secondary in 2006 with their first pick, Jimmy Williams, trading up to land the cornerback with the fifth pick in the second round.

McKay's 2005 draft class played more than expected as rookies, in part because of injuries. Linebacker Michael Boley, the fifth-round pick with the volatile 6.0 predraft rating, proved to be a find. With projected starter Edgerton Hartwell lost for most of the '05 season, Boley started eleven games.

Defensive end Chauncey Davis, the fourth-round pick, started five games, one fewer than defensive tackle Jonathan Babineaux, the second-round selection. First-rounder Roddy White emerged as a starter halfway through the season, ranking fourth on the team with 446 yards receiving on 29 receptions.

The Falcons and Buccaneers continued their spirited rivalry in '05.

Squaring off on Christmas Eve in Tampa, the teams played an epic contest that ended in overtime with the resurgent Bucs eliminating Atlanta from playoff contention and completing a home-and-home sweep. The Bucs finished the year 11–5 and in the playoffs. The Falcons lost six of their last eight as the cold war between McKay and Buccaneers head coach Jon Gruden continued. When the Buccaneers 2006 schedule was unveiled, with a late-season stretch that included three games in eleven days, several Bucs officials privately wondered if McKay was involved.

The most successful person associated with the Falcons' 2005 draft now worked three thousand miles away. Tim Ruskell, the team's assistant general manager who left in February of '05 to become president of football operations for the Seattle Seahawks, overhauled the Seahawks roster. Guided by the character-first philosophy, Ruskell purged the locker room of malcontents and problem children, and eased the front-office tensions that had made head coach Mike Holmgren's life miserable.

Ruskell also appeared to have gotten the biggest steal of the '05 draft in Lofa Tatupu, the undersized linebacker from Southern California. Many NFL personnel people chuckled when Ruskell traded up in the second round to select Tatupu, who proved everyone but Ruskell wrong by becoming the immediate leader of the Seattle defense, making plays all over the field, and earning a spot on the NFC Pro Bowl team. Tatupu led a much-improved defense that included another one of Ruskell's '05 draft picks, third-round linebacker Leroy Hill.

The Seahawks, who had not won a playoff game since 1984, defeated Carolina in the NFC championship before losing Super Bowl XL to the Pittsburgh Steelers in Detroit.

Heath Miller, the former University of Virginia tight end who left school with a year of eligibility remaining, made immediate contributions for the Steelers as a rookie. He earned a Super Bowl ring for his efforts, as did all but one of the Steelers' first six draft picks.

Fred Gibson watched the Super Bowl on television. Pittsburgh's fourth-round pick in 2005, he became the second-highest drafted player cut when the Steelers released him shortly before the season. (Maurice Clarett, the troubled former Ohio State running back chosen at the end of the third round by Denver, also was released.)

Chris Canty, the other main player profiled in *The Draft*, chosen right behind Gibson by the Dallas Cowboys, turned out to be one of the bigger steals of the draft. Though not expected to contribute much in 2005 because of his rehabilitated knee and detached left retina, he missed just a week of training camp. During the season, he led all Cowboys defensive linemen in tackles, mastered the new 3–4 defense installed by Bill Par-cells, and ended up starting by the end of the year. Canty began the 2006 season as the starter at right defensive end, opposite Marcus Spears, a first-round pick in '05. Demarcus Ware, the other first-round defensive end selected by Dallas in '05, was starting at linebacker.

Canty, who played the 3–4 defense at Virginia, already was being touted as the ideal defensive end for the scheme. At 6'7" and 300 pounds, he was the same height and similar build of Mario Williams, the No. 1 overall pick by the Houston Texans.

Canty, of course, would earn just a fraction of what Williams would receive in 2006. But having signed a five-year contract that included two "voidable years" based on minimal playing time, Canty was putting him-self in good position to recoup his draft day losses following the 2007 season.

Gibson wasn't so fortunate. The former Georgia star spent the 2005 season on the Miami Dolphins practice squad, earning $4,700 a week, dealing with an ankle injury, and toiling in anonymity at the team's headquarters in Davie, Florida. Nick Saban, the former LSU coach in his first year with the Dolphins, was a fan of the wide receiver, having faced him in the SEC, and Gibson entered the off-season encouraged about 2006, even after watching the Super Bowl.

Gibson survived until the last round of cuts, was unemployed for less than twenty-four hours, and re-signed to the Dolphins practice squad, where he could remain for the rest of the 2006 season unless he was signed to the active roster or by another team.

If nothing else, the year spent in the NFL no-man's-land of the prac-tice squad in 2005 was the wake-up call Gibson never fully appreciated during the predraft process. He worked tirelessly, realizing he had to learn the offense and not just run routes. Perhaps most tellingly, he put on some weight. He still needed bulk, but at least now was up to 205, nearly ten pounds more than his predraft weight.

The 2006 season began on September 7th, on a Thursday night, with a match-up of the Dolphins and Gibson's former NFL employer, the Steelers. Gibson, as a practice squad player, watched the game in Florida on television.

"I would never have believed coming out of Georgia I'd be a practice squad guy," he said. "I have the talent to play football. But in the NFL, it's tough to break through. I'm just going to have to deal with it and work hard. I don't know, man. I still believe I can play in this league."

ACKNOWLEDGMENTS

'Ve always read acknowledgments and wondered why an author needed to hit up so many people just to get a book done. After writing this book, I know. Trying to weave together the perspectives of NFL teams, college football programs, agents, and athletes was at times like trying to solve a Rubik's Cube.

I did not obtain a publisher for this book, by design, until shortly before the 2005 NFL Draft. I'm grateful to Marc Resnick and the staff at St. Martin's Press for offering me a chance to tell this story. I'm even more thankful for the army of football publicity people and executive assistants who opened the gates to a guy without either a book contract or extensive experience covering the NFL and college football.

That group includes Reggie Roberts, Frank Kleha, Ted Crews, Ryan Moore, Sammie Burleson, and Tina Reinert of the Atlanta Falcons; Rich Murray, Michael Colley, Nancy Bourne, and Darlene Craig at the University of Virginia; Rick Korch at the University of Miami; Jeff Kamis, Tony Morreale, and Julia O'Neal of the Tampa Bay Buccaneers; Harvey Greene of the Miami Dolphins; Rich Gonzales of the Seattle Seahawks; Claude Felton at the University of Georgia; Jeff Purinton, Stacy Wilkshire, and Rachel Curran at Florida State University; Allison George at Georgia Tech; Kirk Sampson at Auburn; Mike Schulze at the Outback Bowl, Joe Galbraith at Florida Citrus Sports, Vic Knight at the Senior

Bowl, Judith Ordehi at the East/West Shrine Game; Ben Crandell at the IMG Academies; the NFL's Steve Alic; Carl Francis of the NFL Players Association; Seth Palansky of the NFL Network; ESPN's Rob Tobias; Dan Bell of Fox Sports; and *Sports Illustrated*'s Rick McCabe.

I'm especially grateful for the more than 150 people who agreed to be interviewed for this book, especially those that let me into their lives frequently during a year. Only one person declined my requests, which I found puzzling, since agent Drew Rosenhaus never turns down a media opportunity. Rosenhaus hinted he might be working on his own draft-related book. We can only hope he finds the time to write a sequel to his memorable 1997 memoir, *A Shark Never Sleeps*.

In the interest of giving credit and full disclosure, I must mention that this book is partially an outgrowth of my work with Mark Verstegen, the founder and owner of the Athletes' Performance training center in Tempe, Arizona. I have coauthored three fitness books with Verstegen, including two that come out in 2006. As recently as February of 2004, I helped players training at Athletes' Performance for the combine to prepare for their interviews with NFL officials. During that time, I met agent Jack Scharf and his Momentum Sports colleague Jeff Griffin and became intrigued by the yearlong process that goes into the evaluation of talent by NFL teams, the recruiting of players by agents, and the often-dramatic shifts in a player's stock between the end of the college football season and the NFL Draft four months later.

Though Verstegen and I continue to write fitness books, and in fact worked on one concurrently while I worked on this project, I agreed that I would not take advantage of my familiarity with his staff and access to his facility. Though I interviewed Scharf and players Chris Canty and Fred Gibson twice each for brief periods at Athletes' Performance in early 2005, I interviewed all three extensively throughout the country between September of 2004 and August of 2005.

Combine preparation is a small but essential part of *The Draft* story, which is why in the interest of balance I twice visited IMG's International Performance Institute in Bradenton, Florida, where Verstegen previously worked. I also interviewed Chip Smith by phone about his precombine work with David Greene and Ray Willis, and spoke extensively with combine prep pioneer Mike Boyle.

Percy Knox, the tireless director of athlete relations at Athletes' Performance, made sure I did not overstep my bounds in Tempe, while at the same time providing insight into combine preparation. I'm grateful for his assistance.

I'm a graduate of the University of Virginia, but my decision to follow the Cavaliers was based solely on the pro philosophies Al Groh has instilled in every aspect of his program, his vast NFL network, and the fact that Virginia uncharacteristically ranked among the top schools for draft talent during the 2004 season. Admittedly, there are few better places to visit on fall afternoons.

Only a few books have tackled the history of the draft, but they were invaluable resources. They are *Sleepers, Busts & Franchise-Makers* by Cliff Christl and Don Langenkamp; *The Meat Market* by Richard Whittingham; *America's Game* by Michael MacCambridge; and the exhaustive *Sporting News Pro Football Draft Encyclopedia*. I'm especially grateful to Christl, who sent me a photocopied version of his hard-to-find book, which a smart publisher would be wise to put back in print.

Several team-related books also were helpful, most notably *When Pride Still Mattered* by David Maraniss, Peter Golenbock's *Cowboys Have Always Been My Heroes*, *Tales from the Bucs Sideline* by Chris Harry and Joey Johnston, and *Patriot Reign* by Michael Holley.

Many friends generously offered or provided lodging during the writing of this book, keeping me from blowing my advance accruing Marriott points. Special thanks to Becky and Joe Lettelleir, Ed Giuliotti, Margee and Tim Mossman, Melissa Mikolajczak, Beth Knowles and Brooks Rathet, Etch Shaheen, and Julie and Brett Benadum.

I'm grateful to old pals Tim Mossman and Bruce Greenbaum for keeping me awake on long drives through Georgia and Florida, providing feedback and insight via cell phone. As for my former collaborator Mike Veeck, a man who does not even watch the Super Bowl, thanks for the proper dose of perspective.

I also owe a debt of gratitude to many media colleagues, including Frank Cooney, who writes for *USA Today Sports Weekly* and runs the fabulous draft Web site NFLDraftScout.com; Neil Stratton, whose InsideTheLeague.com site has a much-deserved following of NFL insiders; Nolan Nawrocki of *Pro Football Weekly;* Russ Lande, who provided me with a copy of his exhaustive *GM Jr.* draft guide; Bill King of *SportsBusiness Journal,* a closeted draft geek whose story of ESPN's draft coverage in 2000 partially inspired this book; Scott Reynolds and Jim Flinn at *The Pewter Report;* I.J. Rosenberg of Score Atlanta; Mark Maske of the *Washington Post;* Roger Mooney of the *Bradenton Herald;* John Romano of the *St. Petersburg Times;* Martin Fennelly and Joe Henderson of the *Tampa Tribune;* and fellow freelance mercenaries Mark Didtler and Bob Andelman, a onetime book collaborator with Arthur Blank.

Since I could only be at one place on draft day, and chose to watch the draft unfold from Atlanta Falcons headquarters, I reconstructed much of the New York action through interviews and ESPN's always-thorough coverage. I'm also grateful for Darren Rovell and Ken Sugiura for providing blow-by-blow accounts of agent Todd France's day on ESPN.com and in the *Atlanta Journal-Constitution,* respectively.

A hearty thank you goes to Falcons scribes Matt Winkeljohn of the *Atlanta Journal-Constitution* and George Henry of the Associated Press, who, during draft week, made me feel like an honorary member of the small but hardworking Falcons media corps.

This book might not exist were it not for Scott Smith and Jonathan Woog at Street & Smith's sports annuals. They provided the assignments and credentials to get me where I needed to be. For many years, NFL teams prepared for the draft with little more than Street & Smith's publications. I am honored to have worn the magazine's credentials at the Outback Bowl, Gridiron Classic, Senior Bowl, and NFL combine, and to have contributed to Street & Smith's wonderful new draft-preview publication. Thanks also to Street & Smith's publisher Mike Kallay and staff writer Matt McKenzie.

Having spent so much time around football agents and players trying to select representation, I am reminded that I have *the* best agent in any field. David Black is everything a writer could hope for, treating this undrafted free agent like a first-round pick. Special thanks to David's All-Pro staff, especially Gary Morris, Dave Larabell, and Jason Sacher.

Then there was my wife, Suzy, who handled my frequent absences while pregnant and with a toddler in tow, never wavering in support of this project. To borrow a phrase from the scouting world, I've overachieved in marriage.

APPENDIX

THE 2005 NFL DRAFT
Round by Round

KEY

Number in parentheses is the overall selection.

Underclassman =*.

Agent as of August 15, 2005 in parentheses.

Key figures in *The Draft* listed in bold type.

FIRST ROUND

San Francisco (1), *Alex Smith, QB, Utah (Tom Condon)

Miami (2), Ronnie Brown, RB, Auburn (Todd France)

Cleveland (3), Braylon Edwards, WR, Michigan (Lamont Smith)

Chicago (4), Cedric Benson, RB, Texas (Eugene Parker, Scott Parker)

Tampa Bay (5), Carnell Williams, RB, Auburn (Ben Dogra)

Tennessee (6), *Adam Jones, CB, West Virginia (Michael Huyghue)

Minnesota (7/from Oakland), *Troy Williamson, WR, South Carolina
(David Canter)

Arizona (8), Antrel Rolle, CB, Miami (Ben Dogra)

Washington (9), Carlos Rogers, CB, Auburn (Todd France)

Detroit (10), *Mike Williams, WR, USC (Tony Fleming, Mitch Frankel)

**Dallas (11), Demarcus Ware, DE, Troy State (Pat Dye, Bill
Johnson)**

San Diego (12/from New York Giants), *Shawne Merriman, DE, Maryland (Kevin Poston)

New Orleans (13/from Houston), Jammal Brown, OT, Oklahoma (Ben Dogra)

Carolina (14), *Thomas Davis, S, Georgia (Todd France)

Kansas City (15), Derrick Johnson, LB, Texas (Vann McElroy, Jeff Nalley, Graylan Crain)

Houston (16/from New Orleans), Travis Johnson, DT, Florida State (Gary Wichard)

Cincinnati (17), David Pollack, DE, Georgia (Ken Kremer)

Minnesota (18), Erasmus James, DE, Wisconsin (Ethan Lock)

St. Louis (19), Alex Barron, OT, Florida State (Roosevelt Barnes)

Dallas (20/from Buffalo), Marcus Spears, DE, LSU (Jimmy Sexton)

Jacksonville (21), Matt Jones, TE, Arkansas (Dave Butz, Alan Herman)

Baltimore (22), Mark Clayton, WR, Oklahoma (Ben Dogra, James Steiner)

Oakland (23/from Seattle), *Fabian Washington, CB, Nebraska (Brian Mackler, Jim Ivler, Jason Chayut)

Green Bay (24), *Aaron Rodgers, QB, California (Mike Sullivan)

Washington (25/from Denver), Jason Campbell, QB, Auburn (Joel Segal)

Seattle (26/from New York Jets through Oakland), *Chris Spencer, C, Mississippi (Ken Kremer)

Atlanta (27), Roddy White, WR, UAB (Neil Schwartz)

San Diego (28), Luis Castillo, DT, Northwestern (Mike McCartney, Rick Smith, Mark Bartelstein)

Indianapolis (29), Marlin Jackson, CB, Michigan (Doug Hendrickson, Mike Sullivan)

Pittsburgh (30), *Heath Miller, TE, Virginia (Tom Condon, Ken Kremer)

Philadelphia (31), Mike Patterson, DT, USC (Gary Uberstine)

New England (32), Logan Mankins, OG, Fresno State (Frank Bauer)

SECOND ROUND

San Francisco (33), David Baas, OG, Michigan (Ethan Lock)

Cleveland (34), *Brodney Pool, S, Oklahoma (Ben Dogra)

Philadelphia (35/from Miami), Reggie Brown, WR, Georgia (Bill Johnson/Pat Dye)

Tampa Bay (36), Barrett Ruud, LB, Nebraska (Ethan Lock, Vance Malinovic)

Detroit (37/from Tennessee), Shaun Cody, DT, USC (Harold Lewis)

Oakland (38), Stanford Routt, CB, Houston (Vann McElroy, Jeff Nalley, Graylan Crain)

Chicago (39), Mark Bradley, WR, Oklahoma (Danny Bradley)

New Orleans (40/from Washington), *Josh Bullocks, S, Nebraska (Josh Luchs, Steve Feldman)

Tennessee (41/from Detroit), Michael Roos, OT, Eastern Washington (Cameron Foster)

Dallas (42), Kevin Burnett, LB, Tennessee (Ricky Lefft)

New York Giants (43), Corey Webster, CB, LSU (Jimmy Sexton)

Arizona (44), J.J. Arrington, RB, California (Fletcher Smith, Kennard McGuire)

Seattle (45/from Carolina), *Lofa Tatupu, LB, Southern Cal (Fletcher Smith, Kennard McGuire)

Miami (46/from Kansas City), Matt Roth, DE, Iowa (Brad Leshnock, Joe Flanagan)

New York Jets (47/from Houston through Oakland), Mike Nugent, K, Ohio State (Ken Harris)

Cincinnati (48), *Odell Thurman, LB, Georgia (John Michels)

Minnesota (49), Marcus Johnson, OG, Mississippi (Rich Moran)

St. Louis (50), Ronald Bartell, CB, Howard (Jeff Griffin, Jack Scharf)

Green Bay (51/from New Orleans), Nick Collins, CB, Bethune-Cookman (Dave Butz, Alan Herman)

Jacksonville (52), Khalif Barnes, OT, Washington (Ken Zuckerman, Rick Smith, Mark Bartelstein)

Baltimore (53), Dan Cody, DE, Oklahoma (Drew Rosenhaus, Jason Rosenhaus)

Carolina (54/from Seattle), *Eric Shelton, RB, Louisville (Peter Schaffer)

Buffalo (55), *Roscoe Parrish, WR, Miami (Drew Rosenhaus, Jason Rosenhaus)

Denver (56), Darrent Williams, CB, Oklahoma State (Jeff Griffin, Jack Scharf)

New York Jets (57), *Justin Miller, CB, Clemson (Eugene Parker)

Green Bay (58), Terrence Murphy, WR, Texas A&M (Doug Hendrickson)

Atlanta (59), Jonathan Babineaux, DT, Iowa (Jack Bechta)

Indianapolis (60), Kelvin Hayden, CB, Illinois (Fletcher Smith, Kennard McGuire)

San Diego (61), Vincent Jackson, WR, Northern Illinois (Neil Schwartz, Jonathan Feinsod)

Pittsburgh (62), Bryant McFadden, CB, Florida State (Roosevelt Barnes)

Philadelphia (63), *Matt McCoy, LB, San Diego State (David Caravantes, Bus Cook)

Baltimore (64/from New England), Adam Terry, OT, Syracuse (Ken Landphere)

THIRD ROUND

San Francisco (65), *Frank Gore, RB, Miami (David Dunn)

St. Louis (66/from Miami), Oshiomogho Atogwe, S, Stanford (Doug Hendrickson, Ken Landphere)

Cleveland (67), Charlie Frye, QB, Akron (Eric Metz, Vance Malinovic)

Tennessee (68), Courtney Roby, WR, Indiana (Peter Schaffer)

Oakland (69), Andrew Walter, QB, Arizona State (Jeff Sperbeck)

Miami (70/from Chicago), *Channing Chowder, LB, Florida (Joel Segal)

Tampa Bay (71), Alex Smith, TE, Stanford (Ken Landphere, Doug Hendrickson)

Detroit (72), Stanley Wilson, CB, Stanford (Ken Zuckerman, Rick Smith, Mark Bartelstein)

Houston (73/from Dallas), *Vernand Morency, RB, Oklahoma State (Drew Rosenhaus, Jason Rosenhaus)

New York Giants (74) *Justin Tuck, DE, Notre Dame (Ken Landphere, Doug Hendrickson)

Arizona (75), Eric Green, CB, Virginia Tech (Craig Domann)

Denver (76/from Washington), Karl Paymah, CB, Washington State (Rocky Arceneaux)

Philadelphia (77/from Kansas City), *Ryan Moats, RB, Louisiana Tech (Mike McCartney, Rick Smith, Mark Bartelstein)

Oakland (78/from Houston), Kirk Morrison, LB, San Diego State (Leigh Steinberg, Bruce Tollner, Ryan Tollner)

Carolina (79), Evan Mathis, OG, Alabama (Kirk Wood, Archie Lamb)

Minnesota (80), Dustin Fox, CB, Ohio State (Neil Cornrich)

St. Louis (81), *Richie Incognito, C, Nebraska (Jack Scharf, Jeff Griffin)

New Orleans (82), Alfred Fincher, LB, Connecticut (Kristen Kuliga)

Cincinnati (83), *Chris Henry, WR, West Virginia (John Frederickson)

New England (84/from Baltimore), Ellis Hobbs, CB, Iowa State (Kevin Omell)

Seattle (85), David Greene, QB, Georgia (Pat Dye, Bill Johnson)

Buffalo (86), Kevin Everett, TE, Miami (Brian Overstreet)

Jacksonville (87), Scott Starks, CB, Wisconsin (Jason Fletcher)

New York Jets (88), Sione Pouha, DT, Utha (Ken Vierra)

Carolina (89/from Green Bay), Atiyyah Ellison, DT, Missouri (Jim Steiner)

Atlanta (90), Jordan Beck, LB, Cal Poly (Leigh Steinberg, Bruce Tollner, Ryan Tollner)

Tampa Bay (91/from San Diego), Chris Colmer, OT, North Carolina State (Jonathan Feinsod, Neil Schwartz)

Indianapolis (92), Vincent Burns, DE, Kentucky (Hadley Engelhard)

Pittsburgh (93), Trai Essex, OG, Northwestern (Roosevelt Barnes)

San Francisco (94/from Philadelphia), Adam Snyder, OG, Oregon (David Dunn)

Arizona (95/from New England), *Darryl Blackstock, LB, Virginia (Ben Dogra)

Tennessee (96/compensatory selection), Brandon Jones, WR, Oklahoma (Craig Domann)

Denver (97/comp selection), Dominique Foxworth, CB, Maryland (Jim Ivler, Brian Mackler)

Seattle (98/comp selection), Leroy Hill, LB, Clemson (Bill Strickland)

Kansas City (99/comp selection), Dustin Colquitt, P, Tennessee (Jimmy Sexton)

New England (100/comp selection), Nick Kaczur, OT, Toledo (Vance Malinovic)

Denver (101/comp selection), *Maurice Clarett, RB, Ohio State (Steve Feldman)

FOURTH ROUND

Philadelphia (102), Sean Considine, FS, Iowa (Rick Smith, Mike McCartney, Mark Bartelstein)

Cleveland (103), Antonio Perkins, CB, Oklahoma (Danny Bradley)

Miami (104), Travis Daniels, CB, Louisiana State (Albert Elias)

Seattle (105/from Oakland), Ray Willis, OT, Florida State (Bill Johnson, Pat Dye)

Chicago (106), Kyle Orton, QB, Purdue (David Dunn)

Tampa Bay (107), Dan Buenning, OG, Wisconsin (Mike McCartney, Rick Smith, Mark Bartelstein)

Tennessee (108), Vincent Fuller, FS, Virginia Tech (Mitch Frankel)

Dallas (109), *Marion Barber, RB, Minnesota (Craig Domann)

New York Giants (110), Brandon Jacobs, RB, Southern Illinois (Justin Schulman, David Dunn)

Arizona (111), Elton Brown, OG, Virginia (Joel Segal)

Minnesota (112/from Washington), *Ciatrick Fason, RB, Florida (Joel Segal)

Tennessee (113/from Detroit), David Stewart, OT, Mississippi State (Bus Cook)

Houston (114), Jerome Mathis, WR, Hampton (Kevin Poston)

Green Bay (115/from Carolina), Marviel Underwood, FS, San Diego State (Jack Bechta)

Kansas City (116), Craphonso Thorpe, WR, Florida State (Matt Couloute)

St. Louis (117), Jerome Carter, SS, Florida State (Dave Butz, Alan Herman)

New Orleans (118), Chase Lyman, WR, California (Marvin Demoff)

Cincinnati (119), Eric Ghiaciuc, C, Central Michigan (Craig Domann)

Washington (120/from Minnesota), Manuel White Jr., FB, UCLA (Leigh Steinberg, Bruce Tollner, Ryan Tollner)

Carolina (121/from Seattle), Stefan Lefors, QB, Louisville (Jerrold Colton)

Buffalo (122), Raymond Preston, C, Illinois (Craig Domann)

New York Jets (123/from Jacksonville), Kerry Rhodes, FS, Louisville (Todd France)

Baltimore (124) Jason Brown, C, North Carolina (Harold Lewis, Kevin Omell)

Green Bay (125), Brady Poppinga, OLG, Brigham Young (Michael Hoffman, Gary Uberstine)

Philadelphia (126/from Denver, through Cleveland, Seattle, Carolina, and Green Bay), Todd Herremans, OT, Saginaw Valley State (Joe Linta)

Jacksonville (127/from New York Jets), Alvin Pearman, RB, Virginia (David Dunn)

Atlanta (128), Chauncey Davis, DE, Florida State (Kevin Conner, Robert Brown)

Indianapolis (129), Dylan Gandy, G, Texas Tech (Scott Smith)

San Diego (130), Darren Sproles, RB, Kansas State, (Gary Wichard)

Pittsburgh (131), Fred Gibson, WR, Georgia (Doug Hendrickson, Demetro Stephens)

Dallas (132/from Philadelphia), Chris Canty, DE, Virginia (Tom Condon, Chris Singletary)

New England (133), *James Sanders, SS, Fresno State (Steve Feldman, Josh Luchs)

St. Louis (134/compensatory selection), Claude Terrell, G, New Mexico (Steve Feldman, Josh Luchs)

Indianapolis (135/comp selection), Matt Giordano, FS, California (Steve Baker)

Tennessee (136/comp selection), Roydell Williams, WR, Tulane (Jeff Guerriero)

FIFTH ROUND

San Francisco (137), Ronald Fields, DT, Mississippi State (Josh Luchs, Steve Feldman)

Kansas City (138/from Miami), Boomer Grigsby, ILB, Illinois State (Vance Malinovic)

Cleveland (139), David McMillan, DE, Kansas (Craig Domann)

Chicago (140), Airese Currie, WR, Clemson (Carl Poston)

Tampa Bay (141), Donte Nicholson, SS, Oklahoma (Ben Dogra)

Tennessee (142), *Damien Nash, RB, Missouri (David Canter)

Green Bay (143/from Oakland), Junius Coston, C, North Carolina A&T (Bardia Ghahremani)

St. Louis (144/from N.Y. Giants through San Diego and Tampa Bay), Jerome Collins, TE, Notre Dame (Mike McCartney, Rick Smith, Mark Bartelstein)

Detroit (145/from Arizona through New England), Dan Orlovsky, QB, Connecticut (David Dunn)

Philadelphia (146/from Washington), Trent Cole, OLB, Cincinnati (Richard Rosa, Anthony Agnone, Edward Johnson)

Kansas City (147/from Detroit), Alphonso Hodge, CB, Miami (Ohio) (Ken Harris)

Indianapolis (148/from Dallas through Philadelphia), Jonathan Welsh, DE, Wisconsin (John Temple)

Carolina (149), Adam Seward, ILB, Nevada-Las Vegas (Michael Hoffman, Gary Uberstine)

Tennessee (150/from Kansas City), Daniel Loper, OT, Texas Tech (Leonard Roth)

Houston (151), Drew Hodgdon, C, Arizona State (Leo Goeas, Craig Domann)

New Orleans (152), *Adrian McPherson, QB, Florida State (Leigh Steinberg, Bruce Tollner, Ryan Tollner)

Cincinnati (153), Adam Kieft, OT, Central Michigan (Dave Butz, Alan Herman)

Washington (154/from Minnesota), Robert McCune, ILB, Louisville (Ken Harris)

Tampa Bay (155/from St. Louis), *Larry Brackins, WR, Pearl River C.C. (Bus Cook, Don Weatherall)

Buffalo (156), Eric King, CB, Wake Forest (Todd France)

Jacksonville (157), Gerald Sensabaugh, SS, North Carolina (Kevin Conner, Robert Brown)

Baltimore (158), Justin Green, FB, Montana (Andrew Baker)

Seattle (159), Jeb Huckeba, OLB, Arkansas (Drew Pittman)

Atlanta (160/from Denver), Michael Boley, OLB, Southern Mississippi (Ethan Lock, Zeke Sandhu)

New York Jets (161), Andre Maddox, SS, North Carolina State (Jason Waugh, Derrick Harrison)

Miami (162/from Green Bay through Kansas City), Anthony Alabi, OT, Texas Christian (Vann McElroy, Jeff Nalley)

Atlanta (163), Frank Omiyale, OT, Tennessee Tech (Mark Slough)

San Diego (164), Wesley Britt, OT, Alabama (David Dunn)

Indianapolis (165), Robert Hunt, C, North Dakota State (Kevin Omell, Harold Lewis)

Pittsburgh (166), *Rian Wallace, ILB, Temple (Edward Johnson, Anthony Agnone, Richard Rosa)

Green Bay (167/from Philadelphia), *Michael Hawkins, FS, Oklahoma (Alex Balic)

Arizona (168/from New England), Lance Mitchell, ILB, Oklahoma (Mason Ashe)

Carolina (169/compensatory selection), Geoff Hangartner, C, Texas A&M (Leonard Roth)

New England (170/comp selection), Ryan Claridge, OLB, Nevada-Las Vegas (David Dunn)

Carolina (171/comp selection), Ben Emanuel, FS, UCLA (James Ivler, Bill Heck)

Philadelphia (172/comp selection), Scott Young, OG, Brigham Young (Patrick Pinkston, Jeff Courtney)

Indianapolis (173/comp selection), Tyjuan Hagler, OLB, Cincinnati (Craig Domann)

San Francisco (174/comp selection), Rasheed Marshall, WR, West Virginia (Ralph Cindrich)

SIXTH ROUND

Oakland (175/from Philadelphia through Green Bay and New England), Anttaj Hawthorne, DT, Wisconsin (Jack Scharf, Jeff Griffin)

Cleveland (176), Nick Speegle, OLB, New Mexico (Jack Bechta)

San Diego (177/from Miami), Wes Sims, OG, Oklahoma (Robb Nelson)

Tampa Bay (178), Anthony Bryant, DT, Alabama (Archie Lamb, Kirk Wood)

Tennessee (179), Bo Scaife, TE, Texas (Kevin Robinson)

Green Bay (180/from Oakland), Mike Montgomery, DT, Texas A&M (Brian Overstreet)

Chicago (181), Chris Harris, SS, Louisiana-Monroe (Albert Elias)

New York Jets (182/from Arizona through Oakland), Cedric Houston, RB, Tennessee (John Michels)

Washington (183), Jared Newberry, OLB, Stanford (Doug Hendrickson, Ken Landphere, Richard Newberry)

Detroit (184), Bill Swancutt, DE, Oregon State (Vance Malinovic)

Jacksonville (185/from Dallas through Oakland and New York Jets), Chad Owens, WR, Hawaii (Leo Goeas, Craig Domann)

New York Giants (186), Eric Moore, DE, Florida State (Adisa Bakari)

Kansas City (187), Will Svitek, OT, Stanford (Steve Baker)

Houston (188), Ceandris Brown, SS, Louisiana-Lafayette (Chad Wiestling, Rich DeLuca)

Carolina (189), *Jovan Haye, DE, Vanderbilt (Jack Scharf, Jeff Griffin)

Cincinnati (190), Tab Perry, WR, UCLA (Jeff Sperbeck)

Minnesota (191), *C. J. Mosley, DT, Missouri (Harold Lewis, Kevin Omell)

St. Louis (192), *Dante Ridgeway, WR, Ball State (Roosevelt Barnes)

New Orleans (193), Jason Jefferson, DT, Wisconsin (Ron Slavin, Brad Leshnock)

Jacksonville (194), Pat Thomas, OLB, North Carolina State (Jason Waugh, Derrick Harrison)

Green Bay (195/from Baltimore through New England), Craig Bragg, WR, UCLA (Michael Hoffman, Gary Uberstine)

Seattle (196), Tony Jackson, TE, Iowa (Cary Fabrikant, Brian Levy)

Buffalo (197), Justin Geisinger, OG, Vanderbilt (Rick Smith, Mark Bartelstein, Mike McCartney)

New York Jets (198), Joel Dreessen, TE, Colorado State (Jeff Sperbeck)

Kansas City (199/from Green Bay), Khari Long, DE, Baylor (Vann McElroy, Jeff Nalley, Graylan Crain)

Denver (200), Chris Myers, OG, Miami (Drew Rosenhaus, Jason Rosenhaus)

Atlanta (201), DeAndra Cobb, RB, Michigan State (Andrew Baker)

Indianapolis (202), Dave Rayner, K, Michigan State (Paul Sheehy)

Cleveland (203/from Tampa Bay), Andrew Hoffman, DT, Virginia (Anthony Agnone, Noel Lamontagne, Edward Johnson)

Pittsburgh (204), Chris Kemoeatu, OG, Utah (Ken Vierra)

San Francisco (205/from Philadelphia), Derrick Johnson, CB, Washington (Jack Scharf, Jeff Griffin)

Detroit (206/from New England), Jonathan Goddard, DE, Marshall (Adam Heller)

Carolina (207/compensatory selection), Joe Berger, OT, Michigan Tech (Tom Tafelski)

Dallas (208/comp selection), Justin Beriault, FS, Ball State (Alan Herman, Dave Butz)

Dallas (209/comp selection), Rob Petitti, OT, Pittsburgh (Ken Kremer)

St. Louis (210/comp selection), Reggie Hodges, P, Ball State (Roosevelt Barnes)

Philadelphia (211/comp selection), Calvin Armstrong, OT, Washington State (Ethan Lock)

Oakland (212/comp selection), Ryan Riddle, DE, California (Josh Luchs, Steve Feldman)

Baltimore (213/comp selection), Derek Anderson, QB, Oregon State (David Dunn)

Oakland (214/comp selection), Pete McMahon, OT (Jack Bechta)

SEVENTH ROUND

San Francisco (215), Daven Holly, CB, Cincinnati (Andy Simms, David Lee)

Miami (216), Kevin Vickerson, DT, Michigan State (Anthony Hilliard)

Cleveland (217), Jon Dunn, OT, Virginia Tech (Ken Harris)

Tennessee (218), Reynaldo Hill, CB, Florida (Ian Greengross)

Minnesota (219/from Oakland), Adrian Ward, CB, Texas-El Paso (Jim Grogan)

Chicago (220), Rodriques Wilson, SS, South Carolina (David Canter)

Tampa Bay (221), Rick Razzano, FB, Mississippi (Jack Reale)

Washington (222), Nehemiah Broughton, FB, The Citadel (Harold Lewis, Kevin Omell)

San Francisco (223/from Detroit), Marcus Maxwell, WR, Oregon (David Caravantes, Bus Cook)

Dallas (224), Jay Ratliff, DE, Auburn (Mark Slough)

Tampa Bay (225/from New York Giants), Paris Warren, WR, Utah (Derrick Fox)

Arizona (226), LeRon McCoy, WR, Indiana (Pa.) (John Rickert)

Houston (227), Kenneth Pettway, OLB, Grambling State (Will Jordan)

Pittsburgh (228/from Carolina), Shaun Nua, DE, Brigham Young (Don Yee, Steve Dubin)

Kansas City (229), James Kilian, QB, Tulsa (Bob Lattinville, Joe Hipskind)

New England (230/from Minnesota through New York Jets and Oakland), Matt Cassel, QB, Southern California (David Dunn)

Tampa Bay (231), Hamza Abdullah, SS, Washington State (Mark Bloom)

New Orleans (232), Jimmy Verdon, DT, Arizona State (Jack Scharf, Jeff Griffin)

Cincinnati (233), Jonathan Fanene, DE, Utah (Angelo Wright)

Baltimore (234), Mike Smith, ILB, Texas Tech (Gary Glick)

Seattle (235), Cornelius Wortham, OLB, Alabama (Mark Slough)

Buffalo (236), Lionel Gates, RB, Louisville (Ken Sarnoff)

Jacksonville (237), Chris Roberson, CB, Eastern Michigan (Anthony Agnone, Richard Rosa, Edward Johnson)

Kansas City (238/from Green Bay), Jeremy Parquet, OT, Southern Mississippi (Reggie Rouzan)

Denver (239), Paul Ernster, P, Northern Arizona (Brett Tessler)

New York Jets (240), Harry Williams, WR, Tuskegee (Harold Lewis, Kevin Omell)

Atlanta (241), Darrell Shropshire, DT, South Carolina (David Canter)

San Diego (242), Scott Mruczkowski, C, Bowling Green (Jack Bechta)

Indianapolis (243), Anthony Davis, RB, Wisconsin (Brian Mackler, Jim Ivler)

Pittsburgh (244), Noah Herron, RB, Northwestern (Mike McCartney, Mark Bartelstein, Rick Smith)

Green Bay (245/from Philadelphia), Kurt Campbell, SS, Albany (New York) (Andrew Baker)

Green Bay (246/from New England), Will Whitticker, G, Michigan State (Reggie Smith, Jim Ryan)

Philadelphia (247/compensatory selection), Keyonta Marshall, DT, Grand Valley State (Angelo Wright)

San Francisco (248/comp selection), Patrick Estes, TE, Virginia (Ron Del Duca)

San Francisco (249/comp selection), Billy Bajema, TE, Oklahoma State (Drew Pittman)

St. Louis (250/comp selection), Ryan Fitzpatrick, QB, Harvard (Jimmy Sexton, Kyle Rote)

St. Louis (251/comp selection), Madison Hedgecock, FB, North Carolina (Tim Irwin)

Philadelphia (252/comp selection), David Bergeron, ILB, Stanford (Josh Luchs, Steve Feldman)

Tampa Bay (253/comp selection), J. R. Russell, WR, Louisville (Jack Scharf, Jeff Griffin)

Seattle (254/comp selection), Doug Nienhuis, OT, Oregon State (Bill Heck)

New England (255/comp selection), Andy Stokes, TE, William Penn (Joe Linta, Tom Klein)

INDEX

Pete Williams writes about the business of sports for such publications as *USA Today* and *Street and Smith's SportsBusiness Journal*. He is the author or coauthor of six books, including the business motivational book *Fun Is Good* (with Mike Veeck). Williams lives in the Tampa Bay, Florida, area with his family. His Web site is www.petewilliams.net.